Fifty Years of Israel

Donald Neff

D1531099

American Educational Trust
Washington, D.C.

Cover photograph: Two-year-old Mohammed Ali Abu-Swai cries in the ruins of his family home in the Arab East Jerusalem neighborhood of Ras Al-Amoud. Israeli bulldozers demolished his home Aug. 4, 1997.
© Khalid Zighari

All of these articles first appeared in the Washington Report on Middle East Affairs, edited by Richard H. Curtiss and Janet McMahon.

Library of Congress Cataloging-in-Publication Data

Neff, Donald, 1930–
    50 years of Israel / by Donald Neff.
        p.   cm.
    Includes bibliographical references and index.
    ISBN 0-937165-08-5 (pbk.)
    1. Israel—History.   2. Arab-Israeli conflict.   3. Palestinian
Arabs—Politics and government.   I. Title.
DS126.5.N37   1998
956.94—dc21   98-25834
                                                                   CIP

To my son, Greg,

my old pals Jim Buckner, Ben Gurtizen,
Fritz Heede & Dick Powell

and to my dear companion,
Suleiman the Magnificent

Also by the author:

Fallen Pillars:
U.S. Policy Toward Palestine and Israel Since 1945

Warriors Against Israel:
How Israel Won the Battle to Become America's Ally 1973

Warriors for Jerusalem:
The Six Days That Changed the Middle East

Warriors at Suez:
Eisenhower Takes America Into the Middle East in 1956

Table of Contents

United Nations And The Palestinians

Israel Abroad

Israel At Home

Arabs

United States

Index

Foreword   By Senator James Abourezk

I once supposed that during the years Don Neff spent as *Time* Magazine's Jerusalem correspondent, he dodged an occasional bullet, and he most certainly dodged the wrath of the Israeli censors and other government watchdogs who were there to make certain he didn't make them look bad. I also supposed that his experience there would make him totally unafraid of anything America could dish out to him.

I supposed wrong.

Following the publication of one of his several excellent histories of the Arab-Israeli conflict, I suggested that he attend the American-Arab Anti-Discrimination Committee's national convention just across the bridge from Washington, in Alexandria, Virginia.

"Your book," I said, "would sell like hotcakes at the convention. All you have to do is get up and make a short talk, then sign away on your books as the money rolls in." At first, he just shuddered, then he began laughing at the notion that anyone would think that he would stand up in front of a crowd to speak, book sales or no book sales.

I tried one more time after that: I suggested he go on a book tour in order to let people know that he had another new book out about the Middle East. This time, he just looked at me, sniffed, and turned back to his computer to continue writing on a new project.

His public shyness is a distinct contrast to his private brilliance when it comes to writing. Not only is his Middle East trilogy the bible of the three Arab-Israeli wars of 1956, 1967, and 1973, but who else, outside of the Israeli Lobby, would even think about collecting significant original documents, including State Department reports, histories and news stories from 1948 onward about the Arab-Israeli conflict, then putting them into a compendium that is without question the best thing available for Middle East researchers. Beyond the research value, it also makes fascinating reading to see how America's policy toward that conflict has been heavily tilted against the Palestinians and other Arab neighbors, squarely in favor of an aggressor Israel. His recall of the recent history of the area helps us to understand why people in the Arab world have become, over the years, so utterly disgusted with American policy in the region.

The United States at one time could draw upon a deep well of trust and love from people in the Arab world, which makes it all the more frustrating for those in the Middle East who seek to understand why successive American governments have acted as they have over the years and up to the present. By now, however, the well of trust and love is nearly drained. Now we are "dulling our pick" in the Arab world with the glaring imbalance of our dealings with the parties to the Israeli-Palestinian conflict. It's as though our policymakers are unable to see over the heads of the Israeli lobbyists who stand between them and the Palestinians, who are asking only for fairness and justice for themselves.

Don Neff's writings on the Middle East have been accurate, unbiased, and highly informative. This new collection will broaden the base of knowledge of Middle East scholars, as well as that of other interested Americans, providing valuable information that most people long ago have forgotten. It is a wonderful primer for those who are just now dipping their noses into the conflict, and it will be a magnificent reference book for those who have been dabbling in it for many years now, to which the heavy footnoting will attest.

In either event, this is a delightful addition to an already great series of books on the Middle East given to us by Don Neff. I call it a gift because hardly anyone else, on either side of the dispute, is providing this kind of information about the conflict in such a neutral and unbiased manner. ❧

James Abourezk served South Dakota in the House of Representatives and the Senate from 1971 to 1979 and was a founder and the national chairman of the American-Arab Anti-Discrimination Committee. He now practices law in South Dakota.

Only Arabs can read this stupid book.

Introduction By Richard H. Curtiss

This is the fifth book on current Middle Eastern history published by Donald Neff during the past 17 years. If this were all that he had done in that period, it would be a commendable achievement in itself. But his published books are only the tip of the iceberg. During the same period he has written a steady stream of journalistic and scholarly articles on Middle Eastern affairs, compiled a unique personal data base in the same field, and has even, I'm told by others, done extensive research and some ghostwriting, based upon that data base, for others. But then, he's a remarkable man.

Although I served in the U.S. Embassy in Beirut and then traveled throughout the Middle East for the U.S. Information Agency from 1975 to 1978 when Don was *Time* bureau chief in Jerusalem, we did not meet until three years after my retirement from the foreign service in 1980.

At that time he was living and working in Washington, DC. After winning the Overseas Press Club's citation for the best magazine article in 1979 for his *Time* magazine cover story "The Colombia Connection," he was assigned by *Time* to work as coordinator with the *Washington Star*, the capital's only remaining evening newspaper, which only two years later closed its doors— leaving a lot of America's top journalists stranded.

At the time, I was executive director of the newly created American Educational Trust, publisher of this book. We were looking for someone who combined both editorial talent and first-hand knowledge of the Middle East, and I had been told that Don Neff might be that person.

He already had published his first book, *Warriors at Suez: Eisenhower Takes America Into the Middle East,* which was an alternate selection for the Book of the Month Club and for the History Book Club.

I also had heard about his now famous Middle East data base. It had an additional cachet since, at the time, computers were still somewhat mysterious. By then most journalists had weaned themselves from typewriters and were pounding out stories on "word processors," but few had ventured into using them for data retrieval—probably because up to then there wasn't much computerized data to be retrieved.

When I telephoned him, Don invited me to join him in a cozy restaurant near his home, where he seemed to have a permanent lease on a corner table for morning coffee. It quickly became apparent, however, that his situation was quite different from that of many other *Washington Star* alumni.

He made it clear there was no way he could take on a full-time job. He was too busy researching and writing another book.

Could he become a regular Washington columnist for our publication, the *Washington Report on Middle East Affairs?* Well, not really, because he already was the regular Washington correspondent for another publication, *Middle East International,* published in London with simultaneous distribution in the United States.

How about occasional articles on subjects other than those he prepared for his London editors? Sure, although it was a little hard to visualize what those subjects would be, since he covered the entire 50 states for his London outlet.

In fact, it appeared, he already was submitting occasional articles to several other publications. I realized I was dealing with an amiable and seemingly laid-back man who, nevertheless, was extremely busy and, in fact, had all the clients he could deal with while still writing his books. Also that he was too honorable to recycle the same material through competing publications, that he was too nice to disappoint me by saying a flat-out no, and that he was far too polite to express any skepticism about how long our brand-new publication would be around. Don, while unfailingly cheerful and accommodating, can also be a little inscrutable.

I didn't press the point and went looking elsewhere. Not long afterward, in 1984, he published his second book, *Warriors for Jerusalem.* It was about the 1967 war, which had given me personally a few very uncomfortable days in the American Embassy in Damascus.

Because his data base was becoming increasingly famous, based on the fact that he spent a part of every day faithfully entering into it items from that day's media as well as historical items turned up in his book research, I did call him from time to time to check a date or a name, or borrow a factoid or two. He was always pleasant and ready to interrupt whatever he was doing. Over the phone I could hear the "click, click" as he entered into his computer—which seemingly always was turned on—the key words that brought up almost instantaneous answers to whatever questions I asked.

On one of those calls, when I wanted to check some facts for an article I planned to write on an upcoming anniversary, he provided such lucid, complete and revealing information that I suggested he write the article instead.

Since it was an event that had happened many years earlier, I pointed out, it wouldn't compete with his work for other publications. He agreed and, if I remember correctly, the article appeared by courier a day or two later. Thus was born his monthly feature "Middle East History: It Happened in..." with the name of the month supplied.

In the early years the articles came in on a disk, and invariably would be the first submission to arrive for each new issue. Don knew that our magazine went into the mail on Fridays. His article for the next issue generally would arrive in the following Monday's mail because, as a professional, he knew the last thing we wanted to deal with at deadline time was a new article for the next issue.

Now, several years later, the articles come in by e-mail, totally fact-checked and accurate, and ready for printing. They still are impeccably written, and always revealing, even to those of us who were in the Middle East and sometimes unhappily involved in the very events described at the time they occurred.

When we proposed to publish a compilation of those articles, Don did the dividing into rough chronological or, in a few cases, subject order. He also was concerned that there still were a few vital links missing from his historical chain that led so clearly to the impasse that was observed in the spring of 1998 by Israelis as 50 years of sovereignty and by Palestinians as 50 years of dispossession.

So Don Neff raced ahead to write those few remaining untold stories, to be published one by one in the appropriate issues of the *Washington Report on Middle East Affairs,* even as his completed book was being printed. The result is an easy, informative and painstakingly accurate account of the key developments in the history of the most significant Middle Eastern event of the 20th century—at least insofar as Middle Eastern events affect Westerners, and Americans in particular.

His book has additional value as a research tool even for those rare scholars who are familiar with the general outlines of the tragic history it records. To realize the book's full potential, the publisher has provided an exhaustive index, occupying 16 additional pages of text, to enable both students and scholars to retrieve quickly all of the facts contained in the 54 separate tales related.

Like all authors, Don Neff undoubtedly has personal viewpoints concerning the information he has compiled. But as a seasoned, highly professional, award-winning journalist he presents the facts as he found and recorded them, and lets the reader choose what uses or interpretations to make of them.

Much of the subject matter will come as a shock to the general American reader and, to a lesser extent, to most Europeans. Many Middle Eastern readers will be shocked as well. Some of the information presented in Middle Eastern media is selectively edited to provide pictures as distorted or incomplete as those presented by much of America's mainstream media to its readers over the first 50 years of Israel's existence, and over the 50 years that preceded May 14, 1948 as well.

I am very proud of my role in encouraging the creation of this clarifying book. My colleague, *Washington Report* managing editor Janet McMahon, may deservedly be proud of her role both in seeing each of the original articles into print in the magazine, and in turn in presenting them between book covers.

Most of all, Donald Neff can be enormously proud of the immense professionalism and personal discipline required to produce such a complete, accurate and readable work of history. It is designed to be equally useful as an introduction for beginners and a research tool for specialists in the past century of Middle Eastern history. The publishers invite readers of both descriptions, and all the categories in between, to find out for themselves. ❧

Richard H. Curtiss, a retired career foreign service offer, is a co-founder of the American Educational Trust and executive editor of the Washington Report on Middle East Affairs.

History

Chapter 1

1912: Justice Brandeis Was the Savior of Zionism in America

O N AUG. 13, 1912, Louis Dembitz Brandeis, a future justice of the U.S. Supreme Court, made a personal decision that would have a profound effect in establishing Zionism in the United States and thereby securing America's eventual support for the Jewish state of Israel. Zionism had been founded 15 years earlier in Europe, but it had failed to gain much support among Jewish Americans. It had probably fewer than 20,000 followers from within the 2.5 million-member American Jewish community before World War I. In the words of a pro-Zionist writer, American Zionism then was "a small and feeble enterprise."[1] A historian of the movement described Zionism at the time as still "small and weak, in great financial distress, and low in morale."[2]

This began to change after an August, 1912, meeting Brandeis had with Jacob de Haas, editor of the *Boston Jewish Advocate* and an early Zionist. A decade earlier, de Haas had been an aide to Zionism's founder, Theodore Herzl. Intrigued by de Haas' tales of Herzl and the beginnings of Zionism, Brandeis hired de Haas to instruct him in Zionism over the winter of 1912-13. At the end of that time Brandeis was a convert to Zionism.[3] Within two years, on Aug. 30, 1914, Brandeis became head of the Provisional Executive for General Zionist Affairs, making him the leader of the Zionist Central Office, which had been removed from Berlin to neutral America just before the outbreak of World War I.

Brandeis, the son of middle-class immigrants from Prague, was a brilliant attorney who had graduated at the top of his law class at Harvard. In 1912 he was 56 years of age, a wealthy Bostonian, a political progressive, a tireless reformer and one of the most famous attorneys in the country, known as the People's Attorney because of his successful litigation against big business on behalf of labor. His courtroom victories brought him riches as well as the enmity of the business establishment, including the wealthy Jewish communities of New York and Boston.[4]

What made Brandeis' conversion so surprising was that he was a non-observant Jew who believed firmly in America's melting pot and had grown up "free from Jewish contacts or traditions," as he put it.[5] It was not until he was in his 50s that Brandeis began paying attention to the Jewish experience. His sense of ethnic kinship had been sharpened by the turn-of-the-century wave of new Jewish immigrants that had led to rising anti-Semitism in America and at the same time had exposed Brandeis to Zionists. These influences came while his popular causes had estranged him from the Brahmin society of Boston and the New York business community, leaving him isolated from the mainline Jew.

New York's and Boston's prosperous upper-class Jews rejected Zionism's pessimistic tenet that anti-Semitism was inevitable. Instead, they believed in keeping an ethnic low profile and seeking social assimilation with other Americans. The elite position and wealth enjoyed by upper-class American Jews proved to them that the American melting pot worked. The last thing they wanted was an ideology that advocated establishment of a foreign country specifically for Jews. They feared this would not only bring into question their place in the melting pot, but also their loyalty to the land that had brought them a comfortable and secure life. Implicit in Zionism was the sensitive issue of dual loyalty toward a Jewish state and toward the nations in which its supporters actually were living.

Opponents of Zionism in America included Jewish socialists and workers, who disdained it as a form of bourgeois nationalism. Ultraorthodox Jewish religious groups went even further, describing Zionism as "the most formidable enemy that has ever arisen among the Jewish people" because it sought to do God's work through politics.[6] Not even the new immigrants streaming out of Eastern Europe were attracted to Zionism, as was obvious from the fact that most of them had chosen to bypass Palestine and go instead to the United States and other Western countries.

Unlike Jews who embraced the melting pot, Zionists openly rejected assimilation. Alienation lay at the heart of Zionism, as explained by Theodore Herzl when he first formulated its purpose
and aims in early 1896 in his seminal pamphlet *Der Judenstaat*: "We
have sincerely tried everywhere to merge with the national communities in which we live, seeking only to preserve the faith of our
fathers," he wrote. "It is not permitted us."[6]

At its core, this was the fundamental rationale of Zionism: a profound despair that anti-Semitism could not be eradicated as long
as Jews lived among Gentiles. Out of this dark vision came the belief
that the only hope for the survival of the Jews lay in the founding
of their own state.

With his conversion came changes in Brandeis' embrace of the
American melting pot. He now preached the "salad bowl," a belief
in cultural pluralism in which ethnic groups maintained their
unique identity. Brandeis maintained:

"America…has always declared herself for equality of nationalities as well as for equality of individuals. America has believed that
each race had something of peculiar value which it can contribute… America has always believed that in differentiation, not in
uniformity, lies the path of progress."[8]

As for the unsettling question of dual loyalty, the foremost suspicion about Zionism among Gentiles, Brandeis asserted there was
no conflict between being an American and a Zionist:

"Let no American imagine that Zionism is inconsistent with
patriotism. Multiple loyalties are objectionable only if they are inconsistent…Every American who aids in advancing the Jewish settlement in Palestine, though he feels that neither he nor his descendants will ever live there, will likewise be a better man and a
better American for doing so…There is no inconsistency between
loyalty to America and loyalty to Jewry. The Jewish spirit, the prod-
uct of our religion and experiences, is essentially modern and essentially American."[9]

Brandeis's Zionism, however, was far from the reality on the
ground in Palestine, where Arabs and Jews viewed each other with
mutual suspicions. He linked Zionists with the early New England
Puritans, declaring that "Zionism is the Pilgrim inspiration and im-

pulse over again. The descendants of the Pilgrim fathers should not find it hard to understand and sympathize with it." To Jewish audiences he said: "To be good Americans, we must be better Jews, and to be better Jews, we must become Zionists."[10]

Brandeis' Zionism, obviously, was different from the passionate and messianic Zionism of Europe, driven as it was by pessimism about the enduring anti-Semitism of the world against Jews and the need for the ethnic cleansing of Palestine's Arabs. His was an ethnic philanthropic vision, a desire to help needy Jews set down a kind of New England town in the Middle East—but with no intention of going to Palestine to live among them. This concept of helping with financial support but not actually moving to Palestine remained central to American Zionists and helps explain why through the years so few Jewish Americans have emigrated to Israel.[11] To European Zionists, it was a pale and anemic version of their life's passion, "Zionism without Zion," they grumbled.[12]

While Brandeis's vision of Zionism was unrealistically idealistic, he would achieve what probably no other Zionist could have. He became instrumental in gaining the support of the United States for a Jewish state in Palestine. Brandeis accomplished this feat by using his friendship with President Woodrow Wilson to advocate the Zionist cause, which he achieved by serving as a conduit between British Zionists and Wilson.

The president was a ready listener. He was the son of a Presbyterian minister and a daily reader of the Bible. Although not particularly interested in the political ramifications of Zionism, he shared the vague sentiment of a number of Christians at the time that there would be a certain biblical justice to have the Jews return to Palestine.

Wilson thought so highly of Brandeis that he appointed him to the Supreme Court on Jan. 28, 1916, thereby enormously increasing Brandeis' prestige and his influence in the White House. In turn, Brandeis resigned from all the numerous public and private clubs and organizations he belonged to, including, ostensibly, his leadership of American Zionism. His resignation, however, did not mean Brandeis had deserted Zionism or active involvement in its promotion. Behind the scenes he continued to play a leadership role. At his Supreme Court chambers in Washington he received daily reports on Zionist activities from the New York headquarters and issued orders to his loyal lieutenants, many of them graduates of Harvard, now heading American Zionism.[13]

While on the court, Brandeis was instrumental in 1917 in gaining Wilson's support for Britain's Balfour Declaration, a seminal document that thereafter served as Zionism's claim to have a legitimate right to settle in Palestine.

The final major diplomatic achievement of Brandeis and American Zionism in the post-World War I period was the passage by Congress on Sept. 11, 1922, of a joint resolution favoring a Jewish homeland in Palestine. The words of the resolution practically echoed the Balfour Declaration:

"Resolved by the Senate and House of Representatives of the United States of America in Congress assembled, that the United States of America favors the establishment in Palestine of a national home for the Jewish people, it being clearly understood that nothing shall be done which may prejudice the civil and religious rights of Christian and all other non-Jewish communities in Palestine, and that the Holy places and religious buildings and sites in Palestine shall be adequately protected."[14]

Zionists trumpeted the resolution as another Balfour Declaration, evidence that a Jewish state had official support not only from Britain but from the United States. After all, it had been sponsored by Senator Henry Cabot Lodge and Representative Hamilton Fish and signed by President Warren G. Harding.

However, during the debate leading up to passage of the resolution, a number of speakers had emphasized that it was merely an expression of sympathy by the Congress, had no force in law and in no way would involve the United States in foreign entanglements. This was the interpretation adopted by the State Department, which had opposed Zionism since its beginning, considering it a minority group interfering in foreign affairs.[15]

Passage of the congressional resolution was the height of Brandeis' brand of American Zionism, and also the end of its heroic period. Under Brandeis the Zionist membership had burgeoned tenfold, reaching around 200,000 after the heralded victory of the Balfour Declaration. The momentum of that historic event carried over into the halls of Congress and resulted in the joint resolution.

But a year before the resolution became a reality, Brandeis himself had been swept from power in Zionist councils in a showdown with European Zionists. Brandeis' tepid form of Zionism was simply too emotionless and sterile for them.[16]

Nonetheless, his contribution to Zionism had been enormous, not only in gaining official U.S. support but also in establishing the intellectual framework for the movement in America. It was from Brandeis' time that American Zionists began a concerted effort to link American ideals and interests with a Jewish state and thereby establish a mutual identity. How successful Brandeis and his successors have been was demonstrated at the two most recent annual meetings of the American Israel Public Affairs Committee (AIPAC), Israel's U.S. lobby.

In 1995 President Bill Clinton had become the first sitting president ever to appear before the lobbying group. On April 28, 1996, appearing before AIPAC for the second time, he told the applauding audience that the relationship between America and Israel was "based on shared values and common strategies."[17] Two days later at the White House, Clinton told visiting Israeli Prime Minister Shimon Peres that America "stands with Israel through good times and bad because our countries share the same ideals— freedom, tolerance, democracy."[18] However astonishing Palestinians and foreign observers might find that description of a country that continues to occupy foreign territories by force and to deprive their occupants of political and civil rights of any kind, the fact is that Zionists have been successful in selling in the United States Brandeis' preposterous claim that the Zionist state and America are basically the same. ᵉᵃ

RECOMMENDED READING:

*Ball, George W. and Douglas B. Ball, *The Passionate Attachment: America's Involvement with Israel, 1947 to the Present,* New York, W.W. Norton & Company, 1992.

*Beit-Hallahmi, Benjamin, *Original Sins: Reflections on the History of Zionism and Israel,* New York, Olive Branch Press, 1993.

Bruce, Allen Murphy, *The Brandeis/Frankfurter Connection: The Secret Political Activities of Two Supreme Court Justices,* Garden City, NY, Anchor Press/Doubleday & Co., 1983.

Grose, Peter, *Israel in the Mind of America*, New York, Alfred A. Knopf, 1983.

Howe, Irving, *World of Our Fathers*, New York, Harcourt Brace Jovanovich, 1976.

Mallison, Thomas and Sally V., *The Palestine Problem in International Law and World Order*, London, Longman Group Ltd., 1986.

Manuel, Frank E., *The Realities of American-Palestine Relations*, Washington, DC, Public Affairs Press, 1949.

*Neff, Donald, *Fallen Pillars: U.S. Policy Towards Palestine and Israel since 1945*, Washington, DC, Institute for Palestiine Studies, 1995.

O'Brien, Lee, *American Jewish Organizations & Israel*, Washington, DC, Institute for Palestine Studies, 1986.

Sachar, Howard M., *A History of Israel: From the Rise of Zionism to Our Time*, Tel Aviv, Steimatzky's Agency Ltd., 1976.

Tivnan, Edward, *The Lobby: Jewish Political Power and American Foreign Policy*, New York, Simon and Schuster, 1987.

*Available through the AET Book Club

NOTES:

[1] Quoted in Howe, *World of Our Fathers*, p. 204. Also see Grose, *Israel in the Mind of America*, p. 45; Manuel, *The Realities of American-Palestine Relations*, p. 112.

[2] Yonathan Shapiro, quoted in O'Brien, *American Jewish Organizations and Israel*, p. 38.

[3] Murphy, *The Brandeis/Frankfurter Connection*, pp. 25-26.

[4] Grose, *Israel in the Mind of America*, p. 48.

[5] Tivnan, *The Lobby*, p. 16.

[6] Grose, *Israel in the Mind of America*, p. 72.

[7] Sachar, *A History of Israel*, p. 40.

[8] Neff, *Fallen Pillars*, p. 11.

[9] Tivnan, *The Lobby*, p. 17.

[10] Neff, *Fallen Pillars*, p. 11.

[11] In the 28 years between Israel's founding in 1948 and 1976, fewer than 60,000 Jewish Americans migrated to Israel. Of these, 80 percent returned to the United States, the highest rate of any immigrant group; see Beit-Hallahmi, *Original Sins*, p. 197.

[12] Tivnan, *The Lobby*, p. 19.

[13]Grose, *Israel in the Mind of America*, p. 57; Murphy, *The Brandeis/Frankfurter Connection*, p. 56.

[14]Manuel, *The Realities of American-Palestine Relations*, p. 282.

[15]*Ibid.*, pp. 281-82.

[16]Neff, *Fallen Pillars*, p. 17.

[17]C-SPAN2.

[18]Thomas W. Lippman, *Washington Post*, 4/30/96.

Chapter 2

1917: Passage of the Balfour Declaration

ON NOV. 2, 1917, Britain issued the Balfour Declaration, a fateful statement that Zionists henceforth claimed gave Jews a legal right to a homeland in Palestine. The statement came in the form of a personal letter from Foreign Secretary Arthur James Balfour to a prominent British Jew, Lionel Walter, the second Lord Rothschild:

> *Foreign Office,*
>
> *November 2, 1917*
>
> *Dear Lord Rothschild,*
>
> *I have much pleasure in conveying to you, on behalf of His Majesty's Government, the following declaration of sympathy with Jewish Zionist aspirations which has been submitted to, and approved by, the Cabinet:*
>
> *"His Majesty's Government view with favour the establishment in Palestine of a national home for the Jewish people, and will use their best endeavours to facilitate the achievement of this object, it being clearly understood that nothing shall be done which may prejudice the civil and religious rights of existing non-Jewish communities in Palestine, or the rights and political status enjoyed by Jews in any other country."*
>
> *I should be grateful if you would bring this declaration to the knowledge of the Zionist Federation.*
>
> *Yours,*
>
> *Arthur James Balfour*[1]

Arabs and anti-Zionists could not help noting the totally pro-Zionist content of the declaration. It failed to mention Christians or Muslims, Arabs or Palestinians, even though they remained by far the majority population in Palestine. At the time, there were about 55,000 Jews and 600,000 Palestinians in Palestine.[2] The declaration spoke of a homeland, but that was widely understood to mean a Jewish state. And it pledged actively to help Jews while merely promising to protect the rights of "the non-Jewish communities."

Arabs far beyond Palestine were alarmed and disappointed. It was clear to them that British wartime promises of Arab independence were being ignored by London. The campaign to chase the Turks from Palestine was being concluded in late 1917 with Arab help. British forces stood at the gates of Jerusalem and soon they would clear the area and Palestine would pass from the Ottoman to the British Empire. But Arab aspirations for independence were being ignored.

Opposition came not only from Arabs and Muslims but within England as well. The only Jew in the Cabinet, Edwin Montague, the secretary of state for India, had opposed the original idea. He supported his position by enlisting the views of one of the greatest Arabists of the time, Gertrude Bell, a colleague of T.E. Lawrence and currently involved in British intelligence in Cairo. She wrote the Cabinet that "two considerations rule out the conception of an independent Jewish Palestine from practical politics. The first is that the province as we know it is not Jewish, and that neither Mohammedan nor Arab would accept Jewish authority; the second that the capital, Jerusalem, is equally sacred to three faiths, Jewish, Christian and Muslim, and should never, if it can be avoided, be put under the exclusive control of any one location, no matter how carefully the rights of the other two may be safeguarded."[3]

Another dissent came from the Middle East from A.P. Albina, a Levantine Catholic merchant from Jerusalem who enjoyed good relations with top British officials. He wrote that it was contradictory for the Western powers to grant freedom to small nationalities while at the same time planning to give Palestine to the Jews. He described the Zionists as:

A foreign and hated race, a motley crowd of Poles, Russians, Romanians, Spaniards, Yemenites, etc., who can claim absolutely no right over the country, except that of sentiment and the fact that their forefathers inhabited it over two thousand years ago[.] The introduction into Palestine of Jewish

rule, or even Jewish predominance, will mean the spoliation of the Arab in-
habitants of their hereditary rights and the upsetting of the principles of na-
tionalities....Politically, a Jewish State in Palestine will mean a permanent
danger to a lasting peace in the Near East.[4]

Despite such concerns, and the opposition of the entire Arab
and Islamic worlds, there were a number of reasons favoring the
Zionist campaign to gain official British sanction. Foremost among
these was the favorable attitude toward a Jewish homeland shared
by both Foreign Secretary Balfour and Britain's prime minister,
David Lloyd George. Welshman Lloyd George was a firm believer
in the Old Testament's claim to the right of the Jews to Palestine.[5]
Balfour had been prime minister in the early 1900s at the time of
the British offer of "Uganda" as a Jewish homeland and, although
not Jewish, he considered himself a Zionist.[6]

Beyond these sentimental and religious reasons, however, there
were other motivations having to do with Britain's interests, among
them a common concern for gaining U.S. support for Britain's post-
war goals in dividing up the tottering Ottoman Empire, including
Britain's ambition of taking over Palestine. In this, they were advised by the British Embassy in Washington that Britain could be
helped in achieving U.S. backing by finding favor with Jewish Americans. Reported the embassy: "They are far better organized than
the Irish and far more formidable. We should be in a position to get
into their good graces."[7]

One obvious way to do this was to follow the natural inclinations
of Lloyd George and Balfour and support Zionist ambitions in Palestine, if only London could be sure President Woodrow Wilson
agreed with such a path. In this they were immeasurably helped, as
well as goaded, by a persistent and persuasive Russian-born Jewish
chemist by the name of Chaim Weizmann. In 1917 he was head of
the Zionist movement in Britain and a tireless worker in that cause.
His achievements were so great that eventually he would be head of
the World Zionist Organization and Israel's first president.

Aware of Lloyd George's and Balfour's desire for U.S. support,
Weizmann sought a backdoor past the anti-Zionist State Department
to the White House via America's foremost Zionist, Louis D. Brandeis, an intimate of President Wilson, who had appointed Brandeis in
1916 to the Supreme Court. On April 8, 1917, Weizmann cabled

Brandeis, advising that "an expression of opinion coming from yourself and perhaps other gentlemen connected with the Government in favor of a Jewish Palestine under a British protectorate would greatly strengthen our hands."[8] A month later, following America's entry into the war, Brandeis had a 45-minute meeting with Wilson. As a son of a Presbyterian clergyman and a daily reader of the Bible, Wilson shared with a number of Christians support for a Jewish homeland in Palestine. Indeed, Brandeis found the president's views of Palestine "entirely sympathetic to the aims of the Zionist Movement" and, moreover, was able to encourage the British by adding that Wilson favored a British protectorate in Palestine.[9]

However, Wilson did not want to make a public declaration because of his concern with French ambitions toward the region and a futile hope that Turkey still could be persuaded to quit the war. Thus, when Britain sought Wilson's endorsement in September, 1917 of a draft declaration, he responded that the time was "not opportune" for him to go public. In desperation, Weizmann cabled Brandeis that it "would greatly help if President Wilson and yourself would support the text. Matter most urgent. Please telegraph."[10] Brandeis was able to use his access to the White House to meet with a Jewish adviser to Wilson, Colonel Edward Mandell House, and together they assured Weizmann that

From talks I have had with President and from expressions of opinion given to closest advisers I feel I can answer you in that he is [in] entire sympathy with declaration quoted in yours of nineteenth as approved by the foreign office and the Prime Minister. I of course heartily agree.[11]

When the British sent a revised draft of the statement for Wilson's examination in early October, he turned it over to Brandeis for his comments. The Justice and his aides redrafted it in slightly stronger and cleaner language, substituting "the Jewish people" for "the Jewish race"–thereby muting the vexing question of who's-a-Jew–and making the final clause read that there would be no prejudice to the "rights and political status enjoyed by Jews in any other country."[12]

Colonel House sent the revision on to Wilson. But, in the midst of world war, he felt no urgency about the matter. It was not until Oct. 13 that he sent a memo to House saying:

I find in my pocket the memorandum you gave me about the Zionist Movement. I am afraid I did not say to you that I concurred in the formula

suggested by the other side. I do, and would be obliged if you would let them know it.[13]

So casual was Wilson about this momentous decision that he never did inform his secretary of state, or publicly announce his decision.[14] Nonetheless, his private assurance to Britain of his support was enough for Lloyd George's Cabinet to adopt the declaration. In the corridors of power, it was well known that the president of the United States quietly supported the Balfour Declaration.

Thus, in the most off-handed way possible, Wilson lent his enormous weight to supporting the Zionist dream of a Jewish state in Palestine. It was a decision that was to have a profound effect on Middle East history and U.S. foreign policy, and especially on the daily lives of Palestinians and the world Jewish community. ❧

RECOMMENDED READING:

Grose, Peter, *Israel in the Mind of America*, New York, Alfred A. Knopf, 1983.

Mallison, Thomas and Sally V., *The Palestine Problem in International Law and World Order*, London, Longman Group Ltd., 1986.

Murphy, Bruce Allen, *The Brandeis/Frankfurter Connection: The Secret Political Activities of Two Supreme Court Justices*, Garden City, New York, Anchor Press/Doubleday & Company, Inc., 1983.

*Neff, Donald, *Fallen Pillars: U.S. Policy Towards Palestine and Israel Since 1945*, Washington, DC, Institute for Palestine Studies, 1995.

Sanders, Ronald, *The High Walls of Jerusalem: A History of the Balfour Declaration and the Birth of the British Mandate for Palestine*, New York, Holt, Rinehart and Winston, 1983.

Tessler, Mark, *History of the Israeli-Palestinian Conflict*, Bloomington, Indiana University Press, 1994.

*Available through the AET Book Club

NOTES:

[1]Sanders, *The High Walls of Jerusalem*, pp. 612-13. The text of the early and the final drafts of the declaration are also in Mallison and Mallison, *The Palestine Problem in International Law and World Order*, pp. 427-29.

[2]Tessler, *A History of the Israeli-Palestinian Conflict*, p. 145.

[3]Sanders, *The High Walls of Jerusalem*, p. 585.

[4] *Ibid.*, p. 586.

[5] *Ibid.*, pp. 119-20.

[6] Grose, *Israel in the Mind of America,* p. 64.

[7] *Ibid.*, p. 63.

[8] Murphy, *The Brandeis/Frankfurter Connection,* p. 57.

[9] *Ibid.*, p. 57; Neff, *Fallen Pillars,* p. 11.

[10] Murphy, *The Brandeis/Frankfurter Connection,* p. 58.

[11] *Ibid.*

[12] *Ibid.*, p. 60; Sanders, p. 598.

[13] Sanders, p. 598.

[14] Grose, p. 64.

Chapter 3

1947: Agony of the Ship *Exodus* Helps Israel

O N JULY 18, 1947, a rickety former Chesapeake Bay ferry-
boat sailed into Haifa harbor in northern Palestine
packed with 4,554 Jewish survivors of the Nazi Holocaust.[1] British troops were waiting for the bedraggled Jews because
they were trying to enter Palestine illegally. The world press also
was there to watch the confrontation. In the melee that followed,
three Jews were killed and scores injured as British troops forcefully removed them from the ship. Not unexpectedly, the incident
received heavy media coverage, picturing brutish British soldiers
manhandling weak and helpless Jews.[2] Thus began the saga of the
Exodus, a piteous incident that helped win unprecedented sympathy for the Zionist cause.

The agony of the *Exodus* was not an accident. The old ferry boat,
originally called *President Wakefield*, had been bought by a group of
Jewish Americans called the Sonneborn Institute after New York
Jewish millionaire Rudolf G. Sonneborn. Its main purpose was to
circumvent U.S. laws against transferring weapons to the Jews in
Palestine.[3]

The voyage of the *Exodus* had been meticulously planned by
Zionist leaders with an eye to gaining sympathy in the world press
for the plight of hundreds of thousands of European Jews left
homeless by World War II. Many of them wanted to migrate to Palestine. They were prevented, however, by the British, who in 1947
were concluding their 30th and final year as Palestine's master.
During their rule, the British had made a number of promises to

Palestine's majority community of Arabs to protect them from waves of Jewish immigrants. Among these promises was a pledge in the White Paper of 1939 that the Arabs would have a de facto veto over Jewish immigration into Palestine after 1944.[4]

The Arabs were adamant after World War II that Britain keep its pledge against new immigrants. They pointed out that since the beginning of the century the demographic balance had changed from an Arab majority of more than 10 to 1 to the current level of 2 to 1. The balance would shift even more dramatically if displaced European Jews were allowed entry to Palestine.[5]

But now, with all the unspeakable details of the Holocaust in full public view–the stark photographs of the concentration camps and crematoria, the shocking stacks of starved bodies, the astounding figure of 6 million dead–the Jews were demanding an open gate to Palestine.

It was a cruel dilemma for Britain. On one level, the two issues had nothing in common. The displaced Jews were a European problem, while immigration into Palestine was a local Middle Eastern problem. But Britain had responsibilities in both regions. Moreover, while it had a commitment to the Palestinians it also was caught up in the humanitarian outpouring of sympathy in the West for the Jews. It was because of such dilemmas that London only five months earlier had announced it was surrendering its Mandate over Palestine and turning the whole difficult matter over to the United Nations.[6] However, until the world body found a solution, British troops would be responsible for maintaining order in Palestine.

On their side, the Zionists launched an organized campaign to transport illegal immigrants to Palestine to challenge the British limits against immigration. As an indication of the magnitude of the operation, 69,878 Jews were sent to Palestine as illegal immigrants between 1945 and May, 1948, and 51,500 of them were intercepted by the British navy and interned on Cyprus.[7]

Predictably, the dramatic story of homeless Jews fresh from Europe's death camps and bound for Palestine in barely seaworthy vessels to face British troops was a running human interest story in the media throughout the immediate postwar years.[8] Little noted by the press was the fact that every able-bodied immigrant added to the military power of the Jews in Palestine, a consideration not overlooked by British Foreign Minister Ernest Bevin. He early warned that new immigrants would be "the beginning of an army which would take Palestine away from the Arabs...."[9]

The saga of the *Exodus* stands out because it was so successful in gaining sympathy for the Zionists. As Ike Aranne, captain of the *Exodus* recalled, Zionist intelligence officers "gave us orders that this ship was to be used as a big demonstration with banners to show how poor and weak and helpless we were, and how cruel the British were."[10]

Britain's frustrated foreign secretary inadvertently aided the secret Zionist scheme by making one of the most insensitive decisions of his distinguished career. Instead of ordering the *Exodus*'s passengers interned with other illegal immigrants being held on Cyprus, he ordered that they be returned to France where the voyage had begun. Few decisions could have been more certain of retaining the attention of the world press. Worse, from Britain's view, the story commanded even larger coverage when many of the Jews refused to disembark when they arrived back in France and the French government declared it would refuse to force them off.

It was not until Sept. 8 that the Jews remaining on board finally were taken to the British zone of Germany and forced off the ships to which they had been transferred under the full glare of the press.[11]

Britain suffered a storm of criticism in the world press for all six weeks of the saga. Britain's government was accused of anti-Semitism, and its officials were called heartless. The French were particularly bitter that the British had tried to throw the problem in their laps. The Communist newspaper *Humanité* charged that the ships returning the Jews were a "floating Auschwitz." *Combat* described them as "cages for wild animals." *Figaro* reported that tensions between London and Paris were higher than at any time since World War II.[12]

British historian Nicholas Bethell later wrote: "Far from 'making an example' of the *Exodus* and rallying the world against the organizers of illegal immigration, Bevin succeeded only in shocking the world community into deeper sympathy for the Zionist enterprise."[13]

The saga of the *Exodus* played out at a time when the United Nations was deciding whether to partition Palestine between Arabs and Jews, and there can be little doubt that the world body's sympathy for the Jews was encouraged by the *Exodus* drama when it voted to create a Jewish state on Nov. 29, 1947. Reverberations of the *Exodus* did not stop there. In the early 1950s, an American public relations man, Edward Gottlieb, seeking to improve Israel's image in the United States, hit upon the idea of hiring a writer to go to Israel and write a heroic novel about the new country. The writer was Leon Uris, and his novel, *Exodus*, became a huge best-seller.[14] Moreover, the highly romanticized novel later became a movie starring Paul Newman. It was a box office smash hit.

The fact that Uris's book totally distorted reality and ignored the basic injustice involved in the West imposing on the Middle East a solution to its own problems was completely overlooked. Instead, the movie inculcated in millions of Americans the image of Zionists as pioneers in search of freedom among fanatical Arabs and perfidious British officials, an image that lingered for many years, in part because of the saga of the *Exodus*.[15]

RECOMMENDED READING:

Cleveland, William L., *A History of the Modern Middle East*, Boulder, Westview Press, 1994.

*Cockburn, Andrew and Leslie, *Dangerous Liaison: The Inside Story of the U.S.-Israeli Covert Relationship*, New York, HarperCollins Publishers, 1991.

Cohen, Michael J., *Palestine and the Great Powers 1945-1948*, Princeton, NJ, Princeton University Press, 1982.

Grose, Peter, *Israel in the Mind of America*, New York, Alfred A. Knopf, 1983.

*Lilienthal, Alfred M., *The Zionist Connection: What Price Peace?* New York, Dodd, Mead & Company, 1978.

Silver, Eric, *Begin: The Haunted Prophet*, New York, Random House, 1984.

Stevens, Art, *The Persuasion Explosion*, Washington, DC, Acropolis Books Ltd., 1985.

U.S. Department of State, *Foreign Relations of the United States, The Near East and Africa, 1945* (Vol. VIII), Washington, DC, U.S. Printing Office, 1969.

*Available through the AET Book Club

NOTES:

[1] Bethell, *The Palestine Triangle*, p. 333. Also see Silver, *Begin*, pp. 85-86.

[2] Gene Currivan, *New York Times*, 7/19/47.

[3] Grose, *Israel in the Mind of America*, pp. 210, 234. Sonneborn was honored in 1972 by the American Friends of Hebrew University for providing arms to the Jews in Palestine in the late 1940s; see *New York Times*, 5/9/72.

[4] Cleveland, *A History of the Modern Middle East*, p. 242.

[5] *Foreign Relations of the United States 1945*, "The Chargé in Egypt (Lyon) to the Secretary of State," Cairo, Nov. 11, 1945, 6 p.m., pp. 817-19.

[6] *New York Times*, 2/19/47.

[7] Cohen, *Palestine and the Great Powers 1945-1948*, p. 250.

[8] Cockburn, *Dangerous Liaison*, p. 22.

[9] Cohen, *Palestine and the Great Powers 1945-1948*, p. 225.

[10] Bethell, *The Palestine Triangle*, p. 331.

[11] *Ibid.*, p. 343.

[12] *Ibid.*, p. 336.

[13] *Ibid.*, p. 343.

[14] Stevens, *The Persuasion Explosion*, pp. 104-105.

[15] Lilienthal, *The Zionist Connection*, pp. 221-22.

Chapter 4

1947: Truman Supports Partition

ON SEPT. 22, 1947, Loy Henderson strongly warned Secretary of State George C. Marshall that partition of Palestine into Arab and Jewish states was not workable and would lead to untold troubles in the future. Henderson was director of the State Department's Office of Near Eastern and African Affairs and his memorandum, coming less than a month after a United Nations special committee had recommended partition, stands as one of the most perceptive analyses of the perils that partition would bring.

Henderson informed Marshall that his views were shared by "nearly every member of the Foreign Service or of the department who has worked to any appreciable extent on Near Eastern problems." Among the points Henderson made:[1]

"The UNSCOP [U.N. Special Committee on Palestine] Majority Plan is not only unworkable; if adopted, it would guarantee that the Palestine problem would be permanent and still more complicated in the future.

"The proposals contained in the UNSCOP plan are not only not based on any principles of an international character, the maintenance of which would be in the interests of the United States, but they are in definite contravention to various principles laid down in the [U.N.] Charter as well as to principles on which American concepts of Government are based.

"These proposals, for instance, ignore such principles as self-determination and majority rule. They recognize the principle of a theocratic racial state and even go so far in several instances as to discriminate on grounds of religion and race against persons outside of Palestine. We have hitherto

always held that in our foreign relations American citizens, regardless of race or religion, are entitled to uniform treatment. The stress on whether persons are Jews or non-Jews is certain to strengthen feelings among both Jews and Gentiles in the United States and elsewhere that Jewish citizens are not the same as other citizens.

"We are under no obligations to the Jews to set up a Jewish state. The Balfour Declaration and the [British] Mandate provided not for a Jewish state, but for a Jewish national home.[2] Neither the United States nor the British Government has ever interpreted the term 'Jewish national home' to be a Jewish national state."

Although the State Department reflected Henderson's anti-partition views, Harry Truman's White House was supporting partition because of strong political pressures. Truman was so unpopular at the time that there was speculation he might not be able to win the Democratic Party's nomination, much less the presidential race.[3] As the vote in the General Assembly on partition approached, Henderson made another effort to change Truman's mind. On Nov. 24, he wrote that "I feel it again to be my duty to point out that it seems to me and all the members of my Office acquainted with the Middle East that the policy which we are following in New York at the present time is contrary to the interests of the United States and will eventually involve us in international difficulties of so grave a character that the reaction throughout the world, as well as in this country, will be very strong."

He continued: "I wonder if the President realizes that the plan which we are supporting for Palestine leaves no force other than local law enforcement organizations for preserving order in Palestine. It is quite clear that there will be wide-scale violence in that country, on both the Jewish and Arab sides, with which the local authorities will not be able to cope....It seems to me we ought to think twice before we support any plan which would result in American troops going to Palestine."[4]

Under Secretary of State Robert A. Lovett was so impressed with the memo that he personally read it to President Truman. But Truman, worried about his election campaign in the coming year and urged by advisers such as Clark Clifford to endorse partition as a way to gain Jewish support, ignored Henderson's warnings.[5] Five days later the U.S. voted for partition in the historic session of the

General Assembly.

As the months passed and Palestine descended into the chaos and violence predicted by Henderson and the State Department, Truman could no longer escape the fact that partition had led to massive bloodshed. George Kennan, the director of policy planning at the State Department, warned on Feb. 24, 1948 that violence in Palestine could only be stopped by the introduction of foreign troops. He urged that the U.S. not be drawn into the quagmire:

"The pressures to which this Government is now subjected are ones which impel us toward a position where we would shoulder major responsibility for the maintenance, and even the expansion, of a Jewish state in Palestine....If we do not effect a fairly radical reversal of the trend of our policy to date, we will end up either in the position of being ourselves militarily responsible for the protection of the Jewish population in Palestine against the declared hostility of the Arab world, or of sharing that responsibility with the Russians and thus assisting at their installation as one of the military powers of the area."[6] Similar views were expressed by the CIA and the Defense Department.

Despite such grave concerns, Clifford continued to urge Truman to maintain support of partition. In a memo on March 6, Clifford argued that if the U.S. deserted it now it would make "...the United States appear in the ridiculous role of trembling before threats of a few nomadic desert tribes....the Arabs need us more than we need them. They must have oil royalties or go bankrupt." Implicit was the underlying message that Jews were more important to Truman's election than Arabs.[7]

By now, Arabs and Jews were slaughtering each other on a daily basis. Jewish forces were gathering strength and were on the verge of major attacks outside the limits defined by the U.N. for the Jewish state. Tens of thousands of Palestinians had already been turned into refugees, presaging the tragedy that soon would result in nearly three-quarters of the total Palestinian community losing their homes.

The horrors unfolding in Palestine could not be ignored. On March, 19, Truman renounced partition. The U.S. announced in the U.N. Security Council that America believed partition was unworkable and that a U.N. trusteeship should be established to replace the British when they ended their withdrawal from Palestine on May 14.*

Reaction in the press and the Jewish community was deafening. Headlines screamed: "Ineptitude," "Weakness," "Vacillating," "Loss of American Prestige."[9] From Jerusalem, the consul general reported: "Jewish reaction...one of consternation, disillusion, despair and determination. Most feel United States has betrayed Jews in interests Middle Eastern oil and for fear Russian designs."[10] Truman tried to shift the blame to the State Department, claiming it had acted without his approval. However, it is clear that he had personally given approval for the change in strategy.[11]

In the end, Truman regained Jewish support two months later when he overrode stiff opposition by the State Department and made the U.S. the first nation to recognize Israel as an independent nation on May 14. Truman's decision had so disgusted Secretary of State Marshall that he told Truman to his face that he believed the president was acting on Clifford's political calculations to win Jewish support, adding: "I said bluntly that if the President were to follow Mr. Clifford's advice and if in the elections I were to vote, I would vote against the President."[12] On Nov. 2, Truman defeated Thomas E. Dewey to win election to a full term as president. ❧

RECOMMENDED READING:

Donovan, Robert J., *Conflict and Crisis: The Presidency of Harry S. Truman, 1945-1948*, New York, W.W. Norton, 1977.

Grose, Peter, *Israel in the Mind of America*, New York, Alfred A. Knopf, 1983.

*Khouri, Fred J., *The Arab-Israeli Dilemma*, Syracuse, NY, Syracuse University Press, third edition, 1985.

Laqueur, Walter and Barry Rubin (eds.), *The Israel-Arab Reader* (revised and updated), New York, Penguin Books, 1987.

Mallison, Thomas and Sally V., *The Palestine Problem in International Law and World Order*, London, Longman Group Ltd., 1986.

Rearden, Steven L., *History of the Office of the Secretary of State: The Formative Years—1947-1950*, Washington, DC, Historical Office, Office of the Secretary of Defense, 1984.

U.S. Department of State, *Foreign Relations of the United States 1947* (vol. 5), *The*

Near East and Africa, Washington, DC, U.S. Printing Office, 1971.

U.S. Department of State, *Foreign Relations of the United States 1948* (vol. 5), *The Near East, South Asia, and Africa*, Washington, DC, U.S. Printing Office, 1975.

Wilson, Evan M., *Decision on Palestine: How the U.S. Came to Recognize Israel*, Stanford, CA, Hoover Institution Press, 1979.

*Available through the AET Book Club.

NOTES:

[1] Foreign Relations of the United States (hereafter referred to as FRUS), "The Director of the Office of Near Eastern and African Affairs (Henderson) to the Secretary of State," Sept. 22, 1947. Text is also in Wilson, *Decision on Palestine*, pp. 117-21.

[2] The Balfour Declaration was issued 11/2/17, saying Britain favored establishment of a "national home" for Jews in Palestine. Its text: "His Majesty's Government view with favor the establishment in Palestine of a national home for the Jewish people, and will use their best endeavors to facilitate the achievement of this object, it being clearly understood that nothing shall be done which may prejudice the civil and religious rights of existing non-Jewish communities in Palestine, or the rights and political status enjoyed by Jews in any other country." Text of the early and the final drafts of the declaration are in Mallison, *The Palestine Problem in International Law and World Order*, pp. 427-9. Text of the Mandate is in Laqueur and Rubin, *The Israel-Arab Reader*, pp. 34-42; a partial text appears in Khouri, *The Arab-Israeli Dilemma* (3rd ed.), pp. 527-28.

[3] Rearden, *History of the Office of the Secretary of Defense*, p. 181.

[4] FRUS 1947, "Memorandum by the Director of the Office of Near Eastern and African Affairs (Henderson) to the Under Secretary of State (Lovett)," Nov. 24, 1947, pp. 1281-82.

[5] Wilson, *Decision on Palestine*, p. 124.

[6] FRUS 1948, "Report by the Policy Planning Staff," Feb. 24, 1948, pp. 656-57.

[7] FRUS 1948, "Memorandum by the President's Special Counsel (Clifford)," March 6, 1948, pp. 687-96.

[8] Thomas J. Hamilton, *New York Times*, 3/20/48; the text of the U.S. statement is in the same edition as well as in FRUS 1948, "Statement Made by the United States Representative at the United Nations (Austin) Before the Security Council on March 19, 1948," March 19, 1948, pp. 742-4.

[9] Grose, *Israel in the Mind of America*, pp. 275-76.

[10] FRUS 1948, "The Consul General at Jerusalem (Macatee) to the Secretary of State," March 22, 1948, p. 753.

[11] Donald Neff, "Palestine, Truman and America's Strategic Balance," *American-Arab Affairs*, Summer 1988.

[12] FRUS 1948, "Memorandum of Conversation, Secretary of State," May 12, 1948, pp. 975-6.

War

Chapter 5

1948: Zionism and Jewish Terrorism

ON JAN. 4, 1948, Jewish terrorists drove a truck loaded with explosives into the center of the all-Arab city of Jaffa and detonated it, killing 26 and wounding around 100 Palestinian men, women and children.[1] The attack was the work of the Irgun Zvai Leumi—the "National Military Organization," also known by the Hebrew acronym Etzel—the largest Jewish terrorist group in Palestine. The Irgun was headed by Revisionist Zionist Menachem Begin and had been killing and maiming Arabs, Britons and even Jews for the previous decade in its efforts to establish a Jewish state.

This terror campaign meant that at the core of Revisionist Zionism there existed a philosophical embrace of violence. It was this legacy of violence that contributed to the assassination of Israeli Prime Minister Yitzhak Rabin on Nov. 4, 1995.

The Irgun was not the only Jewish terrorist group, but it was the most active in causing indiscriminate terror in pre-Israel Palestine. Up to the time of the Jaffa attack, its most spectacular feat had been the July 22, 1946 blowing up of the King David Hotel in Jerusalem, with the killing of 91 people—41 Arabs, 28 Britons and 17 Jews.[2]

The other major Jewish terrorist group operating in Palestine in the 1940s was the Lohamei Herut Israel, "Fighters for the Freedom of Israel," Lehi in the Hebrew acronym, also known as the Stern Gang after its fanatical founder Avraham Stern. Two of its more spectacular outrages included the assassination of British Colonial Secretary Lord Moyne in Cairo on Nov. 6, 1944, and the assassination of Count Folke Bernadotte of Sweden in Jerusalem on Sept. 17, 1948.[3]

Both groups collaborated in the massacre at Deir Yassin, in which some 254 Palestinian men, women and children were slain on April 9, 1948. Palestinian survivors were driven like ancient captives through the streets of Jerusalem by the celebrating terrorists.[4]

Yitzhak Shamir was one of the three leaders of Lehi who made the decision to assassinate Moyne and Bernadotte. Both he and Begin later became prime ministers and ruled Israel for a total of 13 years between 1977 and 1992.

They were both leaders of Revisionist Zionism, that messianic group of ultranationalists founded by Vladimir Zeev Jabotinsky in the 1920s. He prophesied that it would take an "iron wall of Jewish bayonets" to gain a homeland among the Arabs in Palestine.[5] His followers took his slogan literally.

Begin and the Revisionists were heartily hated by the mainline Zionists led by David Ben-Gurion. He routinely referred to Begin as a Nazi and compared him to Hitler. In a famous letter to *The New York Times* in 1948, Albert Einstein called the Irgun "a terrorist, rightwing, chauvinist organization" that stood for "ultranationalism, religious mysticism and racial superiority."[6] He opposed Begin's visit to the United States in 1949 because Begin and his movement amounted to "a Fascist party for whom terrorism (against Jews, Arabs, and British alike), and misrepresentation are means, and a 'leader state' is the goal," adding:

"The IZL [Irgun] and Stern groups inaugurated a reign of terror in the Palestine Jewish community. Teachers were beaten up for speaking against them, adults were shot for not letting their children join them. By gangster methods, beatings, window-smashing, and wide-spread robberies, the terrorists intimidated the population and exacted a heavy tribute."

Ben-Gurion considered the Revisionists so threatening that shortly after he proclaimed establishment of Israel on May 14, 1948, he demanded that the Jewish terrorist organizations disband. In defiance, Begin sought to import a huge shipment of weapons aboard a ship named *Altalena*, Jabotinsky's nom de plume.[7]

The ship was a war surplus U.S. tank-landing craft and had been donated to the Irgun by Hillel Kook's Hebrew Committee for National Liberation, an American organization made up of Jewish-

American supporters of the Irgun.[8] Even in those days it was Jewish Americans who were the main source of funds for Zionism. While few of them emigrated to Israel, Jewish Americans were generous in financing the Zionist enterprise. As in Israel, they were split between mainstream Zionism and Revisionism. One of the best known Revisionists was Ben Hecht, the American newsman and playwright. After one of the Irgun's terrorist acts, he wrote:

"The Jews of America are for you. You are their champions....Every time you blow up a British arsenal, or wreck a British jail, or send a British railroad train sky high, or rob a British bank, or let go with your guns and bombs at British betrayers and invaders of your homeland, the Jews of America make a little holiday in their hearts."[9]

The *Altalena* was loaded with $5 million worth of arms, including 5,000 British Lee-Enfield rifles, more than 3 million rounds of ammunition, 250 Bren guns, 250 Sten guns, 150 German Spandau machine guns, 50 mortars and 5,000 shells as well as 940 Jewish volunteers. Ben-Gurion reacted with fury, ordering the ship sunk in Tel Aviv harbor. Shellfire by the new nation's armed forces set the *Altalena* afire, killing 14 Jews and wounding 69. Two regular army men were killed and six wounded during the fighting.[10] Begin had been aboard but escaped injury. Later that night he railed against Ben-Gurion as "a crazy dictator" and the cabinet as "a government of criminal tyrants, traitors and fratricides."[11]

Ben-Gurion's deputy commander in the *Altalena* affair was Yitzhak Rabin, the same man who as prime minister was assassinated by one of the spiritual heirs of Menachem Begin's Irgun terrorist group. All his life, and especially in his last years, Rabin had opposed Jewish Americans and their radical allies in Israel who continued to embrace the philosophy of the Irgun and who fought against the peace process, thereby earning their enduring hatred.

Thus at the heart of the Jewish state there has been a long and violent struggle between mainline Zionists and Revisionists that continues today. Despite cries after Rabin's assassination that it was unknown for Jew to kill Jew, intramural hatred and occasional violence have marked relations between Zionism's competing groups.

The core of that conflict, one that continues to divide Israel and its American supporters as well, lies in the different philosophies of David Ben-Gurion and Vladimir Jabotinsky. Both were from Eastern Europe, born in the 1880s, and both sought an exclusivist Jewish state. But while Ben-Gurion was pragmatic and secular, Jabotinsky was impatient and messianic, a leader who glorified in the heroic trappings of fascism. Ben-Gurion was usually willing to take less now to get more later, and thus he was content to accept partition of Palestine as a necessary stepping-stone toward a larger Jewish state. Jabotinsky, on the other hand, impatiently preached the right of Jews not only to all of Palestine but to "both sides of the Jordan," meaning the combined area of Jordan and Palestine, or as he called it, Eretz Yisrael, the ancient land of Israel.[12]

Ben-Gurion was a gruff realist who carefully calculated his moves with a wary eye toward the interests of the great European powers and the United States. *Time* magazine, in a profile of Ben-Gurion in August, 1948, described him as "premier and defense minister, labor leader and philosopher, hardheaded, unsociable and abrupt politician, a prophet who carries a gun."[13] Wrote his biographer, Michael Bar-Zohar: "Obstinacy and total dedication to a single objective were the most characteristic traits of David Ben-Gurion."[14]

Jabotinsky, by contrast, was flamboyant and a devoted admirer of Italy's fascist leader Benito Mussolini. His disciple, Menachem Begin, described him as "a speaker, a writer, a philosopher, a statesman, a soldier, a linguist....But to those of us who were his pupils, he was not only their teacher, but also the bearer of their hope." Begin's biographer, Eric Silver, added: "There was a darker side to [Jabotinsky's] philosophy: blood, fire and steel, the supremacy of the leader, discipline and ceremony, the manipulation of the masses, racial exclusivity as the heart of the nation."[15]

One of Jabotinsky's slogans was: "We shall create, with sweat and blood, a race of men, strong, brave and cruel."[16]

Jabotinsky died in 1940 and it was Menachem Begin who refined his wild nationalism into practical political action. Begin concluded: "The world does not pity the slaughtered. It only respects those who fight." He turned Descartes' famous dictum around, saying: "We fight, therefore we exist."[17] Central to Begin's outlook was the concept of the "fighting Jew." As he wrote:

"Out of blood and fire and tears and ashes, a new specimen of human being was born, a specimen completely unknown to the world for over 1,800 years, the 'FIGHTING JEW.' It is axiomatic that those who fight have to hate....We had to hate first and foremost, the horrifying, age-old, inexcusable utter defenselessness of our Jewish people, wandering through millennia, through a cruel world, to the majority of whose inhabitants the defenselessness of the Jews was a standing invitation to massacre them."[18]

From these early leaders of Zionism (Ben-Gurion died in 1973 and Begin in 1992) have emerged their direct descendants in the Israeli political spectrum. Rabin and his successor, Shimon Peres, were both protégés of Ben-Gurion and have carried on his mainstream secular Zionism. On Jabotinsky's and Begin's side, the followers have been Yitzhak Shamir, Ariel Sharon and, now, Binyamin Netanyahu, the current leader of the Likud in 1998.

While the two major factions of Zionism disagree on tactics, their ultimate aim of maintaining a Jewish state free of non-Jews was the same. Rabin explained his strategy shortly before his death during an interview with Rowland Evans and Robert Novak:

"I believe that dreams of Jews for two thousand years to return to Zion were to build a Jewish state and not a binational state. Therefore I don't want to annex the 2.2 million Palestinians who are a different entity from us—politically, religiously, nationally—against their will to become Israelis. Therefore I see peaceful coexistence between Israel as a Jewish state—not all over the land of Israel, on most of it, its capital the united Jerusalem, its security border the Jordan River—next to it a Palestinian entity, less than a state, that runs the life of the Palestinians. It is not ruled by Israel. It is ruled by the Palestinians. This is my goal—not to return to the pre-Six-Day-War lines but to create two entities. I want a separation between Israel and the Palestinians who reside in the West Bank and the Gaza Strip and they will be a different entity that rules itself."[19]

In the Revisionist's vocabulary, the goal was the same, if more expansionist and expressed in more direct and pugnacious words. Former Defense Minister Ariel Sharon, a leading spokesman of Zionism's right wing, commented in 1993: "Our forefathers did not come here in order to build a democracy but to build a Jewish state."[20]

The occupation of all of Palestine, including Jerusalem, in the 1967 war and the coming to power a decade later of Menachem Begin gave a profound boost to Revisionism and its radical philosophy. During this period there arose the firebrand Meir Kahane, a Brooklyn-born rabbi who openly espoused the removal of the Palestinians from all of Palestine. Under the influence of his fiery rhetoric, thousands of Orthodox Jewish Americans were encouraged to emigrate to Israel as settlers on occupied Palestinian land, adding to the radicalization of Israeli politics. After Kahane's assassination in New York in 1990 by an Arab, *New York Times* correspondent John Kifner reported that Kahane had been successful in the sense that many of his ideas "had crept into the mainstream" in Israel.

Dr. Ehud Sprinzak, an Israeli expert on the far right in Israel, observed: "Where [Kahane] has succeeded is in changing the thinking of many Israelis toward anti-Arab feelings and violence. He forced the more respectable parties to change. In the 1970s Kahane was in the political wilderness, but in the 1980s the center had moved toward Kahane." Observed the Jewish Telegraphic Agency: "Rabbi Kahane could die satisfied that his message has impacted deeply and widely throughout Israeli society."[21]

By the mid-1990s, even Kahane's violent ideas seemed somewhat mild in the context of the radicalized politics of Israel. A new strain of religious extremism has been added to the Revisionist ranks. This became obvious on Feb. 25, 1994, when Brooklyn-born Dr. Baruch Goldstein, a Kahane disciple, walked into the Ibrahimi mosque, called the Cave of Machpela by Jews, in Hebron and killed 29 and wounded upwards of 150 Palestinian worshippers.[22] While Rabin and labor Zionists condemned him, Goldstein became a hero for Revisionist Zionists. A shrine was made of his grave and a group of Revisionists grew up called "Goldsteiners." They are dedicated to the "sublime ideals of Goldstein" and urge "all true Jews to follow his footsteps."[23]

While the Revisionists had always had an element of religious messianism, the most radical of their current heirs come fom ultrareligious Orthodox Jews who are less consumed by politics than religion.[24] They believe they are God's messengers. Thus Rabin's assassin, Yigal Amir, cited the authority of God to explain the murder.

This is a sea change in the mindset—if not the violence—of the traditional Revisionists. For instance, in 1943 Yitzhak Shamir ordered the assassination of one of his closest Sternist friends, but offered an entirely different rationale that had nothing to do with God. Mainly the motive stemmed from political and tactical reasons. Shamir wrote in his memoirs, *In the Final Analysis*, that Stern commander Eliyahu Giladi had become "strange and wild" and had wanted to shoot at crowds of Jews and urged the assassination of David Ben-Gurion, acts that would have been highly unpopular. Wrote Shamir: "I was afraid that he had gone completely crazy. I knew that I had to take a fateful decision, and I didn't evade it."[25] Giladi was fatally shot in the back on a beach south of Tel Aviv and his killer was never found.[26]

The new Revisionists have now expanded the right to kill claimed by the early Revisionists in the name of nationalism to include a divine right. In the end, they are less interested in foreign and domestic affairs than in justifying man's acts to God. It is a powerful and inflammatory mix of nationalism and religion that is almost certain to lead to more violence unless Israel is able to look into its own soul. ᴈ

RECOMMENDED READING:

Bar-Zohar, Michael, *Ben-Gurion: A Biography*, New York, Delacorte Press, 1978.

Begin, Menachem, *The Revolt*, Los Angeles, Nash Publications, 1972.

Bell, J. Bowyer, *Terror Out of Zion*, New York, St. Martin's Press, 1977.

Ben-Gurion, David, *Israel: A Personal History*, New York, Funk & Wagnalls, Inc., 1971.

Bethell, Nicholas, *The Palestine Triangle: The Struggle for the Holy Land, 1935-48*, New York, G.P. Putnam's Sons, 1979.

*Brenner, Lenni, *Zionism in the Age of the Dictators*, Westport, CT: Lawrence Hill, 1983.

*Brenner, Lenni, *The Iron Wall: Zionist Revisionism from Jabotinsky to Shamir*, London, Zed Books Led., 1984.

*Halsell, Grace, *Prophecy and Politics: Militant Evangelists on the Road to Nuclear War*, Westport, CT, Lawrence Hill & Company, 1986.

Khalidi, Walid (ed.), *Before Their Diaspora: A Photographic History of the Palestinians 1986-1948*, Washington, DC, Institute for Palestine Studies, 1984.

Khalidi, Walid (ed.), *From Haven to Conquest: Readings in Zionism and the Palestine Problem until 1948*, Washington, DC, Institute for Palestine Studies, second printing, 1987.

Marton, Kati, *A Death in Jerusalem*, New York, Pantheon Books, 1994.

Nakhleh, Issa, *Encyclopedia of the Palestine Problem* (2 vols), New York, Intercontinental Books, 1991.

Palumbo, Michael, *The Palestinian Catastrophe: The 1948 Expulsion of a People from their Homeland*, Boston, Faber and Faber, 1987.

Rubinstein, Ammon, *The Zionist Dream Revisited*, New York, Schocken Books, 1984.

Sachar, Howard M., *A History of Israel: From the Rise of Zionism to Our Time*, Tel Aviv, Steimatzky's Agency Ltd., 1976.

Silver, Eric, *Begin: The Haunted Prophet*, New York, Random House, 1984.

Tillman, Seth, *The United States in the Middle East: Interests and Obstacles*, Bloomington, Indiana University Press, 1982.

*Available through the AET Book Club.

NOTES:

[1] Sam Pope Brewer, *New York Times*, 1/5/48, and Khalidi, *Before Their Diaspora*, p. 316. Also see Palumbo, *The Palestinian Catastrophe*, pp. 83-4. Initial reports put the death toll at 34.

[2] Bethell, *The Palestine Triangle*, p. 263; Sachar, *A History of Israel*, p. 267. Details on the bombing and reaction of British officials are in Nakhleh, *Encyclopedia of the Palestine Problem*, pp. 269-70.

[3] Bethell, *Palestine Triangle*, pp. 181-87, 263; Sachar, *A History of Israel*, p. 267; Marton, *A Death in Jerusalem*, p. 208.

[4] Khalidi, *From Haven to Conquest*, pp. 761-78; Silver, *Begin*, pp. 88-96; Nakhleh, *Encyclopedia of the Palestine Problem*, pp. 271-72.

[5] Silver, *Begin*, p. 12.

[6] *New York Times*, 11/27/48.

[7] Bar-Zohar, *Ben-Gurion*, p. 175.

[8] Silver, *Begin*, p. 98.

[9] Bethell, *The Palestine Triangle*, pp. 308-9. An interview reflecting Hecht's views appeared in *The New York Times*, 5/28/47.

[10] Silver, *Begin*, p. 108.

[11] *Ibid.*

[12] In Hebrew, Eretz Yisrael means the Land of Israel, a phrase invested with strong nationalist feelings.

[13] *Time*, 8/16/48.

[14] Bar-Zohar, *Ben Gurion*, pp. 77, xvii.

[15] Silver, *Begin*, p. 11.

[16] Elfi Pallis, "The Likud Party: A Primer," *Journal of Palestine Studies*, Winter 1992, p. 45.

[17] Begin, *The Revolt*, pp. 36, 46. Also see Tillman, *The United States in the Middle East*, p. 20.

[18] Begin, *The Revolt*, pp. xi-xii. Also see Elfi Pallis, "The Likud Party: A Primer," *Journal of Palestine Studies*, Winter 1992, p. 45.

[19] Evans and Novak, CNN, 10/1/95.

[20] Menachem Shalev, *Forward*, 5/21/93.

[21] John Kifner, *New York Times*, 11/11/90.

[22] David Hoffman, *Washington Post*, 2/28/94.

[23] Khalid M. Amayreh, "Six Months On," *Middle East International*, 9/9/94.

[24] Halsell, *Prophecy and Politics*, p. 75, provides an excellent analysis of the extremist beliefs of Jabotinsky and his followers and their alliance with American fundamentalist Christians such as Jerry Falwell, leader of the Moral Majority.

[25] Clyde Haberman, *New York Times*, 1/15/94.

[26] Glenn Frankel, *Washington Post*, 11/6/95.

Chapter 6

1948: Israel's Capture of Jaffa

ON MAY 13, 1948—two days before Israel's creation—the all-Arab seaside city of Jaffa surrendered to Jewish forces. It was the largest Arab city in Palestine and, under the U.N. Partition Plan, was to have been part of a Palestinian state. But Menachem Begin's terrorist Irgun group began bombarding civilian sectors of the city on April 25, terrifying the inhabitants into panicky flight.

At the time, the city's normal population of around 75,000 was already down to 55,000. On the day of surrender less than three weeks later, only about 4,500 remained.[1] The rest of Jaffa's citizens had fled their homes in terror, becoming part of the 726,000 Palestinian refugees created by the war.

Although Arab armies from neighboring countries did not enter Palestine until May 15, Jewish forces had been active in a campaign of ethnic cleansing since passage of the partition plan the previous Nov. 29. The first effort was aimed at clearing out Palestinians living in cities designated as part of the Jewish state.

This began in a major way on April 18, when Tiberias was captured and its 5,500 Palestinian residents put in flight. On April 22, Haifa fell to the Jewish forces and 70,000 Palestinians fled. On May 10, the 12,000 Palestinians of Safed were routed and the next day Beisan, with 6,000 Palestinians, fell.

Preceding these conquests had been the massacre at Deir Yassin on April 9, where 254 innocent Palestinian men, women and children were killed by a combined force drawn from Irgun and from

Lehi, Jewish terrorist groups. Reports of the savagery of the attack had spread throughout the Palestinian community and caused widespread dread at the advance of Jewish forces.[2]

The capture of Jaffa differed from the earlier conquests in that under the U.N. plan it was supposed to remain as a Palestinian enclave between neighboring Tel Aviv and areas to the south and east designated as part of the Jewish state. Its capture demonstrated that in the future Israelis were not going to observe the limits set on their state by the United Nations.

According to Jewish intelligence officer Shmuel Toledano the reasons for Palestinians fleeing were: "First because the Etzel [Irgun] had been shelling Jaffa for three weeks before the Haganah [regular army] entered, making the Arabs very much afraid; some already began to leave as a result of that shelling by Etzel. [Second,] there were rumors, based on the Etzel reputation, [that] the minute the Jews entered the town, the inhabitants would all be slaughtered."[3]

After the conquest, Irgun forces indulged in widespread looting. Reported Jon Kimche, former editor of the *Jewish Observer* and *Middle East Review,* the official organ of the Zionist Federation of Britain:

"For the first time in the still undeclared war, a Jewish force commenced to loot in wholesale fashion."[4] At first the young Irgunists pillaged only dresses, blouses and ornaments for their girl friends. But this discrimination was soon abandoned. Everything that was movable was carried from Jaffa—furniture, carpets, pictures, crockery and pottery, jewelry and cutlery.

The occupied parts of Jaffa were stripped, and yet another traditional military characteristic raised its ugly head. Historian Michael Palumbo wrote of Jaffa: "Not content with looting, the Irgun fighters smashed or destroyed everything which they could not carry off, including pianos, lamps and window-panes. David Ben-Gurion afterwards admitted that Jews of all classes poured into Jaffa from Tel Aviv to participate in what he called 'a shameful and distressing spectacle.'"[5]

When future Israeli Prime Minister Ben-Gurion learned that Jaffa had fallen, he wrote in his diary: "Jaffa will be a Jewish city. War is war." To accomplish this, Israel set up a housing committee that was to allocate Palestinian homes and apartments to newly arrived Jewish families on certain dates. But Israelis ignored the dates and occupied the abandoned residences on a first-come, first-possess basis. Israeli immigrant chief Giora Yoseftal reported: "Thus the populating of Jaffa was achieved by continuous invasions and counter-invasions [of unauthorized immigrants]." Within a short time some 45,000 Jews had moved into abandoned Palestinian homes in Jaffa.[6] Although no figures appear to be available for Jaffa, Palestinian bank accounts in Haifa containing 1.5 billion Palestinian pounds were seized by Israel.[7]

There was also desecration of Christian churches. Father Deleque, a Catholic priest, reported:

"Jewish soldiers broke down the doors of my church and robbed many precious and sacred objects. Then they threw the statues of Christ down into a nearby garden." He added that Jewish leaders had reassured him that religious buildings would be respected, "but their deeds do not correspond to their words."[8]

Nearly a year after the fall of Jaffa, a group of Palestinian notables from that city who had become refugees in Beirut submitted to U.S. Minister to Lebanon Lowell C. Pinkerton an appeal to the United States to redress their grievances. The appeal included enclosures of agreements with the Haganah and a report on the conditions in Jaffa, the flight of Jaffa's refugees and how they were forced to abandon their land and property. It ended with the warning that "unless they [the refugees] are effectively resettled in their own homes and lands, the peace sought for in this part of the world will never reign, even though it might appear on the surface that the trouble has subsided."[9]

Today, a half-century later, the Palestinians remain refugees. But visitors arriving at Ben-Gurion Airport in Israel can hear about the old abandoned homes in a booklet called *The Opinionated Tourist Guide*. The guide is given to tourists, who can read that "the most beautiful homes in the country are the old Arab ones made of stone, built in the early part of the century, that dot the capital and some streets of Haifa and Jaffa...They cost a fortune, however—$1 million is not uncommon—and there aren't many of them for sale."[10] ❧

RECOMMENDED READING:

Khalidi, Walid (ed.), *From Haven to Conquest: Readings in Zionism and the Palestine Problem until 1948,* Washington, DC, Institute for Palestine Studies, second printing, 1987.

Morris, Benny, *The Birth of the Palestine Refugee Problem,* New York, Cambridge University Press, 1987.

Nakhleh, Issa, *Encyclopedia of the Palestine Problem* (2 vols.), New York, Intercontinental Books, 1991.

Palumbo, Michael, *The Palestinian Catastrophe: The 1948 Expulsion of a People from their Homeland,* Boston, Faber and Faber, 1987.

Quigley, John, *Palestine and Israel: A Challenge to Justice,* Durham, Duke University Press, 1990.

Segev, Tom, *1949: The First Israelis,* New York, The Free Press, 1986.

Silver, Eric, *Begin: The Haunted Prophet,* New York, Random House, 1984.

NOTES:

[1] Morris, *The Birth of the Palestinian Refugee Problem,* pp. 96-101.

[2] Khalidi, *From Haven to Conquest,* contains de Reynier's moving first-hand account as well as accounts of attacks on other Palestinian centers, pp. 761-78. Many writers have discussed the massacre, perhaps none better than Silver, *Begin,* pp. 88-96. Also see details in Nakhleh, *Encyclopedia of the Palestine Problem,* pp. 271-72.

[3] Quigley, *Palestine and Israel,* p. 61.

[4] However, widespread looting had already taken place in Haifa, according to Kimche's own reports; see Palumbo, *The Palestine Catastrophe,* p. 65.

[5] Palumbo, *The Palestinian Catastrophe,* p. 91.

[6] Segev, *1949,* pp. 75-76.

[7] *Ibid.,* p. 73.

[8] Palumbo, *The Palestinian Catastrophe,* p. 91.

[9] Lowell C. Pinkerton, Minister to Lebanon, to the Secretary of State, April 11, 1949, located in U.S. State Department Central Files on Lebanon, 1945-49. Text in *Journal of Palestine Studies,* "Historical Document," Spring 1989, pp. 96-109.

[10] Russell Harris, "Letter from Tel Aviv," *Middle East International,* Jan. 7, 1994.

Chapter 7

1948: From Its Beginning, Israeli Policy Promoted War, Not Peace

O N MAY 14, 1948, Britain ended its mandate over Palestine and Jews declared the establishment of Israel. General Sir Alan Cunningham, the British High Commissioner in Palestine, felt on his departure an "overwhelming sadness....Thirty years and we achieved nearly nothing."[1]

In fact, he and many other Britons felt considerable bitterness toward the Jews. Since the end of World War II, Britain had lost 338 citizens at the hands of Jewish terrorists.[2] Ahead was a half-century of bloodletting.

First there came an attempt by the Jews to complete the ethnic cleansing of Jerusalem. As the British withdrew, Jewish troops completed their occupation of most of southern and western Jerusalem, popularly known as New Jerusalem.[3] Reported Pablo de Azcarate, secretary of the Consular Truce Commission: "Hardly had the last English soldier disappeared than the Jews launched their offensive, consolidating their possession of Katamon which they occupied two weeks before and seizing the German Colony and the other southern districts of Jerusalem. The last remaining Arabs were liquidated, and from henceforth, the Jews were absolute masters of the southern part of the city."[4]

One Palestinian resident, Naim Halaby, reported "an orgy of looting" by Jews. He saw "one group bring a horse and a cart up to his next-door neighbor's abandoned home and systematically strip it bare. Down the street other looters carried away tires, furniture, kerosene and heaps of clothing from another house."[5]

Arabs living in West Jerusalem accounted for more than half of the Arabs in the city, between 50,000 to 60,000 of the 101,000 total in 1948. They were undefended and either fled or were killed, leaving behind only those residing inside the Old City and three nearby districts. Jewish troops tried to capture the Old City—they attacked Jaffa Gate, Damascus Gate, New Gate, Nebi Daoud Gate—but failed to penetrate them.[6]

When the fighting for Jerusalem finally stopped in autumn, Israeli forces occupied 12 of the 15 Arab districts in new, western Jerusalem: Deir Abu Tor, Greek Colony, German Colony, Katamon, Lower Bakaa, Mamillah, Musrarah, Nebi Daoud, Sheikh Bader, Sheikh Jarrah, Talbieh and Upper Bakaa. No Palestinians were left. The conquest of these Arab districts provided Jewish immigrants with some 10,000 homes, most of them fully furnished.[7]

Indicative of how the demographics of Jerusalem changed was the ratio between Jews and Arabs over the next two decades. The Jewish population increased from 99,690 in 1947 to 194,000 in 1967, while the Arabs went from 50,000 to zero in Jewish West Jerusalem and from 50,000 to 70,000 in the Old City and its environs.[8]

At 4 p.m. local time in Tel Aviv, on May 14, 1948, David Ben-Gurion read the proclamation of independence, declaring the birth of Israel as of midnight.[9]

Although Ben-Gurion's proclamation promised in soaring words freedom and justice for all, there was no mention made of the U.N. Partition Plan's call for creation of an Arab state, nor the extent of Israel's borders. The question of Israel's borders went to the heart of the kind of country Israel would be—whether a peaceful state content with its size mandated by the world community or an expansionist Zionist state determined to wrest away the Palestinians' land.

The Jews chose expansion. Two days before declaring independence, the Provisional State Council, the Jewish pre-state government, had voted 5 to 4 not to mention borders. As Ben-Gurion had argued: "If the U.N. does not come into account in this matter, and they [the Arab states] make war against us and we defeat them…why should we bind ourselves?"[10] It was an artful way to say the Jews should grab as much land as they could.

It is clear from its inception that Israel chose not only expansion but also repression of the Palestinians. In its declaration of independence, Israel adopted "the legal system prevailing on May 14, 1948," including the British Defense (Emergency) Regulations.[11] These laws numbered over 160 decrees promulgated by Britain in 1945 to put down Jewish terrorism and gave authorities the right to expel suspects, detain them without trial, restrict their movements, destroy their homes and other extralegal powers.[12]

The martial law regulations gave Israel unfettered power over the 160,000 Palestinians living under Israeli control.[13] When Britain originally imposed the regulations, the Jews had been furious and charged London with inhumanity.

Dr. Bernard Joseph, later Israeli Minister of Justice Dov Yosef, called them "terrorism under official seal." Yaakov S. Shapira, Israel's future attorney general, said: "The regime created by the Emergency Regulations is without precedent in a civilized society. Even Nazi Germany had no such laws...Only one kind of system resembles these conditions—that of a country under occupation."[14] Menachem Begin called the regulations "Nazi laws" and vowed not to obey them, although he had no complaint about them when Israel later used them against the Palestinians.[15]

Israeli writer Tom Segev explained: "Martial law was initially instituted to prevent the return of refugees, or 'infiltrators,' as they were called, and to prevent those who had succeeded in crossing the border from returning to their homes....

"The second role assigned to martial rule was to evacuate semi-abandoned neighborhoods and villages as well as some which had not been abandoned—and to transfer their inhabitants to other parts of the country. Some were evacuated from a 'security cordon' along the borders, and others were removed in order to make room for Jews. The third function of martial rule was to impose political supervision over the Arab population. In the process, the Arabs were isolated from the Jewish population."[16]

The regulations were used to rule over Israeli Palestinians until 1966 when martial law was finally declared ended.[17] Since then Israel has found even more imaginative laws to enforce its occupation.

As for expansionism, Israel's actions said more than any proclamation could. When the 1948 fighting ended, Israel held 8,000 square miles, equal to 77.4 percent, of the 10,434 square miles of Palestine's land. Under the U.N. Partition Plan of 1947, it had been apportioned 56.47 percent even though its population was only half of the Palestinians'.[18]

Surely it was no accident—certainly not the "miraculous" event that Israel's first president, Chaim Weizmann, claimed[19]—that nearly two-thirds of the original 1.2 million Palestinian population was displaced and turned into refugees. Under Israeli pressure they fled their homes and businesses and Israelis took them over, enormously simplifying the task of establishing a new state. The value of immovable property left behind by the Palestinian refugees has been estimated at $4 million to $80 million in 1947 terms, to as high as seven times that amount.[20] This massive loss was the reason that the war became known to Arabs as the *nakba*—the Catastrophe.[21]

Israel completed its conquest of Palestine with the capture of the entire area in 1967, including Syria's Golan Heights. Since then, it has also taken over southern Lebanon and refuses to this day (1998) to surrender it as it does the Golan Heights and much of the West Bank and Gaza Strip.

Suppression of the Palestinians and conquest of Arab land was a formula for war, not peace. And that was what Israel got for the next half-century—and will continue to court until it allows the Palestinians their freedom and the Arabs their land. ❧

RECOMMENDED READING:

Abu-Lughod, Ibrahim (ed.), *Transformation of Palestine* (2nd ed.), Evanston, Northwestern University Press, 1987.

Azcarate, Pablo de, *Mission in Palestine, 1948-1952*, Washington, DC, Middle East Institute, 1966.

Bar-Zohar, Michael, *Ben-Gurion: A Biography*, New York, Delacorte Press, 1978.

Ben-Gurion, David, *Israel: A Personal History*, New York, Funk & Wagnalls, Inc., 1971.

Ben-Gurion, David, *Israel: Years of Challenge*, Jerusalem, Massadah-P.E.C. Press Ltd., 1963.

Bethell, Nicholas, *The Palestine Triangle: The Struggle for the Holy Land, 1935-48*, New York, G.P. Putnam's Sons, 1979.

Cattan, Henry, *Jerusalem*, New York, St. Martin's Press, 1981.

Collins, Larry and Dominique Lapierre, *O Jerusalem!*, New York, Simon and Schuster, 1972.

Davis, Uri & Norton Mezvinsky, *Documents from Israel 1967-73: Readings for a Critique of Zionism*, London, Ithaca Press, 1975.

Epp, Frank, H., *Whose Land is Palestine?*, Grand Rapids, Michigan, William B. Eerdmans Publishing Company, 1974.

Flapan, Simha, *The Birth of Israel: Myths and Realities*, New York, Pantheon Books, 1987.

Forsythe, David P., *United Nations Peacemaking: The Conciliation Commission for Palestine*, Baltimore, The Johns Hopkins University Press, 1972.

Karp, Yehudit, *The Karp Report: Investigation of Suspicions Against Israelis in Judea and Samaria*, Jerusalem, Israeli Government, 1984.

Khalidi, Walid (ed.), *From Haven to Conquest: Readings in Zionism and the Palestine Problem until 1948*, Washington, DC, Institute for Palestine Studies, second printing, 1987.

Laqueur, Walter and Barry Rubin (eds.), *The Israel-Arab Reader* (revised and updated), New York, Penguin Books, 1987.

Lustick, Ian, *Arabs in the Jewish State: Israel's Control of a National Minority*, Austin, Texas, University of Texas Press, 1980.

Morris, Benny, *The Birth of the Palestine Refugee Problem*, New York, Cambridge University Press, 1987.

Nakhleh, Issa, *Encyclopedia of the Palestine Problem* (2 vols), New York, Intercontinental Books, 1991.

Quigley, John, *Palestine and Israel: A Challenge to Justice*, Durham, Duke University Press, 1990.

Sachar, Howard M., *History of Israel: From the Rise of Zionism to Our Time*, Tel Aviv, Steimatzky's Agency Ltd., 1976.

Segev, Tom, *1949: The First Israelis*, New York, The Free Press, 1986.

Shipler, David K., *Arab and Jew: Wounded Spirits in a Promised Land*, New York, Times Books, 1986

Tannous, Izzat, *The Palestinians: A Detailed Documented Eyewitness History of Palestine under British Mandate*, New York, I.G.T. Company, 1988.

NOTES

[1]Collins and Lapierre, *O Jerusalem!* p. 13.

[2]Bethell, *The Palestine Triangle*, p. 360. The text of Britain's withdrawal statement is in *New York Times*, 5/14/48; the text includes a history of Britain's policy during the Mandate.

[3]Azcarate, *Mission in Palestine 1948-1952*, p. 43.

[4]*Ibid.*

[5]Collins and Lapierre, *O Jerusalem!*, p. 412.

[6]Tannous, *The Palestinians*, pp. 565-67.

[7]Cattan, *Jerusalem*, pp. 51, 61.

[8]*Ibid.*, p. 63.

[9]Text of the proclamation is in *New York Times*, 5/15/48; Laqueur and Rubin, *The Israel-Arab Reader*, pp. 125-28; Ben Gurion, *Israel*, pp. 79-81. A total of 37 Jews attended the Tel Aviv independence meeting. Arab critics charged their action had no binding legal force in international law because they represented a minority population and only one of them had been born in Palestine; the others were from European countries. Declared Palestinian scholar Issa Nakhleh: "The Jewish minority had no right to declare an independent state on a territory belonging to the Palestinian Arab nation"; see Nakhleh, *Encyclopedia of the Palestine Problem*, p. 4.

[10]Bar-Zohar, *Ben-Gurion*, p. 161. Also see Flapan, *The Birth of Israel*, pp.34-36, for a detailed examination of early Israeli territorial intentions.

[11]Ben-Gurion, *Israel: Years of Challenge*, p. 43.

[12]Quigley, *Palestine and Israel*, p. 102. Quigley points out that the British had rescinded the emergency relations just before their departure, so strictly speaking Israel did not adopt them. A selection of the regulations can be found in Karp, *The Karp Report*, Appendix II, pp. 65-84.

[13]Lustick, *Arabs in the Jewish State*, p. 49.

[14]Segev, *1949*, p. 50. Also see James J. Zogby, *Palestinians: The Invisible Victims*, American-Arab Anti-Discrimination Committee, 1981, p. 32, and Rabbi Elmer Berger, "A Critique of the Department of State's 1981 Country Report on Human Rights Practices in the State of Israel," Americans for Middle East Understanding, undated.

[15]Segev, *1949*, p. 50n.

[16]*Ibid.*, p. 52.

[17]Lustick, *Arabs in the Jewish State*, p. 123.

[18]Epp, *Whose Land is Palestine?*, p. 195; Sachar, *History of Israel*, p. 350. For details of Israel's plans for occupying Palestinian territory, see Khalidi, *From Haven to Conquest*, pp. lxxv-lxxxiii, 755-61. For an excellent study of Jewish land ownership, see Ruedy in Abu-Lughod, *Transformation of Palestine*, pp. 119-138. Also see Davis & Mezvinsky, *Documents from Israel 1967-1973*, pp. 43-54; Morris, *The Birth of the Palestinian Refugee Problem*, pp. 155, 179; Nakhleh, *Encyclopedia of the Palestine Problem*, pp. 305-45; Shipler, *Arab and Jew*, pp. 32-36; Segev, *1949*, pp. 69-71.

[19]Sachar, *History of Israel*, p. 439.

[20]Forsythe, *United Nations Peacemaking*, pp. 117-19.

[21]Walid Khalidi, "The Palestine Problem: an overview," *Journal of Palestine Studies*, Autumn 1991, p. 9.

Chapter 8

1948: Israel's Capture of Lydda-Ramleh

ON JULY 13, 1948, Israel turned its troops against the all-Palestinian towns of Lydda and Ramleh, forcefully compelling the entire population of as many as 70,000 men, women and children to flee their homes. Systematic looting followed. Swarms of new Jewish immigrants flocked to Lydda and Ramleh, and within days these ancient towns were transformed from Palestinian to Jewish municipalities.

Lydda and Ramleh lay east of Jaffa, between Jerusalem and Tel Aviv, and were to be part of the Palestinian state—as was Jaffa—according to the United Nations Partition Plan of 1947. However, since serious fighting had begun in April, 1948, Israel had not only secured its own territory designated by the U.N. as part of the Jewish state but was now expanding its control into areas designated Palestinian. Jaffa had already been "cleansed" of its Palestinian population and come under Israeli control.

The initial attack against Lydda-Ramleh was led on April 11 by Lt. Col. Moshe Dayan, who was later Israel's defense minister and foreign minister. Israeli historians describe him as driving at the head of his armored battalion "full speed into Lydda, shooting up the town and creating confusion and a degree of terror among the population."[1]

Two American news correspondents witnessed what happened in the ensuing assault. Keith Wheeler of the *Chicago Sun Times* wrote in an article titled "Blitz Tactics Won Lydda" that "practically everything in their way died. Riddled corpses lay by the roadside." Kenneth Bilby of the *New York Herald Tribune* wrote that he saw "the corpses of Arab men, women and even children strewn about in the wake of the ruthlessly brilliant charge."[2]

All men of military age were sent to camps and all transport commandeered. The residents of Lydda were promised that if they congregated in mosques and churches they would be safe. On July 12, a brief firefight broke out in Lydda between Israeli soldiers and a Jordanian reconnaissance team in which two Israelis were killed. In retaliation, the Israeli commander issued orders to shoot anyone on the streets. Israeli soldiers turned their wrath at those cowering in mosques and churches, killing scores of them in Dahmash mosque alone. Palestinians venturing from their homes were also shot and killed. At least 250 Lyddans were killed and many others wounded.[3]

That same day, Prime Minister David Ben-Gurion ordered all the Palestinians expelled. The order said: "The residents of Lydda must be expelled quickly without attention to age." It was signed by Lieutenant Colonel Yitzhak Rabin, operations chief of the Lydda-Ramleh attack and later Israel's military chief of staff and its prime minister in 1974-77 and from 1992 until his assassination in 1995.[4] A similar order was issued about Ramleh.

The next day the massive forced exodus of the Palestinians began. The Ramlehans were luckier than their neighbors from Lydda. Most of the Ramleh expellees were driven into exile in buses and trucks. The Lyddans were forced to walk.

The commander of Jordan's Arab Legion, John Bagot Glubb Pasha, reported: "Perhaps 30,000 people or more, almost entirely women and children, snatched up what they could and fled from their homes across the open fields....It was a blazing day in July in the coastal plains—the temperature about 100 degrees in the shade. It was 10 miles across open hilly country, much of it ploughed, part of it stony fallow covered with thorn bushes, to the nearest Arab village of Beit Sira. Nobody will ever know how many children died."[5]

Israeli historian Benny Morris reported: "All the Israelis who witnessed the events agreed that the exodus, under a hot July sun, was an extended episode of suffering for the refugees, especially from Lydda. Some were looted by soldiers of their valuables as they left town or at checkpoints along the way....One Israeli soldier...recorded vivid impressions of the thirst and hunger of the refugees on the roads, and of how 'children got lost' and of how a child fell into a well and drowned, ignored, as his fellow refugees fought each other to draw water. Another soldier described the spoor left by the slow-shuffling columns, 'to begin with [jettisoning] utensils and furniture and in the end, bodies of men, women and children, scattered along the way.'

"Quite a few refugees died—from exhaustion, dehydration and disease—along the roads eastwards, from Lydda and Ramleh, before reaching temporary rest near and in Ramallah. Palestinian Nimr Khatib put the death toll among the Lydda refugees during the trek eastward at 335.[6]

More than just the murderous sun and rough terrain contributed to the miseries of the displaced Palestinians. Israeli soldiers searched them for valuables and indiscriminately killed those they took a dislike to or thought were hiding possessions. The *London Economist* reported: "The Arab refugees were systematically stripped of all their belongings before they were sent on their trek to the frontier. Household belongings, stores, clothing, all had to be left behind."[7] One youthful Palestinian survivor recalled: "Two of my friends were killed in cold blood. One was carrying a box presumed to have money and the other a pillow which was believed to contain valuables. A friend of mine resisted and was killed in front of me. He had 400 Palestinian pounds in his pocket."[8]

After the forced exit of the Palestinians, looting began in Lydda and Ramleh. Israeli historian Simha Flapan reported: "With the population gone, the Israeli soldiers proceeded to loot the two towns in an outbreak of mass pillaging that the officers could neither prevent nor control....Even the soldiers from the Palmach—most of whom came from or were preparing to join kibbutzim—took part, stealing mechanical and agricultural equipment."[9] Israeli troops carted away 1,800 truck loads of Palestinian property, including a button factory, a sausage factory, a soft drinks plant, a macaroni factory, a textile mill, 7,000 retail shops, 1,000 warehouses and 500 workshops.[10]

In place of the Palestinians came new Jewish immigrants and Lydda and Ramleh quickly "became mainly Jewish towns," in the words of historian Morris.[11] Lydda is now called Lod.

The brutal expulsion of the Palestinians of Lydda and Ramleh long remained a sensitive topic in Israel. Rabin candidly wrote about the incident in his memoirs in the late 1970s but the passage was censored by the Israeli government.[12] In 1978, the Israeli censor canceled a TV film based on Yizhar Smilansky's classic *The Tale of Hirber Hiza,* a novella he wrote under the pen name of S.Yizhar about his experiences as a young Israeli intelligence officer who witnessed in 1948 the expulsion of Palestinians from their homes. Smilansky's offending lines included this one: "We came, shot, burned, blew up, pushed and exiled....Will the walls not scream in the ears lf those who will live in this village?"[13]

The reverberations of the brutal treatment of the residents of Lydda and Ramleh continue to this day. One of the families forced from Lydda was that of George Habash. He later became one of Israel's most feared foes as head of the militant Palestinian guerrilla group Popular Front for the Liberation of Palestine.[14] The PFLP today is among the rejectionist groups opposing peace with Israel. ✍

RECOMMENDED READING:

Flapan, Simba, *The Birth of Israel: Myths and Realities,* New York, Pantheon Books, 1987.

Glubb Pasha (Sir John Bagot Glubb), *A Soldier with the Arabs,* London, Hodder and Stoughton, 1957.

Hirst, David, *The Gun and the Olive Branch: The Roots of Violence in the Middle East,* New York, Harcourt Brace Jovanovich, 1977.

Khalidi, Walid (ed.), *From Haven to Conquest: Readings in Zionism and the Palestine Problem until 1948,* Washington, DC, Institute for Palestine Studies, 1987.

Morris, Benny, *The Birth of the Palestine Refugee Problem,* New York, Cambridge University Press, 1987.

Nakhleh, Issa, *Encyclopedia of the Palesane Problem (2 vole),* New York, Intercontinental Books, 1991.

Palumbo, Michael, *The Palestinian Catastrophe: The 1948 Expulsion of a People From their Homeland,* Boston, Faber and Faber, 1987.

Quigley, John, *Palestine and Israel: A Challenge to Justice,* Durham, Duke University Press, 1990.

Said, Edward W. and Christopher Hitchens (eds.), *Blaming the Victims,* New York, Verso, 1988.

Segev, Tom, *1949: The First Israelis,* New York, The Free Press, 1986.

NOTES:

[1]Childers, "The Other Exodus," in Khalidi, *From Haven to Conquest,* p. 800.

[2]Palumbo, *The Palestinian Catastrophe,* p. 126.

[3]Morris, *The Birth of the Palestinian Refugee Problem,* p. 206; Palumbo, *The Palestinian Catastrophe,* p. 127.

[4]Morris, *The Birth of the Palestinian Refugee Problem,* p. 207.

[5]Glubb, *A Soldier with the Arabs,* p. 162.

[6]Morris, *The Birth of the Palestinian Refugee Problem,* p. 210.

[7]Palumbo, *The Palestinian Catastrophe,* p. 129.

[8]*Ibid.,* pp. 129-30.

[9]Flapan, *The Birth of Israel,* p. 100.

[10]Quigley, *Palestine and Israel,* p. 111.

[11]Morris, *The Birth of the Palestinian Refugee Problem,* p. 211.

[12]It was later published by both *The New York Times,* 10/23/79, and *Newsweek,* 11/9/79, and in a book by Rabin's English translator, Peretz Kidron; see Kidron, "Truth Whereby Nations Live," in Said & Hitchens (eds.), *Blaming the Victims.*

[13]*Time,* "Untimely Story," 2/20/78.

[14]Palumbo, *The Palestinian Catastrophe,* p. 131. Also see Hirst, *The Gun and the Olive Branch,* p. 280.

Chapter 9

1948: Jewish Terrorists Assassinate U.N. Peacekeeper Count Folk Bernadotte

O N SEPT. 17, 1948, Jewish terrorists assassinated Count Folke Bernadotte of Sweden as he sought to bring peace to the Middle East. His three-car convoy had been stopped at a small improvised roadblock in Jewish-controlled West Jerusalem when two gunmen began shooting out the tires of the cars and a third gunman thrust a Schmeisser automatic pistol through the open back window of Bernadotte's Chrysler. The 54-year-old diplomat, sitting on the right in the back, was hit by six bullets and died instantly. A French officer sitting next to Bernadotte was killed accidentally.

The assassins were members of Lehi (Lohamei Herut Is-rael—Fighters for the Freedom of Israel), better known as the Stern Gang. Its three leaders had decided a week earlier to have Bernadotte killed because they believed he was partial to the Arabs. One of those leaders was Yitzhak Shamir, who in 1983 would become prime minister of Israel.[1]

Bernadotte had been chosen the United Nations mediator for Palestine four months earlier in what was the U.N.'s first serious at-tempt at peacemaking in the post-World War II world. As a hero of the war, when his mediation efforts on behalf of the International Red Cross saved 20,000 persons, including thousands of Jews, from Nazi concentration camps, Bernadotte seemed a natural choice for the post.[2] The terms of the mediator's mandate were to "promote a peaceful adjustment of the future situation in Palestine" and to allow him to mediate beyond the terms of the Partition Plan.[3]

It had been only on Nov. 29, 1947 that the U.N. General Assembly had voted to partition Palestine into Arab and Jewish states. Yet, as had been widely predicted, that action had led to war. Fighting intensified after elements of five Arab armies moved into Palestine the day after Israel proclaimed its establishment on May 14, 1948. Bernadotte's first action had been to arrange a truce, which lasted from June 11 to July 9.

During the lull, Bernadotte had put forward his first proposal for solving the conflict. Instead, it was to seal his fate. Bernadotte's transgression, in the view of Jewish zealots, was to include in his June 28 proposal the suggestion that Jerusalem be placed under Jordanian rule, since all the area around the city was designated for the Arab state.[4]

The U.N. partition plan had declared Jerusalem an international city that was to be ruled by neither Arab nor Jew. But the Jewish terrorists, including Shamir and Menachem Begin, the leader of the largest terrorist group, Irgun Zvai Leumi—National Military Organization, also known by the Hebrew acronym "Etzel"—had rejected partition and claimed all of Palestine and Jordan for the Jewish state. These Jewish extremists were horrified at Bernadotte's suggestion.

By July Sternists were already threatening Bernadotte's assassination. New York Times columnist C.L. Sulzberger reported meeting with two Stern members on July 24, who stated: "We intend to kill Bernadotte and any other uniformed United Nations observers who come to Jerusalem." Asked why, "They replied that their organization was determined to seize all of Jerusalem for the state of Israel and would brook no interference by any national or international body."[5]

Since Bernadotte's first set of proposals had caused criticism from all parties, he spent the rest of the summer working up new proposals, which he finally finished on Sept. 16. Unknown publicly was the fact that in his new suggestions Bernadotte dropped his idea of turning over Jerusalem to Jordan and instead reverted to the partition plan's designation of it as an international city.[6] Thus when Shamir's gunmen cut down Bernadotte the next day, they were unaware that he no longer was advocating giving Jerusalem to the Arabs.

The assassination brought an official condemnation from the Israeli government and promises of quick arrests. However, no one was ever brought to trial nor was there any nationwide outcry against the assassination.[7] None of Lehi's leaders or the actual gunmen were ever caught, although they were early known to Israel's leaders.[8]

Israel's obvious reluctance to prosecute the assassins brought the first U.N. Security Council criticism of the new country. On Oct. 19, 1948, the council unanimously passed a resolution expressing its "concern" that Israel had "to date submitted no report to the Security Council or the Acting Mediator regarding the progress of the investigation into the assassination."[9] An official inquiry by Sweden produced a report in 1950 that charged Israel's investigation had been so negligent that "doubt must exist as to whether the Israeli authorities really tried to bring the inquiry to a positive result."[10]

Israel later admitted the laxity of its investigation and in 1950 paid the United Nations $54,628 in indemnity for Bernadotte's murder.[11]

The assassination and Israel's failure to punish the culprits struck a hard blow against the fledgling United Nations. The first secretary-general, Trygve Lie, said: "If the Great Powers accepted that this situation in the Middle East could best be settled by leaving the forces concerned to fight it out amongst themselves, it was quite clear that they would be tacitly admitting that the Security Council and the United Nations was a useless instrument in attempting to preserve peace."[12] To Secretary of State George Marshall, Lie had written on May 15, 1948 that Egypt had warned him it was about to send troops beyond its borders and against the Jewish state in Palestine, saying: "My primary concern is for the future usefulness of the United Nations and its Security Council...I must do everything to prevent this, otherwise the Security Council will have...created a precedent for any nation to take aggressive action in direct contravention to the Charter of the United Nations."[13]

But, as author Kati Marton has observed: "If the United Nations spoke with 'considerable authority' early that summer, by fall its voice was barely above a whisper in Palestine. Unwilling or unable to enforce its own decisions, the U.N. [United Nations Organization, as it was generally called in 1948] became for many Israelis in

Ben-Gurion's memorable putdown, 'UNO, schmuno.'" Marton also observed: "So muted was the world body's reaction, so lacking in any real sanctions against the Jewish state for its failure to pursue the murderers of the United Nations' mediator, that for Israel, 'world opinion' became an empty phrase."[14]

Indeed, the ideal of the U.N. acting as the world's peacemaker and peacekeeper was badly wounded with Bernadotte's death in Jerusalem. After this display of weakness, other nations did not hesitate to thumb their noses at the U.N. when it suited their purposes. ☙

RECOMMENDED READING:

Chomsky, Noam, *Pirates & Emperors: International Terrorism in the Real World*, Brattleboro, VT, Amana Books, 1986.

*Green, Stephen, *Taking Sides: America's Secret Relations with a Militant Israel*, New York, William Morrow and Company, Inc., 1984.

Kurzman, Dan, *Genesis 1948: The First Arab-Israeli War*, New York, The World Publishing Company, 1970.

Lie, Trygve, *In the Cause of Peace*, New York, Macmillan, 1954.

Marton, Kati, *A Death in Jerusalem*, New York, Pantheon Books, 1994.

Persson, Sune O., *Mediation & Assassination: Count Bernadotte's Mission to Palestine in 1948*, London, Ithaca Press, 1979.

Tomeh, George J., *United Nations Resolutions on Palestine and the Arab-Israeli Conflict: 1947-1974*, Washington, DC, Institute for Palestine Studies, 1975.

U.S. Department of State, *Foreign Relations of the United States 1948* (vol. V), The Near East, South Asia, and Africa, Washington, DC, U.S. Printing Office, 1975.

*Available through the AET Book Club.

NOTES:

[1]Marton, *A Death in Jerusalem*, p. 208. Also see Kurzman, *Genesis 1948*, pp. 555, 563; *FRUS 1948* for a contemporaneous report on Bernadotte's assassination, "The Consul General at Jerusalem (Macdonald) to the Secretary of State," Urgent, Jerusalem, Sept. 17, 1948, pp. 1412-13; Avishai Margalit, "The Violent Life of Yitzhak Shamir," *The New York Review of Books*, 5/14/92.

[2]Persson, *Mediation & Assassination*, pp. 225-29. Good background on

Bernadotte is in Marton, *A Death in Jerusalem.*

[3]The text is in Tomeh, *United Nations Resolutions on Palestine and the Arab-Israeli Conflict,* pp. 14-15.

[4]*FRUS 1948,* "Text of Suggestions Presented by Count Bernadotte, at Rhodes, to the Two Parties on June 28, 1948," pp. 1152-54.

[5]C. L. Sulzberger, *New York Times,* 9/18/48.

[6]*FRUS 1948,* "Progress Report of the United Nations Mediator in Palestine" [Extracts], undated but signed and sent to the U.N. on 16 Sept. 1948, pp. 1401-06.

[7]Chomsky, *Pirates and Emperors,* p. 85; Green, *Taking Sides,* pp. 38-44.

[8]Marton, *A Death in Jerusalem,* pp. 233, 238.

[9]Resolution No. 59, 10/19/48; the text is in Tomeh, *United Nations Resolutions on Palestine and the Arab-Israeli Conflict,* p. 129.

[10]*The Middle East Journal,* "Developments of the Quarter: Comment and Chronology," Vol. 4, No. 3, July, 1950, p. 338.

[11]*New York Times,* 6/30/50.

[12]Lie, *In the Cause of Peace,* p. 76.

[13]Marton, *A Death in Jerusalem,* pp. 22-23.

[14]*Ibid.,* pp. 242, 260.

Chapter 10

1968: Battle of Karameh Establishes Claim of Palestinian Statehood

ON MARCH 21, 1968, an Israeli armored force of 15,000 men struck at the Jordanian village of Karameh just across the Jordan River and was humiliatingly repelled by Palestinian guerrillas aided by Jordanian army artillery and armor.[1]

Israel lost at least 28 killed and 90 wounded, and a number of knocked-out tanks and other vehicles were abandoned during the hasty Israeli retreat.[2]

Although militarily the fight was won by Israel—it inflicted at least 10 times more casualties on the Arabs than it suffered itself—Karameh represented the guerrillas' greatest victory up to that time. The battle of Karameh sent a surge of optimism through the Palestinian community and established the Palestinians' claim to being a national liberation organization.[3]

Karameh also was a forceful refutation of the claim by some Israelis that Palestinians did not exist. They had at last enlarged the conflict beyond a contest between refugee and Israeli into a revolutionary context where they were widely regarded, particularly in the Third World, as an authentic political movement.[4]

Yasser Arafat, leader of Fatah, whose troops bore the brunt of the fighting, said: "What we have done is to make the world...realize that the Palestinian is no longer refugee number so and so, but the member of a people who hold the reins of their own destiny and are in a position to determine their own future."[5]

Observed Israeli diplomat Gideon Rafael: "The operation gave an enormous lift to Yasser Arafat's Fatah organization and irrevocably implanted the Palestine problem onto the international agenda, no longer as a humanitarian issue of homeless refugees, but as a claim to Palestinian statehood."[6]

Militarily, however, Karameh was the end of Arafat's strategy to emplace guerrilla bases just inside Jordan for attacks on Israel. Over the previous month Israeli attacks had been vicious, and the massiveness of its assault on Karameh forced Arafat to retreat from the border to hills deeper inside Jordan.[7] Nonetheless, the dimension of the losses inflicted on the Israelis allowed the Palestinians to declare the battle the first Palestinian victory over a regular Israeli army unit.[8]

Never before had Palestinians stood and fought the Israel Defense Forces to a standstill in such a large battle, nor had they ever inflicted such casualties. Refugee camps throughout the Arab world hailed the rebirth of the Palestinian people and volunteers flocked to the guerrilla groups.[9] Fatah reported that 5,000 volunteers applied to join within 48 hours of the battle.[10]

Karameh means "dignity," and to Palestinians everywhere their cause had finally been dignified by the blood of martyrs. So moved by the victory was King Hussein that he proclaimed: "We are all *fedayeen!*"[11]

The psychological boost and international support that Karameh gave the Palestinians more than offset their military casualties. Even outside the region there dawned a recognition that a new force was emerging and a new historic contest forming. The Palestinians were "surely...only doing what brave men always do, whose country lies under the heel of a conqueror," wrote Lady Fisher, the wife of the Archbishop of Canterbury, in a letter to the *Times* of London published five days after Karameh.[12]

The guerrillas discovered in their new popularity that they could operate openly in Jordan, which up to then had severely restricted their movements. After Karameh, they were able to move to Amman, establish recruiting offices in the capital and in other Arab countries and enjoy a degree of respect and legitimacy they had never known.[13]

From the time of the establishment of the Palestine Liberation Organization in 1964, the Palestinians had come a long way. Even the Soviet Union, which in the beginning had shown open opposition to the PLO and Fatah, began to see the guerrilla groups as representing a legitimate political movement.[14]

Before, the Soviets had deplored the extremist statements of the old PLO's leadership, urged restraint and refused to give aid. Moscow repeatedly told Fatah leaders that it supported the existence of Israel, urged them to accept U.N. Security Council Resolution 242 and refused to encourage Fatah's armed struggle.[15] But after Karameh the Soviet attitude began slowly shifting from sympathy to outright support. By 1971 it began giving material assistance to Fatah.[16]

Still, Karameh was an exception. Most of the Palestinian attacks were isolated raids, mining of roads, occasional thrown grenades and hidden bombs, a mortar shell lobbed into a village. These were pinpricks, disturbing but not fatally threatening to Israel, evidence that in the final analysis the guerrillas were no match either in manpower or equipment against the overwhelming might of Israel's military forces.

Ironically, the lesson of the battle of Karameh was that the Palestinians had to win their war not on the battlefield but in world opinion. The Palestinians began winning that battle after Karameh. Within the next decade the United Nations General Assembly would affirm the Palestinians' "inalienable rights" as a people, their right to self-determination and their right to struggle while at the same time repeatedly condemning Israel's occupation. The United States stood by Israel and voted against almost all of these resolutions.

But, tragically, the Palestinian leadership did not get the message. Shortly after Karameh, radical Palestinian groups launched a highly publicized campaign of airplane skyjackings and other high-profile terrorist attacks that had the effect of diverting attention away from their gains in the United Nations. Instead of being recognized in the public imagination as a people with rights, they had a new persona. They no longer were seen as homeless refugees or freedom fighters but as bloodthirsty terrorists. It was only in 1988, when Arafat unequivocally renounced terror, that the Palestinians began recouping the political gains they had earned at Karameh.[17]

Despite their mistakes, who could have imagined that 30 years after Karameh the Palestinians still would not have completely won their legitimate rights? To the shame of Americans, this is mainly because for U.S. domestic political reasons various U.S. administrations have ignored American ideals and continued to stand against the opinion of the entire world by ignoring or defending Israel's flouting of international law decade after decade after decade. ❧

RECOMMENDED READING:

Abu Iyad with Eric Rouleau, *My Home, My Land: A Narrative of the Palestinian Struggle*, New York, Times Books, 1978.

Cobban, Helena, *The Palestinian Liberation Organization*, New York, Cambridge University Press, 1984.

Cooley, John K., *Green March, Black September: The Story of the Palestinian Arabs*, London, Frank Cass, 1973.

Hart, Alan, *Arafat: Terrorist or Peacemaker?*, London, Sidgwick & Jackson, 1985.

Heikal, Mohamed, *The Sphinx and the Commissar: The Rise and Fall of Soviet Influence in the Middle East*, New York, Harper & Row, 1978.

Hirst, David, *The Gun and the Olive Branch: The Roots of Violence in the Middle East*, New York, Harcourt Brace Jovanovich, 1977.

Livingstone, Neil C. and David Halevy, *Inside the PLO: Secret Units, Secret Funds, and the War Against Israel and the United States*, New York, William Morrow and Company, Inc., 1990.

Nakhleh, Issa, *Encyclopedia of the Palestine Problem* (2 vols), New York, Intercontinental Books, 1991.

Rafael, Gideon, *Destination Peace: Three Decades of Israeli Foreign Policy. A Personal Memoir*, London, Weidenfeld and Nicolson, 1981.

Tomeh, George J., *United Nations Resolutions on Palestine and the Arab-Israeli Conflict: 1947-1974*, Washington, DC, Institute for Palestine Studies, 1975.

Yodfat, Aryeh Y. and Yuval Arnon-Ohanna, *PLO: Strategy and Tactics*, London, Croom Helm, 1981.

NOTES:

[1] James Feron, *New York Times*, 3/21-2/68.

[2] Hart, *Arafat*, pp. 261-63.

[3] Hirst, *The Gun and the Olive Branch*, pp. 284-85; Cooley, *Green March, Black*

September, pp. 100-01. For a detailed description of the fierce fighting see Hart, *Arafat*, pp. 261-63.

[4]Hirst, *The Gun and the Olive Branch*, p. 299.

[5]*Ibid.*

[6]Rafael, *Destination Peace*, p. 203.

[7]Livingstone and Halevy, *Inside the PLO*, pp. 80-81.

[8]Cobban, *The Palestinian Liberation Organization*, p. 42.

[9]Thomas F. Brady, *New York Times*, 3/31/68. Also see Hirst, *The Gun and the Olive Branch*, p. 285; Cobban, The *Palestinian Liberation Organization*, pp. 39, 49.

[10]Cobban, *The Palestinian Liberation Organization*, p. 42.

[11]Abu Iyad, *My Land, My Home*, p. 61.

[12]Hirst, *The Gun and the Olive Branch*, p. 286.

[13]Hart, *Arafat*, pp. 270-71.

[14]*Ibid.*, pp. 187, 277-81.

[15]*Ibid.*, pp. 280-81.

[16]*Ibid.*, p. 355. Yodfat and Arnon-Ohanna, *PLO*, pp. 87-88, contend that modest arms aid was promised by Moscow in 1970 but fail to substantiate the claim; also see Heikal, *The Sphinx and the Commissar*, p. 211; Abu Iyad, *My Land, My Home*, pp. 65-66.

[17]The text of Arafat's statement is in *Journal of Palestine Studies*, "Documents and Source Material," Spring 1989, pp. 161-71; excerpts as provided by the PLO appeared in *New York Times*, 11/17/88.

Chapter 11

1982: Begin Describes Israel's Wars of "Choice"

O N AUG. 8, 1982, Prime Minister Menachem Begin admitted in public that Israel had fought three wars in which it had a "choice," meaning Israel started the wars. Begin's admission came in a speech delivered before the Israeli National Defense College. His purpose was to defuse mounting criticism of Israel's invasion of Lebanon, which had begun two months earlier on June 5 and was clearly one of Israel's wars of "choice." The others were in 1956 and 1967.[1]

At the time of Begin's speech, the Israeli siege of Muslim West Beirut was already five weeks old. Israeli U.S.-made aircraft were launching daily air strikes and hundreds of thousands of innocent civilians throughout the country were being killed, wounded, starved, terrorized and uprooted from their homes, most of them by munitions made in America. On July 29, the United Nations Security Council demanded that Israel lift its siege. Only the United States abstained in the 14-0 vote.[2] When Israel refused, the council voted again on Aug. 4 to censure Israel with a vote of 14-0, with the U.S. again abstaining.[3] On Aug. 6, the United States exercised its veto to block a council resolution condemning Israel's occupation practices, the sixth time in 1982 the Reagan administration had used the veto to shield Israel from international criticism.[4]

Despite the Reagan administration's lonely support of Israel, there was increasing disillusionment within Israel itself at the terrible toll being inflicted on Lebanese civilians. An estimated 10,000 Israelis had already staged a protest rally in Tel Aviv as early as June 26.[5] Another hundred thousand Israelis demonstrated against

Begin's Likud government on July 3 under the banner of Peace Now. Other antiwar groups—Yesh Givul (There is a Limit), Soldiers Against Silence, Parents Against Silence—soon sprang up as the siege continued.[6]

The anti-war mood increased when Israeli Colonel Eli Geva, head of an elite armored brigade involved in Israel's invasion of Lebanon, resigned his commission in July to protest the siege of Beirut. It was the first time that a senior Israeli officer had ever resigned in protest during any of Israel's wars.[7] When Prime Minister Begin asked Geva why he had refused to continue in the siege, the tankman replied that he could see children when he looked through his binoculars into Beirut. "Did you receive an order to kill children?" snapped Begin. No, said Geva. "Then what are you complaining about?" demanded the prime minister.[8] Yesh Givul became the strongest of the groups, with 2,000 reservists eventually signing a petition not to serve in Lebanon; 150 of them were court martialed.[9]

In his speech to Israeli security experts on Aug. 8, the prime minister sought to counter these growing anti-war protests by enlisting the military's support. His method was to link the unpopular war in Lebanon with Israel's triumphant victories in 1956 and 1967, which he was careful to point out were also wars of "choice." Now, Begin said, Israel was involved in another war of choice that would finally bring victorious peace.

BEGIN'S WORDS

"The Second World War, which broke out on Sept. 1, 1939, actually began on March 7, 1936. If only France, without Britain (which had some excellent combat divisions), had attacked the aggressor, there would have remained no trace of Nazi German power and a war which, in three years, changed the whole of human history would have been prevented. This, therefore, is the international example that explains what is war without choice, or a war of one's choosing.

"Let us turn from the international example to ourselves. Operation Peace for Galilee [the Israeli name for the invasion of Lebanon] is not a military operation resulting from the lack of an alternative. The terrorists did not threaten the existence of the state of Israel; they 'only' threatened the lives of Israel's citizens and members of the Jewish people. There are those who find fault with the second part of that sentence. If there was no danger to the existence of the state, why did you go to war?

"I will explain why: We had three wars which we fought without an alternative. The first, the war of independence, which began on Nov. 30, 1947 and lasted until January, 1949. What happened in that war, which we went off to fight with no alternative? Six thousand of our fighters were killed. We were then 650,000 Jews in Eretz Israel, and the number fallen amounted to about 1 percent of the Jewish population.

"The second war of no alternative was the Yom Kippur War and the war of attrition that preceded it. Our total casualties in that war of no alternative were 2,297 killed, 6,067 wounded. Together with the war of attrition—which was also a war of no alternative—2,659 killed, 7,251 wounded. The terrible total: almost 10,000 casualties.

"Our other wars were not without an alternative. In November, 1956 we had a choice. The reason for going to war then was the need to destroy the fedayeen, *who did not represent a danger to the existence of the state. Thus we went off to the Sinai campaign. At that time we conquered most of the Sinai Peninsula and reached Sharm el Sheikh. Actually, we accepted and submitted to an American dictate, mainly regarding the Gaza Strip (which Ben-Gurion called 'the liberated portion of the homeland'). John Foster Dulles, the then-secretary of state, promised Ben-Gurion that an Egyptian army would not return to Gaza. The Egyptian army did enter Gaza....After 1957, Israel had to wait 10 full years for its flag to fly again over that liberated portion of the homeland.*

"In June, 1967, we again had a choice. The Egyptian army concentrations in the Sinai approaches do not prove that Nasser was really about to attack us. We must be honest with ourselves. We decided to attack him. This was a war of self-defense in the noblest sense of the term. The Government of National Unity then established decided unanimously: we will take the initiative and attack the enemy, drive him back, and thus assure the security of Israel and the future of the nation.

"As for the Operation Peace for Galilee [the invasion of Lebanon], it does not really belong to the category of wars of no alternative. We could have gone on seeing our civilians injured in Metulla or Qiryat Shimona or Nahariya. We could have gone on countering those killed by explosive charges left in a Jerusalem supermarket, or a Petah Tikvah bus stop. All the orders to carry out these acts of murder and sabotage came from Beirut....True, such actions were not a threat to the existence of the state. But they did threaten the lives of civilians, whose numbers we cannot estimate, day after day, week after week, month after month....

"I—we—can already look beyond the fighting. It will soon be over, we hope, and then I believe, indeed I know, we will have a long period of peace. There is no other country around us that is capable of attacking us."[10]

In reality, it took nearly three more years before Israel was able to disengage its forces. On the third anniversary of the invasion, after suffering 610 dead, Israel withdrew most of its forces from Lebanon, leaving a residual team of about 2,000 combat troops to retain control of a "security belt" in southern Lebanon. The occupied land amounted to nine percent of Lebanon's territory, adding yet several hundred square miles more to the list of Arab land Israel had expanded on since 1948.[11] ❧

RECOMMENDED READING:

Ball, George, *Error and Betrayal in Lebanon*, Washington, DC, Foundation for Middle East Peace, 1984.

Chomsky, Noam, *The Fateful Triangle*, Boston, South End Press, 1983.

Cooley, John K., *Payback: America's Long War in the Middle East*, New York, Brassey's U.S., Inc., 1991.

*Findley, Paul, *Deliberate Deceptions: Facing the Facts about the U.S.-Israeli Relationship*, Brooklyn, NY, Lawrence Hill Books, 1993.

Fisk, Robert, *Pity the Nation: The Abduction of Lebanon*, New York, Atheneum, 1990.

*Friedman, Thomas L., *From Beirut to Jerusalem*, New York, Farrar, Strauss, Giroux, 1989.

Jensen, Michael, *The Battle of Beirut: Why Israel Invaded Lebanon*, London, Zed Press, 1982.

*Khouri, Fred J., *The Arab-Israeli Dilemma*, Syracuse, NY, Syracuse University Press, 1985.

MacBride, Sean, *Israel in Lebanon: The Report of the International Commission to enquire into reported violations of International Law by Israel during its invasion of the Lebanon*, London, Ithaca Press, 1983.

*Mallison, Thomas and Sally V., *Armed Conflict in Lebanon: Humanitarian Law in a Real World Setting*, Washington, DC, American Educational Trust, 1985, and *The Palestine Problem in International Law and World Order*, London, Longman Group Ltd., 1986.

*Randal, Jonathan, *Going all the Way*, New York, The Viking Press, 1983.

Schechla, Joseph, *The Iron Fist: Israel's Occupation of South Lebanon, 1982-1985*,

Washington, D.C., ADC Research Institute, Issue Paper No.17, 1985.

*Schiff, Ze'ev and Ya'ari, Ehud, *Israel's Lebanon War,* New York, Simon and Schuster, 1984.

Silver, Eric, *Begin: The Haunted Prophet,* New York, Random House, 1984.

Simpson, Michael, *United Nations Resolutions on Palestine and the Arab-Israeli Conflict: 1982-986,* Washington, DC, Institute for Palestine Studies, 1988.

Timerman, Jacobo, *The Longest War: Israel in Lebanon,* New York, Vantage Books, 1982.

*Available through the AET Book Club.

NOTES:

[1] Fisk, *Pity the Nation,* pp. 391-93. Excerpts in "Documents and source Material, *Journal of Palestine Studies,* Summer/Fall 1982, pp. 318-19.

[2] Resolution 515; the text is in Simpson, *United Nations Resolutions on Palestine and the Arab-Israeli Conflict: 1982-1986,* p. 220, and Mallison, *The Palestine Problem in International Law and World Order,* p. 482.

[3] Resolution 516; the text is in Simpson, *United Nations Resolutions on Palestine and the Arab-Israeli Conflict: 1982-1986,* p. 220.

[4] U.S. U.N. Mission, "List of Vetoes Cast in Public Meetings of the Security Council," 814/86. The 1982 vetoes, in addition to the one on 8/6, took place on 1/20, 4/2, 4/20, 6/8, and 6/26.

[5] Schiff and Ya'ari, *Israel's Lebanon War,* p. 216.

[6] Khouri, *The Arab-Israeli Dilemma,* p. 433.

[7] Schiff and Ya'ari, *Israel's Lebanon War,* p. 215.

[8] Silver, *Begin,* p. 237.

[9] Spiro, Gideon, "The Israeli Soldiers Who Say 'There is a Limit,'" *Middle East International,* Sept. 9, 1988. Also see "Documents and Source Material," *Journal of Palestine Studies,* Summer 1988, p.201.

[10] Fisk, *Pity the Nation,* pp. 391-93. Excerpts are in "Documents and Source Material," *Journal of Palestine Studies,* Summer/Fall 1982, pp. 318-19.

[11] Augustus Richard Norton, *Washington Post,* 3/1/88.

United Nations &
The Palestinians

Chapter 12

1948: The Right of Return of the Refugees

ON DEC. 11, 1948, the United Nations General Assembly passed Resolution 194, calling for the repatriation or compensation by Israel of the Palestinian refugees. The resolution resolved that the "refugees wishing to return to their homes and live at peace with their neighbors should be permitted to do so at the earliest practicable date, and that compensation should be paid for the property of those choosing not to return and for loss of or damage to property..."[1] The vote was 35-15-8, with the United States voting with the majority.[2]

As late as 1992, the State Department publicly reaffirmed U.S. support of the resolution.[3] In response, Israeli Prime Minister Yitzhak Shamir declared: "It will never happen in any way, shape or form. There is only a Jewish right of return to the land of Israel."[4]

Indeed, Israel has consistently refused either to take back or to compensate the 726,000 Palestinians who were forced from their homes during the fighting in 1948 that led to Israel's creation.[5] The noncombatant residents suddenly turned into refugees amounted to nearly two-thirds of the entire Palestinian population of 1.2 million living in Palestine in 1948.

There is no doubt about the major cause of why so many Palestinians became refugees in their own homeland.[6] It was the fear and panic caused by the massacre at Deir Yassin of 254 Arab women, old men and children on April 9, 1948, by members of the Jewish terrorist group Irgun Zvai Leumi, the National Military Organization, led by Menachem Begin, later one of Israel's prime ministers, and the Stern Gang, whose leadership included Shamir.[7]

Up until the massacre, only about 60,000 Arabs had fled their homes, many of them non-Palestinian employees of the mandate government.[8]

Israel steadfastly maintained for many years that the Palestinians had been urged to flee by their own leaders or had decided themselves to abandon their homes and property. In fact, in most areas, the Palestinians were actively forced to flee by Israelis or deliberately panic stricken into fleeing with reminders of Deir Yassin. The literature by now on the cause and timing of the flight of the refugees is overwhelming.[9]

By Oct. 17, 1948, the U.S. representative in Israel, James G. McDonald, reported urgently and directly to President Truman that the refugees' "tragedy is rapidly reaching catastrophic proportions and should be treated as a disaster."[10] The death rate of Palestinian refugees in the Gaza Strip alone was reported at 230 a day in the winter of 1949. The estimate was by William L. Gower, delegate for the American Red Cross. Gower reported: "Eighty to 85 percent of the displaced persons consist of children, old women, pregnant women and nursing mothers."[11]

As the gigantic dimensions of the refugee problem became apparent, it was increasingly realized that a major part of the problem was that no country, including the United States, was anxious to help the refugees and thereby assume a degree of responsibility for their uncertain future. The attitude of most nations was that Israel should allow the refugees to return to their homes or compensate them for the loss of their property. This Israel firmly refused, maintaining that the bereft Palestinians were the victims of war.

Yet America, by its strong support of the partition plan, had assumed in the eyes of many Arabs as much responsibility for the refugees' flight as Israel itself. Reported Mark F. Ethridge, the U.S. delegate of the Palestine Conciliation Commission which was meeting in Lausanne, Switzerland, to mediate peace treaties: "Since we gave Israel birth we are blamed for her belligerence and her arrogance and for the coldbloodedness of her attitude toward refugees...What I can see is an abortion of justice and humanity to which I do not want to be midwife."[12]

The magnitude of the refugee problem overwhelmed neighboring Arab states, as a U.S. report noted in March, 1949. It said that assistance to the refugees by the Arab governments was $11 million in cash or kind in the last nine months of 1948, a "relatively enormous" sum in "light of the very slender budgets of most of these governments." Israel's "total direct relief...to date consists of 500 cases of oranges."[13]

Israel was not only doing nothing to help the refugees but it was deliberately preventing them from returning to their homes. The U.S. study noted that "Israeli authorities have followed a systematic program of destroying Arab houses in such cities as Haifa and in village communities in order to rebuild modern habitations for the influx of Jewish immigrants from DP camps in Europe [estimated at 25,000 per month]. There are, thus, in many instances, literally no houses for the refugees to return to. In other cases incoming Jewish immigrants have occupied Arab dwellings and will most certainly not relinquish them in favor of the refugees."[14]

In April, 1949, Mark Ethridge had a heated meeting with Israeli Prime Minister David Ben-Gurion over Israel's hard line on the refugee issue. In his report to the State Department, Ethridge wrote: "Israel does not intend to take back one refugee more than she is forced to take and she does not intend to compensate any directly if she can avoid it." Ethridge reported that Israel continued to insist that the number of refugees was exaggerated and that it "refuses to accept any responsibility whatever for creation of refugees...I have repeatedly pointed out political weakness and brutality of their position on refugees but it has made little impression."[15]

President Truman himself replied to Ethridge's messages on April 29: "I am rather disgusted with the manner in which the Jews are approaching the refugee problem. I told the president of Israel in the presence of his ambassador just exactly what I thought about it. It may have some effect, I hope so."[16] It did not.

A few months later, the State Department sought to pressure Israel to soften its policy toward the Palestinian refugees by threatening to withhold $49 million of unallocated funds from a $100 million Export- Import Bank loan to Israel unless Israel took back at least 200,000 refugees. George C. McGhee, the newly appointed U.S. coordinator on Palestine refugee matters, was chosen to deliver the message to the Israeli ambassador in Washington.[17] According to McGhee's account:

"I asked the ambassador [Eliahu Elath] to lunch with me at the Metropolitan Club and put our decision to him in the most tactful and objective way I could...The ambassador looked me straight in the eye and said, in essence, that I wouldn't get by with this move, that he would stop it...Within an hour of my return to my office I received a message from the White House that the president wanted to disassociate himself from any withholding of the Ex-Im Bank loan. I knew of the president's sympathy for Israel, but I had never before realized how swiftly the supporters of Israel could act if challenged."[18]

In the end, Elath was right. Israel received its money without changing its policies.[19]

That humiliating rebuff essentially ended America's efforts on behalf of the Palestinian refugees. Despite the fact that Israel's creation caused the refugee problem, it refused to accept responsibility and does not do so to this day. Thereafter the State Department mainly confined itself to repeating over the decades that the United States still believed the refugees should be allowed to return or be repatriated, but it has made no serious effort to force Israel to take any action. ❧

RECOMMENDED READING:

Davis, John H., *The Evasive Peace*, London, John Murray, 1970

Flapan, Simha, *The Birth of Israel*, New York, Pantheon Books, 1987

Glubb, Pasha, *A Soldier with the Arabs*, London, Hodder and Stoughton, 1957

Khalidi, Walid, *All That Remains* Washington, DC, Institute for Palestine Studies, 1991

Khalidi, Walid, *From Haven to Conquest*, Washington, DC, The Institute for Palestine Studies, 1987

Mallison, Thomas and Sally V., *The Palestine Problem in International Law and World Order*, London: Longman Group Ltd., 1986

Masalha, Nur, *Expulsion of the Palestinians* Washington, DC, Institute of Palestine Studies, 1992

McDowall, David, *Palestine and Israel*, Berkeley, University of California Press, 1989

McGhee, George, *Envoy to the Middle World*, New York, Harper & Row, 1983

Morris, Benny, *The Birth of the Palestine Refugee Problem*, New York, Cambridge University Press, 1987

Nakhleh, Issa, *Encyclopedia of the Palestine Problem*, New York, Intercontinental Books, 1991

Nazzal, Nafez, *The Palestinian Exodus from Galilee 1948*, Beirut, The Institute for Palestine Studies, 1978

Palumbo, Michael, *The Palestinian Catastrophe*, Boston, Faber and Faber, 1987

Said, Edward W. and Christopher Hitchens (eds.), *Blaming the Victims*, New York, Verso, 1988

Segev, Tom, *1949: The First Israelis*, New York, The Free Press, 1986

Silver, Eric, *Begin: The Haunted Prophet*, New York: Random House, 1984

Tannous, Izzat, *The Palestinians*, New York, I.G.T. Company, 1988

Turki, Fawaz, *The Disinherited*, New York, Monthly Review Press, 1972

NOTES:

[1] The General Assembly repeated the rights of Palestinians to return or compensation 19 times in subsequent resolutions between 1950 and 1973; see Ghayth Armanazi, "The Rights of the Palestinians: The Interactional Definition," *Journal of Palestine Studies*, Spring 1974, p. 91.

[2] Resolution 194 (111). The text is in *The New York Times*, Dec. 12, 1948, and Tomeh, George J., *United Nations Resolutions on Palestine and the Arab-Israeli Conflict*, 1: 1947-1974, pp. 15-16. Also see Mallison, *The Palestine Problem in International Law and World Order*, pp. 178-80 and pp. 212-13.

[3] *Washington Times*, 5/14/92.

[4] Clyde Haberman, *New York Times*, 5/15/92.

[5] Thomas J. Hamilton, *New York Times*, 11/19/49. The figure 726,000 was arrived at by the United Nations despite Israeli claims that the number was considerably less, and it has since become the commonly accepted total cited in subsequent documents.

[6] See, for instance, Davis, *The Evasive Peace*, pp. 53-63; Flapan, *The Birth of Israel*, p. 94; McDowall, *Palestine and Israel*, p. 194; Morris, *The Birth of the Palestinian Refugee Problem*, pp. 113-15; Palumbo, *The Palestinian Catastrophe*, pp. 47-57; Segev, *1949*, pp. 25-26. Also see Steven Glazer, "The Palestinian Exodus in 1948," *Journal of Palestine Studies*, Summer 1980, pp. 96-118, and Amnon Kapeliouk, "New Light on the Israel-Arab Conflict and the Refugee Problem and its Origins," *Journal of Palestine Studies*, Spring 1987, pp. 16- 24. Two works focusing on Zionist policy on transfer and

its results are Khalidi, *All That Remains,* and Masalha, *Expulsion of the Palestinians.*

[7]Khalidi, *From Haven to Conquest,* contains a moving first-hand account by International Red Cross representative Jacques de Reynier as well as accounts of attacks on other Palestinian centers, pp. 761-78. Many writers have discussed the massacre, perhaps none better than Silver, *Begin,* pp. 88-96. Also see details in Nakhleh, *Encyclopedia of the Palestine Problem,* pp. 271-72, and Neff, *Warriors at Suez,* pp. 64- 65.

[8]Tannous, *The Palestinians,* p. 754.

[9]Among numerous sources beyond those already cited, see Childers, "The Other Exodus," in Khalidi, *From Haven to Conquest;* Glubb, *A Soldier with the Arabs;* Kidron, "Truth Whereby Nations Live," in Said and Hitchens (eds.), *Blaming the Victims;* Nazzal, *The Palestinian Exodus from Galilee 1948;* and *Foreign Relations of the United States* 1949, Vol. VI., hereafter referred to as *FRUS.*

[10]*FRUS* 1948v, "The Special Representative of the United States in Israel [McDonald] to President Truman," Oct. 17, 1948, 4 p.m., p. 1486. For a touching personal story of the plight of the refugees, see Turki, *The Disinherited.*

[11]*New York Times,* 2/17/49. Also see Beryl Cheal, "Refugees in the Gaza Strip, December, 1948-May, 1950," *Journal of Palestine Studies,* Autumn 1988, pp. 138-57.

[12]*FRUS* 1949vi, "The Minister in Lebanon [Pinkerton] to the Secretary of State" [from Etheridge], March 28, 1949, p. 878.

[13]*FRUS* 1949vi, "Palestine Refugees," Secret, March 15, 1949, pp. 828-42.

[14]*Ibid.,* p. 837.

[15]*FRUS* 1949vi, "Mr. Mark F. Ethridge to the Secretary of State," April 13, 1949, 1 p.m., p. 914.

[16]*FRUS* 1949vi, "The President to Mr. Mark F. Ethridge, at Jerusalem," April 29, 1949, p. 957.

[17]*FRUS* 1949vi, "Memorandum hy William J. McWilliams, assistant to the director of the Executive Secretariat," Aug. 26, 1949, p. 1332; also see pp. 1375, 1389 and 1455.

[18]McGhee, *Envoy to the Middle World,* p. 37.

[19]*FRUS* 1949vi, "The Secretary of State to the United States delegation at Lausanne," Sept. 15, 1949, 8 p.m., pp. 1388-89. Also see McDonald, James G., *My Mission to Israel,* p. 184.

Chapter 13

1949: Lausanne Peace Conference

ON April 27, 1949, the first peace conference on Palestine opened in Lausanne, Switzerland, under the auspices of the U.N. Palestine Conciliation Commission. The PCC had been created the previous year to "achieve a final settlement of all questions outstanding between" Arabs and Jews in Palestine.[1] It was at Lausanne that the dismal future of the Palestinians was decided.

The prospect of forging peace treaties at Lausanne between Israel and its neighbors caused the State Department to delineate clearly U.S. policy on a number of basic issues, including America's attitude toward the boundaries of the new Jewish state, the status of Jerusalem, the fate of 726,000 Palestinian refugees and the question of a Palestinian state. The policy positions were spelled out in top-secret instructions by Acting Secretary of State Robert A. Lovett on Jan. 19 and given to the U.S. delegate to the PCC just before he departed for Palestine.[2]

BOUNDARIES. Lovett revealed that the United States believed the boundaries of the new state of Israel should be those defined by the 1947 U.N. resolution partitioning Palestine into Arab and Jewish states. The instructions specifically noted that "Israel is not entitled" to retain its 1948 conquests beyond those borders. (Israel had been allotted by the U.N. 56 percent of the land but had ended the fighting in control of 77 percent of Palestine.) However, "If Israel desires additions to its territory...Israel should make territorial concessions elsewhere..."

JERUSALEM. Lovett said the status of Jerusalem should remain as called for in the partition plan, a city receiving "special and separate treatment from the rest of Palestine and should be placed under effective United Nations control." In other words, neither Arab nor Jew should call Jerusalem its capital. Lovett said that a U.N. commissioner for Jerusalem should be appointed "to supervise the administration of the area, to guarantee free access to the city and the holy places, and to insure adequate protection of the latter."

REFUGEES. The U.S. position on the Palestinian refugees, Lovett wrote, was the same as expressed in U.N. Resolution 194, passed Dec. 11, 1948. It called for the right of the refugees to return to their homes now occupied by Israel or, if they chose, for compensation and relocation.

PALESTINIANS. Most significantly, Lovett revealed that the United States "favors incorporation of greater part of Arab Palestine in Transjordan. The remainder might be divided among other Arab states as seems desirable." In other words, the United States did not support self-determination for the Palestinians or an independent Palestinian state. In Washington's view, the Palestinians were not a separate people deserving the Wilsonian right to determine their own fate.

Two venues were involved in the Palestine Conciliation Commission's efforts: Jerusalem, to establish an international regime for that city, and Lausanne, where the members met unsuccessfully between April 27 and Sept. 15, 1949, to resolve all other problems in order to achieve overall peace.[3]

Commission members were France (Claude de Boisanger), Turkey (Huseyin Cahit Yalchin) and the United States (Mark F. Ethridge). An Israeli delegation was headed by Dr. Walter Eytan, a veteran negotiator, while the Arabs appeared as one body represented by Egypt, Lebanon, Syria and Transjordan. A "Palestinian Adviser," Ahmad Shuqayri, was attached to the Syrian delegation—meaning the Palestinians did not have their own independent delegate in the discussions that were focused on their future.[4] Mark Ethridge, the U.S. delegate, was a political appointee who had been publisher of the Louisville *Courier Journal* and was a personal friend of President Harry S. Truman. He had no experience in Middle Eastern diplomacy, and therefore displayed a refreshing candor and impatience with the usual coded language that passed for diplomatic practice. It did not take the plain-speaking Kentuckian long to fathom the rigidity of Israel's position.

The most immediate problem faced by the PCC was the desperate situation of the refugees. Israel was totally unyielding on the issue, yet the refugees urgently needed food and housing simply to survive another day. Hundreds were dying daily. It was clear that unless their long-term plight was alleviated they would be an unrelenting source of instability, not to say a humanitarian disgrace. But Israel refused to admit that it had any responsibility for the refugees and refused to allow them to return to their homes or to compensate them.

As early as March 28, 1949, Ethridge reported to the State Department that "Failure of Jews to do so [settle the refugee problem] has prejudiced whole cause of peaceful settlement in this part of world…" On April 11 he wrote a personal letter to his friend Truman:

"The Jews are still too close to the blood of their war…and too close to the bitterness of their fight against the British mandate to exercise any degree of statesmanship yet. They still feel too strongly that their security lies in military might instead of in good relations with their neighbors…The Arabs have made what the Commission considers very great concessions; the Jews have made none so far."[6]

By late April, Israel's stands on the issues at Lausanne had become so inflexible that its rigid position became the subject of news stories. An April 28 report in *The New York Times* said:

"As the Lausanne talks move slowly through their preliminary stages it seems to some observers that for the first time Israel is on the 'wrong' side of almost every point at issue in the eyes of world opinion, as expressed through the United Nations resolutions on Palestine. The observers reason as follows: Israel is occupying territory, notably western Galilee, that has been repeatedly assigned to the Arabs in various partition plans. Israel is acting as if Jerusalem were to be incorporated fully into the new state. Israel is encouraging further immigration of Jewish settlers while rejecting responsibility for the re-establishment of 600,000 to 1,000,000 Palestine Arabs displaced from their former homes."[7]

By the end of May, Truman himself was so disturbed by Israel's "excessive claims" and its refusal to accept any responsibility for the Palestinian refugees that he authorized the sending of a stiff message to the Jewish state. The message warned that the United States was "seriously disturbed by the attitude of Israel with respect to a territorial settlement in Palestine and to the question of Palestinian refugees...The U.S. government is gravely concerned lest Israel now endanger the possibility of arriving at a solution of the Palestine problem in such a way as to contribute to the establishment of sound and friendly relations between Israel and its neighbors.

"The government of Israel should entertain no doubt whatever that the U.S. government relies upon it to take responsible and positive action concerning Palestine refugees and that, far from supporting excessive Israeli claims to further territory within Palestine, the U.S. government believes that it is necessary for Israel to offer territorial compensation for territory which it expects to acquire beyond the boundaries" of the U.N. partition plan. If Israel continued to ignore the advice of the United Nations and the United States, the message sternly warned, "the U.S. government will regretfully be forced to the conclusion that a revision of its attitude toward Israel has become unavoidable."[8]

Despite the stern U.S. warning, U.S. diplomats in the region found that Israel continued to display a "voracious territorial appetite," "expansionist ambitions," a "take it or leave it attitude" interspersed with its threats of force. By July, the consul in Jerusalem reported that "the favorable opportunity for settlement" generated at the time of the Feb. 24 Israel-Egypt armistice agreement "has now passed" because of Israel's "harsh terms."[9]

The Lausanne peace talks ended Sept. 15, 1949, in total failure. In a top-secret report to the State Department, Ethridge placed the primary blame on Israel:

"If there is to be any assessment of blame for stalemate at Lausanne, Israel must accept primary responsibility...Her attitude toward refugees is morally reprehensible and politically shortsighted...Her position as conqueror demanding more does not make for peace. It makes for more trouble...There was never a time in the life of the commission when a generous and far-sighted attitude on the part of the Jews would not have unlocked peace."[10]

In the event, none of the goals sought by the United States at the conference were achieved except the denial of self-determination for the Palestinians. After Lausanne, Israel went on enlarging its frontiers, adopted Jerusalem as its exclusive capital and denied

Palestinian refugees both the right of return and compensation. Moreover, within six months of the collapse of the Lausanne talks, Jordan annexed the remaining Palestinian parts of Palestine, thus creating the West Bank and denying the Palestinians their own state. The U.S. acquiesced in all these acts. The only policy enunciated at Lausanne that the United States retains today is its opposition to a Palestinian state. ❧

RECOMMENDED READING:

Bailey, Sydney D., *Four Arab-Israeli Wars and the Peace Process*, London, MacMillan, 1990.

Forsythe, David P., *United Nations Peacemaking: The Conciliation Commission for Palestine*, Baltimore, The Johns Hopkins University Press, 1972.

Medzini, Meron, *Israel's Foreign Relations: Selected Documents, 1947-1974*, vol. 1, Jerusalem, Ministry of Foreign Affairs, 1976.

Sachar, Howard M., *A History of Israel: From the Rise of Zionism to Our Time*, Tel Aviv, Steimatzky's Agency Ltd., 1976.

Shlaim, Avi, *Collusion Across the Jordan: King Abdullah, the Zionist Movement, and the Partition of Palestine*, New York, Columbia University Press, 1988.

U.S. Department of State, *Foreign Relations of the United States 1949* (vol. 6), *The Near East, South Asia, and Africa*, Washington, DC, U.S. Printing Office, 1977.

NOTES:

[1] For studies of the conference and the commission's problems, see Neil Caplan, "A Tale of Two Cities: The Rhodes and Lausanne Conferences, 1949," *Journal of Palestine Studies*, Spring 1992, and, especially, Shlaim, *Collusion Across the Jordan*, pp. 461-88. Also see Medzini, *Israel's Foreign Relations*, vol. 1, pp. 278-80.

[2] *Foreign Relations of the United States 1949* (hereafter referred to as *FRUS*), untitled, Top Secret, p. 682. For a review of U.S. policy on Palestinian self-determination, see Sally V. Mallison and W. Thomas Mallison, "The Changing U.S. Position on Palestinian Self-Determination and the Impact of the Iran-Contra Scandal," *Journal of Palestine Studies*, Spring 1987, pp. 101-14.

[3] The PCC effort paralleled negotiations between the parties conducted by Acting U.N. Mediator Ralph Bunche on Rhodes, which began Jan. 13, 1949. The Rhodes talks were limited to formalizing the end of the fighting with armistices, which came on Feb. 24 between Egypt and Israel;

March 25 with Lebanon; April 3 with Jordan; and July 20 with Syria. Texts of the armistice agreements are in Bailey, *Four Arab-Israeli Wars and the Peace Process*, pp. 97-106. Iraq refused to enter into talks, thus becoming the only combatant not to sign an armistice with Israel; see Sachar, *A History of Israel*, pp. 347-51; Walid Khalidi, "The Palestine Problem: An Overview," *Journal of Palestine Studies*, Autumn 1991, pp. 5-16.

[4]Forsythe, *United Nations Peacemaking*, pp. 30, 48.

[5]*FRUS*, "The Minister in Lebanon (Pinkerton) to the Secretary of State" (from Ethridge), Top Secret, NIACT (meaning Night Action), Beirut, March 28, 1949, pp. 876, 878.

[6]*FRUS*, "Mr. Mark F. Ethridge to the President," Secret, Jerusalem, April 11, 1949, pp. 905-6.

[7]Michael I. Hoffman, *New York Times*, 4/29/49. Also see *FRUS*, "The Minister in Lebanon (Pinkerton) to the Secretary of State" (from Ethridge), Top Secret NIACT, Beirut, March 28, 1949, 5 p.m., pp. 876-78; *FRUS*, "The Consul at Jerusalem (Burdett) to the Secretary of State," Secret, Jerusalem, Feb. 28, 1949, 9 a.m., p. 775; *FRUS*, "The Consul at Jerusalem (Burdett) to the Secretary of State," Top Secret, Jerusalem, April 20, 1949, 9 p.m., pp. 928-30.

[8]*FRUS*, "The Acting Secretary of State to the Embassy in Israel," Top Secret, Priority, Washington, May 28, 1949, 11 a.m., pp. 1072-74.

[9]*FRUS*, "The Consul at Jerusalem (Burdett) to the Secretary of State," Secret, Jerusalem, July 6, 1949, pp. 1203-05.

[10]*FRUS*, "The Ambassador in France (Bruce) to the Secretary of State," from Ethridge, U.S. delegate at Lausanne commenting separately on Israeli note, Top Secret, Paris, June 12, 1949, 1 p.m., pp. 1124-25.

Chapter 14

1967 : U.N. Resolution 242

ON NOV. 22, 1967, landmark Resolution 242 was unanimously passed by the United Nations Security Council. The resolution was deceptively simple and brief, a mere 292 words. Since then it has been repeatedly cited by all parties to the Middle East conflict as the basic building block for peace.

The text of the resolution is worth recounting in full:

The Security Council,

Expressing its continuing concern with the grave situation in the Middle East,

Emphasizing the inadmissibility of the acquisition of territory by war and the need to work for a just and lasting peace in which every state in the area can live in security,

Emphasizing further that all Member States in their acceptance of the Charter of the United Nations have undertaken a commitment to act in accordance with Article 2 of the Charter,

1. Affirms that the fulfillment of Charter principles requires the establishment of a just and lasting peace in the Middle East which should include the application of both the following principles: (i) Withdrawal of Israeli armed forces from territories* occupied in the recent conflict; (ii) Termination of all claims or states of belligerency and respect for an acknowledgment of the sovereignty, territorial integrity and political independence of every state in the area and their right to live in peace within secure and recognized boundaries free from threats or acts of force;

2. Affirms further the necessity (a) For guaranteeing freedom of navigation through international waterways in the area; (b) For achieving a just settlement of the refugee problem; (c) For guaranteeing the territorial inviolability and political independence of every State in the area, through measures including the establishment of demilitarized zones;

3. Requests the secretary-general to designate a Special Representative to proceed to the Middle East to establish and maintain contacts with the States concerned in order to promote agreement and assist efforts to achieve a peaceful and accepted settlement in accordance with the provisions and principles in this resolution;

4. Requests the secretary-general to report to the Security Council on the progress of the efforts of the Special Representative as soon as possible.[1]

*The French version said *"des territoires occupés"* [from the territories].

The failure to call for the withdrawal of Israeli forces from "the" or "all" territories occupied in the June, 1967 war was considered at the time as an exercise in creative ambiguity. As later events proved, it was a failure of U.S. statesmanship and a triumph of Israeli strategy. The failure to call for total withdrawal, which came at Israel's urgings, has since become the focal point of endless bickering over just what the council meant about the expected extent of withdrawal by Israeli forces. It has also become a classic example of how Israel successfully manipulates U.S. policy to its own ends.

Originally, the justification behind the construction "withdrawal...from territories" was to leave room for Israel and its Arab neighbors to adjust the impractical 1949 armistice lines left over from the 1948 war. Although most council members wanted to demand Israel's total withdrawal, it did seem an eminently practical idea to allow for changes, since there were zigs and zags in the 1948 lines that were potential friction points. Ideally, the post-war period was a time when they could be straightened out to both sides' advantage under a U.S. formula of "minor" and "reciprocal" changes.

One such minor frontier rectification envisioned was the Latrun Salient, a small protrusion of land held by Jordan in the Latrun Plain that blocked direct motoring between Tel Aviv and Jerusalem. Top U.S. officials mentioned the Latrun Salient to Arab officials as an example of the type of minor change in the frontier they envisioned under 242—and of the reciprocity they expected for this concession. For instance, on Nov. 6, less than three weeks before the passage of 242, Secretary of State Dean Rusk privately assured King Hussein of Jordan in a Washington meeting that if Jordan gave up the Latrun Salient, "the United States would then use its diplomatic and political influence to obtain in compensation access for Jordan to a Mediterranean port in Israel." Arthur J.Goldberg, America's ambassador to the U.N., gave Hussein similar assurances at the same time, also citing Latrun as the kind of minor change contemplated.[2] When Hussein met on Nov. 8 with President Lyndon Johnson, who had been briefed by Rusk on the U.S. interpretation, the Jordanian monarch asked how soon Israeli troops would withdraw from most of the occupied land. The president replied: "In six months."[3]

After these assurances from the top echelon of the government, King Hussein pronounced himself "extremely satisfied" with the U.S. interpretation of withdrawal by Israeli forces.[4]

Although Israel would later hotly argue that it did not have to withdraw at all from Arab Jerusalem or the West Bank, it gave every indication in 1967 that it agreed with the U.S. interpretation while it sought America's aid in fashioning a resolution with an undefined withdrawal clause. Israel's less than candid tactics become clear from a study of the U.S. record of conversations, reports and other contemporaneous documents. The State Department conducted such a study in 1978 and concluded:

"At no time did Israel object to this U.S. position....Support for the concept of total withdrawal was widespread in the Security Council, and it was only through intensive American efforts that a resolution was adopted which employed indefinite language in the withdrawal clause. In the process of obtaining this result, the United States made clear to the Arab states and several other members of the Security Council that the United States envisioned only insubstantial revisions of the 1949 armistice lines. Israel did not protest this approach."[5]

While Israel did not immediately challenge Washington's interpretation in public, it lost no time in acting contrary to the assurances America was giving to the Arabs. It embarked on a stealthy program of establishing settlements. By the end of 1967 Israel had begun settlements in all of the occupied territories, including Arab Jerusalem.

At this point Washington made its second big mistake. Although it was the U.S. that made possible passage of a resolution with reference to an indefinite withdrawal, Washington then declined to go public with the assurances it had given in private to the Arabs. There is no official explanation for this reluctance to go public beyond the fact that the Johnson administration, and especially Ambassador Goldberg, an avowed Zionist, were among the most pro-Israel up to that time.

Later Goldberg even claimed that he and other officials had never supported the idea of minor and reciprocal changes.[6] He made this claim despite evidence of the 1978 State Department study and the assertion by no less a friend of Israel's than Henry Kissinger. Kissinger wrote in his memoirs: "Jordan's acquiescence in Resolution 242 had been obtained in 1967 by the promise of our United Nations Ambassador Arthur Goldberg that under its terms we would work for the return of the West Bank to Jordan with minor boundary rectifications and that we were prepared to use our influence to obtain a role for Jordan in Jerusalem."[7] Similarly, Rusk, who personally negotiated with King Hussein, has written: "Resolution 242 never contemplated the movement of any significant territories to Israel."[8]

Secretary of State William Rogers, who was notably evenhanded on the conflict, acknowledged the U.S. interpretation in 1969. On Dec. 9, he remarked that "any changes in the pre-existing lines should be confined to insubstantial alterations required for mutual security. We do not support expansionism."[9] Similarly, Jimmy Carter in the first months of his presidency spoke openly of "minor" border changes. But then he foolishly acceded to a personal request from new Israeli Prime Minister Menachem Begin to stop referring to the U.S. interpretation in public.[10]

Israel then went further in offering a unique interpretation of 242. The Likud government of Begin insisted Israel was under no obligation to withdraw from all three fronts of the Gaza Strip, Golan Heights and West Bank. In fact, the existence of Israel's numerous settlements—around 90 in the West Bank, Golan Heights and Gaza Strip in 1977, when Begin came to power[11]—was eloquent testimony of its claim to the occupied territories. On the issue of whether withdrawal had to occur on all fronts the U.S. has remained steadfast. Successive administrations—at least up to Clinton—have declared in public that Israel must withdraw from all fronts.

However, no president or secretary of state since Carter has repeated in public the original U.S. interpretation—which is what won Arab agreement on the resolution in the first place—that Israel's withdrawal must be total except for minor and reciprocal border changes. While Washington has repeatedly assured the Arabs that there has been no change in policy, its assurances ring hollow when U.S. officials will not even state them in public. ✒

RECOMMENDED READING:

Aronson, Geoffrey, *Creating Facts,* Washington, DC, Institute for Palestine Studies, 1987

Boudrealt, Jody, et al., *U. S. Official Statements Regarding U.N. Resolution 242,* Washington, DC, Institute for Palestine Studies, 1991

First International Conference, 25 Years After the 1967 War, Washington, DC, The Center for Policy Analysis on Palestine, 1992

Kissinger, Henry, *White House Years,* New York, Boston, Little Brown & Co., 1979

Lord Caradon, et al., *U.N. Security Council Resolution 242,* Washington, DC, Georgetown University, 1981

*Neff, Donald, *Warriors for Jerusalem,* New York, Linden Press/Simon & Schuster, 1984

Quandt, William, *Camp David,* Washington, DC, The Brookings Institution, 1986

A Washington Institute Monograph, *U.N. Security Council Resolution 242* (Washington, DC: Washington Institute for Near East Policy, 1993).

*Available through the AET Book Club.

NOTES:

[1]The text is in Tomeh, George J., *United Nations Resolutions on Palestine and the Arab-Israeli Conflict,* Vol. One: 1947-1974, p. 143.

[2]The above examples are all from secret reports made at the time and later cited in a secret State Department study of the U.S. interpretation of Resolution 242 by Nina J. Noring of the Office of the Historian and Walter B. Smith II, director of the Office of Israeli and Arab-Israeli Affairs, Department of State. *The Withdrawal Clause in U.N. Security Council Resolution 242 of 1967,* February, 1978; Secret/Nodis, pp. 12-13.

[3]*Ibid.,* p. 13; author interview with Hussein, Amman, Jordan, Aug. 7, 1983.

[4] *Ibid.*

[5] Noring, Nina J., and Walter B. Smith II, *The Withdrawal Clause in U.N. Security Council Resolution 242 of 1967.* See Neff, *Warriors Against Jerusalem,* p. 337. The study was made at the request of the Carter administration to determine if there was any justice to the Israeli position that the resolution did not include all the occupied territories; it concluded there was not.

[6] See, for instance, Goldberg's article "Hussein's Misreading of History," *Jerusalem Post,* May 28, 1993. Lucius Battle, who was the assistant secretary of state for the Middle East at the time, recalled in a recent interview with the author that Goldberg proved to be on the issue of Resolution 242 "a slippery character."

[7] Kissinger, Henry, *White House Years,* p. 345.

[8] Letter to the author, Aug. 23, 1983.

[9] Boudrealt et al, *U. S. Official Statements Regarding U.N. Resolution 242,* p. 123.

[10] Quandt, *Camp David,* pp. 85, 193.

[11] Foundation for Middle East Peace, *Report on Israeli Settlement in the Occupied Territories,* Special Report, July, 1991; Aronson, *Creating Facts,* p. 70.

Chapter 15

1972: U.S. Vetoes in the United Nations

ON MARCH 17, 1970, the United States cast its first veto in the United Nations Security Council during the presidency of Richard Nixon, when Henry Kissinger was the national security adviser. It was a historic moment, since up to that time Washington had been able to score heavy propaganda points because of the Soviet Union's profligate use of its veto. The first U.S. veto in history was a gesture of support for Britain, which was under Security Council pressure to end the white minority government in southern Rhodesia.

Two years later, however, on Sept. 10, 1972, the United States employed its veto for the second time—to shield Israel.[1] That veto, as it turned out, signaled the start of a cynical policy to use the U.S. veto repeatedly to shield Israel from international criticism, censure and sanctions.

Washington used its veto 32 times to shield Israel from critical draft resolutions between 1972 and 1997. This constituted nearly half of the total of 69 U.S. vetoes cast since the founding of the U.N. The Soviet Union cast 115 vetoes during the same period.[2]

The initial 1972 veto to protect Israel was cast by George Bush in his capacity as U.S. ambassador to the world body. Ironically, it was Bush as president who temporarily stopped the use of the veto to shield Israel 18 years later. The last such veto was cast on May 31, 1990, it was thought, killing a resolution approved by all 14 other council members to send a U.N. mission to study Israeli abuses of Palestinians in the occupied territories. Then President Bill Clinton came along and cast three more.

The rationale for casting the first veto to protect Israel was explained by Bush at the time as a new policy to combat terrorists. The draft resolution had condemned Israel's heavy air attacks against Lebanon and Syria, starting Sept. 6, the day after 11 Israeli athletes were killed at the 1972 Munich Olympic Games in an abortive Palestinian attempt to seize them as hostages to trade for Palestinians in Israeli prisons.[3] Between 200 and 500 Lebanese, Syrians and Palestinians, mostly civilians, were killed in the Israeli raids.[4]

Nonetheless, Bush complained that the resolution had failed to condemn terrorist attacks against Israel, adding: "We are implementing a new policy that is much broader than that of the question of Israel and the Jews. What is involved is the problem of terrorism, a matter that goes right to the heart of our civilized life."[5]

Unfortunately, this "policy" proved to be only a rationale for protecting Israel from censure for violating a broad range of international laws. This became very clear when the next U.S. veto was cast a year later, on July 26, 1973. It had nothing to do with terrorism. The draft resolution affirmed the rights of the Palestinians and established provisions for Israeli withdrawal from occupied territories as embodied in previous General Assembly resolutions.[6] Nonetheless, Washington killed this international effort to end Israel's occupation of Palestinian lands.

Washington used the veto four more times in 1975-76 while Henry Kissinger was secretary of state. One of these vetoes arguably may have involved terrorism, since the draft condemned Israeli attacks on Lebanese civilians in response to attacks on Israel. But the three other vetoes had nothing at all to do with terrorism.

One, in fact, struck down a draft resolution that reflected U.S. policy against Israel's alteration of the status of Jerusalem and establishment of Jewish settlements in occupied territory. Only two days earlier, U.S. Ambassador William W. Scranton had given a speech in the United Nations calling Israeli settlements illegal and rejecting Israel's claim to all of Jerusalem.[7] Yet on March 25, 1976, the U.S. vetoed a resolution reflecting Scranton's positions which had been passed unanimously by the other 14 members of the council.[8]

The two other vetoes during Kissinger's reign also were cast in 1976. One, on Jan. 26, killed a draft resolution calling for recognition of the right of self-determination for Palestinians. The other, on June 29, called for affirmation of the "inalienable rights" of the Palestinians.[9]

The Carter administration cast only one veto. But it had nothing to do with terrorism. It came on April 30, 1980, killing a draft that endorsed self-determination for the Palestinian people.[10]

The all-time abuser of the veto was the administration of Ronald Reagan, with the most pro-Israel secretary of state, George Shultz, since Kissinger. The Reagan team cynically invoked the veto 18 times to protect Israel. A record six of these vetoes were cast in 1982 alone. Nine of the Reagan vetoes resulted directly from Security Council attempts to condemn Israel's 1982 invasion of Lebanon, and Israel's refusal to surrender the territory in southern Lebanon which it still occupies today. The other nine vetoes shielded Israel from council criticism for such illicit acts as the Feb. 4, 1986, skyjacking of a Libyan plane.[11]

Israeli warplanes forced the executive jet to land in Israel, allegedly in an effort to capture Palestinian terrorist Abu Nidal. He was not aboard and, after interrogation, the passengers were allowed to leave.[12] The U.S. delegate explained that this act of piracy was excusable "because we believe that the ability to take such action in carefully defined and limited circumstances is an aspect of the inherent right of self-defense recognized in the U.N. Charter."[13]

Other vetoes employed on Israel's exclusive behalf included the Jan. 20, 1982, killing of a demand that Israel withdraw from the Golan Heights it had occupied in 1967[14]; the April 20, 1982 condemnation of an Israeli soldier who shot 11 Muslim worshippers at the Haram Al-Sharif in the Old City of Jerusalem[15]; the Feb. 1, 1988 call for Israel to stop violating Palestinian human rights in the occupied territories, abide by the Fourth Geneva Convention and formalize a leading role for the United Nations in future peace negotiations[16]; the April 15, 1988 resolution requesting that Israel permit the return of expelled Palestinians, condemning Israel's shooting of civilians, calling on Israel to uphold the Fourth Geneva Convention and calling for a peace settlement under U.N. auspices.[17]

The Bush administration used the veto four times to protect Israel: on Feb. 17, 1989, to kill a draft strongly deploring Israel's repression of the Palestinian uprising and calling on Israel to respect the human rights of the Palestinians[18]; on June 9, 1989, deploring

Israel's violation of the human rights of the Palestinians[19]; on Nov. 7, 1989, demanding Israel return property confiscated from Palestinians during a tax protest and calling on Israel to allow a fact-finding mission to observe Israel's suppression tactics against the Palestinian intifada[20]; and, finally, on May 31, 1990, calling for a fact-finding mission on abuses against Palestinians in Israeli-occupied lands.[21]

The May 31, 1990, veto was the last, presumably, as the result of a secret understanding, if not an official agreement, with Russia and the three other Security Council members with veto power. By then it had become obvious that the council could not be effective in a post-Cold War world if Britain, China, France, Russia and the United States recklessly invoked their vetoes.

Moreover, the international alliances sought by Washington to repel Iraq's invasion of Kuwait in August, 1990 made it necessary for the Bush administration to retain unity in the Security Council. As a result, instead of abstaining on or vetoing resolutions critical of Israel, as it did in 1989 and the first half of 1990, the Bush administration abruptly joined other members in late 1990, 1991 and 1992 in passing six resolutions deploring or strongly condemning Israel's conduct against the Palestinians.[22]

These resolutions brought the total passed by the council against Israel since its birth to 68. If the United States had not invoked its veto, the record against Israel by mid-1998 would total 100 resolutions condemning or otherwise criticizing its behavior or supporting the rights of Palestinians.

The agreement on vetoes held until March, 1995, when President Clinton invoked the veto after all 14 other members approved a U.N. Security Council resolution calling on Israel to rescind a decision to expropriate 130 acres of land in Arab East Jerusalem.[23] The Clinton administration exercised two more vetoes in 1997, both of them on resolutions otherwise unanimously supported by the 14 other Security Council members. The draft resolution was critical of Israel's plans to establish a new settlement at Har Homa/Jabal Abu Ghneim in East Jerusalem in the midst of Palestinian housing.[24]

The three Clinton vetoes brought to 32 the number Washington has cast to protect Israel. ⁂

RECOMMENDED READING:

Cooley, John, *Green March, Black September: The Story of the Palestinian Arabs*, London, Frank Cass, 1973.

Hart, Alan, *Arafat: Terrorist or Peacemaker?* London: Sidgwick & Jackson, 1985.

Hirst, David, *The Gun and the Olive Branch: The Roots of Violence in the Middle East*, New York: Harcourt Brace Jovanovich, 1977.

*Khouri, Fred, *The Arab-Israeli Dilemma*, 3rd ed., Syracuse, NY: Syracuse University Press, 1985.

Livingstone, Neil C. and David Halevy, *Inside the PLO: Secret Units, Secret Funds, and the War Against Israel and the United States*, New York: William Morrow and Company, Inc., 1990.

Nakhleh, Issa, *Encyclopedia of the Palestine Problem*, 2 vol., NY: Intercontinental Books, 1991.

*Neff, Donald, *Warriors Against Israel: How Israel Won the Battle to Become America's Ally*, Brattleboro, VT: Amana Books, 1988.

U.S. State Department, *America's Foreign Policy Current Documents 1986*, Washington, DC: U.S. Government Printing Office, 1987.

*Available through the AET Book Club.

NOTES:

[1] Robert Alden, *New York Times*, 9/12/72; and U.S. U.N. Mission, "List of Vetoes Cast in Public Meetings of the Security Council," 8/4/86. Also Neff, *Warriors Against Israel*, p. 96.

[2] A complete list of the vetoes was printed in Donald Neff, "Vetoes Cast by the United States to Shield Israel from Criticism by the U.N. Security Council," *Washington Report on Middle East Affairs*, March, 1993.

[3] Cooley, *Green March, Black September*, pp. 125-28; Hart, *Arafat*, pp. 350-53; and Livingstone and Halevy, *Inside the PLO*, p. 39 and pp. 104-5.

[4] Hirst, *The Gun and the Olive Branch*, p. 251. Also see Nakhleh, *Encyclopedia of the Palestine Problem*, pp. 450, 790 and 824.

[5] Robert Alden, *New York Times*, 9/12/72. The source was identified as a key member of the American delegation but internal indications in the story strongly suggest the "key member" was Ambassador Bush.

[6] *New York Times*, 7/27/73.

[7] *New York Times*, 3/25/76.

[8] Text of the draft resolutions is in *New York Times*, 1/27/76. Also see U.S. U.N. Mission, "List of Vetoes Cast in Public Meetings of the Security Council," and Khouri, *The Arab-Israeli Dilemma*, p. 382.

[9]U.S. U.N. Mission, "List of Vetoes Cast in Public Meetings of the Security Council," 8/4/86.

[10]*New York Times*, 2/7/86.

[11]U.S. State Department, *American Foreign Policy Current Documents 1986*, p. 374.

[12]U.S. U.N. Mission, "List of Vetoes Cast in Public Meetings of the Security Council," 8/12/86.

[13]*New York Times*, 4/21/82.

[14]Michael J. Berlin, *Washington Post*, 2/2/88.

[15]*New York Times*, 4/16/88.

[16]Paul Lewis, *New York Times*, 2/18/89.

[17]*New York Times*, 6/10/89.

[19]Associated Press, #V0511, 11/7/89, and Nakhleh, *Encyclopedia of the Palestine Problem*, p. 778. Nakhleh has the text of the resolution draft as well as excerpts from the discussion by several delegates and opinions by lawyers and columnist Anthony Lewis.

[20]Associated Press, #V0498, 09:50 EDT, 6/1/90.

[21]The resolutions are #672 of Oct. 12, 1990; #673 of Oct. 24, 1990; #681 of Dec. 20, 1990; #694 of May 24, 1991; #726 of Jan. 6, 1992; and #799 of Dec. 18, 1992.

[22]The resolutions are #672 of Oct. 12, 1990; #673 of Oct. 24, 1990; #681 of Dec. 20, 1990; #694 of May 24, 1991; #726 of Jan. 6, 1992; and #799 of Dec. 18, 1998.

[23]Barbara Crossette, *New York Times*, 5/18/95. Text of U.N. Ambassador Madeleine Albright's remarks is in *Journal of Palestine Studies*, Summer 1995, pp. 160-62.

[24]Ian Williams, "For Second Time, General Assembly Votes to Condemn Israeli Settlements," *Washington Report on Middle East Affairs*, June/July, 1997.

Chapter 16

1974: Palestinians Recognized As a People

O N NOV. 13, 1974, the United States and Israel suffered one of their greatest diplomatic defeats, and the Palestinians and the United Nations one of their greatest victories, when Chairman Yasser Arafat of the Palestine Liberation Organization made a dramatic appearance before the U.N. General Assembly and called on the world community to decide between an "olive branch or a freedom fighter's gun."[1] Arafat declared:

"The difference between the revolutionary and the terrorist lies in the reason for which each fights. Whoever stands by a just cause and fights for liberation from invaders and colonialists cannot be called terrorist. Those who wage war to occupy, colonize and oppress other people are the terrorists....The Palestinian people had to resort to armed struggle when they lost faith in the international community, which ignored their rights, and when it became clear that not one inch of Palestine could be regained through exclusively political means....

"The PLO dreams and hopes for one democratic state where Christian, Jew and Muslim live in justice, equality, fraternity and progress. The chairman of the PLO and leader of the Palestinian revolution appeals to the General Assembly to accompany the Palestinian people in its struggle to attain its right of self-determination....I have come bearing an olive branch and a freedom fighter's gun. Do not let the olive branch fall from my hand."

More than his words, the simple presence of a Palestinian leader in the halls of the U.N. marked a watershed for the Palestinian community. The United States and Israel had opposed Arafat's appearance, as they had for years fought against recognition of Palestinians as a separate people. Washington and Tel Aviv insisted that the Palestinians be identified by their function or position such as refugees or terrorists rather than as a people. Even U.N. Security Council Resolution 242 of 1967 had failed to mention Palestinians and referred only to refugees. And, as late as 1968, Israeli Prime Minister Golda Meir claimed that Palestinians "did not exist."[2]

However, starting in 1968, the same year as Golda Meir's statement, the General Assembly began passing a series of resolutions identifying Palestinians as a people and recognizing their "inalienable rights," including self-determination and the "right to struggle" to achieve it.[3] The United States and Israel voted against all of these resolutions. But year after year in the late 1960s and early 1970s the General Assembly prevailed in slowly establishing the legal and moral framework of a separate Palestinian people. Arafat's 1974 U.N. appearance was the culmination of this process and emphasized how out-of-step the United States was with the world community. But still it took another year before Washington finally admitted the reality of Palestinian identity.

The moment came on Nov. 12, 1975, when Deputy Assistant Secretary of State for Near East and South Asian Affairs Harold H. Saunders testified before the House Foreign Affairs Subcommittee on the Middle East:

"In many ways, the Palestinian dimension of the Arab-Israeli conflict is the heart of that conflict....The Palestinians collectively are a political factor....The legitimate interests of the Palestinian Arabs must be taken into account in the negotiating of an Arab-Israeli peace."[4]

It was the first extensive U.S. statement on the Palestinians since they lost their land in 1948. The Saunders Document, as the statement became known, caused an uproar in Israel, where the Cabinet expressed "grave criticism" and charged that it contained "numerous inaccuracies and distortions."[5] The opposition in Israel to Saunders' statement became so loud that Secretary of State Henry A. Kissinger soon discounted the statement as an "academic and theoretical exercise"—even though Kissinger himself had carefully worked on it before Saunders' appearance.[6]

Although it soon became obvious that the Saunders Document presaged no serious immediate shift in U.S. diplomacy during the rest of Kissinger's tenure as secretary of state,[7] it nonetheless signified an important turning point in the struggle. After this, for the first time, U.S. analysts began identifying Palestinians as a people and the refugee problem, festering since 1948, became only one part of the broader spectrum of concerns Palestinians faced as a people. Observed former Central Intelligence Agency analyst Kathleen Christison: "In many ways the statement changed the bureaucracy's way of looking at the Palestinian issue and set the stage for the Carter Administration's greater concern for Palestinians."[8]

But if Washington was finally willing to recognize the Palestinians, it was not ready to recognize their representative, the PLO, any more than was Israel, even though the leaders of the Arab states had agreed in 1974 that the PLO was the "sole, legitimate representative of the Palestinian people." But the next year, barely a month before the Saunders Document, Kissinger had bowed to Israeli demands and promised that the United States would not recognize the PLO unless it accepted U.N. Security Council Resolution 242 and Israel's right to exist. Thus the gains the Palestinians had made in being recognized at last as a separate people were essentially denied them by Washington's refusal to recognize their sole representative.

Congress moved in 1985 to further marginalize the PLO by passing into law Kissinger's non-recognition pledge to Israel and adding that the PLO also had to "renounce terror."[9] Similarly, Israel passed a law in 1980 making it illegal to express any sympathy to the PLO or other "illegal organizations."[10]

There matters stood until 1988, when Arafat declared the establishment of the state of Palestine, renounced terrorism, accepted Security Council Resolution 242 and called for an international peace conference under U.N. auspices involving Palestinians, Arabs and Israelis.[11] But Arafat's declaration was not considered detailed enough by Secretary of State George P. Shultz, an embarrassingly inept diplomat when it came to the Middle East. In his pro-Israel passion, Shultz's response was essentially to ignore the declaration and defy the U.N. by denying a visa to Arafat and thereby prevent him from accepting an invitation by the General Assembly to address it in November, 1988.

Shultz's petty action was a violation of America's 1947 Headquarters Agreement with the United Nations, which committed the

United States to allow entry to persons invited by the world body.[12] In retaliation, the Assembly took the unprecedented action of holding an extraordinary session in December, 1988 in Geneva, where Arafat appeared once again before the world body.

Given America's embarrassing estrangement from the world community over the Palestinian issue, Shultz finally relented on Dec. 14, 1988, saying the United States would recognize the PLO. Talks began the next day in Tunisia between the PLO and U.S. representatives, but they were so constrained by U.S. restrictions that they made no progress. Under Israeli prodding, they were broken off in 1992.

Meanwhile, in late December, 1988, Pope John Paul II received Arafat in the Vatican, saying that Arabs and Jews had "an identical, fundamental right to their own homelands."[13] And, by the first week of 1989, about 70 countries had recognized the new state of Palestine.[14]

Still, it took until Sept. 13, 1993, with the signing of the Declaration of Principles on Interim Self-Government Arrangements by Prime Minister Yitzhak Rabin of Israel and Arafat before Israel finally recognized "the PLO as the representative of the Palestinian people."[15] After a century of struggle and denial, Israel had at last recognized that there were Palestinians and that they represented a people. And, of course, now that Israel recognized the PLO the United States was finally willing also to fall in line and actually begin to act like it believed the words Harold Saunders had uttered back in 1975. ֍

RECOMMENDED READING:

*Findley, Paul, *Deliberate Deceptions: Facing the Facts About the U.S.-Israeli Relationship*, Brooklyn, NY, Lawrence Hill Books, 1993.

Hart, Alan, *Arafat: Terrorist or Peacemaker?*, London, Sidgwick & Jackson, 1985.

Hirst, David, *The Gun and the Olive Branch: The Roots of Violence in the Middle East*, New York, Harcourt Brace Jovanovich, 1977.

Lukacs, Yehuda (ed.), *The Israeli-Palestinian Conflict: A Documentary Record*, New York, Cambridge University Press, 1992.

Quandt, William B., *Decade of Decisions: American Policy Toward the Arab-Israeli Conflict, 1967-1976*, Berkeley, University of California Press, 1977.

Quigley, John, *Palestine and Israel: A Challenge to Justice*, Durham, Duke University Press, 1990.

Sheehan, Edward R. E., *The Arabs, Israelis, and Kissinger: A Secret History of American Diplomacy in the Middle East*, New York, Reader's Digest Press, 1976.

*Available through the AET Book Club.

NOTES:

[1]Arafat spoke for 100 minutes. See Hirst, *The Gun and the Olive Branch*, p. 335. Also see Sheehan, *The Arabs, Israelis, and Kissinger*, pp. 152-53; Hart, *Arafat: Terrorist or Peacemaker?* pp. 408-13. The text of Arafat's speech is in *Journal of Palestine Studies*, "Palestine at the United Nations," Winter 1975, pp. 181-92.

[2]Hirst, *The Gun and the Olive Branch*, p. 264, quoting the *Sunday Times of London*, 6/15/69.

[3]See, for instance, General Assembly Resolutions 2535, 2672 and 2787.

[4]The text is in Lukacs, *The Israeli-Palestinian Conflict*, pp. 61-64.

[5] *New York Times*, 11/17/75. Also see Findley, *Deliberate Deceptions*, pp. 167-68.

[6]Interview with Harold Saunders, Washington, DC, 5/25/94.

[7]Quandt, *Decade of Decisions*, p. 279. Also see Marwan R. Bubeiry, "The Saunders Document," *Journal of Palestine Studies*, Autumn 1978.

[8]Kathleen Christison, "Blind Spots: Official U.S. Myths About the Middle East," *Journal of Palestine Studies*, Winter 1988, p. 57.

[9]"Codification of Policy Prohibiting Negotiations with the Palestine Liberation Organization," in U.S. Senate and U.S. House of Representatives, Committee on Foreign Relations and Committee on Foreign Affairs, *Legislation on Foreign Relations Through 1987*, vol. 1, Washington, DC, U.S. Government Printing Office, March, 1988, pp. 529-30.

[10]*New York Times*, 7/31/80; Institute For Palestine Studies, *International Documents on Palestine*, p. 435. Also see Quigley, *Palestine and Israel*, p. 146.

[11]The text is in *Journal of Palestine Studies*, Winter 1989, pp. 216-28.

[12]*New York Times*, 11/27/88, includes the text of the State Department statement.

[13]Clyde Haberman, *New York Times*, 12/24/88.

[14]Associated Press, *Wall Street Journal*, 1/9/89.

[15]For an analysis, see Burhan Dajani, "The September, 1993 Israeli-PLO Documents: A Textural Analysis," *Journal of Palestine Studies*, Spring 1994.

Chapter 17

1988: U.N. Forces U.S. to Recognize Palestinians

ON APRIL 26, 1988, the 15-member International Court of Justice at The Hague ruled unanimously against the United States in its attempt to close the Palestine Liberation Organization observer mission at the United Nations.[1] The ruling was yet another setback for Washington in its 20-year struggle with the world community over recognizing the national rights of the Palestinians. Before America finally lost this little-noted but titanic contest at the end of 1988, Secretary of State George P. Shultz and the United States would suffer not only defeat but one of the greatest embarrassments in U.S. diplomatic history.

The PLO had been around since 1964, but the struggle against it only began in earnest after Israel's 1967 war. It was then that Israel more than doubled the territory under its control by launching surprise attacks that ended with the capture of the West Bank, the Gaza Strip, the Sinai Peninsula and the Golan Heights.[2] Israel's occupation of these additional Arab lands elicited the anxious attention of the U.N. General Assembly, where the membership included many nations once under the yoke of colonialism. Starting in 1968, the assembly began passing a series of resolutions that by 1974 had recognized an array of the "inalienable rights" of the Palestinians and effectively established the legal and moral framework for Palestinian nationalism.

During the six-year period, General Assembly resolutions officially recognized the Palestinians as a distinct people "entitled to equal rights and self-determination;"[3] confirmed the "legality of the peoples' struggle for self-determination and liberation...by all available means consistent with the Charter of the United Nations;"[4] and concluded that a "just and lasting peace" could not be achieved unless the Palestinians received their inalienable rights and enjoyed self-determination.[5]

Finally, in 1974, the General Assembly took the historic step of inviting PLO Chairman Yasser Arafat to address it on the political struggle and human suffering caused by Israel's occupation. At the same time it awarded observer status to the PLO, meaning the Palestinians at last had official standing in the international community.[6]

All these actions were ardently opposed by Israel, and it effectively exerted its influence in the U.S. media to help paint the General Assembly as a hotbed of anti-Semitism. Under adverse news coverage and a pro-Israel political climate, American support for the U.N. dropped off even further—it had never been popular among the far-right—and Americans generally kept their backs turned to the plight of the Palestinians.

This widespread indifference to a cruel and illegal occupation was abetted by an astounding growth of Israel's influence in Washington from the mid-1960s onwards. The increased influence was not only in the Congress, accurately described by critics as "Israeli-occupied territory," but in the White House as well.[7] The days of Dwight Eisenhower's coolness toward the Jewish state had been replaced by the Johnson administration. Lyndon Johnson was not only personally a strong supporter of Israel but he was surrounded by Israel's sympathizers keen to do all they could to help the Jewish state. His successor, Richard Nixon, was less so. But one of his principal advisers was Henry Kissinger, one of Israel's greatest friends. By the time of America's supreme embarrassment in 1988, one of the most pro-Israel presidents ever, Ronald Reagan, was in the White House. His secretary of state was George Shultz, who seemed indefatigable in finding new services to render Israel.

Israel's increased influence in Washington was a major reason why the United States was at odds with most of the world community over the issue of the PLO and Palestinian rights. Washington voted against all of the General Assembly resolutions conferring those rights. This thoroughly pro-Israel stand found the United States over the years frequently alone with Israel while all the rest of the world voted another way.

Despite the U.N.'s formidable opposition, Israel had a trump card, which it deftly played during negotiations on the 1975 Sinai II disengagement accords. As a condition for its partial withdrawal from Egyptian territory, Israel demanded that the United States not recognize or deal with the PLO until it met a number of conditions, including the renunciation of terrorism. Kissinger foolishly, or perhaps deviously, agreed, thereby limiting the ability of American diplomats to influence one side of the Palestinian-Israeli conflict. Congress sealed into law this Israeli demand by passing a statute in 1985 that essentially repeated Kissinger's commitment:

"No officer or employee of the United States Government and no agent or other individual acting on behalf of the United States Government shall negotiate with the Palestine Liberation Organization or any representatives thereof (except in emergency or humanitarian situations) unless and until the Palestine Liberation Organization recognizes Israel's right to exist, accepts United Nations Security Council Resolutions 242 and 338 and renounces the use of terrorism."[8]

But the international community was not to be denied its championing of the rights of the Palestinians. The next year, in 1986, the General Assembly on Dec. 4 condemned Israel's continuing occupation and urged all members to cut off all aid to Israel in order to force it to abide by the U.N. Charter.[9] That resolution was just one of 24 passed against Israel that year by the assembly.[10] At about the same time, on Dec. 8, the Security Council "strongly deplored" the recent killings of two Palestinian students by Israeli soldiers. The vote was 14-0 with the United States abstaining.[11]

In 1987 Secretary of State Shultz summarily ordered the PLO information office in Washington closed on Sept. 15. Shultz issued the order despite the fact that there were no allegations of illegal activities. In fact, the office had legally operated in Washington since 1978 as a duly registered foreign agent. Its director, Hassan Abdel Rahman, was a naturalized American citizen from Ramallah. Thus Shultz's order closing the information-dispersing office without cause was a prima facie case of denying an American freedom of speech.

In order to get around this constitutional problem, the State Department unilaterally declared the office a "foreign mission," and claimed that the secretary of state was exercising his authority to order it closed under the Foreign Missions Act. The reason for the closure, said a spokesman for Shultz, was to "demonstrate U.S. concern over terrorism committed and supported by organizations and individuals affiliated with the PLO."

In fact, Shultz had taken his action when anti-PLO bills were pending in both the Senate and the House and it had become clear that Israel's supporters in Congress were going to pass legislation outlawing the PLO.[12]

Less than three months later, the Palestinian intifada erupted in the occupied territories, causing untold suffering. Israel's brutal efforts to suppress the stone-throwing Palestinians brought renewed condemnation from the world community, and even an occasional critical word from the United States. Mostly, however, Washington continued its role as Israel's protector in the U.N.

Shultz finally overreached himself in 1988 by taking a series of actions that brought great embarrassment to himself and his country. The debacle began when he tried to get the PLO's mission kicked out of the U.N. The General Assembly snapped back on March 2, 1988, by declaring that the U.S. effort to close the observer mission was a breach of America's treaty obligations to the United Nations. It ordered that the issue be arbitrated under provisions of the treaty. The vote was an embarrassing 143 to 1 (Israel), with the United States abstaining. In a separate resolution, the General Assembly voted that the International Court of Justice should give an advisory opinion on whether the United States was obliged to enter into arbitration. The vote was 143 in favor, with America and Israel abstaining.

The next day the assembly voted 148 to 2 (Israel and the United States) condemning America's moves and urging it to honor the 1947 Headquarters Treaty. The treaty said that the United States must provide free access to the U.N. headquarters in New York to anyone invited there by the General Assembly.[13]

The matter went to the U.S. federal court as well as the World Court. On June 29, Judge Edmund L. Palmieri of the Federal District Court in Manhattan followed the World Court's lead and ruled against the Shultz effort, saying it was a violation of the Headquarters Agreement.[14] The Reagan administration did not appeal the issue.[15]

The struggle between the United States and the world community intensified in late 1988 when Secretary of State Shultz once again intervened to combat the PLO. On Nov. 26 he personally denied a visa to PLO Chairman Yasser Arafat to enter the United States for an appearance before the U.N. General Assembly. Shultz said the action was justified because Arafat had "associations with terrorism" and therefore was a security threat to America. Arafat had been invited by the General Assembly to address the issue of Palestine in early December.[16]

Shultz's action was not only a violation of the Headquarters Agreement but was widely seen as a petty response to the U.N. support of the PLO. Former CIA analyst Kathleen Christison wrote: "His decision, taken on his own without prior presidential approval, to deny Yasser Arafat a visa…is a striking example of a policy adopted out of personal pique."[17] Nonetheless, 68 senators (33 Democrats, 35 Republicans) signed a letter to him applauding his efforts.[18]

However, international opposition to the United States was overwhelming. Vatican Radio said the decision was like "throwing cold water on the PLO."[19] Clovis Maksoud, Arab League ambassador to the United Nations, said: "It is not for the U.S. to decide who speaks for the Palestinians on a particular issue."[20] PLO spokesman Bassam Abu Sharif wrote an article explaining the evolution of the Palestinians' struggle and urged: "…give peace a visa."[21]

On Nov. 29, the General Assembly expressed its revulsion at Shultz's stand. It voted 121 to 2 (the United States and Israel voting against) to urge the United States to reverse its denial of the visa. But Shultz said: "I think it was the right decision. I stick by it." He said the reason for his decision was his concern with terrorism. "I am afraid that it's too easy for people to forget what an important problem that is and what a threat it is to civilized society."[22]

The General Assembly had other ideas about what constituted a threat to civilized society. It responded with a 152-2-1 vote (U.S. and Israel against, Britain abstaining) "deploring" America's refusal to reconsider. The General Assembly then took a stunning action. It made the unprecedented decision on Dec. 2 to move its regular session to Geneva so Arafat's message could be heard. It was the first time in the U.N.'s history that the General Assembly moved its session outside of New York. The vote was 154-2-1, with the U.S. and

Israel against and Britain abstaining.[23]

Soon more than 150 diplomats representing the governments of the world and hundreds of their aides packed their bags and traveled en masse to Switzerland. It was perhaps the most extraordinary event in the history of the United Nations. Certainly it was the sharpest defiance of the United States ever witnessed in the world body.

The embarrassment for Shultz and the United States did not stop there. On Dec. 13, Arafat appeared before the General Assembly in Geneva and made a dramatic gesture toward peace. He said in an 80-minute speech that "I come to you in the name of my people, offering my hand so that we can make true peace, peace based on justice." He condemned terrorism "in all its forms" and sought a settlement among "Palestine, Israel and other neighbors, within the framework of the international conference for peace in the Middle East on the basis of Resolutions 242 and 338...."[24]

Despite Arafat's public compliance with the demands put forth by Washington to earn its recognition, the State Department made the astonishing assertion that he had failed to accomplish that. Spokesman Charles E. Redman said America's conditions—rejection of terror, acceptance of Resolutions 242 and 338 and recognition of Israel—"must be addressed clearly, squarely, without ambiguity. That didn't happen and, as a consequence, the speech did not meet our conditions."[25]

At a press conference the next day, Arafat unambiguously declared: "...it was clear that we mean...the right of all parties concerned in the Middle East conflict to exist in peace and security, and, as I have mentioned, including the state of Palestine, Israel and other neighbors, according to the Resolutions 242 and 338. As for terrorism, I renounced it yesterday in no uncertain terms, and yet, I repeat for the record...that we totally and absolutely renounce all forms of terrorism, including individual, group and state terrorism."[26]

Such plain language and clear professions of peace could not be ignored. Arafat, backed by the international community, had finally forced Washington's hand. The official response came a few hours later when President Reagan officially announced that as a result of Arafat's pledge, "I have authorized the State Department to enter into a substantive dialogue with PLO representatives."[27]

That same evening, a defeated Shultz called a press conference in the State Department and tried to keep up a proud front. He noted the conciliatory nature of Arafat's remarks and said: "As a result, the United States is prepared for a substantive dialogue with PLO representatives. I am designating our ambassador in Tunisia as the only authorized channel for that dialogue....Nothing here may be taken to imply an acceptance or recognition by the United States of an independent Palestinian state. The position of the U.S. is that the status of the West Bank and Gaza cannot be determined by unilateral acts of either side, but only through a process of negotiations. The United States does not recognize the declaration of an independent Palestinian state. It is also important to emphasize that the United States commitment to the security of Israel remains unflinching."[28]

Despite his words, Shultz proved to the end to be Israel's willing servant.[29] At U.S. insistence, the talks in Tunisia were narrowly focused and the PLO's access to U.S. officials was restricted to Robert H. Pelletreau Jr., the U.S. ambassador in Tunis, not exactly the highest level of U.S. policymakers. Yet even these strict proscriptions did not satisfy Israel.

Under persistent heavy pressure from Israel and its U.S. friends, especially those in Congress such as Senator Jesse Helms of North Carolina,[30] the White House finally succumbed and broke off this modest dialogue. The Bush administration announced on May 30, 1990, it was suspending the talks because the PLO refused to apologize for a terrorist attack against Israel in which no Israelis were killed and even though the PLO probably had nothing to do with it.[31]

Thus by mid-1990, the United States was right back again ignoring the PLO as it had for two decades. It was only after Israel itself accepted in the 1993 Oslo accords the fact that the PLO could no longer be ignored that the White House finally recognized the PLO as a full partner in the peace process.[32]

All told, it was a shameful chapter in U.S. history, largely perpetuated by three secretaries of state, Kissinger, Alexander Haig and Shultz, and three presidents, Lyndon Johnson, Richard Nixon (unintentionally) and Ronald Reagan. If the United States had had the courage of its convictions and had honored its international commitments, many lives would have been saved and America's claim to being an "honest broker" would ring truer. Instead, it was a period of cynical subservience to a foreign country for domestic political gain that no American can be proud of. Yet, under Bill Clinton, this myopic policy of subservience to Israel continues today.

The optimistic note in this doleful tale is that the international community remains committed to seeing justice for the Palestinians. There is, after all, the demonstrable fact that even the United States at its most arrogant can eventually be made to bow somewhat to world opinion and the ideals of the U.N. Charter. Who knows, if the international community keeps up its pressure, the United States might some day actually become an even-handed mediator in the Middle East. ❧

RECOMMENDED READING

Epp, Frank, H., *Whose Land is Palestine?*, Grand Rapids, Michigan, William B. Eerdmans Publishing Company, 1974.

Kimche, David, *The Last Option: After Nasser, Arafat, and Saddam Hussein*, New York, Charles Scribner's Sons, 1991.

*Neff, Donald, *Fallen Pillars: U.S. Policy towards Palestine and Israel since 1945*, Washington, DC, Institute for Palestine Studies, 1995.

Nyrop, Richard F., (ed.), *Israel: a Country Study* (2nd ed.), Washington, DC, U.S. Government Printing Office, 1979.

Simpson, Michael, *United Nations Resolutions on Palestine and the Arab-Israeli Conflict: 1982-1986*, Washington, DC, Institute for Palestine Studies, 1988.

U.S. Senate and U.S. House of Representatives, Committee on Foreign Relations and Committee on Foreign Affairs, *Legislation on Foreign Relations Through 1986* (vol. 1), Washington, DC, U.S. Government Printing Office, March, 1987.

*Available through the AET Book Club.

NOTES:

[1]Paul Lewis, *New York Times*, 4/27/88.

[2]The U.N. 1947 partition plan alloted Israel 5,900 square miles, but Israel had enlarged its frontiers to nearly 8,000 square miles by the end of the 1948-49 war. It captured 20,870 square miles in 1967; see Nyrop (ed.), *Israel: a country study*, p. xix. Also see Epp, *Whose Land is Palestine?* p. 185; Foundation for Middle East Peace, *Report on Israeli Settlement in the Occupied Territories*, Special Report, July, 1991.

[3]#2672 (XXV).

[4]#2787 (XXVI).

[5]#3089 (XXVIII).

[6]Neff, *Fallen Pillars*, p. 114.

[7]*Ibid.*, pp. 119-21.

[8]U.S. Senate and U.S. House of Representatives, *Legislation on Foreign Relations Through 1986*, pp. 359-60. The law's official title is Codification of Policy Prohibiting Negotiations with the Palestine Liberation Organization.

[9]Resolution 41/162 A, B, C. The text is in Simpson, *United Nations Resolutions on Palestine and the Arab-Israeli Conflict*, 1982-1986, pp. 206-09.

[10]Jules Kagian, *Middle East International*, 9/1/87, p. 11.

[11]Resolution 592. The text is in Simpson, *United Nations Resolutions on Palestine and the Arab-Israeli Conflict, 1982-1986*, p. 231; see Frank Collins, "The Iron Fist: A Policy of Provocation," *Middle East International*, 2/6/88.

[12]Elaine Sciolino, *New York Times*, 9/15/87. Texts of the various documents are in *American-Arab Affairs*, Number 22, Fall 1987, pp. 115-20. Also see Richard Curtiss, "US Leaders Protest Palestine Information Office Closure Order," *Washington Report on Middle East Affairs*, Vol. VI, No. 7, November, 1987. For the PLO's side, see Hassan Abdel Rahman in *The Washington Post* Outlook Section, "Evicting the Palestinians," 11/29/87; Rajai M. Abu-Khadra, "The Closure of the PLO Offices," *Journal of Palestine Studies*, Spring 1988, pp. 51-62.

[13]Marvine Howe, *New York Times*, 3/3-4/88. Also see Rajai M. Abu-Khadra, "The Closure of the PLO Offices," *Journal of Palestine Studies*, Spring 1988, pp. 51-62.

[14]Arnold H. Lubasch, *New York Times*, 6/30/88.

[15]Robert Pear, *New York Times*, 8/30/88.

[16]Don Oberdorfer, *Washington Post*, 11/27/88; the same edition carries the text of the State Department statement, as does the *New York Times* of the same date, and Department of State *Bulletin*, Vol. 89, No. 2143, February, 1989.

[17]Kathleen Christison, "The Arab-Israeli Policy of George Shultz," *Journal of Palestine Studies*, Winter 1989, p. 30.

[18]John M. Goshko, *Washington Post*, 12/2/88. Among the signers were Vice President-elect Dan Quayle and Republican Minority Leader Bob Dole; Democratic Majority Leader George Mitchell declined.

[19]Karen DeYoung, *Washington Post*, 11/29/88. For a profile of Arafat and his mood at this time, see Marie Colvin, "The Ambiguous Yasser Arafat," *The New York Times Sunday Magazine*, 12/18/88.

[20]Paul Lewis, *New York Times*, 11/29/88.

[21]Bassam Abu Sharif, "A Message from the PLO: Give Peace a Visa," text in *Journal of Palestine Studies*, Vol. XVIII, No. 3, Spring 1989.

[22]Robert Pear, *New York Times*, 11/30/88.

[23]*Washington Post*, 12/3/88.

[24]The text is in *Journal of Palestine Studies*, "Documents and Source Material," Spring 1989, pp. 161-71; excerpts are in *New York Times*, 11/17/88.

[25]*New York Times*, 12/14/88; the text of Redman's remarks is in the same edition. Also see Kimche, *The Last Option*, p. 298.

[26]Text of Arafat's statement is in *New York Times*, 12/15/88, and "Documents and Source Material," *Journal of Palestine Studies*, Spring 1989, pp. 180-81. For an excellent profile of Arafat at this time, see T.D. Allman, "On the Road with Arafat," *Vanity Fair*, February, 1989, reprinted in *Washington Report on Middle East Affairs*, September, 1989.

[27]The text is in "Documents and Source Material," *Journal of Palestine Studies*, Spring 1989, pp. 184-85.

[28]The text is in *New York Times*, 12/15/88, and Department of State *Bulletin*, Vol. 89, No. 2143, February, 1989. A small group of Jewish Americans including international lawyer Rita Hauser had met personally with Arafat and came away convinced of his sincerity. Despite wide criticism from leaders of organized Jewry, the Hauser group was an influential voice in the debate over recognition; Paula Span, *Washington Post* Style Section, 12/30/88. In addition, President-elect Bush and National Security Adviser Colin Powell pressured Shultz to accept Arafat's pledge; Rowland Evans and Robert Novak, *Washington Post*, 12/16/88.

[29]Shultz went so far in his partisanship in 1987 as to inaugurate the George Shultz doctoral Fellowships at Tel Aviv University and personally contributed $10,000 to the program; see Glenn Frankel, *Washington Post*, 10/19/87. It is unlikely that any sitting secretary ever took such a biased action while trying to mediate in a divided region.

[30]James M. Dorsey, *Washington Times*, 7/21/89. Also see *Journal of Palestine Studies*, "Documents and Source Material," Vol. XIX, No. 1, Autumn 1989, pp. 169-70.

[31]Thomas L. Friedman, *New York Times*, 6/21/90. Texts of official PLO statements on the issue are in *Journal of Palestine Studies*, "Documents and Source Material," Autumn 1990, pp. 159-63, the text of President Bush's comments is in the same journal, pp. 186-90.

[32]The Oslo texts are in *New York Times* and *Washington Post*, 9/10/93. For an analysis of them, see Burhan Dajani, "The September, 1993 Israeli-PLO Documents: A Textural Analysis," *Journal of Palestine Studies*, Spring 1994.

Israel Abroad

Chapter 18

1949: Israel Seeks Neutrality Between U.S. and U.S.S.R.

ON Jan. 13, 1949, *The New York Times* reported Israel sought to steer a neutral course between the United States and the Soviet Union. Correspondent Anne O'Hare McCormick reported from Jerusalem that "It is true that Israel cherishes the ideal of remaining 'neutral' between the United States and the Soviet Union, constantly referred to as 'our two powerful friends...'"[1]

The policy's name in Hebrew was *ee-hizdahut*, "non-identification." Although the Cold War was in full force at the time, Israel hoped to remain friendly with both superpowers because both had assets that Israel needed—money, people and weapons. Israeli Foreign Minister Moshe Sharett said: "Israel will in no case become identified with one of the great blocs of the world as against the other."[2]

This was not good news for the U.S. and its allies. Although Israel by itself was not a significant military factor in the Cold War, its willingness to equate the Soviet Union as the moral equivalent of the United States was a disturbing message to Western Cold Warriors. Their concerns were multiple. One was especially to keep the Soviet Union out of the Middle East, which had been a Western preserve since World War I.

Yet Israel had compelling reasons to embrace the Eastern bloc, as David Ben-Gurion made clear when he formed his first government on March 10, 1949. He informed Israel's legislature that his government would pursue "a foreign policy aimed at achieving friendship and cooperation with the United States and the Soviet Union."[3] He added that the Soviet Union was a "great and growing world power, controlling a number of states not hostile to us...and in it and its satellites lives the second part of the Jewish people."[4]

That was one of the cores of the matter for Israel—some two million Jews living in the U.S.S.R. and Eastern Europe. In the first three years after World War II the Soviet Union allowed 200,000 Jews who had fled Poland for safety in the Soviet Union to emigrate to the West and Palestine.[5]

Israel's interests in the United States were similarly compelling. The United States had the wealth and a generous Jewish community to help finance the fledgling state. Israel's total exports in 1949 were only $40 million, whereas contributions from Jewish Americans accounted for $100 million.[6]

But of more immediate importance were weapons. And it was here that the Soviet Union played a paramount role at this time. Moscow had allowed Czechoslovakia to become Israel's major arms supplier in 1948. In that capacity, Czechoslovakia had provided Israel with all the Messerschmitts and Spitfires that formed its new air force, as well as other weapons and the training of 5,000 of its military personnel by the fall of 1948. And it remained Israel's major arms supplier in 1949.[7]

The significance of the Czech connection to Israel rested on the fact that the U.S. had imposed an arms embargo on the area in 1947. Despite unrelenting pressure from Israel's supporters, the Truman administration continued to observe the embargo in 1949, as did subsequent administrations for more than a decade.

The steadfastness of the Truman administration on the arms issue had less to do with the Arab-Israeli conflict than with the Soviet Union. Keeping Russia out of the Middle East was one of Washington's major goals. Before the Palestine problem grew acute after the end of World War II, the Middle East had been "virtually clean" of Soviet influence, in the words of one British general. But since then it had made some modest gains in Israel because of Moscow's support of partition, its quick recognition of the Jewish state, its decision to allow Jews to emigrate to Israel and its secret supply to Israel of weapons via Czechoslovakia during the fighting.[8]

A mid-1948 report to Secretary of State George C. Marshall from Ambassador to the United Nations Philip C. Jessup observed: "...it is not apparent that communism has any substantial following among the [Arab] masses. On the other hand, there are apparently a substantial number of Communists in the Irgun, the Stern Gang and other dissident [Jewish terrorist] groups. Beyond that, the Soviet Union, through its support of partition and prompt recognition of Israel, must be considered as having a substantial influence with the PGI [Provisional Government of Israel]. The communist influence is, of course, capable of substantial expansion through whatever diplomatic and other missions the Soviet Government may establish in Israel."[9]

In the end, the pressures of the Cold War and the eruption of fighting in Korea forced Israel to choose sides in the early 1950s, a decision that was facilitated by France's decision to replace the Soviet Union as Israel's secret supplier of weapons.[10] Although France had joined with Britain and the United States on May 5, 1950 in the Tripartite Declaration expressing "their opposition to the development of an arms race between the Arab states and Israel" and thereby imposing an arms embargo on the region, France quickly broke the pact.

The reason was that France saw Israel as a natural ally against Arab nationalists opposed to its Algerian policy. By the beginning of 1955, shortly after the Algerian rebellion erupted into open warfare, French arms sales to Israel increased dramatically and included such major items as jet warplanes, battle tanks and heavy artillery.[11]

Israel employed its new strength against Egypt in a series of raids starting on Feb. 28, 1955 in the Gaza Strip against an Egyptian military outpost. Thirty-six Egyptian soldiers and two civilians were killed, making it the largest incident between Egypt and Israel since the 1948 war. The high death toll sent such a shock through Egypt that Gamal Abdul Nasser, the young colonel who had taken power in 1952, was forced into a desperate search for an arms source of his own.[12]

With America, Britain and France officially pledged to an arms embargo and other European nations refusing to deal with Egypt, Nasser had only one source to go to. On Sept. 27, 1955, he announced to a stunned world that Czechoslovakia had agreed to provide Egypt with major weapons systems, including bombers, jet warplanes, tanks and artillery. Instantly, Nasser became a hero throughout the Arab world—and so too did the Soviet Union, the nation everybody knew was behind the deal.

The sudden success of the Soviet Union in gaining entrance into the region caused Secretary of State John Foster Dulles to complain that "we are in the present jam because the past Administration had always dealt with the area from a political standpoint and had tried to meet the wishes of the Zionists in this country and that had created a basic antagonism with the Arabs. That was what the Russians were now capitalizing on."[13]

Despite nearly a decade of effort by Washington and London to keep Moscow out of the region, the Czech arms deal marked the Soviet Union's emergence as a full-blown major player. Henceforth Cold War rivalry would pit Washington and Moscow on opposite sides, confusing what at heart remained the Palestinian-Israeli conflict with what increasingly came to be perceived as the Arab-Israeli conflict.

For Israel, the Czech arms deal marked the moment it decided to provoke a war with Egypt, which it successfully did the next year in secret collusion with Britain and France.[14]

Aside from contributing to Israel's decision to go to war, the Czech arms deal made a Cold War-motivated arms race inevitable in the region.

Nonetheless, with Israel secretly receiving weapons from France, the United States continued over the next seven years its embargo on arms sales. As late as Feb. 17, 1960, President Dwight D. Eisenhower declared that the U.S. had no intention of becoming a major arms supplier to the Middle East, saying: "The United States, as a matter of policy, has never been a major supplier of arms for Israel and doesn't intend to be, nor to any other country in the area."[15]

Two years later, President John F. Kennedy breached this traditional policy for the first time since Israel's existence and opened the floodgates to what eventually became the greatest transfer of weapons in history by the U.S.S.R. and the United States to the region. It began on Sept. 26, 1962, with the State Department announcing the sale of an unspecified number of Hawk antiaircraft missiles to Israel. Considerable emphasis was made that these were defensive weapons.[16]

The fact was this was Israel's greatest achievement in its relations with the United States up to this time. It had finally convinced Washington to sell it American weapons, the most advanced in the world. There was little doubt that the dam, once breached, would unleash more weapons. Indeed, before the decade was out Israel had received the latest in American warplanes and other offensive weapons. From that point on, Israel, with increasing success, sought to define the conflict in Cold War terms: Israel and the United States against the Arabs and the Soviet Union. Long forgotten was Israel's early efforts to be friends to both sides of the Cold War.

The evolution of U.S. arms policy reached a culmination in 1982 when President Reagan declared on Feb. 22 that his administration would maintain Israel's "qualitative edge" over the military power of all other countries in the Middle East.[17] The commitment has been repeated by every president since then, and echoed in national political platforms. From Truman to Reagan, the trajectory of U.S. policy had gone from one of neutrality to commitment to assure Israel's military dominance of the region, a position President Clinton has strongly endorsed. 🙶

RECOMMENDED READING:

Ben-Gurion, David, *Israel: A Personal History*, New York, Funk & Wagnalls, Inc., 1971.

Bialer, Uri, *Between East and West*, New York, Cambridge University Press, 1990.

Brecher, Michael, *Decisions in Israel's Foreign Policy*, London, Oxford University Press, 1974.

Burns, Lt. Gen. E. L. M., *Between Arab and Israeli*, New York, Ivan Obolensky, 1962.

*Cockburn, Andrew and Leslie, *Dangerous Liaison: The Inside Story of the U.S.-Israeli Covert Relationship*, New York, HarperCollins Publishers, 1991.

*Lilienthal, Alfred M., *The Zionist Connection: What Price Peace?*, New York, Dodd, Mead & Company, 1978.

Louis, William Roger, *The British Empire in the Middle East 1945-1951*, Oxford, Clarendon Press, 1988.

Morris, Benny, *The Birth of the Palestine Refugee Problem*, New York, Cambridge University Press, 1987.

Morris, Benny, *Israel's Border Wars: 1949-1956*, Oxford, Clarendon Press, 1993.

*Neff, Donald, *Warriors at Suez: Eisenhower Takes America into the Middle East*, Brattleboro, VT, Amana Books, 1988.

O'Brien, Conor Cruise, *The Siege: The Saga of Israel and Zionism*, New York, Simon and Schuster, 1986.

*Raviv, Dan and Yossi Melman, *Every Spy a Prince: The Complete History of Israel's Intelligence Community*, Boston, Houghton Mifflin Company, 1990.

Schiff, Ze'ev, *A History of the Israeli Army (1870-1974)*, San Francisco, Straight Arrow Books, 1974.

U.S. Department of State, *American Foreign Policy, 1950-1955*: Basic Documents (vol. 2), Washington, DC, U.S. Government Printing Office, 1957.

U.S. Department of State, *American Foreign Policy: Current Documents, 1960*, Washington, DC, U.S. Government Printing Office, 1964.

U.S. Department of State, *Foreign Relations of the United States 1948* (vol. V), The Near East, South Asia, and Africa, Washington, DC, U.S. Printing Office, 1975.

U.S. Department of State, *Foreign Relations of the United States 1955-1957* (vol. XIV), Arab-Israeli Dispute 1955, Washington, DC, U.S. Printing Office, 1989.

*Available through the AET Book Club.

NOTES:

[1] Anne O'Hare McCormick, *New York Times*, 1/14/49. Also see Ben-Gurion, *Israel*, p. 339; Bialer, *Between East and West*, p. 213; Brecher, *Decisions in Israel's Foreign Policy*, p. 166; Cockburn, *Dangerous Liaison*, p. 21; O'Brien, *The Siege*, pp. 370-71.

[2] O'Brien, *The Siege*, p. 370.

[3] Ben-Gurion, *Israel*, p. 33.

[4] Bialer, *Between East and West*, p. 15.

[5] Cockburn, *Dangerous Liaison*, p. 22.

[6] *Ibid.*, pp. 29-30.

[7] *Ibid.*, p. 21.

[8] *FRUS 1948*, "The Ambassador in the United Kingdom (Douglas) to the Acting Secretary of State," Top Secret, London, Oct. 29, 1948, 7 p.m., p. 1531.

[9] *FRUS 1948*, "The Acting United States Representative at the United Nations (Jessup) to the Secretary of State," Top Secret, Priority, New York, July 1, 1948, 4:16 p.m., p. 1182.

[10]Brecher, *Decisions in Israel's Foreign Policy*, p. 166; O'Brien, *The Siege*, p. 371. The actual breakthrough was reported to have come in May, 1951 with a secret agreement between the intelligence services of the two countries, the Mossad and CIA; see Cockburn, *Dangerous Liaison*, p. 49; Raviv and Melman, *Every Spy a Prince*, p. 76.

[11]Neff, *Warriors at Suez*, pp. 162-63.

[12]Burns, *Between Arab and Israeli*, pp. 18, 99-101.

[13]*FRUS 1955-1957*, "Memorandum of Conversation with the Secretary of State," Washington, Oct. 18, 1955, p. 612.

[14]Morris, *Israel's Border Wars*, p. 364.

[15]U.S. State Department, *American Foreign Policy 1960*, "Reply Made by the President (Eisenhower) to a Question Asked at a News Conference, Feb. 17, 1960 (Excerpt)," p. 497.

[16]Max Frankel, *New York Times*, 9/27/62; Schiff, *A History of the Israeli Army (1970-1974)*, pp. 257-59.

[17]*Weekly Compilation of Presidential Documents*, Government Printing Office, Washington, DC, Feb. 22, 1982.

Chapter 19

1954: Israel Conducts First Skyjacking

ON DEC. 12, 1954, Israeli warplanes forced a Syrian Airways Dakota passenger craft carrying four passengers and five crewmen to land at Lydda airport inside Israel.[1] The passengers were interrogated for two days before international protests, including strong complaints from Washington, finally convinced Israel to release the plane and its passengers.[2]

Moshe Sharett, who as Israel's foreign minister had to explain the incident to the international community, was privately appalled. He recorded in his diary: "I have no reason to doubt the truth of the factual affirmation of the U.S. State Department that our action was without precedent in the history of international practice. What shocks and worries me is the narrow-mindedness and the short-sightedness of our military leaders. They seem to presume that the state of Israel may—or even must—behave in the realm of international relations according to the laws of the jungle."[3]

The purpose of the unprecedented skyjacking, according to Sharett, was Chief of Staff Moshe Dayan's ambition "to get hostages in order to obtain the release of our prisoners in Damascus."[4] The reference was to an incident that had occurred four days earlier. Five Israeli soldiers were captured retrieving tapping devices on Syrian telephone lines on the Golan Heights inside Syria. Israel expressed outrage at the imprisonment of the soldiers but Syria refused to release them.[5]

Israeli passions were riled even further the next month when one of the Israeli soldiers, Uri Ilan, son of a former Mapam member of parliament, committed suicide in jail on Jan. 13,

1955. Although the Israeli press loudly charged Syria with torture, an examination by the United Nations showed "no signs of physical ill-treatment."[6]

But still Syria refused to release the prisoners, pointing out that Israel was holding Syrian civilians prisoner. The impasse contributed to an even graver incident toward the end of the year. On Dec. 11, 1955, Israel sent two paratroop battalions backed by artillery and mortar batteries under the command of Ariel Sharon, later Israel's defense minister, against Syrian military posts at Buteiha Farm and Koursi near the northeast shore of Lake Tiberias.

It was Israel's largest military raid inside Syria up to that time and resulted in 56 Syrian deaths, including three women, and nine wounded. Significantly Israel also took 30 prisoners, whom it later used as hostages to exchange for the four Israelis held by Syria.[7] The United States expressed its "shock" at the raid and supported a resolution by the United Nations Security Council that unanimously condemned Israel for its "flagrant violation" of the armistice agreement.[8]

French Ambassador to the U.N. Hervé Alphand observed that the condemnation resolution of Israel was "the strongest ever passed by the council."[9] It was the fifth time the council had condemned, censured, called on and otherwise passed resolutions critical of Israel.

Israel insisted the raid was simply in retaliation for Syrian troops firing at an Israeli patrol boat on Lake Tiberias the previous day, in which there had been no casualties. But the explanation was widely disbelieved. Canadian General E.L.M. Burns, the chief of staff of the United Nations Truce Supervisory Organization, bluntly wrote:

"No one with any knowledge of military affairs would believe that such an elaborate, coordinated attack had not been planned well before, and probably rehearsed. Certainly it was not improvised in a few hours....The reasons given by the Ministry of Foreign Affairs' statement were only an excuse, and not a very good one."[10]

In fact, like most major actions in the Middle East, there was far more than just retaliation behind the raid. At the time, it was widely suspected that Israel's main motive in launching the heavy attack was primarily to punish Syria for keeping the four Israeli soldiers prisoners. But it turned out that was just one of the reasons. Israeli historian Benny Morris reports that primarily the attack was meant as a provocation to goad Egypt into attacking Israel and thus start a war. "This," wrote Morris, "was the thinking behind the strike."[11]

The timing was dictated by two events during the previous three months: Egypt and Syria had signed a mutual defense pact on Oct. 20, 1955, and on Sept. 27 Egypt had announced its historic "Czech" arms deal, shocking Israel by the fact that Egypt was about to start receiving massive quantities of Soviet weapons. In the event, Egypt did not respond to the attack on the Golan and Israel had to wait nearly another year before taking on itself the burden of attacking Egypt to start a war.

There was also another motive behind the attack. It had to do with Israel's long- term policy to establish exclusive control over Lake Tiberias, the biblical Sea of Galilee, which lay within Israeli territory, and the three demilitarized zones (DMZs) that lay along the Israeli-Syrian frontier in the Jordan Valley.

Palestinians and Syrians insisted on fishing in the lake and were a constant source of friction, especially during mid-November to mid-April, which marked the official fishing season. Israel denied Arabs had any rights to fish there, citing the fact that the Mandate governments over Palestine and Syria had agreed in the 1920s that the frontier followed the east shore of the lake at a distance set back 10 meters parallel to the water.

However, the Arabs countered that under Anglo-French agreements of Feb. 3, 1922, June 23, 1923 and Feb. 2, 1926, Syrians were given "the same fishing and navigation rights on Lakes Huleh and Tiberias...as the inhabitants of Palestine" and also the right to "enjoy grazing, watering and cultivations rights" and to "cross the frontier freely."[12]

Nonetheless, Israel insisted on keeping Arab fishermen away from the lake, by force if necessary. It further lacerated relations with Syria by chasing Palestinian farmers out of the DMZs near the lake in violation of the truce of 1949, which held the farmers should be allowed to remain. Israel's forceful takeover of the

DMZs left the Palestinian farmers and fishermen denied access to their fields or fishing grounds embittered and angry. A later UNTSO chief of staff, Norwegian General Odd Bull, who served during the 1960s, wrote:

"I imagine that a number of those evicted settled somewhere in the Golan Heights and that their children have watched the land that had been in their families for hundreds of years being cultivated by Israeli farmers. From time to time they opened fire on these farmers. That, of course, was a violation of the armistice agreement, though I could not help thinking that in similar circumstances Norwegian peasants would almost certainly have acted in the same way. In the course of time all the Arab villages [in the DMZs] disappeared."[13]

So too did the Arab fishermen. In 1967 Israel conquered the whole area, including the Golan Heights, and chased out all of the Arabs. It is Israel's continuing occupation of this land that today remains the major impediment to peace between Israel and Syria. ❧

RECOMMENDED READING:

Bull, Odd, *War and Peace in the Middle East: The Experiences and Views of a U.N. Observer*, London, Leo Cooper, 1976.

Burns, Lt. Gen. E. L. M., *Between Arab and Israeli*, New York, Ivan Obolensky, 1962.

Chomsky, Noam, *The Fateful Triangle*, Boston, South End Press, 1983.

Chomsky, Noam, *Pirates & Emperors: International Terrorism in the Real World*, Brattleboro, VT, Amana Books, 1986.

*Khouri, Fred J., *The Arab-Israeli Dilemma*, Syracuse, NY, Syracuse University Press, 1985.

Morris, Benny, *The Birth of the Palestine Refugee Problem*, New York, Cambridge University Press, 1987.

Morris, Benny, *Israel's Border Wars: 1949-1956*, Oxford, Clarendon Press, 1993.

*Neff, Donald, *Warriors at Suez: Eisenhower Takes America Into the Middle East*, Brattleboro, VT, Amana Books, 1988.

Rokach, Livia, *Israel's Sacred Terrorism: A Study Based on Moshe Sharett's Personal Diary and Other Documents*, Belmont, MA, Association of Arab-

American University Graduates, Inc., 1980.

Von Horn, Carl, *Soldiering for Peace*, New York, David McKay Company, Inc., 1967.

*Available through the AET Book Club.

NOTES:

[1] *New York Times*, 12/13/54.

[2] Associated Press, *New York Times*, 12/15/54.

[3] Rokach, *Israel's Sacred Terrorism*, pp. 20-21. For an analysis of Sharett's lengthy diaries, see "Secrets of State: An Analysis of the Diaries of Moshe Sharett," *Journal of Palestine Studies*, Autumn 1980, pp. 35-57.

[4] Chomsky, *Pirates and Emperors*, p. 84.

[5] Morris, *Israel's Border Wars*, p. 366.

[6] Burns, *Between Arab and Israeli*, p. 109.

[7] *Ibid.*, p. 108; Morris, *Israel's Border Wars*, p. 366n.

[8] Resolution 111. The text is in Tomeh, George J., *United Nations Resolutions on Palestine and the Arab-Israeli Conflict: 1947-1974*, Washington, DC, Institute for Palestine Studies, 1975, p. 137; the text of the U.S. statement is in Boudreault, Jody and Eric Fortin, *U.S. Official Statements: The Golan Heights*, Washington, DC, Institute for Palestine Studies, 1993, pp. 27-28.

[9] Neff, *Warriors for Jerusalem*, 118.

[10] Burns, *Between Arab and Israeli*, p. 108.

[11] Morris, *Israel's Border Wars*, p. 364.

[12] Khouri, *The Arab-Israeli Dilemma*, p. 194.

[13] Bull, *War and Peace in the Middle East*, pp. 50-51.

Chapter 20

1981 : Israel Destroys Iraq's Nuclear Facility

ON JUNE 7, 1981, 16 U.S.-made Israeli warplanes bombed and destroyed Iraq's Osirak nuclear research facility near Baghdad, more than 600 miles from Israel's borders.[1] Prime Minister Menachem Begin claimed the reactor was about to go into operation and was a threat to Israel because it could produce nuclear weapons. Begin's claims were contradicted by a number of experts, but there was considerable circumstantial evidence that Iraq indeed hoped eventually to develop a nuclear weapon.[2] However, Israel's critics pointed out that Iraq was a signatory to the nuclear Non-Proliferation Treaty, which allowed international inspections of the nuclear facility, while Israel itself refused to sign the treaty, refused inspections of its nuclear facility, and was widely believed to have a large nuclear arsenal.[3]

Thus the deeper meaning of the attack was that it amounted to a declaration of war against the Arab world's efforts to enter the atomic age. The attack was Israel's way of declaring that only the Jewish state would be allowed to participate in advanced technology, while the Arabs would be consigned to non-nuclear technology and second-class economies.

Israel was universally condemned. The White House advised Congress that a "substantial" violation of the Arms Export Control Act prohibition against the use of U.S. weapons except in self-defense "may have occurred" in Israel's bombing of Iraq's nuclear facility.[4] It was the third time the act had been invoked against Israel, the first two occurring during the Carter administration because of Israeli attacks on Lebanon.[5] But, as in the prior cases, Congress declined to take any action.[6]

Moreover, President Ronald Reagan soon found extenuating circumstances for Israel's conduct. Reagan said: "Israel might have sincerely believed it was a defensive move," adding: "It is difficult for me to envision Israel as being a threat to its neighbors."[7] While Washington joined in a unanimous U.N. Security Council resolution "strongly" condemning Israel, privately U.S. officials made it known that the United States would veto any article that called for sanctions against Israel. As a result of this pressure, council Resolution 487 stopped short of imposing sanctions and Israel's aggression was let go with a slap on the wrist.[8]

Bobby Inman, the No. 2 man at the Central Intelligence Agency, was less forgiving. He realized that the Israeli warplanes could not have flown to their target without having been guided by aerial photographs supplied by U.S. spy satellites. He was right. Under a secret arrangement worked out with Israeli intelligence by Director of Central Intelligence William J. Casey, Israel had been granted access to U.S. satellite photography.[9]

However, Inman knew that access was to be limited to areas posing potential "direct threats" to Israel, in Inman's words. When he discovered Israel had drawn material on such far-away areas as Iraq, Libya and Pakistan, he made a decision to limit its access to photographs covering areas no farther than 250 miles from Israel's border, thereby reducing Israel's satellite intelligence to its immediate neighbors.[10]

This decision infuriated Israel's supporters, and nearly 13 years later came back to haunt Inman when he was nominated by President Bill Clinton as secretary of defense. Israel's supporters, in particular columnist William Safire of *The New York Times*, took advantage of the occasion to launch harsh personal attacks against Inman, convincing him he could not effectively run the Pentagon amid such powerful criticism. Inman declined the nomination.[11]

Actually, Israel's aggressive intentions toward Iraq should have come as no surprise to anyone, particularly the CIA. Since at least 1979 it had been waging a secret war aimed at disrupting Iraq's nuclear program. The campaign was carried out by Israel's Mossad intelligence agency under the name Operation Sphinx.[12] The operation began at least as early as April 6, 1979, when three bomb

explosions in the nuclear facility of the French firm of Construc-
tions Navales et Industrielles de la Méditerranée in La Seyne-Sur-
Mer near Marseilles blew up reactor cores about to be shipped to
Iraq's facility, setting back Iraq's program by at least half a year.[13]

On June 13, 1980, Dr. Yahya Meshad, an Egyptian nuclear physicist working for Iraq's Atomic Energy Commission, was killed in
his Paris hotel room. Meshad had been in France checking on
highly enriched uranium that was about to be shipped as the first
fuel for Iraq's reactor and, according to Mossad defector Victor
Ostrovsky, was the victim of Mossad agents.[14] Two months later,
starting Aug. 2, a series of bombs exploded at the offices or residences of officials of Iraq's key suppliers in Italy and France: SNIA-
Techint, Ansaldo Mercanico Nucleare, and Techniatome. The
three firms were supplying Iraq with a reactor and hot cells and
their officials and workers were harassed by threatening letters.[15]

The terror campaign against Iraq was similar to one carried out
by Israel 19 years earlier against West German scientists working on
Egypt's rocket program. That campaign was called Operation
Damocles and involved kidnapping and letterbombs which caused
the deaths of at least five persons in 1962-63.[16] By the time Israel
halted its campaign against the German scientists, it had already
become clear that, in the words of Prime Minister David Ben-
Gurion's biographer, they "were a group of mediocre scientists who
had developed antiquated missiles. The panic that had overtaken
the country's leadership...was highly exaggerated."[17] But the damage
was done. Not only did the victims suffer directly, but the operation
convinced Egypt's leadership of Israel's unyielding hostility.

While Israel's suspicions against Iraq may have been more re-
alistic, its disregard of the significant diplomatic effects of its violent action was similarly myopic. Although Israel repeatedly con-
gratulated itself during the 1991 war against Iraq that its attack
represented an early blow to Saddam Hussein's militancy, there can
be little doubt that one result of the attack was to further radical-
ize the Iraqi leader and add to his suspicions of the West and his determination to build up Iraq's war machine.[18]

There can be no certainty, of course, that diplomacy would have
stemmed Saddam's ambitions. But there can be no doubt that once
Israel attacked Iraq with U.S.-made warplanes, Saddam would do

whatever he could to harm America and its Persian Gulf friends like Kuwait. The culmination of Saddam's hatred came a decade later when a half-million American military personnel had to be rushed to the Gulf area to war against Iraq's invasion of Kuwait, and then again in 1997-98 when he provoked a weapons inspections crisis with the U.N. and the U.S. ❧

RECOMMENDED READING:

Bar-Zohar, Michael, *Ben-Gurion: A Biography*, New York, Delacorte Press, 1978.

Ben-Gurion, David, *Israel: A Personal History*, New York, Funk & Wagnalls, Inc., 1971.

*Green, Stephen, *Living by the Sword: America and Israel in the Middle East*, 1968-87, Brattleboro, VT, Amana Books, 1988.

*Hersh, Seymour M., *The Samson Option: Israel's Nuclear Arsenal and American Foreign Policy*, New York, Random House, 1991.

Nakhleh, Issa, *Encyclopedia of the Palestine Problem*, New York, Intercontinental Books, 1991.

*Neff, Donald, *Warriors for Jerusalem: The Six Days That Changed the Middle East*, New York, Linden Press/Simon & Schuster, 1984, and Brattleboro, VT: Amana Books, 1988.

*Ostrovsky, Victor and Claire Hoy, *By Way of Deception*, New York, St. Martin's Press, 1990.

*Raviv, Dan and Yossi Melman, *Every Spy a Prince: The Complete History of Israel's Intelligence Community*, Boston, Houghton Mifflin Company, 1990.

Spector, Leonard S., *Nuclear Proliferation Today*, New York, Vintage Books, 1984.

Steven, Stewart, *The Spymasters of Israel*, New York, Macmillan Publishing Co., Inc., 1980.

Tillman, Seth, *The United States in the Middle East: Interests and Obstacles*, Bloomington, Indiana University Press, 1982.

Weissman, Steve and Herbert Krosney, *The Islamic Bomb: The Nuclear Threat to Israel and the Middle East*, New York, Times Books, 1981.

Woodward, Bob, *Veil: The Secret Wars of the CIA 1981-1987*, New York, Simon and Schuster, 1987.

*Available through the AET Book Club.

NOTES:

[1]Tillman, *The United States in the Middle East,* p. 38; also see Green, *Living by the Sword,* pp. 135-52; Hersh, *The Samson Option,* pp. 8-10; Raviv and Melman, *Every Spy a Prince,* pp. 25-52.

[2]Spector, *Nuclear Proliferation Today,* pp. 167-75; George Lardner Jr., and R. Jeffrey Smith, *Washington Post,* 12/16/92. Also see Elaine Sciolino, *New York Times,* 11/30/92; Jack Anderson and Michael Binstein, Op-ed, "Iran's Nuclear Ambitions," *Washington Post,* 12/20/92.

[3]Tillman, *The United States in the Middle East,* pp. 38-9.

[4]*Ibid.,* p. 39, and Institute for Palestine Studies, *International Documents on Palestine,* 1981, pp. 181-91.

[5]The earlier uses were on April 5, 1978 and Aug. 6, 1979.

[6]*New York Times,* 8/18/81, and Report by the Comptroller General, "U.S. Assistance to the State of Israel," General Accounting Office, GAO/ID-83-51, June 24, 1983, pp. 24-5.

[7]Institute for Palestine Studies, *International Documents on Palestine,* 1981, p. 206.

[8]*Ibid.,* p. 210.

[9]Woodward, *Veil,* p. 160.

[10]Transcript, Inman press conference, Austin, TX, 1/18/94; excerpts are in the *Washington Report on Middle East Affairs,* February/March, 1994.

[11]Transcript, Inman press conference, Austin, TX, 1/18/94.

[12]Ostrovsky and Hoy, *By Way of Deception,* pp. 1-28, and Raviv and Melman, *Every Spy a Prince,* pp. 250-2.

[13]In addition to Ostrovsky and Hoy, and Raviv and Melman, see Weissman and Krosney, *The Islamic Bomb,* pp. 227-8, and Spector, *Nuclear Proliferation Today,* p. 176.

[14]Ostrovsky and Hoy, *By Way of Deception,* p. 23.

[15]Spector, *Nuclear Proliferation Today,* pp. 176-7.

[16]Steven, *The Spymasters of Israel,* pp. 145-71 Also see Bar-Zohar, *Ben-Gurion,* pp. 301-2; Nakhleh, *Encyclopedia of the Palestine Problem,* p. 832; Neff, *Warriors for Jerusalem,* pp. 101-2; and Raviv and Melman, *Every Spy a Prince,* pp. 122-5. Also see Insight Team, the *Sunday Times* of London, 9/23/72, for a history of Israel's introduction of the use of letterbombs in the Middle East.

[17]Bar-Zohar, *Ben-Gurion,* pp. 301-2.

[18]Donald Neff, "The U.S., Iraq, Israel and Iran: Backdrop to War," *Journal of Palestine Studies,* Summer 1991.

Chapter 21

1982: Israeli Spying on U.S.

ON FEB. 1, 1982, *The Washington Post* reported, "Israeli intelligence agencies have blackmailed, bugged, wiretapped and offered bribes to U.S. government employees in an effort to gain sensitive intelligence and technical information."[1] *The Washington Post* report was based on a 47-page secret CIA report, "Israel: Foreign Intelligence and Security Services," issued in March, 1979. The report was published along with other secret documents seized in November, 1979, by militants occupying the U.S. Embassy in Tehran. No serious challenge to the accuracy of its contents has ever been made.

According to the report, Arab countries were Israel's top intelligence targets but "collection of information on secret U.S. policy or decisions...concerning Israel" and "collection of scientific intelligence in the U.S. and other developed countries" ranked second and third in priorities. "The Israelis devote a considerable portion of their covert operations to obtaining scientific and technical intelligence," the CIA report said. "This...included attempts to penetrate certain classified defense projects in the United States and other Western nations. "

Such adverse publicity has not stopped Israel from continuing to steal U.S. secrets. In fact, its biggest spying operation against America began barely two years later, in 1984, when Jonathan Jay Pollard, a civilian navy intelligence analyst, was recruited by Israel. Over the next year and a half he supplied Israel with a steady flow of top-secret U.S. documents, one of the greatest breaches of U.S. secrets ever perpetrated.[2] Author Seymour Hersh labeled Pollard "Israel's first nuclear spy." Hersh claimed Pollard passed on to Israel intelligence about U.S. nuclear targeting and that Israeli Prime Minister Yitzhak Shamir personally decided to pass on some of the information to the Soviet Union, at the time America's greatest enemy.[3]

Defense Secretary Caspar Weinberger later said: "It is difficult for me...to conceive of greater harm to national security than that caused by the defendant, in view of the breadth, the critical importance to the United States and high sensitivity of the information he sold to Israel." The thefts were so extensive that it was estimated it would cost $3 billion to $4 billion to correct security systems and replace exposed operations.[4]

Since the initial CIA revelations of Israeli espionage operations in the U.S., thievery by Israel of U.S. technology has become almost commonplace. In 1985, U.S. businessman Richard K. Smyth was indicted by a federal grand jury in Southern California on charges of illegally exporting 810 krytons to Israel. Krytons are electronic switching devices that can be used to detonate nuclear weapons.[5] Smyth was the president of Milco International, which since 1973 had done 80 percent of its business with Israel through an Israeli middleman, Arnon Milchan, a flamboyant movie producer of such films as "Brazil" and a former arms merchant himself. Smyth and his wife, Emilie, disappeared from California before he could be brought to trial, and he has been reported living in Israel.[6]

In March, 1993, NBC-TV's "Nightly News" aired a two-part report on Arnon Milchan, documenting his role as a top arms supplier to Israel. A weapons expert, Gary Milhollin, head of the Wisconsin Project on Nuclear Arms Control, examined an itemization of Milco's exports to Israel during the mid-1970 to mid-1980 decade and found it filled with material for a nuclear weapons program. "What this list shows is that Israel treated the United States like a nuclear and missile K-Mart for many years," Milhollin said. "They simply swarmed over here for the 'blue plate specials' and took everything home that they weren't supposed to have."

Although Milchan denied over the years that he was providing nuclear or missile technology to Israel, recently he changed his tune. "I was very proud to help my country, but I did nothing wrong," he said in a March 29, 1993, interview with the movie trade paper *Variety*. "That was fifteen years ago."[7]

Other recent cases of Israel's penetration of U.S. secrets:

In 1987, a Connecticut metal-plating firm, NAPCO Inc., of Tarryville, pleaded guilty and paid a $750,000 fine for smuggling equipment and technology to Israel for the chrome-plating of tank cannon barrels. In papers filed in Albany, NY, Federal District Court, the Justice Department revealed that Israel had persuaded the Pentagon in 1984 to pay $1.9 million to build a plant in Israel to manufacture "hydraulic tubes and cylinders, and failed to disclose that the facility would be used to chrome-plate 120mm cannon barrels"—in effect, U.S. funds were used to erect a plant that then employed smuggled U. S. technology.[8]

In 1990, California businessman Ronald Hoffman, 51, of Beverly Hills, owner of Plume Technology, was arrested on charges of selling secret American Star Wars technology to a number of countries, including Israel.[9] William Fahey, the assistant U.S. attorney prosecuting the case, said: "He was dealing with the highest levels of the military government in Israel.'"[10]

Such willingness to violate U.S. laws also has bred corruption at high levels in the U.S. government and private industry. In 1991 Israeli Air Force Brigadier General Rami Dotan, 45, pleaded guilty in an Israeli military court to conspiring with General Electric executive Harold Steindler to divert money from U.S. government-funded contracts between GE and the Israeli air force. Steindler, a career GE executive whom Israeli military prosecutors described as Dotan's partner in illicit schemes, was fired by GE. But GE was not clean itself. On July 22, 1992, GE pleaded guilty in Cincinnati federal court to charges of fraud, money laundering and corrupt business practices and agreed to pay fines and penalties of $69 million.[11]

Rep. John Dingell (D-MI), chairman of the House commerce oversight subcommittee, said his panel had investigated the scandal for more than a year and that Israel had been "markedly uncooperative."[12]

In 1991, former Assistant Secretary of the Navy Melvyn R. Paisley, 66, pleaded guilty to massive fraud involving the awarding of U.S. government-funded defense contracts to an Israeli company and U.S. firms. The three major criminal schemes Paisley admitted to involved the Israeli Mazlat Ltd. firm, Sperry Corp. and Martin Marietta Corp. Paisley was sentenced to four years in prison, two years' probation and fined $50,000.[13] There were allegations that the

Mazlat firm had not only bribed Paisley but had used technology stolen from U.S. manufacturers to produce an Israeli version of an unmanned reconnaissance aircraft that it then sold to the American navy with Paisley's help.[14]

Israel has not only stolen U.S. secrets but it is widely suspected of illegally transferring to other countries secret American technology Washington has voluntarily shared with Israel. Among Israel's prime customers have been China and South Africa. In 1992, a report by the State Department inspector general charged that Israel was engaged in a "systematic and growing pattern" of selling secret U.S. technology in violation of U.S. law. Unnamed U.S. officials added that there was "overwhelming" evidence that Israel was cheating on written promises not to re-export U.S. weapons technology to Third World countries, including China and South Africa, both on America's embargo list.[15] The officials said there was well-founded suspicion Israel also was selling secrets of America's vaunted Patriot antimissile to China.[16]

Dispatch of a 17-member U.S. team to Israel in late March failed to find any proof of transfer of the Patriots or their technology.[17] Nonetheless, Defense Secretary Dick Cheney said there remained "good reason" to believe a diversion had taken place.[18] *The Wall Street Journal* reported that there was "no doubt in the U.S. intelligence community that Israel has repeatedly engaged in diversion schemes."[19] *The Washington Post* confirmed the *Journal's* quotes about U.S. suspicions and added that one official said there were "lots and lots of...clear-cut cases."[20] However, no further action was taken by the Bush administration.

More recently, under the Clinton administration, CIA Director R. James Woolsey reported to Congress in October, 1993 that Israel had been selling advanced military technology to China for more than a decade. Woolsey estimated the value of the trade "may be several billion dollars." The CIA added: "Building on a long history of close defense industrial relations—including work on China's next generation fighter, air-to-air missiles and tanks programs— and the establishment of diplomatic relations in January, 1992, China and Israel appear to be moving toward formalizing and broadening their military technical cooperation."[21] Despite denials by Israel, the disclosure prompted *The New York Times* on Oct. 15, 1993 to write a rare critical editorial on Israel, going so far as to urge a halt in transfers of advanced American technology unless Israel was able to justify its transfers.

Despite such embarrassing disclosures, Israel continued to play fast and loose with U.S. technology. In an August, 1993 report, the General Accounting Office informed Congress that Israel may have understated the actual costs of its vastly expensive Arrow anti-missile missile and suggested that Israel may have transferred to third parties U.S. technology used in the missile. The GAO warned that the United States might be drawn into paying for most of the system without sound information of the Arrow's actual costs. Up to that date, the program had cost $487.6 million, with Israel paying $26.1 million, although the original estimate was that the program would cost a total of only $157 million.

Moreover, in securing U.S. backing for the Arrow program, Israeli officials had assured the United States that the need for American technology would be "relatively minor." In fact, the GAO reported, "the level of U.S. technical assistance has increased significantly over the course of the program." Despite such discrepancies, the GAO reported: "No U.S. government agency or department has monitored or verified Israel's compliance with the restrictive provisions of the Arrow licenses....No U.S. agency has comprehensive information on U.S. hardware and technology licensed for export to the Arrow program. As a result, the U.S. government is unable to fully account for U.S. content in the program."[22]

In other words, Israel was in a position, because of lax U.S. oversight, to do whatever it wished with secret U.S. technology because there was no way Washington could stop it, or even determine how much of the Arrow technology actually belonged to the United States. ≈

RECOMMENDED READING:

Black, Ian, and Benny Morris, *Israel's Secret Wars: A History of Israel's Intelligence Service*, New York, Grove Weidenfeld, 1991.

*Cockburn, Andrew and Leslie, *Dangerous Liaison: The Inside Story of the U.S.-Israeli Covert Relationship*, New York, HarperCollins Publishers, 1991.

*Findley, Paul, *Deliberate Deceptions: Facing the Facts About the U. S.-Israeli Relationship*, Brooklyn, NY, Lawrence Hill Books, 1993.

*Hersh, Seymour, *The Samson Option: Israel's Nuclear Arsenal and American Foreign Policy*, New York, Random House, 1991.

*Ostrovsky, Victor and Claire Hoy, *By Way of Deception*, New York, St. Martin's Press, 1990.

*Raviv, Dan and Yossi Melman, *Every Spy a Prince: The Complete History of Israel's Intelligence Community*, Boston, Houghton Mifflin Company, 1990.

*Available through the AET Book Club.

NOTES:

[1] Scott Armstrong, *Washington Post*, Feb. 1, 1982. For a survey of Israeli spying on America, see a three-part series in *The Wall Street Journal* by Edward T. Pound and David Rogers, Jan. 17, 20, 22, 1992; also see Jeff McConnell and Richard Higgins, "The Israeli Account," *The Boston Globe Magazine*, Dec. 14, 1986. For general stories on Israeli spying on the U.S. see *Washington Post*, Jan. 5, 1986 and *Baltimore Sun*, Nov. 16, 1986; two stories detail efforts by the Reagan administration to play down the seriousness of Israeli espionage: *Los Angeles Times*, June 11, 1986, and *New York Times*, June 12, 1986.

[2] Raviv and Melman, *Every Spy a Prince*, pp. 301-23; Cockburn, *Dangerous Liaison*, pp. 203-09; Hersh, *The Samson Option*, p. 285, p. 297. Text of the government's case against Pollard is in "Documents and Source Material," *Journal of Palestine Studies*, Autumn 1986, pp. 229-34.

[3] Hersh, *The Samson Option*, p. 285, p. 297.

[4] Robert I. Friedman, "The Secret Agent," *New York Review of Books*, Oct. 26, 1989.

[5] Raviv and Melman, *Every Spy a Prince*, pp. 304-5. Also see Jane Hunter, *Israeli Foreign Affairs*, April 11, 1993.

[6] Charles R. Babcock, *Washington Post*, 10/31/86.

[7] NBC-TV, "Nightly News," March 24-25, 1993, quoted in Jane Hunter, *Middle East International*, April 30, 1993.

[8] Charles R. Babcock, *Washington Post*, 11/25/87, and *New York Times*, 11/25/87. Also see Cockburn, *Dangerous Liaison*, p. 197.

[9] *New York Times*, 6/16/90.

[10] *Los Angeles Times* story in *Washington Post*, 6/16/90.

[11] Steven Pearlstein, *Washington Post*, 7/23/92.

[12] John Bennett, *Washington Times*, 7/22/92. Also see "What They Said: The Dotan Affair," *Washington Report on Middle East Affairs*, Aug./Sept. 1992.

[13] Robert F. Howe, *Washington Post*, 6/15/91, 10/19/91.

[14]Ostrovsky and Hoy, *By Way of Deception*, p. 270.

[15]Edward T. Pound, *Wall Street Journal*, 3/13/92; David Hoffman and R. Jeffrey Smith, *Washington Post*, 3/14/92. For a survey of U.S. support of Israel's arms industry, see Bishara A. Bahbah, "The U.S. Role in Israel's Arms Industry," *The Link*, December, 1987.

[16]Bill Gertz and Rowan Scarborough, *Washington Times*, 3/12-13/92.

[17]David Hoffman, *Washington Post*, 4/3/92.

[18]Bill Gertz, *Washington Times*, 4/9/92.

[19]Edward T. Pound, *Wall Street Journal*, 3/13/92.

[20]David Hoffman and R. Jeffrey Smith, *Washington Post*, 3/14/92. Also see David Hoffman, *Washington Post*, 4/2/92.

[21]Michael R. Gordon, *New York Times*, 10/13/93.

[22]General Accounting Office, "U.S.-Israel Arrow/Aces program: Cost, Technical, Proliferation, and Management Concerns," GAO/NSIAD-93.

Chapter 22

1983: Israel "Indirectly Responsible" For Massacres in Lebanon

ON FEB. 7, 1983, the Israeli Commission of Inquiry, better known as the Kahan Commission, issued its report on the 1982 massacres at the Palestinian refugee camps at Sabra and Shatila in Lebanon. It found eight Israeli political and military leaders guilty of "indirect responsibility" for the slaughter by Lebanese Phalange militiamen of as many as 2,000 Palestinian refugees in the two camps during Israel's invasion of Lebanon in 1982.

Those named by the commission: Prime Minister Menachem Begin, Foreign Minister Yitzhak Shamir, Defense Minister Ariel Sharon, Chief of Staff Lieutenant General Rafael Eitan, Director of Military Intelligence Major General Yehoshua Saguy, Major General Amin Drori, Brigadier General Amos Yaron, and the unidentified head of Mossad, Israel's CIA.[1]

Despite the grave nature of the findings, most of those found in the wrong continued to have successful careers. Begin remained prime minister until he voluntarily resigned. He was replaced later in 1983 by Shamir, who remained in power for the next nine years. Sharon lost his ministry but reappeared as the minister of infrastructure under Prime Minister Binyamin Netanyahu. Eitan founded his own political party, Tsomet, which was openly committed to ridding the area of Palestinians, then became minister of agriculture and environment in Netanyahu's government. Yaron went on to become commander of the army's manpower branch and was promoted to major general; in 1986 he was appointed military attaché to the United States.[2]

New York Times correspondent Thomas Friedman, who was at the massacre scene, later commented: "An investigation which results in such 'punishments' is not an investigation that can be taken seriously. The Israelis knew just what they were doing when they let the Phalangists into those camps."[3]

What the Israelis were doing at Sabra and Shatila was indeed clear. They allowed a massacre of Palestinian refugees by Christian Phalange militiamen to occur while the area was in Israel's total control and with a U.S. commitment that civilians would be protected. The basic conclusion of the Kahan Report, eyewitnesses and the international community was that Israel deliberately allowed the slaughter to continue for more than a day before finally ending it.[4]

The slaughter came within the context of Israel's invasion of Lebanon on June 6, 1982. Its aim was to drive out guerrillas of the Palestine Liberation Organization from Israel's northern neighbor. Prime Minister Begin assured the world that Israeli troops would slash no more than 40 kilometers into southern Lebanon to disperse the guerrillas away from Israel's frontier.

Within one week, however, the Israeli invasion forces had linked up with their Phalange allies and were besieging West Beirut, the center of the PLO in Lebanon. On July 3, Israel snapped shut its blockade of West Beirut, stopping all traffic into the area. The next day, it began cutting off water, power, food, gasoline and other essentials to the area in an effort to starve Palestinian guerrillas into submission.

Actress Jane Fonda accompanied Israeli troops to Beirut, witnessed the indiscriminate shelling of the western part of the city and later expressed her support for Israel, as did many of Israel's American supporters.[5]

Despite its severity, Israel's siege failed to subdue West Beirut. On July 22, Israel began daily air attacks with planes given to it by the United States, often accompanied by artillery and naval fire. The attacks grew in ferocity as the siege lengthened. On Aug. 1, the heaviest bombing of the invasion up to that time took place by land, sea and air for 14 hours.[6] The Israeli air force alone launched 127 sorties, dropping an estimated 260 tons of bombs. Some 200 persons were killed and twice that many wounded in the attack.[7]

Worse was in store for the people of West Beirut. On Aug. 12, Defense Minister Sharon ordered the heaviest air and artillery attacks of the war. A massive Israeli artillery attack began at dawn and was accompanied for 11 straight hours by a saturation air bombardment in what became known as "Black Thursday."[8] As many as 500 persons were killed.[9] President Reagan, despite his pro-Israeli sympathies, was so outraged by the slaughter with U.S. weapons that he personally telephoned Begin twice that day, charging that Israel was causing "needless destruction and bloodshed."[10]

International outrage against Israel was such that on Aug. 19 the Jewish state finally agreed to a U.S.-proposed cease-fire. It called for Israel to stay out of West Beirut, where the families of the PLO fighters lived in a series of squalid refugee camps in the southern suburbs, and for the withdrawal from Lebanon of thousands of PLO guerrillas. It also offered U.S. guarantees for the safety of the Palestinians, both the guerrillas withdrawing and their families remaining.[11]

To assure their safety, an international force of troops from the United States, France and Italy arrived in Lebanon. On Aug. 30 PLO Chairman Yasser Arafat sailed away, the last of the Palestinian fighters to leave.[12] The U.S. Marine force followed on Sept. 10, 16 days after they had arrived.[13]

The Marines were barely gone when President-elect Bashir Gemayel, the Maronite Phalangist partner of the Israelis, and 24 others were killed by a powerful bomb in Beirut on Sept. 14.[14] The assassination caused Lebanon to explode with communal hatreds.

Israel reacted quickly. The next morning, it broke the cease-fire and massively invaded West Beirut. By Sept. 16, Israeli troops controlled all of West Beirut, including the sprawling Sabra and Shatila refugee camps in the southern suburbs and all of Beirut's main roads, junctions and strategic heights. Their control was complete and they imposed a total curfew on the area.[15] An official Israeli spokesman declared: "The Israel Defense Force is in control of all key points in Beirut. Refugee camps harboring terrorists concentrations remain encircled and closed."[16]

By remaining in the area—in defiance of a call by Washington to honor the cease-fire agreement—Israel became an occupying power and as such was responsible for the security of the civilian inhabitants under the articles of the Geneva Convention Relative to the Protection of Civilian Persons in Time of War.[17] Israel had signed the convention in 1951.

Israel was well aware of the passions sweeping the Phalangist militia. U.S. Special envoy Morris Draper met Chief of Staff Eitan on Sept. 16 and suggested that the Lebanese army be sent into the Palestinian refugee camps to search for terrorists that Israel insisted were hiding there. However, Eitan said the regular army was not up to the task, adding: "Let me explain to you. Lebanon is at a point of exploding into a frenzy of revenge. No one can stop them. They're [the Phalangists] obsessed with the idea of revenge....I'm telling you that some of their commanders visited me, and I could see in their eyes that it's going to be a relentless slaughter."[18]

On the same day, Eitan explained to the Israeli cabinet that Phalangist forces would soon enter Palestinian refugee camps under Israeli orders to search out terrorists. As summarized by the Israeli inquiry commission:

"He said, inter alia, that he had informed the Phalange commanders that their men would have to take part in the operation and go in where they were told, that early that evening they would begin to fight and would enter the extremity of Sabra, that the IDF [Israel Defense Forces] would ensure that they did not fail in their operation but IDF soldiers would not enter the camps and would not fight together with the Phalangists, rather the Phalangists would go in there 'with their own methods.' In his remarks, the chief of staff explained that the camps were surrounded 'by us,' that the Phalangists would begin to operate that night in the camps, that we could give them orders...."[19]

At 6 p.m. that day, Sept. 16, a company of 150 "special" Phalange forces under Elias Hobeika, the feared intelligence chief of the Christian Phalange militia, moved into the cramped streets of the Shatila Palestinian refugee camp. Darkness was falling and Israeli mortar units and airplanes dropped flares to aid the Phalangists' progress.[20]

The Israeli forward command post in West Beirut was located on the roof of a five-story building about two football fields southwest of Shatila. Next to Shatila was Sabra camp, the two camps merging without clear definition and sprawling over about three square miles. About 90,000 persons lived in the two camps.[21]

At about 7 p.m., an Israeli officer stationed at the forward command post heard a Phalangist receive a radio request for orders on what to do with 50 women and children being held in a section of the camp. "This is the last time you're going to ask me a question like that, you know exactly what to do," replied Hobeika.[22] According to the Israeli inquiry report, the Israeli officer who overheard this exchange "understood that what was involved was the murder of the women and children."[23]

At the same time, a Phalangist liaison officer reported that 300 persons had already been killed by the Phalangists in the camps. When Israeli Chief of Military Intelligence Yehoshua Saguy heard this report he merely asked it to be checked for accuracy. He did not pass it on or take any other action.[24]

At 8:40 p.m., General Yaron's intelligence officer briefed the division's commanders that only two Phalangists had been wounded and that the fighting inside the camps did not seem serious. "...It seems they're trying to decide what to do with the people they find inside. On the one hand, there are evidently no terrorists in the camp; Sabra is empty. On the other, they've gathered up women, children and probably old people and don't know quite what to do with them."[25]

The massacre of the innocents was about to begin in earnest.

Phalangist forces killed civilians indiscriminately inside the camps throughout the night of Sept. 16/17. There were no PLO guerrillas to protect the defenseless women, children and old people nor U.S. forces to make good America's promise to protect the civilians. Whole families were gunned down or knifed to death. One infant was stomped to death by a man wearing spiked shoes. Another refugee was killed by live grenades draped around his neck.[26] Bulldozers were brought in, mass graves hastily dug and truckloads of bodies dumped in them. Throughout the night, the shooting and the screams did not stop.[27]

Israel allowed the Phalangists to remain in the camps until 8 a.m., Sept. 18—even though it was known by the morning of Sept. 17 that a massacre was taking place. When the media pointed a finger at Israel, the Israeli cabinet rejected any blame. A prepared cabinet statement said: "A blood libel has been perpetrated against the Jewish people."[28] Prime Minister Begin memorably declared:

"*Goyim* kill *Goyim* and they blame the Jew."[29]

The Israeli commission of inquiry concluded that 700 to 800 persons had been killed in Sabra and Shatila.[30] Non-Israeli estimates were considerably higher. The Palestine Red Crescent put the number at over 2,000, while Lebanese authorities reported 762 bodies recovered and 1,200 death certificates issued.[31]

It was not until the last week of September that Israeli troops finally withdrew from Beirut. Many West Beirutis complained that the Israelis looted and sacked their homes and businesses as they retreated. Truckloads of plundered booty were seen heading back toward Israel in convoys. Dr. Sabri Jiryis, director of the Palestine Liberation Organization's Research Center in Beirut, complained that Israeli soldiers carted away the center's entire 25,000-volume research library of books in Arabic, English and Hebrew. They also smashed desks, filing cabinets and other equipment and stole a printing press, telephones and electrical appliances.[32]

Left behind by the Israelis were vast death and destruction in Beirut and graffiti saying "Palestinian? What's That?" and "Palestinians, f--- you."[33] ❧

RECOMMENDED READING:

Ball, George W., *Error and Betrayal in Lebanon*, Washington, DC, Foundation for Middle East Peace, 1984.

Chomsky, Noam, *The Fateful Triangle*, Boston, South End Press, 1983.

Cooley, John K., *Payback: America's Long War in the Middle East*, New York, Brassey's (U.S.), Inc., 1991.

Fisk, Robert, *Pity the Nation: The Abduction of Lebanon*, New York, Atheneum, 1990.

*Friedman, Thomas L., *From Beirut to Jerusalem*, New York, Farrar Strass Giroux, 1989.

Hart, Alan, *Arafat: Terrorist or Peacemaker?*, London, Sidgwick & Jackson, 1985.

Jansen, Michael, *The Battle of Beirut: Why Israel Invaded Lebanon*, London, Zed Press, 1982.

MacBride, Sean (chairman), *Israel in Lebanon: The Report of the International Commission to enquire into reported violations of International Law by Israel during its invasion of the Lebanon*, London, Ithaca Press, 1983.

*Mallison, Thomas and Sally V., *Armed Conflict in Lebanon, 1982: Humanitarian Law in a Real World Setting*, Washington, DC, American Educational Trust, 1985.

*Randal, Jonathan, *Going all the Way*, New York, The Viking Press, 1983.

*Schiff, Ze'ev and Ehud Ya'ari, *Israel's Lebanon War*, New York, Simon and Schuster, 1984.

Timerman, Jacobo (trans: Miquel Acoca), *The Longest War: Israel in Lebanon*, New York, Vantage Books, 1982.

*Available through the AET Book Club.

NOTES:

[1] Excerpts in *New York Times*, 2/9/83, and in "Final Report of the Israeli Commission of Inquiry," *Journal of Palestine Studies*, Vol. XII, No. 3, Spring 1983, pp. 89-116.

[2] David Halevy and Neil C. Livingstone, "The Killing of Abu Jihad," *The Washingtonian*, June, 1988.

[3] Friedman, *From Beirut to Jerusalem*, pp. 164-5.

[4] See, for instance, Ball, *Error and Betrayal in Lebanon*; Jansen, *The Battle of Beirut*; MacBride, *Israel in Lebanon*; Mallisons, *Armed Conflict in Lebanon, 1982*; Schiff and Ya'ari, *Israel's Lebanon War*; Timerman, *The Longest War*.

[5] Fisk, *Pity the Nation*, p. 395. Also see Chomsky, *The Fateful Triangle*, pp. 267-68.

[6] Schiff and Ya'ari, *Israel's Lebanon War*, p. 221.

[7] *Ibid.*, p. 221; also see "Chronology of the Israeli Invasion of Lebanon," *Journal of Palestine Studies*, Vols. XI 4, XII 1, Summer/Fall 1982, p. 181.

[8] Schiff & Ya'ari, *Israel's Lebanon War*, p. 225.

[9] "Chronology of the Israeli Invasion of Lebanon," *Journal of Palestine Studies*, Vols. XI 4, XII 1, Summer/Fall 1982, p. 189.

[10] Ball, *Error and Betrayal in Lebanon*, p. 46.

[11] *Ibid.*, pp. 55-56.

[12] Friedman, *From Beirut to Jerusalem*, pp. 152-53.

[13] MacBride, *Israel in Lebanon*, p. 164.

[14] Randal, *Going All the Way*, pp. 1-5; Collins, "Chronology of the Israeli War in Lebanon," *Journal of Palestine Studies*, Winter 1983, p. 99. Also see Schiff & Ya'ari, *Israel's Lebanon War*, pp. 247-8; Friedman, *From Beirut to Jerusalem*, pp. 157-8; Hart, *Arafat*, p. 460; Fisk, *Pity the Nation*, p. 463.

[15]MacBride, *Israel in Lebanon*, p. 166.

[16]*Ibid.*, p. 166.

[17]*Ibid.*, p. 163.

[18]Schiff & Ya'ari, *Israel's Lebanon War*, pp. 259-60.

[19]"Final Report of the Israeli Commission of Inquiry into the Events at the Refugee Camps in Beirut," *Journal of Palestine Studies*, Vol. XII, No. 3, Spring 1983, p. 97.

[20]*Ibid.*, pp. 93-4.

[21]MacBride, *Israel in Lebanon*, p. 162.

[22]"Final Report of the Israeli Commission of Inquiry into the Events at the Refugee Camps in Beirut," *Journal of Palestine Studies*, Vol. XII, No. 3, Spring 1983, p. 95. Also see Cooley, *Payback*, pp. 70-1.

[23]*Ibid.*, p. 95.

[24]*Ibid.*, p. 112.

[25]Schiff & Ya'ari, *Israel's Lebanon War*, p. 262.

[26]*Ibid.*, p. 264.

[27]*Time*, 10/4/82, p. 22.

[28]Ball, *Error and Betrayal in Lebanon*, p. 58.

[29]Silver, *Begin*, p. 236.

[30]"Final Report of the Israeli Commission of Inquiry into the Events at the Refugee Camps in Beirut," *Journal of Palestine Studies*, Vol. XII, No. 3, Spring 1983, p. 105.

[31]Ball, *Error and Betrayal in Lebanon*, p. 57. These figures conform with estimates by the Lebanese government reported by Jack Redden of United Press International on 10/13/82. Also see Carol Collins, "Chronology of the Israeli War in Lebanon," *Journal of Palestine Studies*, Vol. XII, No. 2, Winter 1983, p. 116.

[32]*Washington Post*, 9/29/82. Also see Ihsan A. Hijazi, *New York Times*, 9/30/82; Friedman, *From Beirut to Jerusalem*, p. 159. Israel returned the archives on Nov. 24, 1983; see David Koff, "Chronology of the War in Lebanon, September-November, 1983," *Journal of Palestine Studies*, Vol. XIII, No. 2, Winter 1984, p. 154.

[33]Friedman, *From Beirut to Jerusalem*, p. 159.

Chapter 23

1983: Israelis Endanger U.S. Marines in Lebanon

ON MARCH 14, 1983, the commandant of the Marine Corps sent a highly unusual letter to the secretary of defense expressing frustration and anger at Israel. General R.H. Barrow charged that Israeli troops were deliberately threatening the lives of Marines serving as peacekeepers in Lebanon. There was, he wrote, a systematic pattern of harassment by Israel Defense Forces (IDF) that was resulting in "life-threatening situations, replete with verbal degradation of the officers, their uniform and country."

Barrow's letter added: "It is inconceivable to me why Americans serving in peacekeeping roles must be harassed, endangered by an ally...It is evident to me, and the opinion of the U.S. commanders afloat and ashore, that the incidents between the Marines and the IDF are timed, orchestrated, and executed for obtuse Israeli political purposes."[1]

Israel's motives were less obtuse than the diplomatic general pretended. It was widely believed then, and now, that Israeli Defense Minister Ariel Sharon, one of Israel's most Machiavellian politician-generals, was creating the incidents deliberately in an effort to convince Washington that the two forces had to coordinate their actions in order to avoid such tensions. This, of course, would have been taken by the Arabs as proof that the Marines were not really in Lebanon as neutral peacekeepers but as allies of the Israelis, a perception that would have obvious advantages for Israel.[2]

Barrow's extraordinary letter was indicative of the frustrations and miseries the Marines suffered during their posting to Lebanon starting on Aug. 25, 1982, as a result of Israel's invasion 11 weeks earlier. Initially a U.S. unit of 800 men was sent to Beirut harbor as part of a multinational force to monitor the evacuation of PLO guerrillas from Beirut. The Marines, President Reagan announced, "in no case...would stay·longer than 30 days."[3] This turned out to be only partly true. They did withdraw on Sept. 10, but a reinforced unit of 1,200 was rushed back 15 days later after the massacres at the Palestinian refugee camps at Sabra and Shatila that accompanied the Israeli seizure of West Beirut. The U.S. forces remained until Feb. 26, 1984.[4]

During their-year-and-a-half posting in Lebanon, the Marines suffered 268 killed.[5] The casualties started within a week of the return of the Marines in September, 1982. On the 30th, a U.S.-made cluster bomb left behind by the Israelis exploded, killing Corporal David Reagan and wounding three other Marines.[6]

Corporal Reagan's death represented the dangers of the new mission of the Marines in Lebanon. While their first brief stay had been to separate Israeli forces from Palestinian fighters evacuating West Beirut, their new mission was as part of a multinational force sent to prevent Israeli troops from attacking the Palestinian civilians left defenseless after the withdrawal of PLO forces. As President Reagan said: "For this multinational force to succeed, it is essential that Israel withdraw from Beirut."[7]

Israel's siege of Beirut during the summer of 1982 had been brutal and bloody, reaching a peak of horror on Aug. 12, quickly known as Black Thursday. On that day, Sharon's forces launched at dawn a massive artillery barrage that lasted for 11 straight hours and was accompanied by saturation air bombardment.[8] As many as 500 persons, mainly Lebanese and Palestinian civilians, were killed.[9]

On top of the bombardment came the massacres the next month at Sabra and Shatila, where Sharon's troops allowed Lebanese Maronite killers to enter the camps filled with defenseless civilians. The massacres sickened the international community and pressure from Western capitals finally forced Israel to withdraw from Beirut in late September. Troops from Britain, France, Italy and the United States were interposed between the Israeli army and Beirut, with U.S. Marines deployed in the most sensitive area south of Beirut at the International Airport, directly between Israeli troops and West Beirut.

It was at the airport that the Marines would suffer their Calvary over the next year. Starting in January, 1983, small Israeli units began probing the Marine lines. At first the effort appeared aimed at discovering the extent of Marine determination to resist penetration. The lines proved solid and the Marines' determination strong. Israeli troops were politely but firmly turned away. Soon the incidents escalated, with both sides pointing loaded weapons at each other but no firing taking place. Tensions were high enough by late January that a special meeting between U.S. and Israeli officers was held in Beirut to try to agree on precise boundaries beyond which the IDF would not penetrate.[10]

However, on Feb. 2 a unit of three Israeli tanks, led by Israeli Lt. Col. Rafi Landsberg, tried to pass through Marine/Lebanese army lines at Rayan University Library in south Lebanon. By this time, Landsberg was no stranger to the Marines. Since the beginning of January he had been leading small Israeli units in probes against the Marine lines, although such units would normally have a commander no higher than a sergeant or lieutenant. The suspicion grew that Sharon's troops were deliberately provoking the Marines and Landsberg was there to see that things did not get out of hand. The Israeli tactics were aimed more at forcing a joint U.S.-Israeli strategy than merely probing lines.

In the Feb. 2 incident, the checkpoint was commanded by Marine Capt. Charles Johnson, who firmly refused permission for Landsberg to advance. When two of the Israeli tanks ignored his warning to halt, Johnson leaped on Landsberg's tank with pistol drawn and demanded Landsberg and his tanks withdraw. They did.[11]

Landsberg and the Israeli Embassy in Washington tried to laugh off the incident, implying that Johnson was a trigger-happy John Wayne type and that the media were exaggerating a routine event. Landsberg even went so far as to claim that he smelled alcohol on Johnson's breath and that drunkenness must have clouded his reason. Marines were infuriated because Johnson was well known as a teetotaler. Americans flocked to Johnson's side. He received hundreds of letters from school children, former Marines and from Commandant Barrow.[12] It was a losing battle for the Israelis and Landsberg soon dropped from sight.

But the incidents did not stop. These now included "helicopter harassment," by which U.S.-made helicopters with glaring spotlights were flown by the Israelis over Marine positions at night, illuminating Marine outposts and exposing them to potential attack. As reports of these incidents piled up, Gen. Barrow received a letter on March 12 from a U.S. Army major stationed in Lebanon with the United Nations Truce Supervisory Organization (UNTSO). The letter described a systematic pattern of Israeli attacks and provocations against UNTSO troops, including instances in which U.S. officers were singled out for "near-miss" shootings, abuse and detention.[13] That same day two Marine patrols were challenged and cursed by Israeli soldiers.[14]

Two days later Barrow wrote his letter to Secretary of Defense Caspar W. Weinberger, who endorsed it and sent it along to the State Department. High-level meetings were arranged and the incidents abated, perhaps largely because by this time Ariel Sharon had been fired as defense minister. He had been found by an Israeli commission to have had "personal responsibility" for the Sabra and Shatila massacres.[15]

Despite the bad taste left from the clashes with the Israelis, in fact no Marines had been killed in the incidents and their lines had been secure up to the end of winter in 1983. Then Islamic guerrillas, backed by Iran, became active. On the night of April 17, 1983, an unknown sniper fired a shot that went through the trousers of a Marine sentry but did not harm him. For the first time, the Marines returned fire.[16]

The next day, the U.S. Embassy in Beirut was blown up by a massive bomb, with the loss of 63 lives. Among the 17 Americans killed were CIA Mideast specialists, including Robert C. Ames, the agency's top Middle East expert.[17] Disaffected former Israeli Mossad case officer Victor Ostrovsky later claimed that Israel had advance information about the bombing plan but had decided not to inform the United States, a claim denied by Israel.[18] The Iranian-backed Islamic Jihad claimed responsibility. Veteran correspondent John Cooley considered the attack "the day [Iranian leader Ayatollah] Khomeini's offensive against America in Lebanon began in earnest."[19]

Still, it was not until four months later, on Aug. 28, that Marines came under direct fire by rocket-propelled grenades and automatic weapons at International Airport. They returned fire with M-16 rifles and M-60 machine guns. The firefight resumed the next day with Marines firing 155mm artillery, 81mm mortars and rockets from Cobra helicopter gunships against Shi'i Muslim positions. Two Marines were killed and 14 wounded in the exchange, the first casualties in actual combat since the Marines had landed the previous year.[20]

From this time on, the combat involvement of the Marines grew. Their actions were generally seen as siding with Israel against Muslims, slowly changing the status of the Marines as neutral peacekeepers to opponents of the Muslims.[21] Israel could hardly have wished for more. The polarization meant that increasingly the conflict was being perceived in terms of the U.S., Israel and Lebanon's Christians against Iran, Islam and Lebanon's Shi'i Muslims.

Israel accelerated the building conflict on Sept. 3, 1993, by unilaterally withdrawing its troops southward, leaving the Marines exposed behind their thin lines at the airport. The United States had asked the Israeli government to delay its withdrawal until the Marines could be replaced by units of the Lebanese army, but Israel refused.[22] The result was as feared. Heavy fighting immediately broke out between the Christian Lebanese Forces and the pro-Syrian Druze units, both seeking to occupy positions evacuated by Israel, while the Marines were left in the crossfire.[23] On Sept. 5, two Marines were killed and three wounded as fighting escalated between Christian and Muslim militias.[24]

In an ill-considered effort to subdue the combat, the Sixth Fleet frigate USS *Bowen* fired several five-inch naval guns, hitting Druze artillery positions in the Chouf Mountains that were firing into the Marine compound at Beirut airport.[25] It was the first time U.S. ships had fired into Lebanon, dramatically raising the level of combat. Despite such firepower, the Marines' exposed location on the flat terrain of the airport left them in an impossible position. On Sept. 12, three more Marines were wounded.[26]

On Sept. 13, President Reagan authorized what was called aggressive self-defense for the Marines, including air and naval strikes.[27] Five days later the United States essentially joined the war against the Muslims when four U.S. warships unleashed the heaviest naval bombardment since Vietnam into Syrian and Druze positions in eastern Lebanon in support of the Lebanese Christians.[28] The bombardment lasted for three days and was personally ordered by National Security Council director Robert McFarlane, a Marine Corps officer detailed to the White House who was in Lebanon at the time and was also a strong supporter of Israel and its Lebanese Maronite Christian allies. McFarlane issued the order despite the fact that the Marine commander at the airport, Colonel Timothy Geraghty, strenuously argued against it because, in the words of correspondent Thomas L. Friedman, "he knew that it would make his soldiers party to what was now clearly an intra-Lebanese fight, and that the Lebanese Muslims would not retaliate against the Navy's ships at sea but against the Marines on shore."[29]

By now, the Marines were under daily attack and Muslims were charging they were no longer neutral.[30] At the same time the battleship USS *New Jersey*, with 16-inch guns, arrived off Lebanon, increasing the number of U.S. warships offshore to 14. Similarly, the Marine contingent at Beirut airport was increased from 1,200 to 1,600.[31]

The fight now was truly joined between the Shi'i Muslims and the Marines, who were essentially pinned down in their airport bunkers and under orders not to take offensive actions. The tragic climax of their predicament came on Oct. 23, when a Muslim guerrilla drove a truck past guards at the Marine airport compound and detonated an explosive with the force of 12,000 pounds of dynamite under a building housing Marines and other U.S. personnel. Almost simultaneously, a car-bomb exploded at the French compound in Beirut. Casualties were 241 Americans and 58 French troops killed. The bombings were the work of Hezbollah, made up of Shi'i Muslim guerrillas supported by Iran.[32]

America's agony increased on Dec. 3, when two carrier planes were downed by Syrian missiles during heavy U.S. air raids on eastern Lebanon.[33] On the same day, eight Marines were killed in fighting with Muslim militiamen around the Beirut airport.[34]

By the start of 1984, an all-out Shi'i Muslim campaign to rid Lebanon of all Americans was underway. The highly respected president of the American University of Beirut, Dr. Malcolm Kerr, a distinguished scholar of the Arab world, was gunned down on Jan. 18 outside his office by Islamic militants aligned with Iran.[35] On Feb. 5, Reagan made one of his stand-tall speeches by saying that "the situation in Lebanon is difficult, frustrating and dangerous. But this is no reason to turn our backs on friends and to cut and run."[36]

The next day Professor Frank Regier, a U.S. citizen teaching at AUB, was kidnapped by Muslim radicals.[37] Regier's kidnapping was the beginning of a series of kidnappings of Americans in Beirut that would hound the Reagan and later the Bush administrations for years and lead to the eventual expulsion of nearly all Americans from Lebanon where they had prospered for more than a century. The U.S. government imposed a ban on travel by U.S. citizens to Lebanon that remained in effect until 1997.

The day after Regier's kidnapping, on Feb. 7, 1984, Reagan suddenly reversed himself and announced that all U.S. Marines would shortly be "redeployed." The next day the battleship USS *New Jersey* fired 290 rounds of one-ton shells from its 16-inch guns into Lebanon as a final act of U.S. frustration.[38] Reagan's "redeployment" was completed by Feb. 26, when the last of the Marines retreated from Lebanon.

The mission of the Marines had been a humiliating failure—not because they failed in their duty but because the political backbone in Washington was lacking. The Marines had arrived in 1982 with all sides welcoming them. They left in 1984 despised by many and the object of attacks by Muslims. Even relations with Israel were strained, if not in Washington where a sympathetic Congress granted increased aid to the Jewish state to compensate it for the costs of its bungled invasion, then between the Marines and Israeli troops who had confronted each other in a *realpolitik* battlefield that was beyond their competence or understanding. The Marine experience in Lebanon did not contribute toward a favorable impression of Israel among many Americans, especially since the Marines would not have been in Lebanon except for Israel's unprovoked invasion.

This negative result is perhaps one reason a number of Israelis and their supporters today oppose sending U.S. peacekeepers to the Golan Heights as part of a possible Israeli-Syrian peace treaty. A repeat of the 1982-84 experience would certainly not be in Israel's interests at a time when its supporters were seeking to have a budget-conscious Congress continue unprecedented amounts of aid to Israel. ≉

RECOMMENDED READING:

Ball, George, *Error and Betrayal in Lebanon*, Washington, DC, Foundation for Middle East Peace, 1984.

*Cockburn, Andrew and Leslie Cockburn, *Dangerous Liaison: The Inside Story of the U.S.-Israeli Covert Relationship*, New York, Harper Collins, 1991.

Cooley, John K., *Payback: America's Long War in the Middle East*, New York, Brassey's U.S., Inc., 1991.

*Findley, Paul, *Deliberate Deceptions: Facing the Facts About the U.S.-Israeli Relationship*, Brooklyn, NY, Lawrence Hill Books, 1993.

Fisk, Robert, *Pity the Nation: The Abduction of Lebanon*, New York, Atheneum, 1990.

Frank, Benis M., *U.S. Marines in Lebanon: 1982-1984*, History and Museums Division, Headquarters, U.S. Marine Corps, Washington, DC, 1987.

*Friedman, Thomas L., *From Beirut to Jerusalem*, New York, Farrar, Strauss, Giroux, 1989.

*Green, Stephen, *Living by the Sword*, Amana, 1988.

Jansen, Michael, *The Battle of Beirut: Why Israel Invaded Lebanon*, London, Zed Press, 1982.

MacBride, Sean, *Israel in Lebanon: The Report of the International Commission to enquire into reported violations of international law by Israel during its invasion of Lebanon*, London, Ithaca Press, 1983.

*Ostrovsky, Victor and Claire Hoy, *By Way of Deception*, New York, St. Martin's Press, 1990.

Peck, Juliana S., *The Reagan Administration and the Palestinian Question: The First Thousand Days*, Washington, DC, Institute for Palestine Studies, 1984.

*Randal, Jonathan, *Going all the Way*, New York, The Viking Press, 1983.

Schechla, Joseph, *The Iron Fist: Israel's Occupation of South Lebanon, 1982-1985*, Washington, DC, ADC Research Institute, Issue Paper No. 17, 1985.

*Schiff, Ze'ev and Ehud Ya'ari, *Israel's Lebanon War*, New York, Simon and Schuster, 1984.

Timerman, Jacobo, *The Longest War: Israel in Lebanon*, New York, Vantage Books, 1982.

Woodward, Bob, *Veil: The Secret Wars of the CIA 1981-1987*, New York, Simon and Schuster, 1987.

* Available through the AET Book Club.

NOTES:

[1] *New York Times*, 3/18/83. For a detailed review of these clashes, see Green, *Living by the Sword*, pp. 177-92, and Clyde Mark, "The Multinational

Force in Lebanon," Congressional Research Service, 5/19/83.

[2]See "NBC Nightly News," 6:30 PM EST, 3/17/86; also, George C. Wilson, *Washington Post,* 2/5/83.

[3]Ball, *Error and Betrayal in Lebanon,* p. 51; Cooley, *Payback,* pp. 69-71.

[4]Frank, *U.S Marines in Lebanon: 1982-1984,* p. 137.

[5]*Ibid.,*Appendix F.

[6]*New York Times,* 10/1/82. Also see Cooley, *Payback,* p. 71; Green, *Living by the Sword,* pp. 175-77

[7]The text is in *New York Times,* 9/30/82. Also see Peck, *The Reagan Administration and the Palestinian Question,* p. 76.

[8]Schiff & Ya'ari, *Israel's Lebanon War,* p. 225.

[9]"Chronology of the Israeli Invasion of Lebanon," *Journal of Palestine Studies,* Summer/Fall 1982, p. 189.

[10]Green, *Living by the Sword,* pp. 178-80.

[11]Frank, *U.S Marines in Lebanon: 1982-1984,* pp. 45-46.

[12]*Ibid.*

[13]Green, *Living by the Sword,* p. 182.

[14]Frank, *U.S Marines in Lebanon: 1982-1984,* p. 56.

[15]*New York Times,* 2/9/83; "Final Report of the Israeli Commission of Inquiry," *Journal of Palestine Studies,* Spring 1983, pp. 89-116.

[16]Frank, *U.S Marines in Lebanon: 1982-1984,* p. 56.

[17]*New York Times,* 4/22/83 and 4/26/83. For more detail on CIA victims, see Charles R. Babcock, *Washington Post,* 8/5/86, and Woodward, *Veil,* pp. 244-45.

[18]Ostrovsky, *By Way of Deception,* p. 321.

[19]Cooley, *Payback,* p. 76.

[20]*New York Times,* 8/30/83.

[21]Ball, *Error and Betrayal in Lebanon,* pp. 75-77.

[22]*New York Times,* 9/5/83.

[23]Fisk, *Pity the Nation,* pp. 489-91; Friedman, *From Beirut to Jerusalem,* p. 179.

[24]*New York Times,* 9/6/83.

[25]Fisk, *Pity the Nation,* p. 505.

[26]*New York Times,* 9/14/83.

[27]*New York Times,* 9/13/83.

[28]Philip Taubman and Joel Brinkley, *New York Times,* 12/11/83. Also see Cockburn, *Dangerous Liaison,* p. 335; Fisk, *Pity the Nation,* p. 505; Friedman, *From Beirut to Jerusalem,* p. 210.

[29]Friedman, *From Beirut to Jerusalem*, pp. 200-01. Also see Green, *Living by the Sword*, pp. 190-92.

[30]*New York Times*, 9/29/83.

[31]*New York Times*, 9/25/83; David Koff, "Chronology of the War in Lebanon, Sept.-November, 1983," *Journal of Palestine Studies*, Winter 1984, pp. 133-35.

[32]Philip Taubman and Joel Brinkley, *New York Times*, 12/11/83. Also see Cooley, Payback, pp. 80-91; Fisk, *Pity the Nation*, pp. 511-22; Friedman, *From Beirut to Jerusalem*, pp. 201-4; Woodward, *Veil*, pp. 285-87.

[33]*New York Times*, 1/4/84; Cooley, *Payback*, pp. 95-97.

[34]*New York Times*, 12/4/83.

[35]*New York Times*, 1/19/84. Also see *New York Times*, 1/29/84, and Cooley, *Payback*, p. 75. For a chronology of attacks against Americans in this period, see the *Atlanta Journal*, 1/31/85.

[36]Fisk, *Pity the Nation*, p. 533.

[37]*New York Times*, 4/16/84. Also see Cooley, *Payback*, p. 111; Fisk, *Pity the Nation*, p. 565.

[38]Cooley, *Payback*, p. 102; Fisk, *Pity the Nation*, p. 533; Friedman, *From Beirut to Jerusalem*, p. 220.

Chapter 24

1986: Israel's Nuclear Weapons

ON OCT. 5, 1986, the *Sunday Times* of London reported that Israel was a nuclear superpower. The tiny country had in its possession "at least 100 and as many as 200 nuclear weapons," making it a nuclear power rivaling Britain, China and France. The story said Israel had been producing the weapons at Dimona in the Negev Desert for 20 years.[1]

The *Sunday Times* article was based o the testimony of a disaffected Israeli nuclear technician, Mordechai Vanunu, 31. He had worked at Dimona for 10 years before he became disillusioned by Israel's nuclear policy and, after living in Australia, went to England to tell his story. Although it had long been speculated that Israel had a nuclear arsenal, Vanunu revealed details of Israel's nuclear program never before made public. He provided the

with a cross-section drawing of the entire Dimona underground nuclear complex and photographs Vanunu said he had secretly taken of the control room. Vanunu said bombs were assembled in an underground complex called Machon that extended six stories beneath the ground under a two-story building.

Vanunu's details were so convincing that nuclear experts pronounced themselves satisfied as to his accuracy. Frank Barnaby, former director of the Stockholm International Peace Research Institute and physicist at Britain's Atomic Weapons Research Establishment, said Vanunu's evidence convinced him that Israel had both fission and fusion weapons.[2]

Vanunu was later lured from Britain to Rome by an American

blonde Mossad agent named "Cindy" and kidnaped back to Israel aboard a ship in the fall of 1986.[3] On Nov. 9, 1986, Israel admitted Vanunu was a prisoner in Israel. But it has refused ever since to say how he had been brought there.[4] On March 24, 1988, after a seven-month trial closed to the public, he was found guilty of espionage and treason and sentenced to 18 years in prison.[5]

A later book, *Triple Cross: Israel, the Atomic Bomb and the Man Who Spilled the Secrets* by Louis Toscano, claimed Likud leader Yitzhak Shamir proposed assassinating Vanunu but was turned down by Prime Minister Shimon Peres. Instead, Peres saw disclosure of the nuclear information as delivering a forceful deterrent to the Arabs without Israel having to publicly admit possession of such weapons. The book claimed Peres ordered Vanunu's kidnapping.

Only in early 1998 was Vanunu released from the cramped cell in solitary confinement where he had been kept since his apprehension. His family fears Israeli authorities may be trying to drive him insane so that when his sentence expires he can be transferred directly to an asylum and his comments could be discounted as those of a lunatic. There are indications Israel has employed this inhumane technique in the past to discredit other Israeli dissidents.[6]

While the general public may have found Vanunu's revelations sensational, they were not news to the CIA or American leaders. As early as 1968, the Central Intelligence Agency concluded that Israel possessed nuclear weapons. According to records of a 1976 classified briefing given by Carl Duckett, the CIA's deputy director for science and technology from 1967 to 1976, the agency informed President Johnson of this in early 1968. Johnson's response was to order the CIA not to inform any other members of the administration, including Defense Secretary Robert McNamara and Secretary of State Dean Rusk.[7]

In 1978, another CIA document on Israel's nuclear program became public. This one was a Sept. 14, 1974 five-page report that said: "We believe that Israel already has produced nuclear weapons." It said its conclusion was "based on Israeli acquisition of large quantities of uranium, partly by clandestine means." Other evidence cited by the CIA for its belief that Israel was producing nuclear weapons included "the ambiguous nature of Israeli efforts in the field of uranium enrichment, and Israel's large investment in a costly missile system designed to accommodate nuclear warheads."[8]

Over the years Israel has done everything it could to mislead or hide from the United States its nuclear program. When questions first arose in 1960, Israel claimed the Dimona nuclear plant was a textile mill. Later that year it had to admit the nuclear nature of the plant but insisted that it was devoted to peaceful research. On Dec. 19, 1960, the State Department announced it had received assurances that "Israel has no intention of producing nuclear weapons and that its [nuclear] program is concerned exclusively with the peaceful uses of atomic energy."[9]

Despite Israeli denials and Washington's public acceptance of them, informed American officials suspected even then that Israel was embarked on a major nuclear weapons program. Early in 1961, Sen. Bourke Hickenlooper exploded at a secret session of the Senate Foreign Relations Committee:

"I think the Israelis have just lied to us like horse thieves on this thing. They have completely distorted, misrepresented and falsified the facts in the past. I think it is very serious, for things that we have done for them to have them perform in this manner in connection with this very definite production reactor facility [meaning it was specifically designed to produce plutonium] which they have been secretly building, and which they have consistently, and with a completely straight face, denied to us they were building."[10]

Although Israel continued to insist the Dimona plant was dedicated to peaceful research, it refused repeated urgings by the United States to sign the Non-Proliferation Treaty or accept IAEA (International Atomic Energy Agency) safeguards.[11] To this day it has not signed the Non-Proliferation Treaty or allowed free inspection of its Dimona facilities by the United States. Between 1963 and 1969, American scientists were allowed to make limited inspections, but they halted when the scientists reported they were so severely constrained by Israeli authorities that they could not certify there were no bombs being made at Dimona. In fact, reported investigative reporter Seymour Hersh, the Israelis went to the extent of building a false control room in Dimona to mislead the U.S. inspectors.[12]

Despite such actions, it was an open secret in Washington well before Vanunu's revelations that Israel had the bomb.[13] In fact, two legislators, Democratic Representatives Stephen J. Solarz and Jonathan B. Bingham, both of New York, dropped their amendment to ban U.S. aid to countries manufacturing nuclear weapons after admitting they were afraid it would affect Israel. Their action followed a private briefing by Under Secretary of State James L. Buckley on Dec. 8, 1981.

"We didn't want to find ourselves in a position where we had inadvertently and gratuitously created a situation that might lead to a cutoff of aid for Israel," Solarz said. "They left us with the impression that such a requirement might well trigger a finding by the administration that Israel has manufactured a bomb."[14] ❧

RECOMMENDED READING:

Beit-Hallahmi, Benjamin, *The Israeli Connection*, New York, Pantheon Books, 1987.

Cervenka, Zdenck, and Barbara Rogers, *The Nuclear Axis*, New York, Times Books, 1978.

*Cockburn, Andrew and Leslie, *Dangerous Liaison*, New York, Harper Collins Publishers, 1991.

*Findley, Paul, *Deliberate Deceptions*, Brooklyn, NY, Lawrence Hill Books, 1993.

*Gaffney, Mark, *Dimona: The Third Temple?* Brattleboro, VT, Amana Books, 1989.

Hersh, Seymour, *The Samson Option*, New York, Random House, 1991.

Jabber, Fuad, *Israel and Nuclear Weapons*, London, Chatto and Windus, 1971.

Raviv, Dan and Yossi Melman, Every Spy a Prince: The Complete History of Israel's Intelligence Community, Boston, Houghton Mifflin Company, 1990.

Spector, Leonard S., *Nuclear Proliferation Today*, New York, Vintage Books, 1984.

Weissman, Steve and Herbert Krosney, *The Islamic Bomb*, New York, Times Books, 1981.

*Available through the AET Book Club.

NOTES:

[1] *Sunday Times* of London, 10/5/86.

[2] Frank Barnaby, "The Nuclear Arsenal in the Middle East," *Journal of Palestine Studies*, Autumn 1987, pp. 98-99, p. 102.

[3] Glenn Frankel, *Washington Post*, 10/29/86, 3/24/88. The CBS-TV program "Sixty Minutes" had an excellent report on March 27, 1988, on how Vanunu was kidnaped. Also see Cockburn, *Dangerous Liaison*, pp. 94-96; Hersh, *The Samson Option*, pp. 307-315; Raviv and Melman, *Every Spy a Prince*, pp. 360-372.

[4] Thomas L. Friedman, *New York Times*, 10/10/86.

[5] Glenn Frankel, *Washington Post*, 3/25/86.

[6] Ian Williams, "A Tale of Two Spies, " *Washington Report on Middle East Affairs*, July/August, 1993.

[7] *Washington Post*, 3/2/78; David Burnham, *New York Times*, 3/2/78.

[8] *New York Times*, 6/25/81. The document was released under a Freedom of Information Act request; the CIA later said the release had been a "mistake."

[9] Dana Adams Schmidt, *New York Times*, 12/22/60; State Department, *American Foreign Policy 1960*, "Statement Issued by the Department of State, Dec. 19, 1960," p. 501.

[10] Spector, *Nuclear Proliferation*, p. 121.

[11] *Ibid, p.* 126. Also see Beit-Hallahmi, *The Israeli Connection*, pp. 129-136; Cockburn, *Dangerous Liaison*, pp. 86-92.

[12] Hersh, *The Samson Option*, pp. 111, 210-211.

[13] See, for instance, Robert Manning and Stephen Talbot, "American Cover-Up on Israeli Bomb," *The Middle East*, June, 1980; Ali A. Mazrui et al., "Study on Israeli Nuclear Disarmament," United Nations Publication, 1982; Gary Milhollin, "Israel's Nuclear Shadow, *Wisconsin Project on Nuclear Arms Control*, University of Wisconsin, Nov. 10, 1986.

[14] Judith Miller, *New York Times*, 12/9/81.

Chapter 25

1990: Israel Briefly Succeeds in Banning Spy Book

ON SEPT. 12, 1990, an extraordinary legal order was handed down by New York State Supreme Court Judge Michael J. Dontzin at 1 a.m. in his Fifth Avenue Manhattan apartment. At the request of the government of Israel, Dontzin issued an unprecedented restraining order against publication of a kiss-and-tell book by a former case officer of Mossad, Israel's main foreign spying agency. Lawyers representing Israel had convinced Judge Dontzin that the book contained information that would, in the language of Dontzin's order, "endanger the lives of various people in the employ of the state of Israel, and would be detrimental to the government of the state of Israel."[1]

Legal experts were stunned. New York attorney Floyd Abrams, a leading First Amendment expert, said it was the "first time that any foreign state has sought or obtained a prior restraint against the publication of a book."[2] Roy Gainsburg, president of St. Martin's Press, publisher of the book, added: "But can you imagine a book being banned in the United States because it's detrimental to some other government?"[3]

Cooler heads quickly prevailed. The next day the New York State Appeals Court lifted the ban, concluding that Israel "failed to substantiate...its claim that the safety of Israeli intelligence agents is endangered."[4] The book was *By Way of Deception* by Victor Ostrovsky, written with Canadian journalist Claire Hoy. When it was published on schedule, it quickly became obvious why Israel did not want it released.

By Way of Deception was nothing less than an exposé of the basic elements of spycraft as practiced by Israel. This included details of Mossad training exercises, the methods of tailing and detecting a tail, covert communications, techniques of enlisting agents, and vivid descriptions of old professionals indoctrinating new spies to the unsavory game that includes sexual blackmail, lying and assassination. Ostrovsky's description of one particularly evil Mossad assassin is a classic portrayal of the psychopaths attracted to the spy game.

By Ostrovsky's account, Mossad spies were anything but "princes among men." He found them just the reverse of being disciplined, scrupulous or defenders of democracy. He revealed that it was leaks by Mossad that brought down Prime Minister Yitzhak Rabin in 1976 on the relatively minor infraction of having a foreign bank account. Mossad leaked the information because it did not like Rabin's insistence on seeing raw intelligence data and thus bypassing Mossad analyses.

By Way of Deception also revealed that Israel kept 24 to 27 Mossad agents in the United States belonging to a super secret division known as Al, which in Hebrew means "above" or "on top." Ostrovsky wrote: "[The Mossad is] actively spying, recruiting, organizing and carrying out covert activities, mainly in New York and Washington, which they refer to as their playground." He revealed that Israel lied to Washington when it said it had closed down the special unit that recruited U.S. civilian naval intelligence analyst Jonathan Jay Pollard to spy on America for Israel. What actually happened, he wrote, was that Israel simply changed the name of the unit.

Ostrovsky wrote that Israel influences Congress in part by searching for Jewish aides to congressmen serving on such committees as the Armed Services Committee and then trying to recruit them. In fact, he added, Mossad routinely exploited the Jewish community around the world to assist, usually unwittingly, its operations abroad. He revealed Mossad had advance information about a Mercedes truck-bomb used in the killing of 241 U.S. Marines in Beirut in 1983 but failed to pass on a warning to the United States.

Ostrovsky described himself as coming from "an ardent Zionist background" and said he only undertook the book "out of love for Israel." It was necessary for Israel's own good, he wrote, to expose how cynically Mossad had betrayed its trust and in the process had helped "turn the Zionist dream into the present-day nightmare." Predictably, Israel claimed his book contained many errors, and even claimed he had been a spy for only 17 months. However, Ostrovsky spent three years of training before becoming a spy and his details of the Mossad culture are completely convincing.

Not surprisingly, *By Way of Deception* became an instant bestseller, thanks to Israel's well-publicized efforts to ban it. Not only did Israel's legal action draw attention to the book, but its admission that he had been a spy gave Ostrovsky added credibility. To the con-spiracy-minded. the mere fact that Israel would have taken such actions certain to draw attention to the book raised the question of whether there wasn't a deeper conspiracy at work here aimed for some hidden reason at actually promoting *By Way of Deception*. Israel, after all, is not exactly without talent when it comes to manipulating public opinion.

However suspicious all this sounds, a close reading of Ostrovsky's vivid Mossad memoirs quickly dispels the idea. There is nothing here to make either Israel or its super spy agency proud. Perhaps the best explanation for Israel's bumbling legal action is that the Jewish state had gotten so used to receiving special treatment in America that its arrogance overwhelmed its common sense.

Note: A caveat that applies to all books by spies applies to this one as well: spies are trained liars. &

RECOMMENDED READING:

*Victor Ostrovsky and Claire Hoy, *By Way of Deception: The Making and Unmaking of a Mossad Officer*, New York, St. Martin's Press, 1990.

*Available through the AET Book Club.

NOTES:

[1]Roger Cohen, *New York Times*, 9/13/90.

[2]*Ibid.*

[3]Associated Press, *Washington Post*, 9/13/90.

[4]Howard Kurtz and William Claiborne, *Washington Post*, 9/14/90.

Chapter 26

1990: Israel Sells U.S. Secrets to China

O N JUNE 13, 1990, the *Los Angeles Times* reported Israel had become the largest supplier of advanced military technology to China since the United States banned military sales in the wake of the Chinese suppression of the democracy movement a year earlier. An unnamed U.S. official told the newspaper that Israel was a "back door to U.S. technology that the United States won't sell them."[1]

The meaning was that Israel was not only breaching America's embargo, but selling to China technology that the United States had given to it for the Jewish state's own defense. With the technology came restrictions that Israel would not re-export. What was especially interesting about the *Times* account was that it cited anonymous U.S. sources. There had been stories over the past decade about the growing Sino-Israeli relationship but few, if any, came from recognizable U.S. sources, who usually hesitated to criticize Israel, even anonymously.

The story was a strong indicator that Israel's relations with China had grown so massive and intimate that they were becoming too close for comfort for the administration of President George Bush. This was particularly so at a time when China was under worldwide criticism for its antidemocracy policy. Washington was especially loud in its condemnation of China.

Nonetheless, Israel was not deterred. Shortly before the *Times* report, Israel, which had no official diplomatic relations with China, opened an office of the Israeli Academy of Sciences in Beijing. It was no doubt that blatant act that caused U.S. officials to begin leaking information. The *Times*' source said Israel's supposedly academic office in Beijing was actually "facilitating a whole range of military-to-military cooperation between Israel and China."

The newspaper said intelligence experts in the West and Asia believed Israel in recent years had provided China with some of the advanced technology needed to modernize China's jet planes and missiles. It said U.S. officials had told Israel they strongly opposed the military cooperation because it undercut the intended effect of U.S. sanctions against China. "This is over our objections," a senior administration official told the newspaper. U.S. officials insisted that Israel was not operating as a proxy for the United States in the military sales, as it did when it supplied arms to Iran during the Iran-Contra arms-for-hostages affair.

The story had no discernible impact on Israel, perhaps because the administration had decided to take a low-profile approach by leaking it to a West Coast newspaper rather than *The New York Times* or *Washington Post*. Over the next few years an undeclared battle raged as Washington, in its frustration, became increasingly aggressive in its criticism and Israel went on blithely selling arms technology to China and upgrading relations between the two countries.

A year after the *Times* report, in June, 1991, China and Israel signed a bilateral agreement on scientific cooperation, the only area in which they had official relations. Israel was represented in Beijing by a liaison officer of its Academy of Science office in Beijing.[2]

On Nov. 20, 1991, the East Coast press finally caught up with the story. Israeli Defense Minister Moshe Arens was reported to have made a secret official visit to China in early November, the first Israeli minister to visit China. The four-day visit gave an unprecedented boost to the rapidly growing relations.[3] By the end of 1991, China's Deputy Foreign Minister Yang Fuchang visited Israel, the highest Chinese official to do so.[4]

How fast Sino-Israeli relations were increasing became apparent on Jan. 24, 1992, when China and Israel established formal diplomatic relations in ceremonies in Beijing. The occasion was attended by Chinese Foreign Minister Qian Qichen and Israeli Foreign Minister David Levy.[5]

The Sino-Israeli relationship was a strange one. China traditionally favored the Arabs in the Arab-Israel conflict, and just the day before the establishment of full relations, Chinese spokesman Wu Jianmin said: "It has been China's consistent position that the legitimate rights of the Palestinian people should be restored, the Arabs' occupied territories should be returned, and the sovereignty and security of all the Middle East countries, including Israel, should be guaranteed and respected."[6] Moreover, while Israel based its pleas for enormous amounts of U.S. aid on the danger from Arab countries, its selling of weapons technology to China was indirectly helping strengthen the Arabs because China was a major supplier of missiles to Iran and such Arab countries as Saudi Arabia and Syria.[7]

In an obvious effort to dampen the burgeoning Sino-Israeli relationship, U.S. officials stepped up their leaks. Unnamed officials revealed in early March, 1992, that there was "overwhelming" evidence of Israel's cheating on written promises not to re-export U.S. weapons technology to Third World countries, including China.[8] They added there was well-founded suspicion that Israel was also selling secrets of America's vaunted Patriot anti-missile missile to China.[9] The issue was so serious that a U.S. team of experts was dispatched to Israel in late March but it failed to find any proof of Israeli cheating. The State Department said on April 2 that "the Israeli government has a clean bill of health on the Patriot issue."[10]

But there was clearly disagreement in the government. Defense Secretary Dick Cheney said there remained "good reason" to believe a diversion had taken place.[11] CIA Director Robert Gates agreed, saying, "There is some indication that they [the Chinese] have some of the [Patriot] technology."[12]

About the same time, a study by the Pentagon-supported think tank RAND Corp. became public, with the conclusion that Israel had become "China's leading foreign supplier of advanced technology." It said there had been reports that Israel had helped China develop the HQ-61 surface-to-air missile, the CSS-2 intermediate missile, the PL-8 air-to-air and surface-to-air missile as well as advanced armor for battle tanks and an air-borne early warning radar system. It added Israel was currently cooperating with China to develop an advanced fighter jet.[13]

These disclosures were followed by a major report in *The Wall*

Street Journal that significantly broadened the scope of the charges. It mentioned illegal Israeli re-exports of an array of technology to a number of countries beyond China, including Chile, Ethiopia, South Africa and Thailand. The story said there was "no doubt in the U.S. intelligence community that Israel has repeatedly engaged in diversion schemes."[14] *The Washington Post* joined the fray by adding that one official said there were "lots and lots of...clear-cut cases." The clear impression was that the U.S. had more than enough evidence to convict Israel, if it had the political will to do so.[15]

The leaks by unnamed but official sources came just days before Israeli Defense Minister Moshe Arens was due to meet on March 16, 1992, in Washington with his counterpart, Dick Cheney. Arens' initial public reaction was outrage: "There is not a grain of truth. No truth in it at all." But as the volume of charges grew, his statements changed to questioning the motives of the leakers: "The real story is who are these unnamed individuals who are floating these malicious rumors?"[16] Defense Secretary Cheney and his spokesmen declined any comment.[17]

Israel was hit with another major blow on April 1, 1992, when the State Department released a report by its inspector general charging that a "major recipient" of U.S. military aid was engaged in a "systematic and growing pattern" of selling secret U.S. technology in violation of U.S. law. The public report did not directly name Israel, but officials left no doubt that it was the subject of the report. The report said Israel's violations began about 1983 and that Israel sought to conceal the violations.[18]

State Department Inspector General Sherman M. Funk said he notified Secretary of State James A. Baker III about intelligence reports of Israel's violations in June, 1991, and that new procedures to prevent future violations were then put in force under an operation called Blue Lantern. Funk said U.S. officials previously had depended on verbal assurances from Israel that it was not retransferring, adding that such assurances from Israel "are not an effective mechanism for providing end-use verification. We identified instances where U.S. items and technology were retransferred or were used in violation of the assurances."

He added that he had recommended that Israel be forced to repay the money illicitly earned from the transfers but Deputy Secretary of State Lawrence S. Eagleburger rejected the proposal as being an impossible chore. Eagleburger was a protégé of former Secretary of State Henry Kissinger and a strong supporter of Israel.

The succession of charges sent a shockwave through Israel, as they no doubt were intended to, because the subject went to the heart of the economic prosperity of the Jewish state. Arms sales of around $1.5 billion annually accounted for 40 percent of Israel's exports and were based almost entirely on U.S. technology.[19]

The background on how Israel became so advanced in technology was revealed in a study by the General Accounting Office.[20] They began in 1970 with the signing of an important and far-reaching Master Defense Development Data Exchange Agreement that provided for the greatest transfer of technology to Israel, or any other country, ever undertaken. Transfer of U.S. technology was provided by what was known as Technical Data Packages, the entire complex of blueprints, plans and types of materials required to actually construct new weapons.

More than 120 such packages were given to Israel over the next eight years, according to a 1979 study by the official Middle East Arms Transfer Panel.[21] Such a massive infusion of technology provided a boon to Israel's economy. By 1981, Israel had emerged from being a technologically backward arms importer to the seventh largest exporter of military weapons in the world, with overseas sales of $1.3 billion.[22]

An Israeli writer observed, "The Americans have made virtually all their most advanced weaponry and technology—meaning the best fighter aircraft, missiles, radar, armor, and artillery—available to Israel. Israel, in turn, has utilized this knowledge, adapting American equipment to increase its own technological sophistication, reflected tangibly in Israeli defense offerings."[23]

Despite the number of reports over the years that Israel was illicitly profiting from U.S. technology at the cost of American companies and U.S. security, Washington continued providing ever-increasing amounts of technology to Israel. According to a report in 1992, there were 322 separate cooperative U.S.-Israeli ventures at that time, valued at $2.9 billion. In addition, there were 49 country-to-country programs involving Israel in co-development or co-production and research with the United States, and there existed

36 active data exchange agreements and 11 new proposed accords. The report concluded: "The magnitude of existing cooperative efforts with Israel is extensive and growing rapidly."[24] Despite that magnitude, when Bill Clinton became president in 1993 he promised to lift the "technological barrier" by granting Israel even more sophisticated technology.[25]

Meanwhile Sino-Israeli relations flourished. Israeli President Chaim Herzog visited China between Dec. 24 and 30, 1992. In January, 1993, with the administration of President Bill Clinton taking over in Washington, Israel and China signed a contract permitting Israel to buy Chinese coal. On Feb. 14, 1993, the two countries signed a scientific agreement for joint research projects in electronics, medical technology, renewable energy, agriculture and civilian uses of space technology.[26]

On Oct. 12, 1993, the CIA added its weight to the controversy by revealing to the Senate Governmental Affairs Committee that Israel had been selling advanced military technology to China for more than a decade. Central Intelligence Director R. James Woolsey estimated that the trade "may be several billion dollars." Woolsey added: "Building on a long history of close defense industrial relations—including work on China's next-generation fighter, air-to-air missiles and tank programs—and the establishment of diplomatic relations in January, 1992, China and Israel appear to be moving toward formalizing and broadening their military technical cooperation."[27]

Israeli Prime Minister Yitzhak Rabin denied that the trade reached billions of dollars, adding that the figure for 1992 was about $60 million. "All these stories of billions of dollars of arms business in the past 10 years are total nonsense," he said. "We have made it clear time and again that we have never done a thing against American law...never transmitted items of technology that we got from the United States. We are not stupid enough" to endanger Israel's annual $3 billion in U.S. aid. He issued his statement in Beijing, where he was on an official four-day visit, the first public visit by Israel's prime minister.[28]

The CIA said that new indications of stronger Sino-Israeli ties were the opening of a number of Israeli military sales offices in China, the Feb. 14, 1993, signing by the two countries of an agreement to share technology, and the current visit to Beijing of Rabin. The report stated: "We believe the Chinese seek from Israel advanced military technologies that the U.S. and Western firms are unwilling to provide. Beijing probably hopes to tap Israeli expertise for cooperative development of military technologies, such as advanced tank power plants and airborne radar systems, that the Chinese would have difficulty producing on their own."[29]

In 1994, another serious report documented Israel's sales to China. Professor Duncan L. Clarke of The American University in Washington, DC, reported in a study: "For years, Israel had violated the Arms Export Control Act and related executive agreements.[30]...Israel has employed U.S. weaponry contrary to U.S. law and policy, incorporated U.S. technology into Israeli weapons systems without prior approval, and made improper transfers of U.S. missile and other defense systems and technologies to other countries, including Chile, China, and South Africa."[31]

The issue climaxed in early 1995 with yet another series of media reports on Israel's China trade. These led to official denials by Israel. David Ivri, the director-general of the Israeli Defense Ministry, admitted on Jan. 3 that Israel had sold China "some technology on aircraft" but added that it was not U.S. technology and that the contracts were "very small in magnitude."[32]

State Department spokesperson Michael McCurry said the next day that "those types of reports concern us very much....This has been an item on our agenda for some time....This has been going around for some time." He said Undersecretary of State for International Security Lynn E. Davis had had "substantive discussions with the government of Israel on a range of these types of issues." McCurry added that he was unaware of any authorization being given to Israel to share any U.S. technology with China.[33]

On Jan. 6, Aded Ben-Ami, the spokesperson for Prime Minister Yitzhak Rabin, again denied that Israel had illegally transferred any U.S. technology to China. "Israel did not transfer any American technology or American components to China," he said.[34] Two days later Defense Secretary William Perry discussed the issue with Prime Minister Rabin in Jerusalem, but the Israeli leader again denied any U.S. technology was involved.[35]

Then, suddenly, the issue disappeared from the public eye.

The controversy had visibly begun in 1990 with anonymous leaks and had grown into official charges by the United States, culminating at the beginning of 1995 with serious discussions between the two countries at the highest levels. After Perry's meeting with Rabin, the subject dropped from public sight. Whatever action, if any, was taken was not announced. But that was not uncommon. Washington would not want to embarrass its "most reliable" Middle East ally. ❧

RECOMMENDED READING:

Black, Ian, and Benny Morris, *Israel's Secret Wars: A History of Israel's Intelligence Service*, New York, Grove Weidenfeld, 1991.

Beit-Hallahmi, Benjamin, *The Israeli Connection*, New York, Pantheon Books, 1987.

Brecher, Michael, *Decisions in Israel's Foreign Policy*, London, Oxford University Press, 1974.

*Cockburn, Andrew and Leslie, *Dangerous Liaison: The Inside Story of the U.S.-Israeli Covert Relationship*, New York, HarperCollins Publishers, 1991.

El-Khawas, Mohammed and Samir Abed-Rabbo, *American Aid to Israel: Nature and Impact*, Brattleboro, VT, Amana Books, 1984.

*Findley, Paul, *Deliberate Deceptions: Facing the Facts about the U.S.-Israeli Relationship*, Brooklyn, NY, Lawrence Hill Books, 1993.

Hersh, Seymour M., *The Samson Option: Israel's Nuclear Arsenal and American Foreign Policy*, New York, Random House, 1991.

Klieman, Aaron S., *Israel's Global Reach: Arms Sales and Diplomacy*, Washington, DC, Pergamon-Brassey's, 1985.

*Ostrovsky, Victor and Claire Hoy, *By Way of Deception*, New York, St. Martin's Press, 1990.

Raviv, Dan and Yossi Melman, *Every Spy a Prince: The Complete History of Israel's Intelligence Community*, Boston, Houghton Mifflin Company, 1990.

*Available through the AET Book Club.

NOTES:

[1]United Press International, #0543, 6/13/90.

[2]Jackson Diehl, *Washington Post*, 11/20/91. Also see *Israeli Foreign Affairs*, "Defense Minister Arens Visited China," Vol. VII, No. 10-11 (Special Double Issue), 12/16/91.

[3]Jackson Diehl, *Washington Post,* 11/20/91; Clyde Haberman, *New York Times,* 1/9/92.

[4]Clyde Haberman, *New York Times,* 1/9/92.

[5]Lena H. Sun, *Washington Post,* 1/25/92. A discussion of early Sino-Israeli relations is in Brecher, *Decisions in Israel's Foreign Policy,* pp. 111-172. For more recent relations, see Beit-Hallahmi, *The Israeli Connection,* pp. 36-37.

[6]*New York Times,* 1/24/92.

[7]Richard A. Bitzinger, "Chinese Arms Production and Sales to the Third World," RAND Corp., 1991.

[8]Edward T. Pound, *Wall Street Journal,* 3/13/92; David Hoffman and R. Jeffrey Smith, *Washington Post,* 3/14/92. For a survey of U.S. support of Israel's arms industry, see Bishara A. Bahbah, "The US Role in Israel's Arms Industry," *The Link,* Vol. 20, No. 5, December, 1987.

[9]Bill Gertz and Rowan Scarborough, *Washington Times,* 3/12-13/92.

[10]David Hoffman, *Washington Post,* 4/3/92.

[11]Bill Gertz, *Washington Times,* 4/9/92.

[12]Bill Gertz, *Washington Times,* 1/5/93.

[13]Richard A. Bitzinger, "Chinese Arms Production and Sales to the Third World," RAND Corp., 1991.

[14]Edward T. Pound, *Wall Street Journal,* 3/13/92.

[15]David Hoffman and R. Jeffrey Smith, *Washington Post,* 3/14/92.

[16]Thomas L. Friedman, *New York Times,* 3/15/92.

[17]Eric Schmidt, *New York Times,* 3/17/92.

[18]David Hoffman, *Washington Post,* 4/2/92.

[19]Cockburns, *Dangerous Liaison,* p. 7.

[20]See "U.S. Assistance to the State of Israel, Report by the Comptroller General of the United States," GAO/ID-83-51, June 24, 1983, U.S. Accounting Office. The report was, up to 1983, the most comprehensive survey ever made of the extraordinary special arrangements provided for Israel's profit. When it was released, the report was heavily censored, but uncensored versions quickly leaked to such organizations as the American-Arab Anti-Discrimination Committee. An uncensored early draft of the report can be found in El-Khawas and Abeh-Rabbo, *American Aid to Israel,* pp. 114-91.

[21]Middle East Arms Transfer Panel, "Review of Israel's Military Requirements, 1979-84"; prepared in 8/79; secret.

[22]Drew Middleton, *New York Times*, 3/15/81. For a report on the state of Israel's arms industry in 1986, see Thomas L. Friedman, *New York Times*, 12/7/86.

[23]Kleiman, *Israel's Global Reach*, p. 175.

[24]*Near East Report*, 2/10/92.

[25]Clinton press conference, C-SPAN, 11/12/93; Thomas L. Friedman, *New York Times*, 11/13/93.

[26]*Israeli Foreign Affairs*, 2/26/93.

[27]Michael R. Gordon, *New York Times*, 10/13/93.

[28]Patrick E. Tyler, *New York Times*, 10/14/93.

[29]Bill Gertz, *Washington Times*, 10/13/93; Michael R. Gordon, *New York Times*, 10/13/93.

[30]The act, PL 94-329, requires that no defense article or service shall be transferred by the U.S. to a foreign country unless that country agrees not to transfer the article to a third country or use it for purposes other than those for which it was furnished, without prior approval of the U.S.

[31]Duncan L. Clarke, "The Arrow Missile: The United States, Israel and Strategic Cooperation," *Middle East Journal*, Summer 1994, pp. 483-84.

[32]Associated Press, *Washington Times*, 1/4/95.

[33]*Ibid.*, 1/5/95.

[34]*Washington Times*, 1/7/95.

[35]Associated Press, *Washington Times*, 1/9/95.

Chapter 27

1993: Israel Behind U.S. Policy on Iran

O N FEB. 13, 1993, less than a month after Bill Clinton was sworn in as president, the media in Israel and Israel's supporters in the United States began a coordinated campaign to enlist America into an alliance against Iran. The effort was so successful that by 1996 U.S. Secretary of State Warren Christopher had publicly described Iran as "public enemy No. 1,"[1] and the Clinton administration had imposed a total trade ban against the country.

What was interesting about this evolution of U.S. policy was that Israel's motives and intentions were largely played out in the media as it drew Washington into its strategic web. The Israeli campaign began in February, 1993, when Israeli academic Israel Shahak alerted readers of the *Washington Report on Middle East Affairs* that various Israeli newspapers had begun warning about the potential threat to Israel from Iran. They urged that the United States be "persuaded" to contain Iran by adopting a tougher policy.[2]

Shahak cited several news stories in the Hebrew press that clearly laid out the Israeli position. One especially revealing article was an interview with former intelligence official Daniel Leshem in the leftist *Al Hamishmar* on Feb. 19, 1993. He was quoted as saying that Israel alone could not deter Iran. Instead it should try to "create the situation so that it will appear similar to that of Iraq before the Gulf crisis...We should hope that, emulating Iraq, Iran will...start a war [with its Arab neighbors]...This prospect is, in my view, quite likely, because the Iranians lack patience. But if, nevertheless, they should refrain from starting a war, we then should take advantage of their involvement in the Islamic terror which already troubles the entire world...We should take advantage of this by explaining persistently to the world at large that, by virtue of its involvement in terrorism, no other state is as dangerous as Iran."[3]

An article in the right-wing *Ma'ariv* had sounded a similar theme a week earlier, urging that Israel "persuade the United States" to enforce an embargo on exports of weaponry and other industrial goods to Iran from any source.[4]

Although *The New York Times* failed to note this emerging campaign, *The Washington Post* did and it reported in mid-March that "Israel is attempting to convince the United States that Iranian-inspired Islamic extremism and Iran's military rearmament drive have become a major threat to the stability of the Middle East and the interests of the West." The story also pointed out that both the Anti-Defamation League of B'nai B'rith and the American Jewish Committee had recently released studies warning of the Iranian threat, with the latter asserting that "we cannot run away or avoid" the possibility that Iran by the end of the decade may become the "dominant force in the Middle East."[5]

By the end of that month, on March 30, just over two months after the coming to power of the pro-Israel Clinton administration, Secretary of State Christopher publicly called Iran "a dangerous country" and an "international outlaw" because of what he claimed was its support for international terrorism and its efforts to develop nuclear and other weapons of mass destruction.[6]

Two weeks later another Israeli, Professor Shlomo Aharonson, further elaborated Israel's strategic thinking. He wrote that Israel classified its enemies as those nearby and those more remote, among the latter being Iran, Iraq and Libya, with Iran the most threatening.

"Israel cannot mobilize its entire army to fight a ground war in Iran, in line with its doctrine of a pre-emptive first strike," he explained. Likewise, Israel's air force is not capable of devastating Iran with conventional weapons. So Aharonson concluded that "against its distant enemies Israel will have to rely not so much on conventional components of the Israeli army as on nuclear deterrence, long-range missiles and improved cooperation with the U.S. and some neighboring states like Egypt or Turkey."[7]

By April 30 the State Department's annual report on terrorism cited Iran as "the most dangerous sponsor of terrorism in 1992, with over 20 acts in 1992 attributable to it or its surrogates." It blamed Iran for 1992's most dramatic attack, the bombing of the Israeli Embassy in Argentina which killed 29 people and wounded 242, although the report offered no evidence.[8]

In another two weeks, the National Security Council's Middle East adviser, Martin Indyk, a former employee of the American Israel Public Affairs Committee (AIPAC), Israel's principal Washington, DC lobby, and subsequently U.S. ambassador to Israel, outlined the Clinton administration's new policy toward the Persian Gulf. It was, he said, "dual containment" of both Iran and Iraq.

"'Dual containment' derives from an assessment that the current Iraqi and Iranian regimes are both hostile to American interests in the region," Indyk explained. "Accordingly, we do not accept the argument that we should pursue the old balance of power game, building up one to balance the other...As long as we are able to maintain our military presence in the region; as long as we succeed in restricting the military ambitions of both Iraq and Iran; and as long as we can rely on our regional allies—Egypt, Israel, Saudi Arabia and the GCC [Gulf Cooperation Council], and Turkey—to preserve the balance of power in our favor in the wide Middle East region, we will have the means to counter both the Iraqi and Iranian regimes."

He added: "When we assess Iranian intentions and capabilities, we see a dangerous combination for Western interests...The necessity to act now derives from the fact that Iran's threatening intentions for the moment outstrip its capabilities...If we fail in our efforts to modify Iranian behavior, five years from now Iran will be much more capable of posing a real threat to Israel, the Arab world, and Western interests in the Middle East."[9]

Secretary of State Christopher followed Indyk on June 9 by urging Western nations to curb technology sales that would help Iran develop nuclear and other advanced weapons. Christopher, referring to Iran as "the most worrisome" of countries engaged in secret weapons development, said at a meeting of the European Community in Luxembourg: "We need to adopt a collective policy of containment. Iran must be persuaded to abandon its nuclear, chemical-biological and missile programs."[10]

Thus, after being in office less than five months, the Clinton administration had already echoed all of Israel's charges against Iran and, on the basis of them, embarked on a harsh anti-Iran policy. It was a policy that made little sense in terms of finding a viable balance of power in the oil-rich Persian Gulf. It was unlikely to add to regional stability or allay suspicions of U.S. motives. The one thing it did do, however, was totally align U.S. policy in support of the perceived interests of Israel.

As *Washington Report on Middle East Affairs* publisher and former Ambassador Andrew I. Killgore wrote in September, 1995:

"The simplest explanation of Washington's anti-Iranian policy is domestic politics. Bill Clinton believes that he cannot be re-elected without overwhelming media and financial support from the Israel lobby and those who take their cues from it. Thus he and Warren Christopher are ready to 'buy' Israeli exaggerations of the dangers emanating from Iran, whether they really believe them or not."[11]

Whatever its motives, and the Killgore thesis seems the most likely, the administration continued to ratchet up its anti-Iran policy. When Iran did not cower before the new U.S. policy by halting its efforts to purchase nuclear technology or withdrawing its support of Hezbollah guerrillas in southern Lebanon, Washington's anti-Iran measures became dramatically harsher.

Starting in February, 1995—exactly two years after Israel launched its anti-Iran campaign—Washington began leveling a number of provocative charges against Tehran. It claimed Iran had placed Hawk anti-aircraft missile launchers on the island of Abu Musa near the Strait of Hormuz and recently had put missiles on them. The U.S. also claimed that Iran had put Chinese-made Seersucker ground-to-ground missiles on the island of Greater Tunb while artillery was emplaced on Lesser Tunb. In addition, it was reported that there had been an increase of Iranian troops on Lesser Tunb to nearly 4,000 from 700 the previous October.[12]

So suspect were the administration's policy and motives, however, that several top U.S. military men anonymously told the *Washington Times* that they feared the Clinton administration was manufacturing a crisis with Iran, by using "inflated" figures about Iranian deployments. One army officer said: "I think the Iranians have taken action purely as a defensive countermeasure to what we've been trying to do. They're afraid of what we might do."[13]

The next month, on March 22, Defense Secretary William Perry said Iran had installed near the Strait of Hormuz 6,000 men as well as poison gas that could threaten the flow of oil from the Persian Gulf.[14] He said other weapons included two Russian-made Kilo-class submarines, cruise missiles with a 60-mile range and five Chinese-made Houdong missile boats. Half of the world's oil supplies go through the strait.[15]

Not to be left out of the Iran-bashing, Christopher authorized his spokesman to assure the press that "there's nobody more of a hawk on Iran than Secretary of State Warren Christopher."[16]

It was not only the White House, Pentagon, State Department and CIA that were consumed by hatred of Iran. The Congress, where Israel exercises overwhelming influence, became rabid on the subject, in part because AIPAC worked hard on the Hill during early 1995 preaching against Iran. Among AIPAC's activities was the compilation and distribution to congressmen of a 74-page booklet outlining Israel's case against Tehran and calling for a complete halt to all trade with Iran.[17]

By early spring of 1995 the subject had become so hot that there was what *The Washington Post* described as an "anti-Iran fever" in Congress, where bills were introduced in both houses not only banning any U.S. business with Iran, but also banning Americans from doing business with any company worldwide that conducts business with Iran.[18]

On April 11, the Central Intelligence Agency let it be known that it was seeking $19 million from Congress to continue covert operations to undermine Iran and Iraq and to curb what the administration called Iran's expansionist ambitions.[19]

Then, on April 30, President Clinton, wearing a skullcap, announced at a meeting of the World Jewish Congress that he was taking an action long advocated by Israel—the banning of all trade with Iran. The reasons, he said, were those that Israel had been citing all along: Iran was a major exporter of terrorism, a threat to the Middle East peace process and was seeking nuclear weapons. The ban essentially hurt only American workers and businessmen.

It ended all U.S. oil purchases from Iran, then about $4 billion annually for resale overseas, and Iranian purchases of U.S. products, which in 1994 equaled $326 million, mainly in oil service equipment and corn and rice. About 3,000 U.S. jobs were lost in the oil services industry. Moreover, Iran owed U.S. firms about $500 million and it became questionable whether they would be paid.[20]

Since Clinton cited no new information to justify his action, it was no surprise that many questioned the wisdom of the new policy.[21] Even Alexander Haig, who had been a strong supporter of Israel when he was Ronald Reagan's first secretary of state, said he knew of no recent terrorist activity sponsored by Iran, adding: "In fact, all the evidence points to a major change of heart in Tehran about state-sponsored terrorism."[22]

Not surprisingly, America's major allies rejected the embargo and happily picked up the extra business. They contended a better way to influence Iran was through diplomatic dialogue. The European Union, including members Britain, France and Germany, called for a "critical political dialogue." They complained that the United States had not bothered informing them before imposing its embargo.[23]

But that was missing the point, which was that Clinton was acting to please Israel, not America's European allies. *The New York Times*, no longer able to ignore the story, noted with understatement: "Mr. Clinton's new announcement brings the United States policy on Iran more into line with Israel's."[24]

In fact, *The Washington Post* had already reported how Israel was behind Washington's claims about Iran's nuclear efforts. It said the CIA had confirmed that Israel was the original source of information that Iran was seeking the capacity to make nuclear weapons fuel and that the United States had acted only after receiving this Israeli-supplied information.[25]

Nor was the anti-Iran campaign over. Christopher let it be known that he planned to harm Tehran in any way he could. According to *The Washington Post*:

"Christopher has concluded that Iran's behavior—what Washington views as its support for terrorism and quest for nuclear weapons—is not only outside the bounds of acceptability but also a direct threat to many vital interests of the United States and its allies...In Iran, according to friends and colleagues, Christopher sees not a diplomatic abstraction but a living menace, a terrorist state that if left to its own devices will soon have nuclear weapons and use them to bully its neighbors, subvert Israel and dominate oil transport routes essential to global commerce."[26]

With Israel calling the shots and Washington only too happy to comply, there was little hope that America's relations with the strongest power in the Persian Gulf would improve while Bill Clinton remained in the White House. ✍

RECOMMENDED READING:

Beit-Hallahmi, Benjamin, *The Israeli Connection*, New York, Pantheon Books,1987.

*Bill, James A., *The Eagle and the Lion: The Tragedy of American-Iranian Relations*, New Haven, Yale University Press, 1988.

Keddie, Nikki, *Roots of Revolution: An Interpretive History of Modern Iran*, New Haven, Yale University Press, 1981.

Roosevelt, Kermit, *Counter Coup: The Struggle for the Control of Iran*, New York, McGraw-Hill Book Company, 1979.

Segev, Samuel, *The Iranian Triangle*, New York, Free Press, 1988.

Stewart, Richard A., *Sunrise at Abadan: The British and Soviet Invasion of Iran*, 1941, New York, Praeger, 1988.

*Available through the AET Book Club.

NOTES:

[1]Thomas W. Lippman, *Washington Post*, 5/8/95.

[2]Israel Shahak, "With Iraq Neutralized, Israelis Seek Catalyst for War with Iran," *Washington Report on Middle East Affairs*, April/May, 1993.

[3]Yo'av Kaspi, *Al Hamishmar*, 2/19/93.

[4]Ya'akov Erez, *Ma'ariv*, 2/12/93.

[5]David Hoffman, *Washington Post*, 3/13/93.

[6]Elaine Sciolino, *New York Times*, 3/31/93.

[7]Israel Shahak, "Israel Seeks to Build a Coalition Against Iran," *Middle East International*, Aug. 6, 1993.

[8]*New York Times*, 5/1/93. The text is in U.S. State Department, "Patterns of Global Terrorism 1992," April, 1993.

[9]The text is in National Security Council release, May 18, 1993, and "Documents and Source Material," *Journal of Palestine Studies*, Summer 1994,

pp. 159-61. Also see John Law, "Martin Indyk Lays Out the Clinton Approach," *Middle East International,* June 11, 1993; excerpts in "Special Report #84," Washington Institute for Near East Policy, May 21, 1993. Also see Douglas Jehl, *New York Times,* 5/27/93.

[10]John M. Goshko, *Washington Post,* 4/10/93.

[11]Andrew I. Killgore, "Israeli-Inspired U.S. Pressure May Backfire in Iran," *Washington Report on Middle East Affairs,* September, 1995.

[12]Eric Schmitt, *New York Times,* 3/1/95.

[13]Rowan Scarborough, *Washington Times,* 3/27/95.

[14]Associated Press, *Boston Globe,* 3/23/95.

[15]Reuters, *Boston Globe,* 3/22/95.

[16]Thomas W. Lippman, *Washington Post,* 4/2/95.

[17]Elaine Sciolino, *New York Times,* 4/5/95.

[18]Thomas W. Lippman, *Washington Post,* 4/2/95.

[19]Elaine Sciolino, *New York Times,* 4/12/95.

[20]Barnaby J. Feder, *New York Times,* 5/2/95.

[21]Ann Devroy, *Washington Post,* 5/1/95; Todd S. Purdum, *New York Times,* 5/1/95.

[22]Arnaud de Borchgrave, *Washington Times,* 5/3/95.

[23]Martin Sieff, *Washington Times,* 5/3/95.

[24]Todd S. Purdum, *New York Times,* 5/1/95.

[25]Thomas W. Lippman, *Washington Post,* 4/17/95.

[26]Thomas W. Lippman, *Washington Post,* 5/8/95.

Israel at Home

Chapter 28

1954: Israel Takes Land of the Bedouins

ON MARCH 17, 1954, 11 Israelis riding in a bus were killed in an ambush at Scorpion Pass in Israel's eastern Negev desert. The slaughter caused intense outrage and anti-Arab hatred inside Israel. Arabs and Palestinians were widely suspected and there was hot talk about revenge. It was only later that investigators discovered the attackers had been Bedouin nomads retaliating because Israeli troops had driven them from their traditional Negev grazing grounds.[1]

Although the plight of the Bedouins has been largely ignored, their treatment by Israel has been no kinder, and no less systematic, than the dispossession of the Palestinians.[2] When Israel came into being in 1948, there were 108 Bedouin villages and localities with a population of about 135,000. By 1961, only 22,578 Bedouins remained inside Israel in 41 villages and localities.[3] Today there are only a few thousand scattered Bedouins left in the Negev.

In their place are 280,000 Jews living in 114 villages and towns.[4] Before 1948, there were at most around 4,000 Jews in the large Beersheba-Negev southern districts.[5]

Israel's campaign to rid the Negev of the Bedouins began the same year the Jewish state came into being. By the time the fighting ended in late 1948, Israel had destroyed 67 Bedouin villages and localities and routed hundreds and perhaps thousands of the nomads from their grazing areas—as it had dispossessed three-quarters of a million Palestinians.[6] The next year 500 Bedouin families were chased out by Israeli troops from an area south of Hebron, just north of the Negev.[7] In 1950, Egypt complained to the United

Nations that 4,000 Bedouins had been driven from their homes in the Negev into its territory. Egypt charged that atrocities had been committed against the Bedouins by Israeli troops and that the Bedouins' herds of goats had been killed.[8]

While Israel's major concern was to get rid of the Bedouins and take their land, there were strategic military considerations as well in moving some of the nomads. This was noted at the time by the chief of staff of UNTSO, the U.N. Truce Supervision Organization, Lt. Gen. E.L.M. Burns. He reported that 3,500 of those expelled in 1950 were from the Azazme tribe who were the original inhabitants of the El Auja demilitarized zone, an old Turkish garrison area renamed by Israel as Nitzana. It was a strategic 145-square-kilometer juncture between Israel and Egypt at the western Negev-Sinai frontier that had been demilitarized in the 1949 armistice between Egypt and Israel because it was a major invasion route along the Cairo-Beersheba-Jerusalem axis.[9]

When members of the Azazme tribe drifted back to El Auja they attracted the fiery attention of Ariel Sharon, at the time the commander of Israel's terrorist Unit 101 and later a defense minister. Sharon led the unit in September, 1953, in an attack on the Bedouins in the demilitarized zone. An unknown number of Bedouins were killed.[10] Israel eventually took over much of the zone by hook or crook, and used it to considerable advantage in two wars against Egypt when the Jewish state launched surprise attacks across the Sinai in 1956 and 1967.[11]

Israel's campaign against the Bedouin reached a new height of brutality in 1959 when troops forcibly drove out 350 Bedouins from the Negev. On Oct. 6, the United Nations Egyptian-Israeli Mixed Armistice Commission condemned Israel for the action. The commission accused the Israelis of killing some Bedouins, burning their tents and taking their property, including camels, donkeys and sheep.[12]

Such brutal behavior eventually achieved Israel's aims. Israeli anthropologist Clinton Bailey reported at the end of 1993 that during the past four decades Israel had forced 99 percent of the Bedouins off their lands and confiscated their herds. Now, he wrote, Israel was conducting a "discriminatory policy designed to get all the Bedouins off the land....the last 1 percent of the Bedouins still living in their native area in the central Negev are fighting expulsion."

In order to escape criticism for driving the Bedouins into Egypt or Jordan, Israel over the years also had attempted to gain their land by congregating them in seven development towns in northern Negev. But, according to Bailey, "most never got beyond the sprawling desert slums of shanties and ragged tents around Beersheba, because Israel has never provided the necessary finances to develop the townships....Many in the townships are unemployed, and some have become dependent on welfare and turned to drugs."

Bailey added: "To cover up its land-grabbing, the government presents the expulsions as benevolent. The Bedouins, it says, must be brought into the 21st century. If they are concentrated in the townships, the argument goes, they will have access to proper schools and medical care....And if critics say that benevolence alone doesn't justify the expulsions, the government trots out the sacred cow: the army needs all the land for training.

"The cynicism is clear. No one asks whether Hasidic Jews are ready for the 21st century, so why ask it about Bedouins?"[13] ◗◣

RECOMMENDED READING:

Abu-Lughod, Ibrahim (ed.), *Transformation of Palestine* (2nd ed.), Evanston, Northwestern University Press, 1987.

Benziman, Uzi, *Sharon: An Israeli Caesar*, New York, Adama Books, 1985.

Burns, Lt. Gen. E.L.M., *Between Arab and Israeli*, New York, Ivan Obolensky, 1962.

Hutchison, Commander E.H., *Violent Truce*, New York, The Bevin-Adair Company, 1956.

Love, Kennett, *Suez: The Twice-Fought War*, New York, McGraw-Hill Book Company, 1969.

Lustick, Ian, *Arabs in the Jewish State: Israel's Control of a National Minority*, Austin, University of Texas Press, 1980.

Morris, Benny, *The Birth of the Palestine Refugee Problem*, New York, Cambridge University Press, 1987.

Nakhleh, Issa, *Encyclopedia of the Palestine Problem* (2 vols.), New York, Intercontinental Books, 1991.

*Neff, Donald, *Warriors at Suez: Eisenhower Takes America Into the Middle East*, New York, Linden Press/Simon & Schuster, 1981, and Brattleboro, VT, Amana Books, 1988.

1954: Israel Takes Land of the Bedouins 183

*Available through the AET Book Club.

NOTES:

[1]Love, *Suez*, p. 61. Also see Hutchison, *Violent Truce*, pp. 47-59.

[2]For a detailed examination of Israel's treatment of the Bedouins, see Kurt Goering, "Israel and the Bedouin of the Negev," *Journal of Palestine Studies*, Autumn 1979, pp. 3-20; Nakhleh, *Encyclopedia of the Palestine Problem*, pp. 311-14 and 420.

[3]Nakhleh, *Encyclopedia of the Palestine Problem*, pp. 311 and 332. Nakhleh provides a short history of the expulsions and testimony on the subject before the United Nations, pp. 311-14.

[4]Clinton Bailey, *New York Times*, 12/29/93.

[5]Janet L. Abu-Lughod, "The Demographic Transformation of Palestine," p. 153, in Abu-Lughod, *Transformation of Palestine.*

[6]Nakhleh, *Encyclopedia of the Palestine Problem*, p. 332. Also see Lustick, *Arabs in the Jewish State*, p. 135.

[7]Morris, *The Birth of the Palestinian Refugee Problem*, pp. 247-48.

[8]*New York Times*, 9/16/50. Quotes from Egypt's complaint to the Security Council are in Nakhleh, *Encyclopedia of the Palestine Problem*, p. 313. Also see Benziman, *Sharon*, p. 49.

[9]Burns, *Between Arab and Israeli*, pp. 92-93; Love, *Suez*, pp. 11 and 108-9; Neff, *Warriors at Suez*, p. 112.

[10]Morris, *Israel's Border Wars*, p. 242.

[11]Neff, *Warriors at Suez*, pp. 112-14.

[12]Reuters, *New York Times*, 10/7/59; Jay Walz, *New York Times*, 10/18/59.

[13]Clinton Bailey, *New York Times*, 12/19/93.

Chapter 29

1967 : Jewish Settlements Begin

O N JULY 15, 1967—just five weeks after the end of the Six-Day War—Israel quietly established its first settlement in the occupied territories, despite promises to Washington that it had no intention to do so. The settlement was Kibbutz Merom Hagolan near Quneitra on the Golan Heights.[1] Although Israel continued to indicate it wanted peace more than land, its aggressive actions became suspect in Washington. A secret cable drafted in the State Department for transmission to the U.S. Embassy in Tel Aviv on Sept. 14 noted that Israeli policy seemed to be hardening toward retention of the occupied territories: "Israeli objectives may be shifting from original position seeking peace with no repeat no territorial gains toward one of territorial expansionism," said the cable.

It continued: "Israel's refusal to authorize the return of all refugees desiring to resume residence on West Bank...and statements by senior Israeli officials quoted in American press give rise to impression that Israeli government may be moving toward policy of seeking security simply by retaining occupied areas rather than by achieving peaceful settlement with Arabs." The cable noted Israel now seemed to be putting more emphasis on "form of settlement (direct negotiations and formal peace treaties) rather than substance....There is concern [this stance] could in fact become rationale for territorial acquisitions." The cable concluded that it was important for Israel to demonstrate "that Israel sincerely wishes peaceful settlement above all."[2]

Despite protests from the United Nations and the United States that settlements were a violation of the Fourth Geneva Convention, Israel continued establishing Jewish settlements. Within six months,

Israel had expropriated 838 acres for new settlements, expelled hundreds of Arabs from the Jewish Quarter in the Old City of Jerusalem, razed Palestinian refugee towns at Tiflig and near Jericho as well as 144 homes in Gaza, and secretly embarked on a major plan for founding four large settlements in Arab East Jerusalem.[3] By the beginning of 1968, Israel had placed settlements in all the occupied lands of Egypt, Jordan and Syria.[4]

Under its Labor governments Israel pursued a steady but deliberately quiet policy of establishing settlements, disguising them as "*nahals*," paramilitary outposts manned by youths. The subterfuge served the purpose of muting international criticism. However, by mid-1976 the number of settlements had grown to 68 and no longer could be ignored. Finally, on March 23, 1976, the United States went public with its concerns about Israel's actions. On that date, U.S. Ambassador to the United Nations William W. Scranton declared in the Security Council that Israel's settlements in the occupied territories were illegal and that its claim to all of Jerusalem was void.

Scranton said: "The United States position on the status of Jerusalem has been stated here on numerous occasions since the Arab portion of that city was occupied by Israel in 1967.... [T]he future of Jerusalem will be determined only through the instruments and processes of negotiation, agreement and accommodation. Unilateral attempts to predetermine the future have no standing.

"Next, I turn to the question of Israeli settlements in the occupied territories. Again, my government believes that international law sets the appropriate standards. An occupier must maintain the occupied areas as intact and unaltered as possible, without interfering with the customary life of the area, and any changes must be necessitated by the immediate needs of the occupation and be consistent with international law. The Fourth Geneva Convention speaks directly to the issue of population transfer in Article 49: 'The occupying power shall not deport or transfer parts of its own civilian population into the territory it occupies.' Clearly, then, substantial resettlement of the Israeli civilian population in occupied territories, including East Jerusalem, is illegal under the convention and cannot be considered to have prejudged the outcome of future negotiations between the parties or the location of the borders of states of the Middle East. Indeed, the presence of these settlements is seen by my government as an obstacle to the success of the negotiations for a just and final peace between Israel and its neighbors."[5]

The settlements issue between the United States and Israel grew more heated under President Carter. He personally declared them "illegal" during a press conference on July 28, 1977. Said Carter: "The matter of settlements in the occupied territories has always been characterized by our government, by me and my predecessors as an illegal action."[6]

Finally, on April 21, 1978, the State Department legal adviser, Herbert Hansell, rendered an official opinion on the issue of Israel's settlements in occupied territories, saying they were "inconsistent with international law." The opinion also asserted that the Fourth Geneva Convention applied to the West Bank and Gaza, against Israeli claims that it did not because sovereignty over those areas was in dispute.[7] Despite this official finding, the Carter administration did not have the political will to support a 1979 U.N. Security Council resolution saying Israeli settlements on Arab land, including East Jerusalem, had no legal status and "constitute a serious obstruction in achieving a comprehensive, just and lasting peace in the Middle East." The vote was 12-0-3 with the United States, Britain and Norway abstaining.[8]

U.S. policy was significantly weakened with the coming to power of Ronald Reagan. On Feb. 2, 1981, less than two weeks after he became president, Reagan declared: "I disagreed when the previous administration referred to them [settlements] as illegal—they're not illegal."[9] This odd language left the issue in something of a semantic limbo, since Reagan never actually declared the settlements legal. Throughout his two terms Reagan maintained the attitude that settlements were simply "not illegal."[10]

The result of this astonishing turn-about was reported by David A. Korn, who was the State Department's director for Israel and Arab-Israeli affairs at the time. He noted that Reagan's pronouncement left the United States without a coherent policy toward settlements: "For more than a year afterward, the United States remained mute on Israeli settlements. American silence was all the signal Mr. Begin's Likud government needed to initiate an accelerated settlements program. By September, 1982, the administration realized what damage it had done to its Middle East peace efforts and the formula 'settlements are an obstacle to peace' became standard State Department usage. However, at no time during the Reagan administration's eight years in office did it revert to the stronger position that settlements are illegal."[11] In fact, Secretary of State George Shultz went further in weakening the U.S. position on Sept. 9, 1982, when he told Congress that "the status of Israeli settlements must be determined in the course of the final status negotiations."[12]

The Bush administration adopted Reagan's formulation that the settlements were obstacles to peace. Despite Bush's conflict with the government of Yitzhak Shamir over the use of U.S. loan guarantees in the occupied territories, at no time did his administration express the earlier language describing settlements as illegal. This reluctance by the president to invoke the stronger language was ruefully referred to publicly by Secretary of State James Baker in 1991 when he referred to the settlements that "we used to characterize as illegal, and which we now moderately characterize as an obstacle to peace."[13]

The Clinton administration has retreated even further by calling them "complicating" factors.[14] &

RECOMMENDED READING:

Abu-Lughod, Ibrahim, "Israeli Settlements in Occupied Arab Lands: Conquest to Colony," *Journal of Palestine Studies*, Winter 1982, pp. 16-54.

Adams, Michael, "Israel's Treatment of the Arabs in the Occupied Territories," *Journal of Palestine Studies*, Winter 1972, pp. 19-40.

Aronson, Geoffrey, *Creating Facts: Israel, Palestinians and the West Bank*, Washington, DC, Institute for Palestine Studies, 1987.

Foundation for Middle East Peace, *Report on Israeli Settlement in the Occupied Territories* (bimonthly newsletter), Washington, DC.

*Khouri, Fred J., *The Arab-Israeli Dilemma*, 3rd ed. Syracuse, NY, Syracuse University Press, 1985.

Lesch, Ann Mosley, "Israeli Settlements in the Occupied Territories, 1967-1977," *Journal of Palestine Studies*, Autumn 1977, pp. 26-47.

*Lilienthal, Alfred M., *The Zionist Connection*, New York, Dodd Mead, 1978.

Mallison, William T. and Sally V., *The Palestine Problem in International Law and World Order*, London, Longman Group Ltd., 1986.

Matar, Ibrahim, "Israeli Settlements in the West Bank and Gaza Strip," *Journal of Palestine Studies*, Autumn 1981, pp. 93-110.

*Neff, Donald, *Warriors for Jerusalem*, Battleboro, Vt., Amana Books, 1984.

Thorpe, Merle Jr., *Prescription for Conflict*, Washington, DC, Foundation for Middle East Peace,1984.

Tillman, Seth, *The United States in the Middle East*, Bloomington, Indiana University Press, 1982.

*Available through the AET Book Club.

NOTES:

[1]Aronson, *Creating Facts*, p. 16. Also see Israel Shahak, "Memory of 1967 'Ethnic Cleansing' Fuels Ideology of Golan Settlers," *Washington Report on Middle East Affairs*, November, 1992.

[2]State to American embassy Tel Aviv, Secret cable 2942, 9/14/67; declassified 3/5/79. The cable is quoted in Neff, *Warriors for Jerusalem*, p. 322.

[3]Israeli Housing Minister Ze'ev Sharef revealed details of the Jerusalem settlements 2/18/71, see *Facts on File 1971*, p. 123.

[4]Lesch, Ann. "Israeli Settlements in the Occupied Territories," *Journal of Palestine Studies*, Autumn 1978.

[5]Excerpts in *New York Times*, 3/25/76. See Bernard Gwertzman, *New York Times*, 3/13/80, for list of U.S. statements over the years of the U.S. position on Jerusalem.

[6]Text is in *New York Times*, 7/29/77, and U.S. State Department, *American Foreign Policy 1977-1980* (1983), p. 618.

[7]Department of State, Office of the Legal Adviser, *Digest of United States Practice in International Law 1978*, pp. 1575-83. Text is in *Israeli Settlements in the Occupied Territories: Hearings Before the Subcommittee of International Organizations and on Europe and the Middle East of the Committee on International Relations*, House of Representatives, 95th Congress, 1st Ses., 1978, 167-72, and in Thorpe, *Prescription for Conflict* (1984), 153-58. Major excerpts are in Foundation for Middle East Peace, *Report on Israeli Settlement in the Occupied Territories*, Special Report, July, 1991. For a detailed discussion, see Mallison, *The Palestine Problem in International Law and World Order* (1986). Chapter 6.

[8]Resolution 446, passed March 22, 1979. The text is in Sherif, *United Nations Resolutions on Palestine and the Arab-Israeli Conflict* (1988), Volume Two: 1975-1981, p. 188.

[9]*New York Times*, 2/3/81.

[10]See, for instance, *New York Times*, 8/28/83.

[11]David A. Korn, letter, *New York Times*, 10/10/91.

[12]Thorpe, *Prescription for Conflict*, p. 160.

[13]David Hoffman and Jackson Diehl, *Washington Post*, 9/18/91.

Chapter 30

1971: Repression of Palestinians in Gaza

ON JAN. 2, 1971, Palestinian guerrillas attacked an Israeli car in occupied Gaza, killing two Jewish children and wounding their mother. In reaction, Israel launched its most massive and intense military operation up to this time to try to pacify the nearly 400,000 Palestinians, most of them refugees from 1948 or 1967, crowded in the 5-by-28-mile Gaza Strip.[1] Ultimately, the effort, although exceedingly brutal and lasting for a year, failed and Gaza remained a seething center of opposition. It was Gaza's unrelenting opposition over a quarter-century to occupation that helps explain why Israel was so ready in September, 1993 to surrender Gaza to the Palestine Liberation Organization.

Among the measures Israel imposed in 1971 was a month-long curfew on the Gaza Strip, the dismissal of Mayor Raghed Alami of Gaza City and a series of destructive searches of the region's teeming refugee camps.[2] The drastic Israeli actions provoked loud protests charging brutality and Gestapo tactics from critics ranging from the Israeli left to the Soviet Union.[3] Israeli writer Amos Elon toured Shati refugee camp shortly after it was searched by Israeli troops in 1971. He wrote in the major Hebrew daily *Ha'aretz:*

"Some of the houses look as if an earthquake has struck them...We see opened walls and poor furniture broken into pieces, floors split by axes, and broken closets...torn mattresses, boxes and wooden closets broken, glasses smashed and doors broken from their hinges...Many were arrested...The families of certain suspects, sought for a long time by the security forces, were exiled to south Sinai."[4]

The Israeli League for Human and Civil Rights reported that during searches Israeli troops "strip women...and stand them nude or almost nude against a wall...Jewelry and watches of the women are robbed in broad daylight, and the few belongings of poor families are savagely shattered and destroyed."[5]

However, despite their ruthlessness, such tactics were ineffective. When guerrilla attacks continued into the summer, General Ariel Sharon, one of Israel's most ruthless commanders, was ordered by Defense Minister Moshe Dayan to "establish order" in the Gaza Strip.[6]

In his autobiography, Sharon paints a rosy picture of his activities. He claims he pacified Gaza within the seven months between July, 1971 and February, 1972 "with an absolute minimum of harm to the civilian population. Specifically, two Gaza civilians had died accidentally...On two separate occasions we deported a small number of people, less than 30 altogether. That was all that was necessary. Soldiers did not beat students, let alone shoot at them, and students did not stone soldiers. Overall, I got tremendous satisfaction from our success in Gaza. I felt I had brought quiet to a place that had been suffering the tortures of the damned."[7]

However, the facts tell a different story. Even by Sharon's own statistics, 104 "terrorists" were killed and 742 captured.[8] One of Sharon's biographers, Uzi Benziman, an Israeli newsman, wrote that Sharon had in fact conducted "a reign of terror" against Gazans.[9]

"Sharon achieved his goals by working systematically and relentlessly...On his orders, every adult male in Gaza was stopped and subjected to thorough search. Periodically, curfews were imposed on the refugee camps, and all residents were assembled for hours on end for purposes of identification. Paths through the refugee camps were widened and the population thinned out, to make it harder for terrorists to find refuge...Sharon was accused by Palestinian organizations of secretly killing *fedayeen* who had been captured alive. He adamantly denied this, although he admitted that his soldiers had orders to shoot to kill all terrorists and not to make an effort to capture them alive."[10]

One of Sharon's tactics was "thinning out" of the population, which meant that families were given short notice to leave their homes and relocated in housing selected by Israel. *The New York*

Times described the process: "Every day Israeli jeeps roll up to 35 or 40 of the cinder-block houses. A soldier paints a black cross on the wall and another tells the family they will have to move. Twenty-four hours later, after the families have loaded their possessions onto trucks furnished by the army and departed, the bulldozer arrives and knocks the houses down."[11]

Hundreds of refugee homes were bulldozed. The process was described by a Quaker field worker, Anne Lesch: "In July, the army began to 'thin out' the refugee camps, demolishing almost 40 houses daily in Jabalya, which housed 40,000 persons....The army bulldozed wide streets through the Jabalya and Shati refugee camps in order to seal off and separate each section.... After U.N. Secretary-General U Thant protested against the demolitions and evacuations, the army temporarily ceased them. By then over 13,000 people had been uprooted."[12]

Although Sharon's tactics brought about a dramatic drop in guerrilla attacks—from 34 in June to only one in December—the "pacification" was only temporary.[13]

Over the years since then, opposition to Israel's occupation grew along with Gaza's burgeoning population, which today totals nearly 800,000.[14] Gaza became the cauldron of Palestinian resistance, making it an area where Israeli civilians feared to go and soldiers ventured only reluctantly. It was in Gaza where in December, 1987, the historic uprising, the intifada, against Israeli occupation began.

Despite all of Israel's efforts to suppress resistance in Gaza over a quarter-century, the guerrilla movement remained strong and a serious threat to Israel's control. By 1992, many Israelis openly admitted they were ready to wash their hands of Gaza. Indicative of how troublesome maintaining the occupation in Gaza had become, Yitzhak Rabin declared shortly after he became prime minister in 1992: "I would like to see Gaza drown in the sea."[15]

But Gaza refused to drown. It is no surprise, then, that when Israel finally agreed to recognize the Palestinians as a separate people, the first area it was ready to surrender was Gaza. ໜ

RECOMMENDED READING:

Benziman, Uzi, *Sharon: An Israeli Caesar,* New York, Adama Books, 1985.

Davis, Uri and Norton Mezvinsky, *Documents from Israel 1967-73: Readings for a Critique of Zionism,* London, Ithaca Press, 1975.

Lesch, Ann M., "Gaza: Forgotten Corner of Palestine," *Journal of Palestine Studies,* Autumn 1985.

Locke, Richard and Anthony Stewart, *Bantustan Gaza,* London, Zed Books Ltd., 1985.

Nakhleh, Issa, *Encyclopedia of the Palestine Problem,* New York, Intercontinental Books, 1991.

Roy, Sara, *The Gaza Strip Survey,* Boulder, CO, Westview Press, 1986.

Roy, Sara, "Gaza: Dynamics of Civic Disintegration," *Journal of Palestine Studies,* Summer 1993.

Sharon, Ariel (with David Chanoff), *Warrior: The Autobiography of Ariel Sharon,* New York, Simon and Schuster, 1989.

NOTES:

[1]Benziman, *Sharon,* p. 115.

[2]In Alami's place Israel later appointed as mayor Rashad Shawa, the elder of a prominent local landowning family; see *New York Times,* 9/24/71. For a detailed review of Israeli actions against refugees in Gaza since the 1967 war, see Nakhleh, *Encyclopedia of the Palestine Problem,* pp. 425-32.

[3]Peter Grose, *New York Times,* 2/2/71.

[4]Davis and Mezvinsky, *Documents from Israel,* pp. 155-60.

[5]*Ibid.,* p. 154.

[6]Benziman, *Sharon,* p. 115.

[7]Sharon, *Warrior,* pp. 260-61.

[8]*Ibid., p.* 260.

[9]Benziman, *Sharon, p.* 118.

[10]*Ibid.,* pp. 115-16.

[11]Richard Eder, *New York Times,* 8/20/71.

[12]*Facts on File 1971,* p. 608, p. 673, and letter by Edward W. Said, "Pacification of Gaza," in *New York Times,* 2/5/88, which quotes Anne Lesch's "Political Perceptions of the Palestinians on the West Bank and Gaza Strip," published in 1980 by the Middle East Institute Journal, Washington, DC

[13]Benziman, *Sharon,* p. 116.

[14]Foundation for Middle East Peace, *Report on Israeli Settlement in the Occupied Territories,* January, 1993.

[15]Clyde Haberman, *New York Times,* 3/3/93.

Chapter 31

1977: The Exposure of Torture by Israel

ON JUNE 19, 1977, the Insight Team of the *Sunday Times* of London reported Israel's use of torture against Palestinians was "systematic" and "appears to be sanctioned at some level as deliberate policy." Although Palestinian prisoners had been complaining for years that they were tortured while in Israeli custody, the report by the prestigious newspaper caused a sensation. Israel vehemently denied the charge, touching off a major controversy between Israel and the newspaper. The *Times* stuck by its story and so too did Israel stay with its version that torture did not exist as an official policy.[1] While Israel's strong official denials somewhat muted the impact of the *Times* report, the controversy it generated had the result of touching off investigations by other groups, both foreign and Israeli. It took another 10 years before an Israeli judicial panel finally confirmed that Israeli security officials did indeed routinely torture Palestinian prisoners.

However, instead of demanding the medieval practice be stopped, it agreed that "moderate physical pressure" could be employed against prisoners. Those are the general guidelines that Israel follows today, meaning it is the only self-professed democracy in the world that sanctions the use of torture. The practice puts Israel in violation of the 1984 International Convention Against Torture, which Israel signed in 1991. Israel was strongly criticized in 1994 by the U.N. Committee Against Torture for failing to enact in its domestic law terms of the convention, thus "its provisions cannot be invoked in Israeli courts."[2]

To this day Israel condones torture despite international criticism. However, there is little doubt that the practice has been at least somewhat moderated under the glare of the international community. The credit for documenting and pressuring Israel to admit its practice of torture goes largely to Amnesty International.

AI had been a consistent critic of Israel's torture since 1970, but with little impact. After the 1977 *Times* exposé, AI decided to send its own team of investigators to the occupied territories. On Sept. 1, 1980, it reported: "Amnesty International reaffirms its view stated on several occasions since 1970 that there is sufficient prima facie evidence of ill-treatment of security suspects in the Occupied Territories by interrogators and detaining officials to warrant the establishment of a public inquiry into this matter."

The AI report reviewed in detail the *Times'* exposé, concluding that Israel's denials were unsatisfactory. It strongly urged Israel "to investigate the allegations of ill-treatment in their totality..."

Once again Israel officially denied the allegations. In a long response dated Dec. 31, 1980, Israeli Attorney General Itzhak Zamir rejected Amnesty International's recommendations and contended the present Israeli practices adequately protected prisoners from torture and mistreatment. Amnesty International renewed its recommendations after Zamir's reply but Israel again rejected them.[3] It was not until 1987 that Israel accepted AI's recommendation and appointed a special commission to look into the torture charges. While it was gathering evidence, *The Washington Post*'s Jerusalem correspondent, Glenn Frankel, was reporting that recent allegations of torture by the Shin Bet, Israel's domestic secret police, "lent credence to longstanding Palestinian charges that [Israeli] agents frequently torture Arab prisoners and perjure themselves in court." Added the story: "...now some Shin Bet operatives are conceding publicly that illegal methods have been used regularly. Those techniques include sleep deprivation, ice cold showers, suffocation by hooding, verbal threats and, in many instances, punches, kicks to the groin and face-smacking, designed usually to frighten more than wound."[4]

Finally, on Oct. 30, the government-appointed commission headed by former Supreme Court Justice Moshe Landau released a report confirming that members of the Shin Bet had systematically lied to Israeli courts since 1971 about using torture against Palestinians to gain confessions.[5]

Though Israeli laws were violated, no prosecutions were recommended. Instead, the commission took the extraordinary step of actually endorsing the use of "moderate physical pressure" and "nonviolent psychological pressure."[6]

Observed *The Post's* Frankel: "The [apologetic tone of the] report seemed to reflect a consensus among Israelis that although abuses of power were unfortunate, the Shin Bet nonetheless deserves public support...."[7] Just how approving most Israelis were of torture of Palestinians was evident two years later when another case of severe torture became public without causing an outcry. *New York Times* columnist Anthony Lewis recounted the details. The case involved a Palestinian human rights worker, Shawan Jabarin, 29, arrested Oct. 10, 1989: "They blindfolded him and handcuffed him with his hands behind his back. Soldiers whispered in his ear, 'You are a dog.' After putting a cloth in his mouth to keep him from screaming, they burned him with a cigarette on his ear and hand. Then they took him into a bathroom and made him lie on the tile floor. 'One soldier...stepped on my head, my chest and my hands. The soldier grabbed on to something located above him and began to jump on me. This went on for approximately 10 minutes, and I felt I was going to die.'" Lewis concluded: "It is time for [Israel's supporters] to speak out about the injustice that burdens the occupied territories and corrupts the occupiers."[8]

But still the torture continued. On July 29, 1991, Amnesty International released another major report on Israel's human rights violations, urging Israel to halt its "routine" use of torture and ill-treatment of Palestinian prisoners. It expressed serious concerns about Israel's entire system of military justice in the occupied territories, calling it basically flawed. The report said: "We believe either that the government endorses these interrogation practices, which amount to torture or ill-treatment, or interrogators have been routinely violating official guidelines as international standards which prohibit all torture and ill-treatment."

AI said some 30,000 Palestinians had been tried before military courts since the start of the intifada at the end of 1987, adding: "The odds are stacked against Palestinian civilians getting a fair trial in military courts...because of fundamental flaws in the system, including the routine torture or ill-treatment of suspects during interrogation."[9]

The following year a leading Israeli human rights group reported torture by Israeli security forces had become so routine that Palestinian prisoners often no longer bothered complaining about it. The Israeli Center for Human Rights in the Occupied Territories, B'Tselem (In the Image), reported that at least 5,000 of the 20,000 Palestinians arrested in the past year had been tortured. B'Tselem said Palestinians under arrest had been severely beaten, deprived of sleep for days and tied up in painful positions with hoods over their heads. The report said that torture and violations of international agreements by security forces "have now become so routine that we would describe them as standard practice for most Palestinians who are seriously interrogated."[10]

Despite such criticism Israel has refused to abandon torture. As late as 1995, Scottish Doctor Derrick Pounder reported that Palestinian Abdel Zamed Hassan Harizat, 30, of Hebron, had died while under Shin Bet torture. Pounder said: "As far as I know, this is the first absolutely clear-cut case where there can be no debate that this is a death as the result of torture and nothing else.....He died as a result of physical injury and that injury was the result of torture and that the method of torture is one commonly used by the Shin Bet."[11] The cause of death was violent shaking of the head, a method used by Shin Bet. Other methods included shackling prisoners in painful positions, placing foul-smelling sacks over their heads and depriving them of sleep.[12]

Pounder said two Israeli doctors helped him conduct the autopsy and agreed with his findings. As it turned out, Israel had not only refused to halt torture but it was revealed that the rules of interrogation had been relaxed for the Shin Bet in November, 1994.[13] So, after more than two decades of scrutiny and condemnation, Israel perversely remains committed to employing a practice that is abhorred by all democratic countries. It is a practice that helps explain why young Palestinians are willing to turn themselves into suicide bombers to strike back at their tormentors. ❧

RECOMMENDED READING:

Nakhleh, Issa, *Encyclopedia of the Palestine Problem* (2 vols), New York, Intercontinental Books, 1991.

Tillman, Seth, *The United States in the Middle East: Interests and Obstacles*, Bloomington, Indiana University Press, 1982.

NOTES:

[1] Texts of the *Times* story and Israel's response are in *Journal of Palestine Studies*, "Special Document," Summer 1977, pp. 191-219. See Nakhleh, *Encyclopedia of the Palestine Problem*, pp. 593-672, for personal accounts of torture in Israeli prisons and mistreatment of Palestinian women. Also see Tillman, *The United States in the Middle East*, pp. 192-93, for a review of how such reports were received in the U.S.

[2] Reuters, *Washington Times*, 4/19/94.

[3] Amnesty International, *Report and Recommendations of an Amnesty International Mission to the Government of the State of Israel: 3-7 June, 1979*, London: An Amnesty International Publication, September, 1980. Also see "Israel and Torture," a compilation of U.S. Consulate reports on Israeli torture, in the *Journal of Palestine Studies*, Vol. IX, No. 2, Winter 1980, pp. 79-117, as well as a history of reports on Israeli torture, Ghassan Bishara, *Journal of Palestine Studies*, Vol. VIII, No. 4, Summer 1979, pp. 3-30.

[4] Glenn Frankel, *Washington Post*, 7/2/87.

[5] Glenn Frankel, *Washington Post*, 10/31/87; also see Thomas L. Friedman, *New York Times*, 11/8/87; *New York Times*, 11/2/87; Amnesty International, *Amnesty Report: 1988*, p. 239; Stanley Cohen, "Talking About Torture in Israel," *Tikkun*, November/December, 1992.

[6] Glenn Frankel, *Washington Post*, 10/31/87.

[7] *Ibid.*

[8] Anthony Lewis, "The Week in Review," *New York Times*, 10/22/89.

[9] Reuters, *Washington Times*, 7/30/91.

[10] Clyde Haberman, *New York Times*, 4/3/92.

[11] Reuters, *Washington Times*, 5/29/95.

[12] Joel Greenberg, *New York Times*, 5/1/95.

Chapter 32

1977: Christians Discriminated Against by Israel

ON DEC. 29, 1977, Christians in Israel and the occupied territories protested a new law passed by the Israeli parliament making it illegal for missionaries to proselytize Jews. Protestant churches charged that the law had been "hastily pushed through parliament during the Christmas period when Christians were busily engaged in preparing for and celebrating their major festival." The law made missionaries liable to five years' imprisonment for attempting to persuade people to change their religion, and three years' imprisonment for any Jew who converted. The United Christian Council complained that the law could be "misused in restricting religious freedom in Israel."[1]

Nonetheless, it came into force on April 1, 1978, prohibiting the offering of "material inducement" for a person to change his religion. A material inducement could be something as minor as the giving of a Bible.[2] Although the Likud government of Menachem Begin assured the Christian community that the law applied equally to all religions and did not specifically mention Christians, the United Christian Council of Israel charged that it was biased and aimed specifically at Christians since only Christians openly proselytized. Council representatives also cited anti-Christian speeches made in the parliament during debate on the law. Parliament member Binyamin Halevy had called missionaries "a cancer in the body of the nation."[3]

The next year Rabbi Ovadiah Yosef, considered a political moderate, issued a religious ruling that copies of the New Testament should be torn and destroyed out of any edition of a Bible owned by a Jew.[4] Israeli scholar Yehoshafat Harkabi wrote that he was disturbed by "these manifestations of hostility—the designation of Christians as idolaters, the demand to invoke the 'resident alien' ordinances, and the burning of the New Testament." Observed Harkabi: "Outside of the Land of Israel Jews never dared behave in this fashion. Has independence made the Jews take leave of their senses?"[5]

Desecration of Christian property and churches—arson, window-breaking, burning of the New Testament—had long marred relations between the two communities. A small but fanatical group of Jews wanted no Christians, whom they considered fallen Jews, in Israel. This virulent strain of prejudice had been present since before the Jewish state was founded.

For instance, after the capture by Jewish forces of Jaffa on May 13, 1948, two days before Israel's birth, there was desecration of Christian churches. Father Deleque, a Catholic priest, reported: "Jewish soldiers broke down the doors of my church and robbed many precious and sacred objects. Then they threw the statues of Christ down into a nearby garden." He added that Jewish leaders had reassured that religious buildings would be respected, "but their deeds do not correspond to their words."[6]

On May 31, 1948, a group of Christian leaders comprising the Christian Union of Palestine publicly complained that Jewish forces had used 10 Christian churches and humanitarian institutions in Jerusalem as military bases and otherwise desecrated them. They added that a total of 14 churches had suffered shell damage, which killed three priests and made casualties of more than 100 women and children.[7]

The group's statement said Arab forces had abided by their promise to respect Christian institutions, but that the Jews had forcefully occupied Christian structures and been indiscriminate in shelling churches. It said, among other charges, that "many children were killed or wounded" by Jewish shells on the Convent of Orthodox Copts on May 19, 23 and 24; that eight refugees were killed and about 120 wounded at the Orthodox Armenian Convent at some unstated date; and that Father Pierre Somi, secretary to the Bishop, had been killed and two wounded at the Orthodox Syrian Church of St. Mark on May 16.[8]

Churches again were desecrated during the 1967 war when Israel captured East Jerusalem, the West Bank and Gaza, completing the occupation of all of Palestine. On July 21, 1967, the Reverend James L. Kelso, a former moderator of the United Presbyterian Church and long-time resident in Palestine, complained of extensive damage to churches, adding: "So significant was this third Jewish war against the Arabs that one of the finest missionaries of the Near East called it 'perhaps the most serious setback that Christiandom has had since the fall of Constantinople in 1453.'"[9]

Kelso continued: "How did Israel respect church property in the fighting...? They shot up the Episcopal Cathedral [in Jerusalem], just as they had done in 1948. They smashed down the Episcopal school for boys....The Israelis wrecked and looted the YMCA...They wrecked the big Lutheran hospital...The Lutheran center for cripples also suffered..."

Nancy Nolan, wife of a physician at the American University Hospital in Beirut, who was in Jerusalem during and after the fighting, charged that "while the Israeli authorities proclaim to the world that all religions will be respected and protected, and post notices identifying the Holy Places, Israeli soldiers and youths are throwing stink bombs in the Church of the Holy Sepulchre.

"The Church of St. Anne, whose crypt marks the birthplace of the Virgin Mary, has been severely damaged and the Church of the Nativity in Bethlehem also was damaged. The wanton killing of the Warden of the Garden Tomb followed by the shooting into the tomb itself, in an attempt to kill the warden's wife, was another instance that we knew first-hand which illustrated the utter disregard shown by the occupation forces toward the Holy Places and the religious sensibilities of the people in Jordan and in the rest of the world.[10]

"The desecration of churches...includes smoking in the churches, littering the churches, taking dogs inside and entering in inappropriate manner of dress. Behavior such as this cannot be construed other than as a direct insult to the whole Christian world."[11]

Desecration has occurred not only in times of war. As recently as 1995, an Israeli soldier, Daniel Koren, 22, entered St. Anthony Catholic Church in Jaffa and went on a shooting rampage, firing more than 100 bullets in the altar and the cross above it but causing no injuries. Koren said his Judaic convictions forced him to destroy all physical images of God, and admitted that he had staged a prior attack in Jerusalem's Gethsemane Church.[12]

Perhaps the worst outbreak of organized desecration of Christian institutions came on Sept. 10, 1963, when hundreds of ultra-orthodox Jews simultaneously attacked Christian missions in Jaffa, Haifa and Jerusalem.[13] (One has to say "perhaps" because reporting on this sensitive subject in the U.S. media has been so poor over the decades.) At any rate, the attacks were a concerted effort to intimidate Christians in Israel by a religious vigilante group called Hever Peelei Hamahane Hatorati, the Society of Activists of the Torah Camp.[14] In an attack on the Church of Scotland school in Jaffa, Christian children were beaten and considerable damage was caused to the school by at least 200 rampaging Jews.

Other attacks occurred at two nearby church schools, the Greek Catholic missionary school of St. Joseph and a Christian Brothers school. In Jerusalem, attacks occurred at the St. Joseph convent and the Finnish Lutheran mission school. In Haifa, the American-European Beth El Messianic Mission Children's Hostel and School was attacked. No serious damage occurred in any of the attacks except at the Scotland school.[15] More than 100 Jews were convicted in the attacks, none of them receiving more than small fines and suspended sentences.[16]

The first half of the 1980s, with Likud governments in control, was a particularly active period for Jewish bigots. On Oct. 8, 1982, the Baptist Church in Jerusalem was burned down. Kerosene had been sprinkled on the church's wooden chapel, constructed in 1933. Although no one was ever charged in the arson, the Baptist Center's bookstore had been vandalized a dozen times in previous years, and Jews were suspected.[17] When the Baptists sought to re-build the church, Jews demonstrated against the project and the Jewish district planning commission refused to grant a building permit. In 1985, the Israeli Supreme Court advised the Baptists to leave the all-Jewish area.[18]

On Christmas Day in 1983, a hotel in Tiberias where Christians held meetings was set afire, the latest in a series of attacks on a small group of about 50 Christians. Two Jews were arrested in the arson incident. Other attacks included stones thrown through windows at the hotel while the group was meeting and break-ins at the homes of members of the group. The anti-missionary group Yad Le'Achim complained that Christian missionary work in Israel was on the increase and that missionaries were offering money, clothes, jewelry and tennis shoes to Jews to listen to Christian lectures.[19]

Just over a fortnight later, on Jan. 11, 1984, suspected Jewish extremists stacked hymnals on a piano in a Christian prayer room in Jerusalem and set them afire. Also in the same week angry Jews protesting Christian proselytizing caused Beth Shalom, a Christian evangelical group, to withdraw its plans to build a multimillion-dollar hotel in Jerusalem. Beth Shalom took its action after about 150 Jews showed up at a city council meeting with placards reading "You can't buy me" and "I didn't immigrate to live next to missionaries." A leader of the protest, Rabbi Moshe Berliner, compared Christian missionaries to Trojan horses.[20]

Jewish infringements on Christian rights became so bad by 1990 that on Dec. 20 the leaders of Christian churches in Jerusalem took the extraordinary decision to restrict Christmas celebrations to protest "the continuing sad state of affairs in our land," including encroachment by Israel on traditional Christian institutions. Among concerns expressed by the patriarchs and heads of churches were attempts by Jewish settlers to move into the Old City and an "erosion of the traditional rights and centuries-old privileges of the churches," including imposition by Israel of municipal and state taxes on the churches.

The statement added: "We express our deep concern over new problems confronting the local church. They interfere with the proper functioning of our religious institutions, and we call upon the civil authorities in the country to safeguard our historic rights and status honored by all governments."[21]

Anti-Christian prejudice helps account for the fact that the number of Christian Palestinians in all of former Palestine had dwindled to only 50,000 in 1995. They no longer were a major presence in either Jerusalem or Ramallah, and they were fast losing their majority status in Bethlehem.[22]

When Israel was established in 1948, the Palestinian Christian community had numbered 200,000, compared to roughly 600,000 Jews in Palestine at the time.[23] Now the Christians are not even one percent of the population of Israel/Palestine. Of today's estimated

total of 400,000 Christian Palestinians, most now are living in their
own diaspora, mainly in the Americas.[24] ❧

RECOMMENDED READING:

*Halsell, Grace, *Journey to Jerusalem*, New York, Macmillan Publishing Co., Inc.,
1981.

*Halsell, Grace, *Prophecy and Politics: Militant Evangelists on the Road to Nuclear
War*, Westport, CT, Lawrence Hill & Company, 1986.

*Harkabi, Y., *Israel's Fateful Hour*, New York: Harper & Row, Publishers, 1988.

Nakhleh, Issa, *Encyclopedia of the Palestine Problem* (2 vols), New York, Intercontinental Books, 1991.

Nyrop, Richard F. (ed.), *Israel: a Country Study* (2nd ed.). Washington, DC,
U.S. Government Printing Office, 1979.

Palumbo, Michael, *The Palestinian Catastrophe: The 1948 Expulsion of a People
from their Homeland*, Boston: Faber and Faber, 1987.

*Available through the AET Book Club.

NOTES:

[1] *New York Times*, 12/30/77.

[2] Nyrop (ed.), *Israel: a Country Study*, p. 105.

[3] *New York Times*, 2/14/78.

[4] Harkabi, *Israel's Fateful Hour*, p. 159. A review of Zionism's relations with
Christians is in Nakhleh, *Encyclopedia of the Palestine Problem*, pp. 395-412.

[5] Harkabi, *Israel's Fateful Hour*, p. 159.

[6] Palumbo, *The Palestinian Catastrophe*, p. 91.

[7] Associated Press, *New York Times*, 6/1/48.

[8] Text of the lengthy statement is in Nakhleh, *Encyclopedia of the Palestine Problem*, pp. 396-8. Nakhleh contains a chronology of Israeli attacks against
Christian institutions up to 1989, pp. 396-412.

[9] James L. Kelso, letter, *Christianity Today*, 7/21/67, cited in Nakhleh, *Encyclopedia of the Palestine Problem*, p. 400.

[10] The Reverend S.J. Mattar, the warden of the Garden Tomb in Jerusalem,
was shot dead by Israeli soldiers at his home on June 6 without apparent cause.

[11] Nakhleh, *Encyclopedia of the Palestine Problem*, pp. 399-400.

[12]*Washington Times*, 5/24/95. The story was not carried by either *The Washington Post* or *The New York Times*.

[13]W. Granger Blair, *New York Times*, 9/11/63.

[14]*New York Times*, 10/1/63.

[15]W. Granger Blair, *New York Times*, 9/11/63.

[16]*New York Times*, 3/27/64.

[17]*Washington Post*, 10/9/82.

[18]*Baptist Church News*, 6/13/85, cited in Nakhleh, *Encyclopedia of the Palestine Problem*, pp. 409-10.

[19]*Jerusalem Post*, 12/27/83, cited in Nakhleh, *Encyclopedia of the Palestine Problem*, p. 406.

[20]*New York Times*, 1/15/84.

[21]Text in *Journal of Palestine Studies*, Spring 1991, p. 139.

[22]Serge Schmemann, *New York Times*, 12/31/95.

[23]*New York Times*, 8/12/48.

[24]Serge Shmemann, *New York Times*, 12/31/95.

Chapter 33

1983: Israel's Likud Prime Ministers

ON OCT. 10, 1983, former pre-state terrorist Yitzhak Shamir became Israel's new prime minister, making him the second leader from the nationalist Likud party to rule the Jewish state.[1] At the time Shamir was 67, a dedicated member of the Likud who in his inaugural speech vowed to continue the "holy work" of establishing settlements on Palestinian land in the territories occupied by Israeli forces since 1967.[2] He was as good as his word, as had been the Likud party's first prime minister, Menachem Begin, and as its third and latest prime minister, Binyamin Netanyahu, who came to power in 1996.

The right of settlement is a core belief of the revisionist Zionist Likud, and both Begin and Shamir were passionate in their efforts to establish and expand Jewish settlements in the occupied territories.

When Begin came to power in 1977, there were about 50,000 Jews living in Arab East Jerusalem and about 7,000 in 45 settlements in the West Bank and in an additional 45 Jewish settlements in the Gaza Strip and Golan Heights.[3] When Begin left office six years later, there were close to 200 settlements in all the occupied territories, with about 22,000 Jewish settlers in the territories and 100,000 in Arab East Jerusalem. Under Begin, the pattern of settlements essentially established the central points for Jewish settlement throughout the territories.

Shamir's contribution over the next decade was to substantially thicken and expand the carefully laid out settlements.[4] When Shamir finally left office in mid-1992, there were some 245,000 Jews in some 250 settlements, including Arab East Jerusalem.[5]

The ambitious settlement programs of Begin and Shamir stemmed from the belief that Jews have a God-given right to Eretz Yisrael, all of the Land of Israel ruled by ancient Israelites. That claim is central to the Likud manifesto, which unequivocally states: "The right of the Jewish people to Eretz Yisrael is eternal and indisputable, and linked to our right to security and peace. The State of Israel has a right and a claim to sovereignty over Judea, Samaria, and the Gaza Strip. In time, Israel will invoke this claim and strive to realize it. Any plan involving the hand-over of parts of western Eretz Yisrael to foreign rule, as proposed by the Labor Alignment, denies our right to this country."[6]

The reference to "western Eretz Yisrael" is to Palestine. Begin and Shamir were both firm believers that the rest of Eretz Yisrael lay to the east—modern-day Jordan. Like all Likudniks, Netanyahu most likely also believes that, although he has been diplomatically silent on the subject.

While Begin was no slouch in invoking the right of settlement, Shamir brought a new level of arrogance to it in his public declarations asserting the Jews' birthright to Eretz Yisrael. He became notorious for his repeated declaration that "for the sake of the Land of Israel it's all right to lie." His critics say he followed his own advice with a vengeance.[7]

Shamir's passion about the settlement issue became particularly intense in the first half of 1992 when he faced June elections and, at the same time, a concerted effort by President George Bush to link the granting of $10 billion in U.S. loan guarantees to a halt to Israel's establishment of new settlements. In defiance of Bush, Shamir on Jan. 20, 1992, launched his re-election campaign in the settlement of Betar Illit on the occupied West Bank. He told the Jewish settlers: "No force in the world will stop this construction. We say to ourselves, and to the Gentiles of the world and to the next generations, here will be our homeland, here will be our home, forever and ever."[8]

It was reported President Bush "went ballistic" when he heard of Shamir's remarks. No public comment was made by the White House, but clearly the battle had been joined by Shamir and Bush.[9] The bitterness of the fight over the next six months was eventually to contribute to Shamir's loss of the election.

On Jan. 26, Shamir returned to the settlement theme in a speech to Jewish journalists in Jerusalem. Though he had been speaking in Hebrew, he switched to English when he said: "To avoid any misunderstandings, Israel and all those people who represent Israel are not talking or not speaking about any freeze of settlements. Please forget about it."[10] On Feb. 13, Shamir said: "Even an implicit understanding that there be no housing starts is out of the question. Anything that can be perceived as a freeze is something that this government cannot live with."[11]

When the State Department announced on May 12 that the United States continued to support United Nations General Assembly Resolution 194 of 1948, which called for the return or compensation for the nearly three-quarters of a million Palestinians driven from their homes in the 1948 war, Shamir responded in public, defiantly declaring: "It will never happen in any way, shape or form. There is only a Jewish right of return to the land of Israel."[12] A week later Shamir earmarked $470 million for new development, including $40 million for industrial development in the territories and $430 million for new housing, with 10,000 of the 17,000 new units in the territories.

During the election campaign Shamir openly spelled out the underlying reason why settlements were necessary. It was, he explained, aimed at preventing a territorial compromise with the Palestinians. This was to be accomplished by having so many settlers live in the territories that "the dream of territorial compromise will disappear, like a dream," Shamir said.[13]

It was this strategy that explains Shamir's and Likud's intense insistence that Jews have a right and a duty to settle the occupied territories. Shamir and his Likud colleagues hope that at some point the number of Jewish settlers will become so great that no government would be strong enough to dislodge them. That in turn explains why Likud governments have traditionally been so careful to stretch out any talks about peace. As Shamir himself admitted after his defeat by Yitzhak Rabin on June 23, 1992: "I would have conducted [peace] negotiations for 10 years, and in the meantime we would have reached half a million souls in Judea and Samaria [the West Bank]....Without such a basis there would be nothing to stop the establishment of a Palestinian state."[14]

Thus when the new Likud prime minister, Binyamin Netanyahu, insists that peace talks "have to advance very slowly" and at the same time insists that Jews have a right to settle anywhere in the occupied territories,[15] he is doing more than merely repeating old Likud campaign slogans. He is saying that he, like his Likud predecessors, wants enough time to move so many Jews onto Palestinian land that there will be no future possibility for the Palestinians to establish their own state. ❧

RECOMMENDED READING:

Bell, J. Bowyer, *Terror Out of Zion*, New York, St. Martin's Press, 1977.

Bethell, Nicholas, *The Palestine Triangle: The Struggle for the Holy Land, 1935-48*, New York, G.P. Putnam's Sons, 1979.

Brenner, Lenni, *The Iron Wall: Zionist Revisionism from Jabotinsky to Shamir*, London, Zed Books Ltd., 1984.

Frank, Gerald, *The Deed*, New York, Simon and Schuster, 1963.

Marton, Kati, *A Death in Jerusalem*, New York, Pantheon Books, 1994.

Quigley, John, *Palestine and Israel: A Challenge to Justice*, Durham, Duke University Press, 1990.

Sprinzak, Ehud, *The Ascendance of Israel's Radical Right*, New York, Oxford University Press, 1991.

NOTES:

[1]An interesting probe into the beliefs of the Stern Gang, of which Shamir was a leader, and of Shamir's character is in Israel Shahak's "Yitzhak Shamir, Then and Now," *Middle East Policy*, Vol. 1, No. 1, 1992. Shahak recalls the assassination of Lehi commander Eliyahu Giladi on Shamir's orders, and concludes that Shamir should be "perceived as an individual ready to murder his closest friends without any residual misgivings," p. 38. Shamir's direct involvement in the 1948 assassination of Count Bernadotte and his early career are detailed in Marton, *A Death in Jerusalem*. For a profile of Shamir's governing style, see Glenn Frankel, *Washington Post*, 10/16/88. A good study of Shamir's beliefs is in Avishai Margalit, "The Violent Life of Yitzhak Shamir," *The New York Review of Books*, 5/14/92. A general profile of Shamir can be found in Sol Stern & Louis Rappoport, "Israel's Man of the Shadows," *The Village Voice*, 7/3/84, while his early career is detailed in Gerald Frank's *The Deed*. A sympathetic profile by one of his aides is given in a story by Sarah Honig, *Jerusalem Post* International Edition, 1/6/90. Also see Mark Tessler, "The

Political Right in Israel: Its Origins, Growth, and Prospects," *Journal of Palestine Studies*, Winter 1986, pp. 12-55.

2Quigley, *Palestine and Israel*, p. 176.

3Foundation for Middle East Peace, *Report on Israeli Settlement in the Occupied Territories*, Special Report, July, 1991 (Washington, DC); Aronson, "Creating Facts."

4Author interview with Geoffrey Aronson, 1/24/94.

5Associated Press, *Washington Times*, 5/9/92.

6Elfi Pallis, "The Likud Party: A Primer," *Journal of Palestine Studies*, Winter 1992, pp. 42-43.

7Avishai Margalit, "The Violent Life of Yitzhak Shamir, *The New York Review of Books*, 5/14/92.

8Clyde Haberman, *New York Times*, 1/21/92.

9Rowland Evans and Robert Novak, *Washington Post*, 1/24/92.

10*New York Times*, 1/27/92.

11Clyde Haberman, *New York Times*, 2/14/92.

12Clyde Haberman, *New York Times*, 5/15/92.

13Jackson Diehl, *Washington Post*, 5/28/92.

14Clyde Haberman, *New York Times*, 6/27/92; David Hoffman, *Washington Post*, 6/27/92.

15Edward Cody, *Washington Post*, 6/26/96.

Chapter 34

1984: Israeli Commission: Occupation Unjust

ON FEB. 9, 1984, a report prepared by a special commission appointed by the Israeli attorney general was released deploring violence by Jewish settlers against Palestinians living under occupation. To the outrage of many Israeli government officials, the report added that Israeli occupation troops and Jewish settlers were engaged in a massive miscarriage of justice against Palestinians.

Known as the Karp Report after commission chairman Deputy Attorney General Yehudit Karp, the report declared that the Israeli administration of justice in the occupied territories was in need of "a radical reform of the basic concept of the rule of law in its broadest and most profound sense."[1]

The report found that Jewish settlers were regularly protected by the army and seldom arrested for offenses ranging from shootings to massive destruction of property against Palestinian residents in the occupied territories. In essence, the report found that settlers considered themselves above the law and refused to cooperate with Israeli police investigating Palestinian complaints. The report commented:

"Israeli residents of the territories are given to understand that they are soldiers to all intents and purposes...Israeli residents of Judea and Samaria, explicitly relying on this assurance, refuse to cooperate with the police or provide information; they reject any contact with the police, basing themselves on 'high-level policy' and declaring that they are under no obligation to cooperate in this matter."[2]

Particularly cited in the report were the radical settlers living in Kiryat Arba and the adjoining Palestinian city of Hebron. The report said the settlers' refusal to cooperate with civilian police was "tantamount to civil rebellion."[3]

The report was considered so critical of Israel's occupation policies that the government kept it secret after its initial submission on May 25, 1982, meanwhile charging that it was unfair and misleading. But public pressure and Karp's resignation from the commission in protest of the suppression of the report finally caused release of a censored version 20 months later. The full report has never been released.

Still, on the basis of the censored report, the *Jerusalem Post* editorialized:

"The Karp Report bears out the initial suspicion that a systematic miscarriage of justice is being perpetrated in the West Bank. Jewish settlers, wishing to assert their rights to the area, take the law into their own hands and refuse…to cooperate in police investigations…The police, deferring to the army, fail to stand on their own rights, and the army tends to look benignly on those it views as its soldiers. The result…is that files are closed without anyone being booked."[4]

Although Israeli officials roundly condemned the report as exaggerated, its essential charge that settlers were taking the law in their own hands and were being protected by occupation authorities was dramatically confirmed a decade later. In the aftermath of the 1994 massacre of 29 Palestinian worshippers in Hebron's Ibrahimi mosque by Jewish settler Dr. Baruch Goldstein, Israeli police and troops openly admitted that there were different laws for Jews and Palestinians.

Chief Inspector Meir Tayar of the border police stationed in Hebron testified before a special commission investigating the Feb. 25 massacre that troops had standing orders never to shoot at Jewish settlers even if the settlers were shooting at Palestinians. Tayar said of the massacre: "Even if I had been there I would not have been able to do a thing because there were special instructions regarding this. The open-fire orders were that if a settler in Hebron fires purposefully, under no circumstances should he be shot at." He added that the order applied even if the settler was shooting at Israeli troops, saying: "The order, as I interpret it, is to take cover so as not to be hit, wait until the gun jams or the clip is empty and try to overpower him with other means."[5]

Similar revelations had been made several months earlier by reserve paratrooper Amit Gurevitz. But, like the Karp Report itself, they were ignored by the government. Gurevitz revealed in a newspaper interview that the beating of Palestinians, vandalizing their property or otherwise humiliating them in front of soldiers was not cause for arrest.[6]

In January, 1994, the Hebrew daily *Ha'aretz* reported a radio broadcast in which an Israeli officer identified as Colonel Y said that the standing orders of the army in the occupied territories were "never, under any circumstances, and in no case whatsoever, to shoot at any Jew." The author of the article, correspondent Amnon Denkner, commented that "when an Arab is thought to be a danger to the life of a Jew, there is no problem. Just kill him and feel good."[7]

On March 15, 1994, the Israeli human rights group B'Tselem reported that the Israeli army, police and courts failed to enforce the law against Jewish settlers who killed Palestinians. The report said 62 Palestinians had been killed by settlers between 1988 and 1993. During the same period, 1,145 Palestinians were killed by Israeli security forces, compared to 117 Israeli civilians and 64 security personnel killed by Palestinians.

The B'Tselem report said a study of 48 cases in which Palestinians were killed by settlers showed that Israeli authorities "apply an unstated policy of tolerance, compromise and failure in bringing about full justice" against settlers. In the cases studied, only 13 settlers were brought to trial. Only one was convicted of murder, one of manslaughter, six of causing death by negligence and two of shooting in a residential area. Another 27 cases were closed without prosecution. The report said: "In many cases...no investigation at all is carried out...Israeli authorities have failed in the task of protecting the life, person and property of the Palestinians."[8]

Said B'Tselem researcher Eitan Feiner: "A settler can act with virtual impunity in committing violent acts against Palestinians."[9] Thus, 11 years after the Karp Report, the same abuses, the same favoritism toward settlers and the same violations of law were still endemic in the occupied territories. Things had not changed in 1998. ✇

RECOMMENDED READING:

Amnesty International, *Amnesty Report: 1988*, p. 239

Cohen, Stanley, "Talking About Torture in Israel," *Tikkun*, November/ December, 1992.

*Findley, Paul, *Deliberate Deceptions: Facing the Facts about the U.S.-Israeli Relationship*, Brooklyn, NY, Lawrence Hill Books, 1993.

Karp, Yehudit, *The Karp Report: Investigation of Suspicions Against Israelis in Judea and Samaria*, Jerusalem, Israeli Government, 1984, reprinted by the Institute for Palestine Studies, Washington, DC, 1984.

*Shahak, Israel, "Israel's State-Assisted Terrorism: 'Settlers' as Armed Combatants," *Washington Report on Middle East Affairs*, February/March, 1994.

*Sprinzak, Ehud, *The Ascendance of Israel's Radical Right*, New York, Oxford University Press, 1991.

U.S. Department of State, *Country Reports on Human Rights Practices for 1993*, Washington, DC, Government Printing Office, February, 1994.

*Available through the AET Book Club.

NOTES:

[1] Karp, *The Karp Report*, p. 49. Also see Sprinzak, *The Ascendancy of Israel's Radical Right*, pp. 87-88.

[2] *The Karp Report*, p. 41.

[3] *Ibid.*, p. 46.

[4] *Jerusalem Post*, 2/9/84, quoted on the back page of *The Karp Report* printed by the Institute of Palestine Studies.

[5] Joel Greenberg, *New York Times*, 3/11/94.

[6] Amit Gurevitz, Haolam Haze, 11/17/93, quoted in Israel Shahak, "Israel's State-Assisted Terrorism: 'Settlers' as Armed Combatants," *Washington Report on Middle East Affairs*, February/March, 1994.

[7] Amnon Denkner, *Ha'aretz*, 1/9/94, quoted in Israel Shahak, "Israel's State-Assisted Terrorism: 'Settlers' as Armed Combatants," *Washington Report on Middle East Affairs*, February/March, 1994.

[8] David Hoffman, *Washington Post*, 3/15/94.

[9] Joel Greenberg, *New York Times*, 3/15/94.

Chapter 35

1987 : The Palestinian Intifada Erupts

O N DEC. 9, 1987, the Palestinian intifada, the uprising, erupted in the territories occupied by Israel. The violence was the worst since the fighting of 1948. But in this case the Palestinians had no arms and no help from the neighboring Arab countries.[1] The uprising would continue until late 1993, with great suffering by the Palestinians and considerable damage to Israel's international image. In the end, the Palestinians gained the recognition of the world community they had so long sought, but failed to get Israel to live up to its commitments.

The immediate cause of the uprising came on Dec. 8, when an Israeli army truck ran into a group of Palestinians near the Jabalya refugee camp in the Gaza Strip, killing four and injuring seven. A Jewish salesman had been stabbed to death in Gaza two days earlier and there were suspicions among the Arabs that the traffic collision had not been an accident.[2] The day after the traffic deaths, Palestinians throughout the territories exploded with pent-up rage.

Observers speculated that Palestinian rioters were motivated in part by a dramatic event of the previous month: the daring attack on a northern Israel army base by a solo Palestinian hang-glider, who killed six Israeli soldiers and wounded seven others.[3] Another factor fanning Palestinian passions had been a recent increase in pressure by Jewish militants to take over Islam's third holiest site, the Haram Al-Sharif, the revered Temple Mount to Jews, in Arab East Jerusalem.[4]

Daily, the riots escalated throughout the territories, and were particularly severe in the Gaza Strip, a 5-by-28-mile area packed with about 550,000 people, mostly refugees. By Dec. 16, Gaza director

Bernard Mills of the United Nations Relief and Works Agency (UNRWA) said: "We're in a situation of either total lawlessness or a popular uprising."[5]

There soon could be no doubt that what was happening was a national uprising against a colonial power that had been subjugating Palestinians by military occupation since 1967.

Palestinian outrage was inflamed on Dec. 18 when Israeli troops killed two and wounded 20 Muslims leaving Friday religious services, then invaded the Shifa Hospital in Gaza and beat doctors and nurses and dragged off wounded Palestinians.[6] Casualties quickly mounted as Israeli troops responded to stone-throwing Palestinians with live ammunition. By Dec. 21, Israel was reporting a total of 15 killed and 70 wounded, while U.N. officials counted 17 killed and Palestinian sources reported 20 killed and 200 wounded.[7]

The televised beatings and killings of unarmed Palestinians by Israeli troops heavily equipped with U.S. weapons brought protests worldwide. The American Friends Service Committee on Dec. 21 deplored Israel's continued occupation and brutal suppression of the uprising. The Quaker statement also criticized Washington's "continued support of a policy that has acquiesced in occupation and failed to engage in a serious peace process."[8]

The next day the U.N. Security Council voted 14-0-1 to "strongly deplore [Israel's] policies and practices which violate the human rights of the Palestinian people in the occupied territories." The United States was the lone abstainer.[9] It was the 58th time the Security Council had passed a resolution critical of Israel since 1948.

The U.N. action brought immediate criticism from Israel's U.S. supporters. Republican Representative Jack F. Kemp of New York, a presidential candidate, said the U.N. was "picking on Israel."[10] Jewish-American leaders denounced the vote, calling it, in the words of Rabbi Alexander Schindler, president of the Union of American Hebrew Congregations, an action that "will be seen by the Palestinians as a license for further violence."[11]

Nonetheless, the emotional impact of Israel's violent suppression of the Palestinians caused the Reagan administration, on the same day that it abstained in the Security Council, to scold Israel for its "harsh security measures and excessive use of live ammunition."[12] The next day Washington urged Israel to use nonlethal riot control methods.[13] (On Dec. 24, leaders of some two dozen American-Jewish organizations went to the State Department to complain that the administration's criticism was unfair.[14])

Despite the White House criticism, Congress on Dec. 22 passed provisions that expanded U.S. aid to Israel by agreeing to refinance Israel's $9 billion debt to reduce its interest rates. The measure saved Israel as much as $2 billion in interest payments.[15] In addition, Israel was granted its traditional $3 billion in economic and military aid, allowed to use $150 million of its military aid on an advanced aircraft research and development program in the United States and to use another $400 million of its military aid for defense procurement in Israel. Israel also received an additional $5 million for U.S.-Israel cooperative aid and $25 million for refugee resettlement.[16]

It was as though Congress was rewarding Israel for its cruel treatment of the Palestinians. That apparently was how Israel's Likud government saw it. Its response to international criticism was to impose a new "iron fist" policy on Dec. 23. This meant manhandling and arresting Palestinians en masse.

Defense Minister Yitzhak Rabin said: "We will fight with all our power against any element that tries by violence to upset our full control over Judea, Samaria and the Gaza Strip. I know the descriptions of what is going on in the territories, the way it is interpreted in the media, is not helping the image of Israel in the world. But I am convinced that above and beyond the temporary problem of an image, the supreme responsibility of our government is to fight the violence in the territories and to use all the means at our disposal to do that. We will do that, and we will succeed."[17]

In defense of the army's use of marksmen and high-powered sniping rifles against rioters, Rabin added: "They can shoot to hit leaders of disorder, throwers of firebombs, as much as possible at the legs after firing in the air fails to disperse the riot."[18] U.S. officials urged Israel not to carry out its threat to expel ringleaders, but Prime Minister Yitzhak Shamir said with sarcasm: "We thank them for their advice but we shall act according to our own understanding."[19]

Under the tougher new policy, Israeli troops broke into homes, smashed furniture, hit women with rifle butts and dragged off suspects. Palestinian sources reported 350 arrested during the first day of the "Iron Fist" policy. Deaths were reported at 21 as of Dec. 23.[20] On Dec. 25, Israel admitted that nearly 1,000 Palestinians had been arrested, most of them in the previous three days. The Palestine Press Service put the number at more than 2,000 since Dec. 9. Casualties were placed at 21 dead and more than 150 wounded.[21]

Amnesty International's annual report for 1987 criticized Israel for using brutal methods to suppress the Palestinian uprising. It reported: "In December at least 23 Palestinian demonstrators in the West Bank and Gaza were shot and killed by soldiers during the widespread violent protests against Israeli occupation. There were also severe and indiscriminate beatings of demonstrators, and hundreds were summarily tried and imprisoned. There was an increase in reports of ill-treatment and torture of detainees by members of the Israel Defense Force and the General Security Service. Political activists, including prisoners of conscience, continued to be administratively detained or restricted to towns or villages or imprisoned in violation of their right to freedom of expression."[22]

Despite such criticism, Israeli Defense Minister Rabin on Jan. 19 announced a new policy of "broken bones." He said Israel would use "force, power and blows" to suppress the Palestinian intifada.[23] He added: "The goal is to act against violence with punches and blows and not live ammunition."[24]

Prime Minister Yitzhak Shamir, an old terrorist from the pre-Israel days, later said: "Our task now is to re-create the barrier of fear between Palestinians and the Israeli military, and once again put the fear of death into the Arabs of the areas so as to deter them from attacking us anymore."[25]

Israeli troops certainly tried to achieve that goal. Israeli press accounts said 197 Palestinians had been treated in the Gaza Strip for fractures as a result of beatings in the three days following Rabin's announcement. *The New York Times* added that the toll in all of the occupied areas "clearly runs well into the hundreds and perhaps higher."[26]

An UNRWA official in the Gaza Strip, acting director Angela Williams, said: "We are deeply shocked by the evidence of the brutality with which people are evidently being beaten. We are especially shocked by the beatings of old men and women."[27] The State Department said on Jan. 21 that it was "disturbed" by the new policy.[28]

Such complaints had no outward effect on Israel. It continued its brutal tactics, often caught in the glare of world television. In turn, however, the Palestinians, the "children of the stones," as they became called, continued their struggle, no doubt encouraged by the TV coverage. The fact is Israel was receiving influential advice to continue its cruel suppression. *The New York Times* reported that Henry A. Kissinger, the former U.S. secretary of state, had urged at a small private meeting of Jewish leaders in early February that Israel bar newsmen from the occupied territories and use force to end the uprising quickly.[29]

Kissinger recommended that Israel put down the Palestinian uprising "as quickly as possible—overwhelmingly, brutally and rapidly. The insurrection must be quelled immediately, and the first step should be to throw out television, à la South Africa. To be sure, there will be international criticism of the step, but it will dissipate in short order." He added: "There are no awards for losing with moderation." Kissinger's remarks were contained in a three-page, single-spaced memorandum of the meeting made by one of the participants, Julius Berman, former head of the Conference of Presidents of Major American Jewish Organizations. Kissinger later denied he made the remarks, saying they were a "gross distortion of the truth."[30]

Despite Israel's cruel tactics, the intifada went on month after month, year after year, unarmed youngsters against heavily equipped Israeli troops. Despite Israel's superior power, the unequal struggle was debilitating for the Jewish state, and especially its image abroad. The little country that so long had presented itself as a "light unto other nations" and pleaded for international support because of its small population was now seen as the cruel suppressor of another people.

Behind the scenes, Israel under a Labor government secretly sought a way out of its image-destroying predicament. At the start of 1993, without informing Washington, Israel and the Palestinians began meeting secretly in Oslo, with Norway acting as the mediator. By late August, 1993 the two sides had come to an agreement and the Clinton administration was finally informed.[31]

Two weeks later, on Sept. 13, amid great ceremony on the South Lawn of the White House, Israel and the Palestine Liberation Organization signed the Declaration of Principles on Interim Self-

Government Arrangements, generally referred to as the Oslo accords. Its aim was to "establish a Palestinian Interim Self-Government Authority...for the Palestinian people in the West Bank and the Gaza Strip, for a transitional period not exceeding five years, leading to a permanent settlement based on Security Council Resolutions 242 and 338."[32]

The signing of the Oslo accords was an enormously celebratory moment. There were euphoric, indeed unrealistic, expectations of peace in the Middle East. This became clear when Israel in mid-1996 returned to another Likud leader, Binyamin Netanyahu. Like his predecessors, Menachem Begin and Yitzhak Shamir, Netanyahu displayed the arrogant disregard of Palestinian rights that brought on the intifada in the first place. The Oslo accords basically died with Netanyahu's election.

But before then, during the initial enthusiasm for Oslo, with all its shining promises, the intifada essentially ended. Cost of the uprising to the Palestinians had been heavy. The Palestine Human Rights Information group reported at the end of 1993 that since the start of the intifada Israeli troops and settlers had killed 1,283 Palestinians. An estimated 130,472 Palestinians had been injured, 481 expelled, 22,088 held without trial, 2,533 houses demolished or sealed and, equally important for the eventual division of the land, 184,257 Palestinian trees uprooted.[33]

All told during the six-year uprising, 120,000 Palestinians were arrested and spent varying amounts of time in inhospitable Israeli jails.[34] It is these veterans who will likely form the cadre for the next generation of Palestinian freedom fighters if the two sides cannot find an accommodation soon. ❧

RECOMMENDED READING:

Nakhleh, Issa. *Encyclopedia of the Palestine Problem* (2 vols), New York, Intercontinental Books, 1991.

Roy, Sara, *The Gaza Strip: The Political Economy of De-development*, Washington, DC, Institute for Palestine Studies, 1995.

Michael Simpson, George J. Tomeh and Regina S. Sherif (eds.), *United Nations Resolutions on Palestine and the Arab-Israeli Conflict*, three volumes, Washington, DC, Institute for Palestine Studies, 1988.

NOTES:

[1] Glenn Frankel, *Washington Post*, 12/12/87. Also see Roy, *The Gaza Strip*, S.K.L., "The Gaza Strip," *I&P, Israel & Palestine Political Report*, No. 139, 1/88, pp. 4-5; Ann M. Lesch, "Prelude to the Uprising in the Gaza Strip," *Journal of Palestine Studies*, "Documents and Source Material," Autumn 1990, pp. 1-23; Nakhleh, *Encyclopedia of the Palestine Problem*, pp. 735-88.

[2] John Kifner, *New York Times*, 12/15/87.

[3] Glenn Frankel, *Washington Post*, 11/27/87.

[4] Stephen J. Sosebee, "Seeds of a Massacre: Israeli Violations at Haram al-Sharif," *American-Arab Affairs*, No. 36, Spring 1991, p. 114.

[5] John Kifner, *New York Times*, 12/16/87.

[6] Patrick J. Tyler, *Washington Post*, 12/19/87.

[7] Dan Fisher, *Washington Post*, 12/21/87.

[8] The text is in the *Journal of Palestine Studies*, "Documents and Source Material," Spring 1988, pp. 201-2.

[9] *New York Times*, 12/23/87, Resolution No. 605. For earlier abstentions see entries above and Michael Simpson, George J. Tomeh and Regina S. Sherif (eds.). *United Nations Resolutions on Palestine and the Arab-Israeli Conflict*, three volumes, Washington, DC, Institute for Palestine Studies, 1988.

[10] David E. Rosenbaum, *New York Times*, 12/31/87.

[11] *New York Times*, 1/18/88.

[12] *New York Times*, 12/23/87.

[13] *New York Times*, 12/24/87.

[14] *New York Times*, 12/25/87.

[15] David K. Shipler, *New York Times*, 12/24/87. Also see Clyde Mark, "Israel: U.S. Foreign Assistance Facts," Foreign Affairs and National Defense Division, Congressional Research Service, updated 7/5/91.

[16] Clyde Mark, "Israel: U.S. Foreign Assistance Facts," Foreign Affairs and National Defense Division, Congressional Research Service, updated 7/5/91.

[17] John Kifner, *New York Times*, 12/24/87. Thomas L. Friedman, *New York Times*, 12/25/87 and 12/31/87, had particularly insightful pieces on how Israel regarded the riots as a public relations problem and how the Palestinians failed to offer a political solution.

[18] Glenn Frankel, *Washington Post*, 12/24/87.

[19]Juan O. Tamayo, *Washington Post,* 12/30/87.

[20]Glenn Frankel, *Washington Post,* 12/22-23/87; Frankel's reporting from Gaza was particularly descriptive.

[21]Thomas L. Friedman, *New York Times,* 12/26/87; Glenn Frankel, *Washington Post,* 12/26/87.

[22]Amnesty International, *Amnesty Report: 1988,* p. 239.

[23]John Kifner, *New York Times,* 1/20/88; 1/21/88; Glenn Frankel, *Washington Post,* 1/23/88.

[24]Jonathan C. Randal, *Washington Post,* 1/21/88.

[25]*Time,* 2/8/88, p. 39.

[26]John Kifner, *New York Times,* 1/23/88.

[27]*Ibid.*

[28]Chronology 1988, "America and the World 1988/89," *Foreign Affairs,* Vol. 68, No. 1, Winter 1989, p. 233.

[29]Robert D. McFadden, *New York Times,* 3/5/88. A copy of the memo was obtained and circulated among the membership by the American-Arab Anti-Discrimination Committee of Washington, DC. The text is in *American-Arab Affairs,* No. 24, Spring 1988, pp. 158-61, and *Journal of Palestine Studies,* Summer 1988, pp. 184-7.

[30]Barbara Vobejda, *Washington Post,* 3/6/88.

[31]Clyde Haberman, *New York Times,* 8/29/93.

[32]The text is in *New York Times,* 9/1/93; "Documentation," *Middle East Policy,* Number 2, Volume II, 1993. For an analysis, see Burhan Dajani, "The September, 1993 Israeli-PLO Documents: A Textural Analysis," *Journal of Palestine Studies,* Spring 1994.

[33]Palestine Human Rights Information of Jerusalem and Washington, "Living Under Israeli Occupation," *Washington Report on Middle East Affairs,* April/May, 1994.

[34]Barton Gellman, *Washington Post,* 10/3/95.

Chapter 36

1990: The Struggle for Jerusalem

ON OCT. 8, 1990, Israeli police killed 17 and wounded more than 150 Palestinian worshippers within the Muslim sanctuary known as the Haram Al-Sharif—which Jews call the Temple Mount—in the Old City of Jerusalem. There, amid the golden Dome of the Rock and Al Aqsa mosque, the third holiest shrine in Islam, Israeli police fired into a crowd of 3,000 worshippers to stop what they claimed were attacks on Jews. Police said they opened fire to prevent Muslims from throwing stones down on Jews worshipping in the plaza below at the Western (Wailing) Wall, the remnant of the ancient Jewish temple sacred to Judaism. The police reported that 11 Jews were hurt by rocks.[1]

Early media reports all reflected the version of events reported by Israeli police. But later investigation told a different story. There had been no injury-causing attacks on Jewish worshippers; no Jewish victims could be found. Nor had there been a premeditated plot by Palestinians to start a riot.

Instead, the melee was touched off when reports spread that radical Zionists were planning to lay the cornerstone of a new Jewish temple on the sanctuary plateau to replace the Muslim mosques. The tense atmosphere became charged when hundreds of Palestinians rushed to the site in response to an appeal by the Islamic Mufti of Jerusalem, Sheikh Saad El Dine Alami, for Muslims "to defend the mosque."

The Palestinians' nervousness was well founded. The day marked the Jewish holiday of Succot, the Feast of the Tabernacles. For the past several years, members of the extremist group Temple Mount Faithful had used the holiday to try to place a three-ton cornerstone on the mount as the foundation of a proposed Third Temple. In their fervor to restore the temple, the Temple Mount Faithful were determined to rid the sanctuary of Muslims.

Unknown to the Palestinians was the fact that police had obtained a court order preventing the Temple Mount Faithful from trying to lay the cornerstone that year. But the group had vowed its members would visit the site anyway, causing the Muslims to believe another attempt was being made to desecrate their mosques.[2]

Although Israeli police placed the blame for the resulting bloodshed on Palestinian provocations, an investigation by Mike Wallace of the CBS-TV news show "60 Minutes" told a different story. He determined that 11 of the 17 Palestinians slain had been struck by bullets in the head or neck, despite police claims that orders had been issued to fire at legs. Film showed that Israeli police fired at Palestinian ambulances seeking to aid the wounded. Wallace also asserted that, contrary to Israeli claims that Muslim leaders had urged the Palestinians to fight against the police, the reality was that the Palestinians were implored to seek safety inside mosques. Police fired inside at least one mosque.[3]

Major inquiries by both The New York Times and The Washington Post also concluded that the events were not premeditated nor ordered by outside groups, as claimed by Israeli police.[4]

The New York Times reported that "it was a spontaneous result of developments that day, particularly the threats by a group of Jews called the Temple Mount Faithful to march on Al Aqsa plaza that morning."[5]

Israel appointed a three-man commission to study causes of the massacre but it had no subpoena power. The commission released its report on Oct. 26, absolving police of the use of deadly force. However, it blamed senior police officials for not acting on information that there was likely to be a demonstration. The report found that police opened fire long after Jewish worshippers at the base of the Temple Mount had fled from stoning by Palestinians, but said the police acted because they feared for their lives.[6] Despite criticism of police leaders in the government report, the officer in charge of the Jerusalem police district, Deputy Police Commander Aryeh Bibi, was promoted the next month to full commander.[7]

It was not until July the next year that the full story emerged. Israeli Judge Ezra Kama concluded a nine-month judicial inquiry by charging that Israeli police had provoked the violence, that the deaths were unjustified, and that police claims that they had opened fire because they feared for their lives were "exaggerated and strange." Nonetheless, he ruled no charges should be brought against any policeman because it was impossible to determine which one had fired first.[8]

The Israeli government of Yitzhak Shamir displayed no remorse over the massacre. But it did not hesitate to show its displeasure at the U.S. administration of President George Bush when, the day after the massacre, it introduced a resolution before the U.N. Security Council condemning Israel. Israel's U.N. ambassador, Johanan Bein, said the draft resolution showed "again Israel is the sacrificial lamb," adding: "I think it will give the impression the Security Council stands behind those who instigated those disturbances, that is, the PLO and some other elements in Jerusalem who prepared this cold-bloodedly."[9]

However, President Bush openly criticized Israel, calling the deaths "this needless loss of life" and saying: "Israeli security forces need to be better prepared for such situations, need to act with greater restraint, particularly when it comes to the use of deadly force."[10]

On Oct. 12, the Council unanimously condemned Israel for "acts of violence" against Palestinians. The resolution called on Israel to "abide scrupulously" with the Fourth Geneva Convention and asked the secretary-general to send a mission to the region and report before the end of October on "his findings and conclusions."[11]

On Oct. 14, the Israeli cabinet unanimously rejected the resolution and said it would not cooperate with the U.N. mission. "We have read the Security Council's decision and it is completely unacceptable," said a cabinet statement. "As a result, Israel will not receive the delegation of the U.N. secretary-general." Foreign Minister David Levy said that "accepting the delegation" would also mean accepting that "Jerusalem is not our legal capital and questioning our sovereignty over it....Our relations with the United States are very important, but we should not accept and we should not ignore the sorrowful fact that the U.S. administration has made a mistake...."[12]

The cabinet statement added: "Jerusalem is not, in any part, 'occupied territory.' It is the sovereign capital of the State of Israel. Therefore there is no room for any involvement on the part of the United Nations in any matter relating to Jerusalem, just as the United Nations does not intervene in events, some even more severe, that occur in other countries."[13]

The Israeli statement came despite the fact that Secretary of State James Baker had sent a blunt letter to Israel on the morning of the cabinet meeting, urging Israel to cooperate with the U.N. mission.[14]

On the same day as the cabinet meeting, a cabinet committee headed by Housing Minister Ariel Sharon recommended that Israel build 15,000 new apartments for immigrants in Arab East Jerusalem. The move was seen as "a clear, defiant response" to the U.S. support for the U.N. resolution condemning Israel.[15]

In response to Israel's intransigence, President Bush said: "We want to see that U.N. resolution fully implemented. We are a part of it and we think it's the right step."[16] In Israel, Prime Minister Shamir's response was to open the autumn session of the parliament by criticizing the United States and the U.N. for "daring to presume that they could question anything Israel does in its capital."[17]

Given Israel's adamant opposition, U.N. Secretary-General Javier Perez de Cuellar announced on Oct. 19 that he would not send an investigative mission to Israel: "I cannot send a mission if I am not persuaded that the mission will get all the necessary facilities in order to complete their mission." In view of Perez de Cuellar's stand, Arab and nonaligned nations proposed a new resolution based on Article 25 of the Charter, which requires member countries to obey Security Council orders. The U.S. opposed the draft and it failed passage.[18]

Privately, President Bush pleaded with Shamir to accept a U.N. mission, but Shamir continued to refuse.[19] As a result, on Oct. 24 the Council unanimously passed Resolution 673 "deploring the refusal of the Israeli government" to accept a U.N. mission to investigate the Oct. 8 killing of 17 Palestinians in Jerusalem. The resolution urged Israel to reconsider its refusal and "insists that it comply fully with the October 12 resolution authorizing the mission."[20] Israel immediately rejected it.[21]

In the midst of all this wrangling, the U.S. Senate gave Israel every reason to believe it could thumb its nose at the White House and still retain access to America's Treasury. On Oct. 22, the Senate voted 97 to 1 (the only naysayer was Democrat Robert Byrd of West Virginia) to give Israel $700 million worth of used weapons being withdrawn from Europe. The new aid was on top of Israel's annual $3 billion aid package. The measure's sponsor, Democrat Daniel Inouye of Hawaii, one of Israel's most devoted friends in the Senate, said Israel deserved the aid because "it is the best ally we have."[22]

Thus the matter ended with Israel being portrayed as an ally although it had defied the U.S. and its president personally. Moreover, it had violated its pledge as a U.N. member to obey all resolutions by the Security Council. Nonetheless, the council took no further action, and the U.S. continued granting Israel unprecedented amounts of aid over the following years. ✒

RECOMMENDED READING:

Friedman, Robert I., *The False Prophet: Rabbi Meir Kahane*, Brooklyn, NY, Lawrence Hill Books, 1990.

*Friedman, Robert I., *Zealots for Zion: Inside Israel's West Bank Settlement Movement*, New York, Random House, 1992.

*Halsell, Grace, *Journey to Jerusalem*, New York, Macmillan Publishing Co., Inc., 1981.

*Halsell, Grace, *Prophecy and Politics: Militant Evangelists on the Road to Nuclear War*, Westport, CT, Lawrence Hill & Co., 1986.

*Sprinzak, Ehud, *The Ascendance of Israel's Radical Right*, New York, Oxford University Press, 1991.

Stephen J. Sosebee, "Seeds of a Massacre: Israeli Violations at Haram al-Sharif," *American-Arab Affairs*, No. 36, Spring 1991, pp. 116-7.

Journal of Palestine Studies, "Special File," Winter 1991, pp. 134-59.

*Available through the AET Book Club.

NOTES:

[1] Jackson Diehl, *Washington Post*, 10/14/90, and Stephen J. Sosebee, "Seeds of a Massacre: Israeli Violations at Haram al-Sharif," *American-Arab Affairs*, No. 36, Spring 1991, pp. 116-7. Texts of various reports and comments on the incident in *Journal of Palestine Studies*, "Special File," Winter 1991,

pp. 134-59.

[2]Jackson Diehl, *Washington Post*, 10/9/90. Also see Halsell, *Prophecy and Politics.*

[3]Mike Wallace, "60 Minutes," 12/2/90. Also see Grace Halsell, *Arab News,* 11/19/90, and Michael Emery, *Village Voice,* 11/13/90.

[4]See Jackson Diehl, *Washington Post,* 10/14/90, and Joel Brinkley, *New York Times,* 10/15/90.

[5]Joel Brinkley, *New York Times,* 10/12/90.

[6]Joel Brinkley, *New York Times,* 10/27/90. The same edition carries excerpts from the report. Major excerpts are in *Jerusalem Post International Edition,* 11/3/90.

[7]Joel Brinkley, *New York Times,* 11/13/90.

[8]Joel Brinkley, *New York Times,* 7/19/90.

[9]David Hoffman, *Washington Post,* 10/10/90.

[10]*Ibid.*

[11]Resolution 672; text in *New York Times,* 10/14/90.

[12]Jackson Diehl, *Washington Post,* 10/15/90.

[13]Joel Brinkley, *New York Times,* 10/16/90.

[14]Thomas L. Friedman, *New York Times,* 10/16/90.

[15]Joel Brinkley, *New York Times,* 10/16/90, and Jackson Diehl, *Washington Post,* 10/16/90.

[16]Thomas L. Friedman, *New York Times,* 10/16/90.

[17]Joel Brinkley, *New York Times,* 10/16/90.

[18]Paul Lewis, *New York Times,* 10/20/90.

[19]Paul Lewis, *New York Times,* 10/25/90, and Trevor Rowe, *Washington Post,* 10/25/90.

[20]Alan Cowell, *New York Times,* 10/25/90.

[21]Joel Brinkley, *New Tork Times,* 10/26/90; text in same edition.

[22]Associated Press, #V0161, 21:37 EDT, 10/22/90.

Chapter 37

1991 : Jews From Ethiopia Face Discrimination on Arrival in Israel

ON MAY 25, 1991, Israel airlifted the last 15,000 Jews from embattled Ethiopia and flew them to Israel in a daring emergency operation. The action, called Operation Solomon, lasted 36 hours and involved 35 cargo planes flying the 1,500-mile route to Israel with the black Jews, called Falashas in Ethiopia.[1] The rescue operation came as rebel forces were closing in on the capital of Addis Ababa amid frantic diplomatic efforts by Israel and the United States to have the tottering government grant permission for the Jews to leave. In the end, a $35 million bribe by Israel and direct pleas to Ethiopia by President George Bush secured their release.[2]

Prime Minister Yitzhak Shamir was on hand in Israel to greet the first of the arrivals in 1984, saying: "It's a great moment for all our people, all our country, for Jewish people all over the world. Now they are here and they are Israeli citizens, so no one will persecute them anymore."[3] Eleven years later the Falasha community rioted, charging that Israel systematically discriminated against them because they were black.

The odyssey of the Falashas is a tale of daring and social inequity in present-day Israel. It began in the mid-1980s and was not completed for six years.

An ancient tribe, the Falashas kept their Jewish faith over the millennia in isolation in Ethiopia. Their long history and unique form of Judaism gripped the imagination of some Israelis, casting the Falashas in a romantic and even mythic aura. Ethiopia had long served as a way station for covert Israeli activities in Africa and the Middle East. Moreover, its location was important to Israel because of Ethiopia's strategic position on the Horn of Africa at the narrow entrance to the Red Sea at Bab el Mandeb. Activities in Ethiopia were frequently coordinated between the United States and Israel. In addition, Israeli foreign policy for a time saw Ethiopia as a counterbalance on the African continent to Egypt.[4] Because of these strategic interests, Israeli officials traveled regularly to Ethiopia, where they became acquainted with the Falashas and their sufferings. Out of these meetings grew the ambitious idea to bring the entire impoverished community of around 30,000 to Israel. Adding urgency to the plan was the fact that by the 1980s Ethiopia was being torn apart by the Tigre rebellion. Thousands of Falashas were already refugees on the Sudanese border.

The original grandiose enterprise was appropriately named Operation Moses. Begun in deep secrecy in November, 1984, it lasted only to the first week of 1985 when an official of the Jewish Agency carelessly referred to it at a public meeting, much to the embarrassment of the governments of Ethiopia and Sudan. Both governments were so weak that to be seen as favoring one ethnic group over another was a threat to their hold on power. The flights were halted immediately.

About 10,000 Ethiopian Jews had been transported to Israel. But there were still some 20,000 left in Ethiopia and Sudan. Israel called on the United States for help. Under the personal intervention of Vice President George Bush, 1,000 stragglers were allowed by Sudan to be picked up by six U.S. military planes on March 28, 1985. With that, Operation Moses ended, at best only a partial success.[5] It was not until the late 1980s that the Jewish state managed to reopen the pipeline for immigrant Falashas. Marxist President Mengistu Haile Mariam agreed to allow the legal emigration of the Falashas at the rate of 500 per month in exchange for weapons to fight the Tigran rebels. The emigration continued from 1989 until the early summer of 1990, when the flow suddenly stopped. Mengistu demanded that Israel provide Ethiopia with more weapons, including cluster bomb units. Israel agreed.[6]

The deadly bombs took a devastating toll among Tigran and other rebel groups, causing an international uproar and again bringing attention to the Falashas and Israel. Congressional aide Steve Morrison prepared a study of the situation for Democrat Rep. Howard Wolpe of Michigan, noting that there was "a certain cynical logic that underlies the tradeoff between Israeli military assistance—likely to contribute to the deaths of thousands of Ethiopians—and the humanitarian interests of Ethiopian Jews. Apart from the question of whether this exchange is truly in the best interests of Ethiopian Jews, one must ask: how many Ethiopian lives can be justified for the sake of an Ethiopian Jew having the opportunity to reunify with his family in Israel? Is this implicitly racist?"[7]

The flow of Falashas to Israel resumed in July, 1990, shortly before the State Department finally agreed to Israel's repeated request for it to hold a high-level meeting with Ethiopia. Ethiopian Foreign Minister Tesfaye Dinka met with Undersecretary of State Lawrence Eagleburger for an hour July 27. A U.S. spokesman said the "emigration issue was discussed very forcefully."[8]

By Nov. 1, the Ethiopian government announced that all of the estimated 15,000 remaining Falashas were free to depart. The announcement came after Secretary of State James Baker and Israeli officials warned that relations between the U.S. and Ethiopia would not improve until the Jews were allowed to leave.[9] By this time, however, Tigran rebels were on the march. President Mengistu's position was crumbling under the pressure of the rebel forces advancing on Addis Ababa. On May 21, 1991, Mengistu fled the country, finally opening the way for the mass exodus. Mengistu's successor, acting President Tesfaye Gebre-Kidan, said he was "ready to make a deal," which included the payment of $35 million by Israel.[10] What the United States may have secretly given is unknown.

The effort that had begun in 1984 was finally completed in mid-1991. Nearly the entire Falasha community of Ethiopia now had a new home in Israel. But there was trouble in paradise. While from a distance many Israelis regarded the Falashas as a romanticized ancient tribe, up close they seemed to see only the color of their skin. Discrimination against the black Jews became widespread, tainting even government policies toward the new immigrants. They were settled in isolated "development towns" in the Negev desert and Galilee, and soon became afflicted by unemployment, drug problems and crime. One American Jewish activist in Israel noted: "The fact is that there is a color problem, in the sense that a lot of Israelis don't really identify with these people."[11]

A 1995 government education study reported that many Ethiopian elementary schoolchildren were needlessly channeled into classes for the learning-disabled, and teenage Ethiopians were largely schooled in subjects that prepared them for Israel's least rewarding jobs. A majority of the Ethiopians remained housed in the grim trailer parks in the distant development towns, where some of them had been living since the mid-1980s. Moreover, their religious leaders still were not recognized by Israel's government-sponsored rabbinate, implying that theirs was a less pure form of Judaism than that of other Israelis.[12]

Pent-up resentment in the Falasha community finally erupted in fury on Jan. 24, 1996, when it was learned that Falasha donations to Israel's national blood bank were routinely thrown away. They were not pacified by the excuse given. Zvi Ben Yishai, chairman of the National AIDS Committee, said it was because the Falashas had 50 times the incidence of AIDS as other Israelis. He said the practice was "justified for the protection of the public."

However, Yoram Lass, a member of parliament and former director general of the health ministry, described the policy as "racist and unfounded scientifically." He said Americans had a much higher AIDS rate but Israel would never consider banning blood donations by American Jews.

The revelation horrified the Falashas, who now numbered around 50,000. Adiso Masala, head of the Organization of Ethiopian Immigrants, said: "This is pure racism. We are blood brothers with the Israelis but our blood is thrown in the garbage because we are black." Benny Mekonnen, 30, a reserve army major, said he was so mad that he was going to leave Israel: "I gave blood every year, once a year. They took our blood and threw it in the garbage...I am very, very angry."[13]

On Jan. 28, some 10,000 Falashas protested at the prime minister's office in Jerusalem and were brutally met by riot police who used batons, rubber bullets, water cannon and tear gas against them. The Falashas carried placards reading "Apartheid in Israel" and "Our blood is as red as yours and we are just as Jewish as you are."[14] Prime Minister Shimon Peres promised to investigate their complaints. But on the basis of their experience during more than a decade in Israel, the Falashas seemed doomed to a fate of suffering the same isolation in Israel that they fled in Ethiopia. ✜

RECOMMENDED READING:

Beit-Hallahmi, Benjamin, *The Israeli Connection*, New York, Pantheon Books, 1987.

*Ostrovsky, Victor and Claire Hoy, *By Way of Deception*, New York, St. Martin's Press, 1990.

Raviv, Dan and Yossi Melman, *Every Spy a Prince: The Complete History of Israel's Intelligence Community*, Boston, Houghton Mifflin Company, 1990.

*Available through the AET Book Club.

NOTES:

[1]Joel Brinkley, *New York Times*, 5/26/91.

[2]Jackson Diehl, *Washington Post*, 5/25/91.

[3]*Ibid.*

[4]A survey of relations between Israel and Ethiopia is in Beit-Hallahmi, *The Israeli Connection*, pp. 50-54.

[5]Raviv and Melman, *Every Spy a Prince*, pp. 236-44; Ostrovsky and Hoy, *By Way of Deception*, pp. 287-301.

[6]On Israel's supply of cluster bombs, see Elaine Sciolino, *New York Times*, 1/21/90. For a fuller discussion of Israel's actions and motives, see Rachelle Marshall, "Israel Arms Ethiopia," *Washington Report on Middle East Affairs*, Vol. VIII, No. 11, March, 1990.

[7]*The Economist*, 7/21/90, and *Israel Foreign Affairs*, Vol. VI, No. 7, July, 1990.

[8]Nora Boustany, *Washington Post*, 7/28/90.

[9]Clifford Kraus, *New York Times*, 11/2/90.

[10]Jackson Diehl, *Washington Post*, 5/25/91.

[11]Jackson Diehl, *Washington Post*, 5/27/91. For more on the difficulties experienced by the earlier arrivals, see Henry Kamm, *New York Times*, 3/30/86.

[12]Barton Gellman, *Washington Post*, 1/25/96.

[13]*Ibid.*

[14]Serge Schmemann, *New York Times*, 1/29/96.

Arabs

Chapter 38

1952: Nasser Comes to Power

ON JULY 23, 1952, corrupt King Farouk of Egypt, an Albanian on his paternal side, was overthrown by a group of young military men calling themselves the Free Officers. The next day, one of the officers, Anwar Sadat, informed the nation by radio that for the first time in 2,000 years Egypt was under the rule of Egyptians. Sadat spoke in the name of General Mohammed Neguib, the revolution's titular head. In fact, the real leader was Gamal Abdul Nasser. He was 34 at the time and would rule Egypt for the next 18 turbulent years. Because of his youth, Nasser hid his power behind the older Neguib for the first two years of the new regime. It was not until 1954 that he officially became prime minister and not until June 23, 1956, that he assumed the presidency.[1]

The coming to power in Egypt of the energetic young warrior sent shockwaves through Britain, France and Israel. Leaders in all three countries feared him as a galvanizing ruler who had the potential to unify the shattered Arab world at the expense of the West and Israel. As Israel's David Ben-Gurion put it: "I always feared that a personality might rise such as arose among the Arab rulers in the seventh century or like [Mustafa Kemal Ataturk] who rose in Turkey after its defeat in the First World War. He raised their spirits, changed their character, and turned them into a fighting nation. There was and still is a danger that Nasser is this man."[2]

Britain and France held similar concerns. The rise of a strong Arab leader could not have come at a worse time for both nations. Drained by World War II, they were both in the process of losing their vast colonial empires. Both countries had already lost their mandates in the Middle East and both were desperately trying to maintain their influence in North Africa.

Nasser, above all else, wanted Egypt rid of British troops stationed along the Suez Canal, London's passage to India. In 1954, Britain finally gave in to Nasser's demand and agreed to withdraw its 80,000 British troops since, indeed, there no longer existed any reason for their presence. India was now independent and the canal had lost its strategic importance to Britain.[3] The troops had been there since 1882 and their departure, the last foreign troops on Egyptian soil, was an enormous boost to Nasser's prestige. The historic agreement meant, in British diplomat Anthony Nutting's words: "For the first time in two and a half thousand years the Egyptian people would know what it was to be independent and not to be ruled or occupied or told what to do by some foreign power."[4]

Israel, however, was greatly distressed by the agreement. The presence of British troops along the canal acted as a buffer against any rash action by Egypt, Israel's strongest Arab neighbor. Israel was so disturbed by the withdrawal that it had acted directly to ruin the talks by sending a sabotage team to Egypt to attack British and U.S. facilities. However, the covert effort backfired when Egyptian counterintelligence agents captured the spy ring and the embarrassing mission known as the Lavon Affair became public.[5]

The Anglo-Egyptian Suez agreement was reached Oct. 19, 1954, and was widely regarded as a strategic defeat for Britain. Two weeks later, on Nov. 1, Algerian Arabs, their morale boosted by Nasser's success, began their revolt against French colonial rule, which dated back to 1830. One of the many results of the insurrection was to convince France and Britain that Egypt, and specifically Nasser, was aiding the Algerians and therefore a dangerous common enemy of the West.[6] France had long seen Israel as a natural ally against the Arabs, and indeed was Israel's major friend at the time. The close friendship included France secretly sending weapons to the Jewish state in violation of the arms embargo agreed to by Western nations, including the United States.[7]

Thus was born the fiasco that has ignominiously gone down in history as the Suez Crisis of 1956. Little remembered in the United States, it was a watershed event in the Middle East. It involved one of the most cynical schemes ever hatched by Britain, France and Israel—and one of the highest points of American diplomacy. It also made Nasser the most idolized Arab leader of his time.

The crisis began when the leaders of Britain, France and Israel decided to collude secretly to get rid of Nasser. Just how to do that was never really clear. But, somehow, they wistfully hoped that by sending vast navies and armies against Egypt they would cause Nasser to be overthrown or to resign in humiliation. The plan was to pretend Israel had been hit by an Egyptian raid and in retaliation its army would race across the Sinai Peninsula and occupy the east bank of the Suez Canal. In response, Britain and France would pretend to intervene to stop a new Egyptian-Israeli war. All the while, of course, their warships and troops would actually be attacking Egypt. It was a preposterously transparent and shameless ploy but the three nations acted on it nonetheless.In its broader context, the Suez Crisis was a concerted attack by Europe and Israel against Islam.

A massive armada of French and British warships gathered off Egypt in late summer 1956 as the colluders went ahead amid growing international concern. No one was more concerned than President Dwight D. Eisenhower. The colluders had failed to take him into their scheme, presumably in the mistaken belief that since they were all U.S. friends the United States would not oppose their ill-conceived machinations.

In this they were fatally mistaken. Although facing presidential elections in November, Eisenhower publicly and privately opposed the three countries. Using every power short of military force at his command, Eisenhower compelled them to stop their naval bombardment and invasion of Egypt and to withdraw without gaining any profit from their misadventure. Not only did Nasser not fall but his prestige soared in the Arab world as the leader who had faced down the West and Israel.

Failure of the Suez plot had disastrous consequences for the colluders. The attack by Britain and France on Egypt drained moral authority from those two countries and spelled the end of their empires. Iraq, Britain's last major ally in the region, fell to Arab nationalists in 1958. And France finally lost Algeria in 1962. After Suez, the United States became the major Western power in the Middle East—not a position President Eisenhower had sought. As he noted in his memoirs, before the Suez war "...we felt that the British should continue to carry a major responsibility for its [Middle East] stability and security. The British were intimately familiar with the history, traditions and peoples of the Middle East;

we, on the other hand, were heavily involved in Korea, Formosa, Vietnam, Iran, and in this hemisphere."[8]

Not only did Britain and France lose their position in the region, but their rash actions helped the Soviet Union cement its presence in such countries as Egypt, Iraq and Syria. Moscow was able to strut as the defender of the Arabs against the perfidious West, earning Russia considerable popular support in the Arab world.

Israel's leaders pronounced themselves satisfied with the gains achieved. It had secured U.S. support for free maritime passage through the Strait of Tiran, connecting the Red Sea with the Gulf of Aqaba and the Israeli port of Eilat, and the stationing of UNEF troops at Gaza, where they prevented *fedayeen* raids into Israel. Prime Minister Ben-Gurion thought he had profited by humiliating Nasser and by raising domestic morale and intensifying a sense of national identity among Israel's diverse Jewish population. However, on closer examination Israel had sowed the whirlwind with its aggressive actions. The government of Gamal Abdel Nasser had initially shown little interest in the Arab-Israeli conflict. Its main interests were narrowly focused on its own demanding domestic problems. But after Israel's aggressive actions, which started well before the Suez outrage, Egypt diverted its resources to a major buildup of its armed forces.

The war also released aggressive forces within Israel that fed on dreams of conquest and expansion. These dreams would be realized 11 years later when Israel launched another surprise attack against both Egypt and Syria, drawing in Jordan, which was bound to both Arab countries by military treaty. That aggression, in turn, made Israel a pariah state in the world community because of its continued occupation of Arab land and made inevitable the 1973 war, which cost Israel unrelieved suffering and shook the country's self-confidence to the core. By then Nasser was gone. He had died of a heart attack on Sept. 28, 1970, at the age of 52.

Although widely reviled by Israel and its supporters, Nasser, the son of a postal clerk, had been a great Arab leader. While he was a compulsive conspirator, suspicious of others and thin-skinned to criticism, he was also charismatic, a natural leader and eventually the most beloved and admired Arab of his time. Nasser was described by his friend and chronicler, Mohamed Heikal, as "always a rebel [who] remained a conservative in his personal life....He was never interested in women or money or elaborate food. After he came to power the cynical old politicians tried to corrupt him but they failed miserably. His family life was impeccable....The world itself had found in him one of its most controversial statesmen and the Arabs had chosen him as the symbol of their lost dignity and their unfulfilled hopes."[12]

In the judgment of diplomat Anthony Nutting, who knew Nasser and wrote a biography of him: "For all his faults, Nasser helped to give Egypt and the Arabs that sense of dignity which for him was the hallmark of independent nationhood....Egypt and the whole Arab world would have been the poorer, in spirit as well as material progress, without the dynamic inspiration of his leadership."[13]

RECOMMENDED READING:

Eisenhower, Dwight D., *Waging Peace: 1956-61*, Garden City, NY, Doubleday & Company, Inc., 1965.

Heikal, Mohamed, *Nasser: The Cairo Documents*, London, New English Library, 1973.

Horne, Alistair, *A Savage War of Peace: Algeria 1954-1962*, New York, Viking, 1977.

Love, Kennett, *Suez: The Twice-Fought War*, New York, McGraw-Hill Book Company, 1969.

*Neff, Donald, *Warriors at Suez: Eisenhower takes America into the Middle East*, New York, Linden Press/Simon & Schuster, 1981.

Nutting, Anthony, *Nasser*, London, Constable, 1972.

Nyrop, Richard F. (ed.)., *Area Handbook for Egypt* (3rd ed.), Washington, DC, U.S. Government Printing Office, 1976.

Rubenberg, Cheryl A., *Israel and the American National Interest: A Critical Examination*, Chicago, University of Illinois Press, 1986.

Stephens, Robert, *Nasser: A Political Biography*, London, Allen Lane/The Penguin Press, 1971.

*Available through the AET Book Club.

NOTES:

[1]Nutting, *Nasser*, p. 37; Nyrop (ed.), *Area Handbook for Egypt*, p. 36. The best

biographies remain Anthony Nutting's and Robert Stephens' books, both titled *Nasser* and both published in the early 1970s.

[2]Love, *Suez*, p. 676.

[3]Nutting, *Nasser*, pp. 69-72; Neff, *Warriors at Suez*, pp. 17-18, 59.

[4]Nutting, *Nasser*, p. 71.

[5]Neff, *Warriors at Suez*, pp. 56-58.

[6]*Ibid.*, p. 161. The bitter war lasted until July 1, 1962, when Algerians voted to establish an independent Arab nation. The fighting took the lives of 17,456 French and upward of a million Arabs. See Horne, *A Savage War of Peace*, p. 538.

[7]*Ibid.*, pp. 235, 238.

[8]Eisenhower, *Waging Peace*, pp. 22-23.

[9]Rubenberg, *Israel and the American National Interest*, p. 84.

[10]Neff, *Warriors at Suez*, p. 439.

[11]Love, *Suez*, pp. 13-14.

[12], *The Cairo Documents*, pp. 1, 20.

[13]Nutting, *Nasser*, p. 481.

Chapter 39

1966: Assad Enters Road to Power in Syria

O
N FEB. 23, 1966, Hafez al-Assad gained his first cabinet post, a position he used to become what he remains today—Syria's most enduring modern leader. The event was another bloody coup, the 13th in the 20 years since Syria received its independence from France in 1946. At least 50 people were killed. Assad's reward for taking part was promotion from chief of the air force to Syria's minister of defense.[1] He was 35 at the time.[2]

It was from this period that the deep animosity that apparently continues today developed between Assad and Palestinian leader Yasser Arafat. The two men quarreled over strategy to confront Israel and the role of Arafat's fledgling Fatah guerrillas. Arafat wanted to spark a general war with Israel before it became stronger, while Assad and the Syrian government recognized Syria's weakness and sought to substitute a guerrilla people's war for a conventional war. The argument became so heated that on May 6, 1966, Assad ordered Arafat imprisoned for six weeks.[3] The incident caused what Assad biographer Patrick Seale called "intense mutual antipathy" between Arafat and Assad.[4]

Israel's successful launching of a surprise war against both Egypt and Syria in 1967 traumatized the new defense minister. Assad vowed that Syria would never again suffer such humiliation. As Patrick Seale noted: "The importance of this moment of national ruin in Assad's career cannot be overestimated. Without a doubt, the defeat was the decisive turning point in his life, jolting him into political maturity and spurring the ambition to rule Syria free from constraints of colleagues and rivals who he felt had led the country to disaster...After the war, as the lessons of the defeat sank in, Assad's good nature gave way to something more steely, and it was from this time on that he set about in earnest building a personal power base in the armed services."[5]

By the fall of 1970, Assad was ready to make his move. On Nov. 13, Assad staged a bloodless coup.[6] Three days later, his appointment as Syria's prime minister was announced and his rule began. Assad was officially elected president on March 12, 1971, and two days later was sworn in for a seven-year term.

Assad, a member of the Alawite minority sect of Islam, representing only about 11 percent of Syria's population, was to prove Syria's most long-lasting and effective modern leader. His rule was stern. When well-armed radical Islamists revolted in early 1982 in the conservative city of Hama, starting a month-long insurrection, Assad responded with overwhelming force. Syrian troops killed anywhere from 5,000 to 20,000 people in the city.[7] At least 15,000 machine guns were taken from the rebels. Assad cited the capture of sophisticated U.S. communications gear as evidence of America's complicity, a charge Washington denied.[8]

One of Assad's first acts as ruler was to reaffirm Syria's rejection of the U.N. Security Council land-for-peace Resolution 242. He believed the resolution would freeze the conflict at the cost of the Palestinians' claims arising from their expulsion in 1948 and he doubted Israel would return to Syria the Golan Heights it occupied in 1967. Only war could deliver those claims, Assad believed.[9] He, along with other Arab states and the Palestinians, has since embraced the resolution.

Seale observed: "From the moment of coming to power Assad was in the grip of an obsession. He was convinced that Israel had won the Six-Day War by ruse, catching the Arabs napping, but that it was not inherently unbeatable. He longed to wipe away the stain of defeat, which had affected him personally and profoundly, restore the confidence of his troops, recover the land, and show the world that, given a chance, the Arabs could acquit themselves honorably. The need to fight another round was his obsession."[10] Thus were planted the seeds for another war—the 1973 earthquake. This time the Arabs launched war with a surprise attack of their own.

While Syria and Egypt ultimately lost the 1973 war, their troops fought valiantly and inflicted such enormous losses on Israel that the Arabs felt vindicated for the 1967 defeat. Henceforth, diplomacy and scrimmages, verbal and otherwise—rather than all-out war—would rule relations between Syria and Israel. Syria has been scrupulous in observing the terms of the 1973 cease-fire. Not even Israel's massive invasion of neighboring Lebanon in 1982 provoked Syria to go to war.

Assad denies he sponsors terrorism against Israel and he bristles at Syria's inclusion on the U.S. list of terror-sponsoring states. He said at a 1994 press conference that he had asked a senior U.S. official to mention "one incident in which Syria has committed a terrorist action, and he was helpless. He was not able to mention one single incident in which Syria supported terrorism."[11] Nonetheless, Syria remained on the list in 1998.

Since the 1973 war, Assad has met with four U.S. presidents: Nixon in Damascus in 1974, Carter and Bush in Geneva in 1977 and 1990, and Clinton in Geneva and Damascus, both in 1994. Assad has assured each that Syria desires peace. But he has emphasized over the years that it must be a fair peace that returns to Syria all of its territory and that does not allow Israel to retain any gain it achieved on the field of battle. His adamant insistence that Israel return all of Syria's land has made him the favorite of many Arabs, and the most implacable foe facing Israel.

As he put it in eloquent terms at a press conference after his Jan. 16, 1994, meeting with President Clinton in Geneva: "Syria seeks a just and comprehensive peace with Israel as a strategic choice that secures Arab rights, ends the Israeli occupation and enables our peoples in the region to live in peace, security and dignity...We want the peace of the brave—a genuine peace which can survive and last—a peace which secures the interests of each side and renders all their rights...We are ready to sign peace now....If the leaders of Israel have sufficient courage to respond to this kind of peace, a new era of security and stability with normal peaceful relations shall dawn."

Clinton responded: "I believe that President Assad has made a clear, forthright and very important statement on normal, peaceful relations...This is an important statement—the first time that there has been a clear expression that there will be a possibility of that sort of relationship."[12]

Syria and Israel appeared to be moving toward peace under the Labor governments of Yitzhak Rabin and Shimon Peres. They held regular talks in Washington, exchanged ideas with U.S. officials, and Israel hinted broadly that it was ready to return the Golan Heights in return for full peace. All that ended with the terrorist attacks in Israel in February and March, 1996. Israel broke off the talks, saying it was too traumatized by the carnage caused by Palestinian terrorists.

Still, the hope remained that once things settled down Israel would return to the bargaining table and the circle of peace finally could be secured. Then came the May 29, 1996, election of Binyamin Netanyahu of the nationalist Likud Party. He quickly made clear he had no intention of returning the Golan Heights.[13]

Now, instead of talk, Syria has begun conducting military exercises around the Heights. After all these years in power, no one can believe that Hafez al-Assad will settle for anything less than the return of all of the territory. An ominous period lay ahead. ❧

RECOMMENDED READING:

*Friedman, Thomas L., *From Beirut to Jerusalem*, New York, Farrar, Strauss, Giroux, 1989.

Hart, Alan, *Arafat: Terrorist or Peacemaker?*, London, Sidgwick & Jackson, 1985.

Nyrop, Richard F. (ed.), *Syria: A Country Study* (3rd ed.), Washington, DC, U.S. Government Printing Office, 1979.

Petran, Tabitha, *Syria*, New York, Praeger Publishers, 1972.

Rabinovich, Itamar, *Syria Under the Ba'th 1963-66*, Jerusalem, Israel University Press, 1972.

*Seale, Patrick, *Asad of Syria: The Struggle for the Middle East*, Berkeley, University of California Press, 1988.

*Available through the AET Book Club.

NOTES:

[1]Seale, *Asad*, p. 104; Petran, *Syria*, p. 182; Rabinovich, *Syria Under the Ba'th 1963-66*, pp. 204-8.

[2]Assad's birth date is generally given as 1930—the date used by his major biographer, Patrick Seale—although various works such as Nyrop, *Syria*,

p. 42, place it as early as 1926.

[3]Hart, *Arafat*, p. 208.

[4]Seale, *Asad*, p. 125.

[5]*Ibid.*, p. 144.

[6]Petran, *Syria*, p. 249.

7Seale, *Asad*, p. 334; Friedman, *From Beirut to Jerusalem*, pp. 76-87.

[8]Seale, *Asad*, p. 334.

[9]*Ibid.*, pp. 185-6.

[10]*Ibid.*, p. 185.

[11]Douglas Jehl, *The New York Times*, 10/28/94.

[12]Douglas Jehl, *The New York Times*, 1/17/94.

[13]See, for instance, Nasser H. Aruri, "Netanyahu and the Peace Process," *Middle East International*, 6/16/96; Associated Press, *The New York Times*, 9/10/96.

[14]Barton Gellman, *The Washington Post*, 8/28/96.

Chapter 40

1977: Sadat Makes Historic Trip to Jerusalem

ON NOV. 19, 1977, Anwar Sadat made his historic visit to Jerusalem and declared the next day before Israel's parliament: "We really and truly welcome you to live among us in peace and security."[1]

It was a spectacular moment, a personal commitment of the Egyptian leader's desire for peace. However, deep suspicions remained in Israel even on the day of his arrival. Atop a roof at Ben-Gurion International Airport where Sadat landed were Israeli sharpshooters. Absurd as it seems in retrospect, they were there in part in fear that the Egyptian airplane was not carrying Sadat at all but a planeload of terrorists.[2] Despite such exaggerated suspicions, the visit led within a year and a half to the first peace treaty between Israel and an Arab country, mainly because of American largess.

It was not an easy journey. In public, Sadat expressed optimism that his "sacred mission" had essentially solved the Arab-Israeli conflict. But privately he was deeply disappointed by his realization that he had not managed to solve the conflict with one grand gesture. Israeli Prime Minister Menachem Begin showed no willingness to match Sadat's imaginative gesture or even to make any serious concessions, and the Palestinians and other Arab states roundly condemned him for going to Jerusalem.[3] All factions of the Palestine Liberation Organization joined in calling his visit to Jerusalem "treasonous."[4]

Instead of gaining the instant freedom of the Palestinians and Egypt's land occupied by Israel, as he had hoped, Sadat found himself in the following months increasingly isolated. On Dec. 5, 1977, Algeria, Iraq, Libya, Syria and South Yemen jointly condemned the visit and vowed to "work for the frustration of the results of President Sadat's visit to the Zionist entity...."[5] The nations said they were freezing political and diplomatic relations with Egypt and would refuse to attend meetings of the Arab League held in Egypt. Sadat's angry reaction was to sever diplomatic ties with all of them.[6]

Less than a week later, on Dec. 14, Sadat suffered another major embarrassment when he called for a conference in Cairo to unify the Arab position and receive international support for his efforts. The Arab nations refused to attend, as did the Soviet Union.[7] Only Israel, the United States and the United Nations attended. No agreements emerged from the conference, adding to Sadat's humiliation.[8]

Sadat's disillusionment was obvious when he hosted a reciprocal visit to Egypt for the Israelis on Dec. 25, 1977. Gone was the magic and drama of his visit to .[9] Instead of personally meeting Begin and his group, Sadat sent his vice president to greet them. There were no bands, no Israeli flags, no placards of greeting for the Israeli delegation. Even Defense Minister Ezer Weizman, who had established the warmest relations of any of the Israelis with Sadat the previous month, found the reception "frosty." Given Begin's well-known love of pomp and ceremony and his excessive concern with dignity, Weizman concluded: "The chilly welcome, the indifference toward Begin, the flouting of the most elementary rules of protocol and courtesy—all these could only be harmful to our talks."[10]

Sadat met the Israeli delegation not in Cairo but at Ismailiya on the western bank of the Suez Canal. He and Begin immediately retired for brief private talks. Sadat accepted a Begin proposal to form two separate committees to discuss military and political issues. The Egyptian leader made a considerable concession in agreeing that the political committee would meet in Jerusalem, implying to the Israelis "some measure of recognition that Jerusalem was Israel's capital."[11]

The concession was typical of Sadat—a grand gesture, an open show of conciliation, and underneath an impatience with details, a concentration on general principles, and most of all, a hard determination to regain every inch of Egypt's land. Unhappily, no two negotiators could have been less suited to deal with each other.

Unlike Sadat, Begin delighted in the parsing of sentences, the splitting of words, the elaboration of nuances. He was a subtle and wily negotiator enamored with the rhetorical flourish but trustful only of the technicalities of negotiation. He was as wedded to the concept of Israeli retention of Eretz Yisrael, the land of Israel, meaning Jewish control over Samaria and Judea, the West Bank, as Sadat was to getting back Egyptian land. As Ezer Weizman noted:

"Anyone observing the two men could not have overlooked the profound divergence in their attitudes. Both desired peace. But whereas Sadat wanted to take it by storm, capitalizing on the momentum from his visit to Jerusalem to reach his final objective, Begin preferred to creep forward inch by inch. He took the dream of peace and ground it down into the fine, dry powder of details, legal clauses, and quotes from international law."[12]

The talks dragged on into the next day. But there was no progress. Begin refused to consent to the issuance of general principles on withdrawal and self-determination for the Palestinians, and Sadat refused to accept the idea of Israel retaining Jewish settlements in Sinai. The two-day meeting ended in stalemate and a further worsening of the atmosphere that had seemed so promising only the month before.[13]

The major problem was not the return of Egypt's Sinai Peninsula, which had little significance for Begin, but retention of the West Bank with its Jewish settlements. Sadat had vowed that he would not only regain the Sinai but also gain self-determination for the Palestinians. As he said publicly shortly before going to Jerusalem: The Palestinian problem was the "core and crux" of the Arab-Israeli conflict and that "no progress" could be achieved without its solution.[14]

President Jimmy Carter shared these views. He was the first president to declare publicly that settlements in the occupied territories were illegal.[15] In order to help Sadat, and goad Begin to be more forthcoming, Carter visited Egypt on Jan. 4, 1978. He enunciated what later became known as the Aswan Declaration, a formula that seemed to grant the Palestinians self-determination. Carter said that any solution must "enable Palestinians to participate in the determination of their own future."[16]

On that same day, Israel revealed it was establishing four new settlements in the Sinai. Carter and Sadat were both furious, suspecting that Begin was purposefully fouling the peace process.[17]

Things degenerated. On Jan. 18, 1978, the first—and last—meeting of the joint Egyptian-Israeli Political Committee ended in mutual recrimination. The foreign ministers of Egypt and Israel could not get past the first item on the agenda, a declaration of intentions.[18] Sadat ordered home his delegation the next day, saying Israel wanted land more than peace.[19]

Carter met in Washington with Sadat for four days starting Feb. 4 to work out a joint strategy to press Israel to make concessions.[20] Carter by then had "little real trust or confidence" in Begin, according to the National Security Council's Middle East expert, William Quandt.[21] At the end of their talks, Carter and Sadat agreed that Egypt would put forth in writing its proposals for the future of the Palestinians. It was assumed that Israel would reject the proposals and that the United States would then put forward its plan for a West Bank settlement.[22]

But there was a problem that foiled the plan. Israel's supporters adamantly opposed U.S. pressure against the Jewish state. Their hand was strengthened by the coincidence that controversial treaties on Panama, on which Carter had worked so hard, were about to come before the Senate. Carter still did not have enough votes, and several of the senators whose votes the president needed were strong supporters of Israel. Thus, the domestic dimension of the Arab-Israeli conflict once again influenced the White House's actions. In this case it meant the president did not believe he had the political power to apply the necessary pressure on Israel to make it bow to U.S. policy.[23]

So it went month after month. The momentum of Sadat's bold gesture drained away and relations between Egypt and Israel returned to mutual animosity. The final straw came on July 23, 1978, when Begin, in reply to a plea from Sadat that Israel make some modest goodwill gesture in support of the peace process, rudely turned down the Egyptian leader. Replied Begin: "Not even one grain of desert sand. Nobody can get anything for nothing."[24]

On July 30, a flash cable from Ambassador Hermann Eilts in Cairo informed Carter that Sadat told him in great agitation that he was at the end of his patience. The Egyptian leader demanded that the United States press Israel to abide by the basic principles of U.S. policy: withdrawal, sovereignty for the Palestinians and the illegality of settlements. Sadat said this was his final word.[25]

On that same day, Carter, desperate for some achievement, decided he would invite both Sadat and Begin to a summit meeting at Camp David.[26] It was in this mood of despair that the celebrated Camp David meeting among Begin, Carter and Sadat took place between Sept. 5 to Sept. 17. In the end, it resulted in just what Sadat's critics suspected—a bilateral deal between Egypt and Israel with only empty words about the Palestinians.

Under the framework dealing with the West Bank and Gaza (the Golan Heights was not mentioned), "full autonomy" was promised the Palestinians after a transitional period "not exceeding five years." The transitional period was to begin with the election by the Palestinians of a "self-governing authority (administrative council)," at which time "the Israeli military government and its civilian administration will be withdrawn" and the self-governing authority would establish "a strong local police force."

Then, "as soon as possible, but not later than the third year after the beginning of the transitional period," negotiations would begin "to determine the final status of the West Bank and Gaza...and to conclude a peace treaty between Israel and Jordan by the end of the transitional period."[27]

Arab reaction was harshly negative, especially among Palestinians. As usual, they had not been allowed to participate in negotiations that presumed to represent their fate.

Their criticisms pointed out that there was no elaboration of what Begin meant by "full autonomy;" there was no detailed plan on just how the administrative council was to be elected or which Palestinians would be eligible to serve on it. Nor was there any mention of the principles that Sadat had sought such as "self-determination" or "the inadmissibility of the acquisition of territory by war." In addition, there was no challenge to Israel's claim of sovereignty over Jerusalem, nor had Begin committed Israel to anything more than a temporary freeze on settlements, an implicit acceptance of his contention that they were legal. Finally, the PLO, the body designated by the Arab world to represent the Palestinians, was not mentioned.[28]

In the end, none of this mattered. Begin had no intention of honoring the parts of the agreement dealing with the West Bank and Palestinians, as he quickly made clear. Almost immediately after signing the accords, the Israeli leader began to reinterpret them in such a narrow way that they lost all meaning in their application to the Palestinians and the West Bank.[29]

Although the accords said that the question of sovereignty of the West Bank and Gaza would be negotiated after five years, Begin went before Congress two days after the accords had been signed and declared: "I believe with all my heart that the Jewish people have a right to sovereignty over Judea and Samaria."[30]

The following day, Begin told Jewish American leaders in New York: "I hereby declare the Israeli Defense Forces will stay in Judea, Samaria and the Gaza Strip to defend our people and make sure Jewish blood is not shed again. I hereby declare they will stay beyond five years."[31]

As for the phrase "legitimate rights of the Palestinians," which was used in the agreements as an acknowledgement of Palestinian interests, Begin declared that it "has no meaning." He had accepted the phrase only to please Carter and Sadat "and because it does not change reality."[32]

In reality, no serious effort was made by Begin in the five additional years he remained as Israel's leader, and none during the seven years his Likud successor, Yitzhak Shamir, was in power. Instead, the practical result of the accords was to neutralize Egypt, the Jewish state's most powerful Arab neighbor. As anticipated by Sadat's critics, this freed Israel to pursue aggressive policies such as the annexation of Jerusalem in 1980, the bombing of Iraq's nuclear facility in 1981 and the invasion of Lebanon in 1982.

At the same time, Begin enormously expanded Jewish settlements in the territories occupied in 1967, which was his main priority. When he came to power in 1977, there were about 50,000 Jews living in Arab East Jerusalem and about 7,000 in 45 settlements in the West Bank and in an additional 45 in the rest of the occupied territories. When he left office six years later, there were close to 200 settlements in all the occupied territories, with about 100,000 Jewish settlers in East Jerusalem and 22,000 Jewish settlers in the territories.[33]

The positioning of the settlements essentially established the central points for Jewish settlement throughout the territories. His Likud successor, Yitzhak Shamir, then pursued an aggressive program that substantially thickened and expanded these focal points.[34] When Shamir left office in mid-1992, there were about 245,000 Jews in some 250 settlements, including East Jerusalem.[35]

The NSC's William Quandt, who attended the Camp David meetings, concluded: "Begin was no doubt the most able negotiator at Camp David."[36]

Camp David was a triumph for Israel and Begin's settlements policy, and it was accordingly widely hailed by the U.S. media and in Congress. But for Carter and Sadat it was a disaster waiting to happen. Despite all the hype, the fact was that Israel showed no more willingness to make concessions after Camp David than before. Talks between Egypt and Israel to implement the accords quickly broke down and the Middle East returned to gridlock. Carter and Sadat had spent a huge amount of time in search of peace but by the beginning of 1979 it was as elusive as ever.

In desperation, President Carter himself flew off to the Middle East in March, 1979. He spent a week shuttling between Egypt and Israel before finally gaining a peace agreement between the two countries.

It did not come cheaply. The treaty not only cost the president his time but the American taxpayer unprecedented amounts of money. The United States promised Israel in a far-reaching Memorandum of Understanding a variety of major transfers of technology and aid, including $3 billion to relocate two Israeli air bases out of the Sinai, where they had no right to be in the first place.[37] Egypt also profited. It was given $1.5 billion in military aid over three years.[38]

Following the treaty, which was signed in Washington on March 26, 1979, U.S. aid climbed until 1985, when it reached $3 billion annually for Israel and $2.1 billion for Egypt, all of it in nonrepayable grants. These levels remained the same in 1998, giving Egypt and Israel the distinction of being the two largest recipients of U.S. aid in the world.

The treaty did nothing to help Carter's political fortunes. He went down to defeat the next year at the hands of Ronald Reagan, a strong supporter of Israel who immediately declared as president that Israeli settlements were not illegal. Anwar Sadat paid for his efforts with his life. He was gunned down by Muslim fundamentalists on Oct. 6, 1981, while celebrating the eighth anniversary of his war against Israel. Begin remained in power until Sept. 15, 1983, when he voluntarily resigned, successful in his life's aim to establish the master plan for Jewish settlements in Palestine. ✌

RECOMMENDED READING:

Boudreault, Jody, and Yasser Salaam. *U.S. Official Statements: Status of Jerusalem*, Washington, DC, Institute for Palestine Studies, 1992.

Boutros-Ghali, Boutros, *Egypt's Road to Jerusalem: A Diplomat's Story of the Struggle for Peace in the Middle East*, New York, Random House, 1997.

Brzezinski, Zbigniew, *Power and Principle: Memoirs of the National Security Adviser*, New York, Farrar, Strauss, Giroux, 1983.

Dayan, Moshe, *Breakthrough*, New York, Alfred A. Knopf, 1981.

Fahmy, Ismail, *Negotiating for Peace in the Middle East*, Baltimore, The Johns Hopkins University Press, 1983.

*Khouri, Fred J., *The Arab Israeli Dilemma* (3rd ed.), Syracuse, NY, Syracuse University Press, 1985.

Kimche, Jon, *There Could Have Been Peace*, New York, Dial Press, 1973.

Medzini, Meron, *Israel's Foreign Relations: Selected Documents, 1977-1979* (vols. 4 and 5), Jerusalem, Ministry of Foreign Affairs, 1981.

O'Brien, Conor Cruise, *The Siege: The Saga of Israel and Zionism*, New York, Simon and Schuster, 1986.

Quandt, William B., *Camp David: Peacemaking and Politics*, Washington, DC, The Brookings Institution, 1986.

Riad, Mahmoud, *The Struggle for Peace in the Middle East*, New York, Quartet Books, 1981.

Rubenberg, Cheryl A., *Israel and the American National Interest: A Critical Examination*, Chicago, University of Illinois Press, 1986.

Sadat, Anwar, *In Search of Identity*, New York, Harper & Row, 1978.

Safty, Abdel, *From Camp David to the Gulf: Negotiations, Language & Propaganda, and War*, New York, Black Rose Books, 1992.

Sicherman, Harvey, *Palestinian Self-Government (Autonomy): Its Past and Its Future*, Washington, DC, The Washington Institute for Near East Policy, 1991.

Silver, Eric, *Begin: The Haunted Prophet*, New York, Random House, 1984.

Tillman, Seth, *The United States in the Middle East: Interests and Obstacles*, Bloomington, Indiana University Press, 1982.

U.S. Department of State, *American Foreign Policy: Basic Documents, 1977-1980*, Washington, DC, U.S. Government Printing Office, 1983.

Weizman, Ezer, *The Battle for Peace*, New York, Bantam Books, 1981.

*Available through the AET Book Club.

NOTES:

[1]The text is in *New York Times*, 11/21/77, and Quandt, *Camp David*, Appendix C. Also see Sadat, *In Search of Identity*, p. 309; Brzezinski, *Power and Principle*, p.

111; Fahmy, *Negotiating for Peace in the Middle East*, p. 277; Rubenberg, *Israel and the American National Interest*, p. 217.

[2]Quandt, *Camp David*, p. 147.

[3]Safty, *From Camp David to the Gulf*, p. 68.

[4]The text is in State Department, *American Foreign Policy 1977-1980*, p. 635.

[5]Text in State Department, *American Foreign Affairs 1977-1980*, pp. 636-38.

[6]Riad, *The Struggle for Peace in the Middle East*, p. 308.

[7]O'Brien, *The Siege*, p. 580; Safty, *From Camp David to the Gulf*, pp. 71, 72.

[8]Dayan, *Breakthrough*, p. 99.

[9]Quandt, *Camp David*, p. 159; Safty, *From Camp David to the Gulf*, pp. 69-70; Sicherman, *Palestinian Self-Government (Autonomy)*, pp. 11-12. Also see Dayan, *Breakthrough*, pp. 102-05; Weizman, *The Battle for Peace*, pp. 122-35.

[10]Weizman, *The Battle for Peace*, pp. 123-24.

[11]*Ibid.*, p. 126.

[12]*Ibid.*, pp. 136-37.

[13]The text of their joint news conference is in *New York Times*, 12/27/77.

[14]*New York Times*, 4/5/77.

[15]The text is in *New York Times*, 7/29/77. Previous administrations had taken this position through statements by various spokesmen but Carter was the first president to say it in public. See Boudreault and Salaam. *U.S. Official Statements: Status of Jerusalem.*

[16]The text of Carter's and Sadat's statements are in *New York Times*, 1/5/78, and Medzini, M. *Israel's Foreign Relations, Selected Documents, 1977-79*, pp. 289-90. Also see Brzezinski, *Power and Principle*, p. 239; Quandt, *Camp David*, p. 161; Sicherman, *Palestinian Self-Government (Autonomy)*, pp. 12-13; Tillman, *The United States in the Middle East*, pp. 220-21. Tillman observes that Carter never embraced the idea of an independent Palestinian state and that the declaration actually put the Palestinians on notice that while "they might 'participate' in deciding their own future, Israel and perhaps others would participate as well, guaranteeing that there would be no independent Palestinian state." See Brzezinski, *Power and Principle*, pp. 234-39, for background on U.S. attitudes toward the Middle East at the start of the year; compare with Quandt, *Camp David*, p. 168.

[17]Quandt, *Camp David*, p. 161; Safty, *From Camp David to the Gulf*, pp. 70-71.

[18]Dayan, *Breakthrough*, p. 112; Safty, *From Camp David to the Gulf*, pp. 71-72.

[19]Quandt, *Camp David*, p. 165.

[20]Brzezinski, *Power and Principle*, pp. 243-44; Quandt, *Camp David*, p. 175; Safty,

From Camp David to the Gulf, p. 73. Kimche, *The Last Option,* pp. 95-110, has a particularly sensational account of this joint effort.

[21]Quandt, *Camp David,* p. 167.

[22]*Ibid.,* p. 175. Also see Rubenberg, *Israel and the American National Interest,* pp. 221-23. The text of the joint Carter-Sadat public statement is in *New York Times,* 2/9/78.

[23]Quandt, *Camp David,* p. 174.

[24]Rubenberg, *Israel and the American National Interest,* p. 231.

[25]Quandt, *Camp David,* pp. 201-02.

[26]*Ibid.,* p. 202; Brzezinski, *Power and Principle,* pp. 251-562. Also, Khouri, *The Arab-Israel Dilemma,* p. 406.

[27]For a detailed comparison of the differences between the accords and Begin's original Home Rule plan offered in December, 1977, see Sicherman, *Palestinian Self-Government (Autonomy),* pp. 13-14.

[28]Quandt, *Camp David,* pp. 255-56; Khouri, *The Arab-Israel Dilemma* (3rd ed.), pp. 407-08. Also see Safty, *From Camp David to the Gulf,* pp. 78-84.

[29]Quandt, *Camp David,* pp. 260-61.

[30]Tillman, *The United States in the Middle East,* p. 134.

[31]*Ibid.*

[32]*Ibid.,* p. 132. Also see Rubenberg, *Israel and the American National Interest,* pp. 138-39.

[33]Foundation for Middle East Peace, *Report on Israeli Settlement in the Occupied Territories,* Special Report, July, 1991 (Washington, DC); Aronson, *Creating Facts,* p. 70.

[34]Author interview with Geoffrey Aronson, Washington, DC, Jan. 24, 1994.

[35]Associated Press, *Washington Times,* 5/9/92.

[36]Quandt, *Camp David,* p. 255.

[37]State Department, *American Foreign Policy 1977-1980,* p. 667; "U.S. Assistance to the State of Israel, Report by the Comptroller General of the United States," GAO/ID-83-51, US Accounting Office, June 24, 1983.

[38]Quandt, *Camp David,* p. 316; Safty, *From Camp David to the Gulf,* pp. 85-88.

United States

Chapter 41

1953: Dulles' Tour of the Middle East

ON JUNE 1, 1953, President Dwight D. Eisenhower's secretary of state, John Foster Dulles, reported to a national radio and television audience on the extraordinary adventures on his just-completed 20-day tour of the Middle East, the first by an American secretary of state.

Dulles' major conclusion was perhaps as much a surprise to the strongly anti-Communist secretary as it was to his audience: The Arabs, he reported, were "more fearful of Zionism than communism." What makes Dulles' speech memorable today is its reminder of how much U.S. policy has shifted toward Israel since then—and how the problems of the region have worsened.

The election of Dwight D. Eisenhower had brought to office in 1953 an administration that was determined to be even-handed and fair. This was made clear in Dulles' speech when he declared the United States would continue to oppose any nation arming for an attack on its neighbors. He also declared that the United States opposed both Israeli and Arab claims to Jerusalem, preferring instead to see Jerusalem as an international city.

During his journey, Dulles visited 12 nations and Jerusalem. He reported he found Jerusalem "divided into armed camps split between Israel and the Arab nation of Jordan. The atmosphere there is heavy with hate. As I gazed on the Mount of Olives, I felt anew that Jerusalem is, above all, the holy place of the Christian, Muslim and Jewish faiths. That's been repeatedly emphasized by the United Nations, and that fact does not necessarily exclude some political status in Jerusalem for Israel and Jordan. But the world religious community has claims in Jerusalem which take precedence over the political claims of any particular state."

Dulles also described the "bitter fate" of the Palestinian refugees: "Closely huddled around Israel are most of the over 800,000 Arab refugees who fled from Palestine as the Israelis took over. They mostly exist in makeshift camps, with few facilities either for health, work or recreation. Within these camps the inmates rot away, spiritually and physically. Even the Grim Reaper offers no solution, for as the older die, infants are born to inherit their parents' bitter fate. Some of these refugees could be settled in the area presently controlled by Israel. Most, however, could more readily be integrated into the lives of the neighboring Arab countries. This, however, awaits on irrigation projects, which will permit more soil to be cultivated. Throughout the area the cry is for water for irrigation....Irrigation needs became most vivid as we motored from Jerusalem to Amman, the capital of Jordan. The road goes through the Dead Sea area, a scene of desolation with no sign of life other than the tens of thousands of refugees who survive precariously on the parched land largely by aid of U.N. doles."

Secretary Dulles' conclusions from his trip make bittersweet reading today. Had the U.S. followed along the lines proposed, the Middle East would be a safer place for all of its inhabitants today, and the U.S. might have regained the widespread trust and respect it had so abruptly lost in 1947 and 1948. Dulles observed:

"The United States should seek to allay the deep resentment against it that has resulted from the creation of Israel. In the past we had good relations with the Arab peoples. American educational institutions there had built up a feeling of goodwill, and also American businessmen had won a good reputation in this area. There was mutual confidence to mutual advantage.

"Today the Arab peoples are afraid that the United States will back the new state of Israel in aggressive expansion. They are more fearful of Zionism than of communism, and they fear the United States, lest we become the backer of expansionist Zionism. On the other hand, the Israelis fear that ultimately the Arabs may try to push them into the sea."

In an effort to calm these contradictory fears the United States joined with France and Britain in a declaration of May 25, 1950, which stated that "the three governments, should they find that any of these states of the Near East was preparing to violate frontiers or armistice lines, would...immediately take action...to prevent such violations...It must be made clear that the present United States administration stands fully behind that declaration. We cannot afford to be distrusted by millions who should be sturdy friends of freedom....And the leaders of Israel themselves agreed with us that United States policies should be impartial so as to win not only the respect and regard of the Israeli but also of the Arab peoples. We shall seek such policies."[1]

Both the key policies enunciated by Dulles—arms control and support of the internationalization of Jerusalem—have since been abandoned by Washington. Official policy now is to guarantee Israel's qualitative superiority over all of its Arab neighbors, a commitment made formal by President Reagan on Feb. 22, 1982, just months before Israel's unprovoked invasion of Lebanon.[2] (The commitment was repeated in the Republican Party national platform adopted on Aug. 21, 1984.[3] Reagan adopted the pro-Israel policy despite the fact of Israel's proven military superiority as demonstrated by its unilateral launching of wars in 1956 and 1967, and its steady expansion of its frontiers onto Arab lands.

Equally important, Washington no longer insists that neither side should control Jerusalem. President Johnson changed that after Israel captured all of Jerusalem in 1967 by decreeing that the city's final status should be determined by the parties themselves. This weakening of Washington's traditional policy was revealed by U.S. Ambassador Arthur J. Goldberg on July 14, 1967, when he told the United Nations that the city's future must be settled through negotiations "of all problems arising out of the recent conflict."[4] The change was made despite the fact that Israel since its founding has defied world opinion, and U.S. policy, by claiming Jerusalem as its capital.

After Johnson's change, U.S. policy nonetheless remained that Arab East Jerusalem was occupied territory, the same as other territories Israel had occupied during the 1967 war. This designation was enshrined in a number of United Nations Security Council resolutions supported by various administrations between 1971 and 1991.

However, even that position has now been diluted by the Clinton administration. It opposes the description of Arab Jerusalem as occupied territory, apparently as a result of a secret promise Clinton made to Jewish American leaders during his presidential campaign.[5] It accepted the Israeli position that the area is "disputed" territory. ❧

RECOMMENDED READING:

Cattan, Henry, *Jerusalem*, New York, St. Martin's Press, 1981.

Gerson, Louis L., *John Foster Dulles*, New York Cooper Square Publishers Inc., 1967.

Hoopes, Townsend, *The Devil and John Foster Dulles*, London, Andre Deutsch, 1974.

*Neff, Donald, *Warriors at Suez: Eisenhower Takes America into the Middle East*, Brattleboro, VT, Amana Books, 1988.

Rubenberg, Cheryl A., *Israel and the American National Interest: A Critical Examination*, Chicago, University of Illinois Press, 1986.

*Available through the AET Book Club.

NOTES:

[1] The Text of Dulles' report is in *The New York Times*, June 2, 1953, and U.S. Department of State, *American Foreign Policy, 1950-1955* (1957), 2,368-75.

[2] *Weekly Compilation of Presidential Documents*, Government Printing Office, Washington, DC, Feb. 22, 1982, p. 177.

[3] The text is in *The New York Times*, Aug. 22, 1984.

[4] Cattan, *Jerusalem*, p. 112. Also see Bernard Gwertzman, *The New York Times*, March 13, 1980.

[5] John M. Goshko, *The Washington Post*, March 14, 1994.

Chapter 42

1957 : Eisenhower Forces Israel Out of Sinai

O N MARCH 16, 1957, Israel withdrew under unrelenting U.S. pressure from all the territory it had occupied in the Sinai peninsula during its invasion of Egypt less than five months earlier. As Israeli forces pulled out, they ignored pleas from U.N. Secretary-General Dag Hammarskjold and displayed their contempt for U.S. President Dwight D. Eisenhower's policy by systematically destroying all surfaced roads, railway tracks and telephone lines. All buildings in the tiny villages of Abu Ageila and El Quseima were destroyed, as were the military buildings around El Arish.[1]

Israel's dogged insistence on keeping by military occupation parts of the Sinai had led to increasingly tense relations between Eisenhower and Israeli Prime Minister David Ben-Gurion. From the very beginning of what became known as the Suez crisis Eisenhower had forcefully opposed the secret plot by Britain, France and Israel to invade Egypt. Against great political pressures, Ike had managed to stop the ill-considered invasion—but not before Israeli troops grabbed Egypt's Sinai peninsula in a lightning surprise attack starting Oct. 29, 1956.

Britain and France followed Eisenhower's firm advice and quickly removed their troops from Egypt. But Israel insisted on retaining parts of the peninsula. Despite repeated U.S. urgings, Ben-Gurion refused to withdraw Israeli troops. In retaliation, Eisenhower joined with 75 other nations in the U.N. General Assembly in passing a resolution on Feb. 2, 1957, "deploring" Israel's occupation. Only two nations opposed: France and Israel.[2]

Still, Ben-Gurion refused to move his troops. On Feb. 11, Eisenhower sent a forceful note to Ben-Gurion to withdraw. Again Ben-Gurion refused. At the same time, the influence of Israel's supporters became intense. The White House was besieged by efforts to halt its pressure on the Jewish state; 41 Republican and 75 Democratic congressmen signed a letter urging support for Israel.[3]

In reaction to mounting pressures against his policy, Eisenhower on Feb. 20 called a meeting of the congressional leadership to seek their support for his position. But the lawmakers, sensitive to the influence of the Israeli lobby, refused to help, causing Secretary of State John Foster Dulles to complain to a friend:

"I am aware how almost impossible it is in this country to carry out a foreign policy [in the Middle East] not approved by the Jews." In other conversations around the same time, Dulles remarked on the "terrific control the Jews have over the news media and the barrage which the Jews have built up on congressmen....I am very much concerned over the fact that the Jewish influence here is completely dominating the scene and making it almost impossible to get Congress to do anything they don't approve of. The Israeli Embassy is practically dictating to the Congress through influential Jewish people in the country."[4]

Disgusted with Congress's timidity, Eisenhower boldly decided to take his case directly to the American people. He went on national television on the evening of Feb. 20 and explained:

"Should a nation which attacks and occupies foreign territory in the face of United Nations disapproval be allowed to impose conditions on its own withdrawal? If we agreed that armed attack can properly achieve the purposes of the assailant, then I fear we will have turned back the clock of international order.

"If the United Nations once admits that international disputes can be settled by using force, then we will have destroyed the very foundation of the organization and our best hope of establishing world order. The United Nations must not fail. I believe that in the interests of peace the United Nations has no choice but to exert pressure upon Israel to comply with the withdrawal resolutions."[5]

Ike did not depend only on words. While he expressed his principled position in public, privately that same day he sent a stern message to Ben-Gurion warning of punitive actions if Israel did not withdraw. Eisenhower threatened that he would approve trade sanctions against Israel and might also cut off all private assistance to Israel, which amounted to $40 million in tax-deductible donations and $60 million annually in the purchase of bonds.[6]

This combination of public diplomacy and private grit paid off. On Feb. 27, Israel announced it accepted the U.S. position on withdrawal.[7]

Although Zionists continue to criticize Eisenhower to this day, painting his policy as flawed and short-sighted, his actions in the Suez crisis represent one of the brightest, most principled victories of U.S. diplomacy. Eisenhower had acted, as he later recalled, on the basis of his belief that "change based on principle is progress; constant change without principle becomes chaos."[8]

In detailing his thinking, Ike wrote in his memoirs: "Some critics have said that the United States should have sided with the British and French in the Middle East, that it was fatuous to lean so heavily on the United Nations. If we had taken the advice, where would it have led us? Would we now be, with them, an occupying power in a seething Arab world? If so, I am sure we would regret it. During the campaign, some political figures kept talking of our failure to 'back Israel.' If the administration had been incapable of withstanding this kind of advice in an election year, could the United Nations thereafter have retained any influence whatsoever? This, I definitely doubt."[9]

America and Eisenhower emerged from the crisis with enhanced moral authority and prestige around the world. Noted Eisenhower's major biographer, Stephen E. Ambrose: "Eisenhower's insistence on the primacy of the U.N., of treaty obligations, and of the rights of all nations gave the United States a standing in world opinion it had never before achieved."[10]

This became immediately clear to American diplomats. Ike's U.N. ambassador, Henry Cabot Lodge, telephoned the president and reported at one point during the crisis: "Never had there been such a tremendous acclaim for the president's policy. Absolutely spectacular." From Cairo, Ambassador Raymond Hare cabled: "The U.S. has suddenly emerged as a real champion of right."[11]

Added Ambrose: "The small nations of the world could hardly believe that the United States would support a Third World country, Egypt, in a struggle with colonial powers that were America's two staunchest allies, or that the United States would support Arabs against Israeli aggression. But it was true, and the small nations were full of admiration and delight. The introduction of the American [cease-fire] resolution to the U.N. was, indeed, one of the great moments in U.N. history."[12]

Eisenhower's handling of the crisis was a high point of his presidency. It upheld the authority and moral stance of the United Nations and the ideals of the United States. As difficult and painful as his actions were to take against such traditional allies as Britain and France, Eisenhower nonetheless had spurned short-term political gain and instead acted out of principle.

It was a far different story when Israel lashed out again 11 years later, this time occupying not only the Sinai but lands of Jordan and Syria. Lyndon B. Johnson was president and he had neither Ike's international experience nor his political strength. Instead Johnson was a fervent supporter of Israel, acutely aware of its influence in domestic politics, and made the fateful mistake of not taking any action to oppose Israel's acquisition of territory by force in 1967.

This led directly to the 1973 war in which Egypt and Syria sought to regain their land. After that war, Secretary of State Henry A. Kissinger, a critic of Ike's Suez policy, made another fateful mistake. He accepted Israel's "right" to use the territories it illegally held in occupation as bargaining chips for a number of conditions for withdrawal.

Before Kissinger was through, he had managed to give to Israel the largest transfer of U.S. treasury, technology and diplomatic support ever voluntarily granted by one country to another. In return, Israel surrendered minor tracts of land but maintained its occupation over nearly two million Palestinians for two decades more.

This astonishing bargain reached its culmination on Sept. 4, 1975, with the signing of the second Sinai disengagement agreement between Egypt and Israel.[13]

Beyond promises of aid to Israel at around a $2 billion annual level for each of the next five years,[14] Kissinger signed a sweeping series of secret understandings providing a broad array of pledges to Israel. One of these committed the United States to "make every effort to be fully responsive...on an on-going and long-term basis to Israel's military equipment and other defense requirements, to its energy requirements and to its economic needs." The memorandum officially committed American support against threats by a "world power," meaning the Soviet Union.

In essence, Sinai II, as it became known, formally allied the United States with Israel and its occupation of Arab lands.

As then-Defense Minister Shimon Peres observed at the time: "The...agreement has delayed [an international peace conference in] Geneva, while...assuring us arms, money, a coordinated policy with Washington and quiet in Sinai....We gave up a little to get a lot."[15]

Indeed, in return for all this Israel gave up only a few miles of desert territory in the Sinai that nearly every nation in the world believed it had no right to keep under military occupation. It retained all of Jordan's West Bank, all of Syria's Golan Heights and about half of Egypt's Sinai. But unlike Eisenhower, who did not pay a penny for Israel's 1957 withdrawal, Kissinger and President Gerald Ford paid a fortune, mainly because they had failed to stand by principle and instead favored Israel to gain partisan political advantage.

Kissinger's policy was prohibitively costly to the United States. By making Israel the military superpower of the region, the Kissinger policy also led to tragic events. These included Israel's bloody 1982 invasion of Lebanon, an action based on its new arrogance of power stemming from U.S.-supplied weaponry.

Even graver, however, was the fact that Israel was allowed by Washington to continue its occupation and settlement of Jordanian and Syrian land. This occurred during the same period that the United States became Israel's major patron and supporter starting in the 1970s under President Richard M. Nixon and Kissinger.

The dramatic increase of U.S. aid while Israel violated official U.S. policy against military occupation was a declaration to the world that where the Jewish state was concerned politics outweighed principle.

These events eventually contributed to the assassination of Prime Minister Yitzhak Rabin in 1995. Yigal Amir, the murderer, was one of the Jewish fanatics who emerged during the long occupation and were dedicated to retaining the occupied territories. Had Kissinger, like Ike, driven Israel off the occupied land, Amir's motive for the assassination would never have existed. The occupation would not have lasted three decades and the extremist cult devoted to keeping the land that began growing strong in Israel in the 1970s would not have come into being.

As a final irony, Kissinger to this day is considered a great statesman for his Sinai agreement, while the Suez crisis and Ike's brave actions are barely remembered. David Halberstam did not even bother mentioning the 1956 crisis in his recent bestselling book *The Fifties*, dedicated to the major events of that decade. That is more than a sad commentary on the relative merits of the policies pursued by the two men. It is a stunning reminder of how strong Zionist influence is in the American media when it comes to molding perceptions of U.S. policy in the Middle East. 🖈

RECOMMENDED READING:

Ambrose, Stephen E., *Eisenhower: The President*, New York, Simon & Schuster, 1984.

Burns, Lt. Gen. E.L.M., *Between Arab and Israeli*, New York, Ivan Obolensky, 1962.

Eisenhower, Dwight D., *Waging Peace: 1956-61*, Garden City, N.Y., Doubleday & Company, Inc., 1965.

*Lilienthal, Alfred M., *The Zionist Connection: What Price Peace?*, New York, Dodd, Mead & Company, 1978.

Love, Kenneth, *Suez: The Twice-Fought War*, New York, McGraw-Hill Book Company, 1969.

Medzini, Meron, *Israel's Foreign Relations: Selected Documents, 1974-1977* (vol. 3), Jerusalem, Ministry of Foreign Affairs, 1982.

*Neff, Donald, *Warriors at Suez: Eisenhower takes America into the Middle East*, New York, Linden Press/Simon & Schuster, 1981, and Brattleboro, VT, Amana Books, 1988.

Rubenberg, Cheryl A., *Israel and the American National Interest: A Critical Examination*, Chicago, University of Illinois Press, 1986.

Sheehan, Edward R.E., *The Arabs, Israelis, and Kissinger: A Secret History of American Diplomacy in the Middle East*, New York, Reader's Digest Press, 1976.

Tomeh, George J., *United Nations Resolutions on Palestine and the Arab-Israeli Conflict: 1947-1974* (vol. 1). Washington, DC, Institute for Palestine

Studies, 1975.

U.S. Department of State, *American Foreign Policy: Current Documents, 1957,* Washington, DC, U.S. Government Printing Office, 1961.

*Available through the AET Book Club.

NOTES:

[1]Burns, *Between Arab and Israeli,* p. 243.

[2]Resolution 1124 (XI); text in Tomeh, *United Nations Resolutions on Palestine and the Arab-Israeli Conflict,* Volume One: 1947-1974, p. 39.

[3]Rubenberg, *Israel and the American National Interest,* p. 78.

[4]Transcripts of Dulles' telephone conversations on Feb. 11, 12 and 19, 1957, quoted in Neff, *Warriors at Suez,* p. 433.

[5]Text is in State Department, *American Foreign Policy: Current Documents, 1957,* pp. 923-28. Also see Love, *Suez,* p. 666.

[6]Neff, *Warriors at Suez,* pp. 433-35.

[7]Dana Adams Schmidt, *New York Times,* 2/28/57.

[8]Eisenhower, *Waging Peace,* p. 13.

[9]*Ibid.,* p. 99.

[10]Ambrose, *Eisenhower,* p. 361.

[11]Neff, *Warriors at Suez,* p. 417.

[12]Ambrose, *Eisenhower,* p. 361.

[13]Text of the agreement and of the MOU and its secret addenda are in Medzini, *Israel's Foreign Relations, Selected Documents, 1974-77,* 3: pp. 281-90. Also see Sheehan, *The Arabs, Israelis, and Kissinger,* Appendix Eight.

[14]Over the next five years the State Department reported total aid to Israel equalled $1.742 billion in 1977, $1.792 billion in 1978, $4.790 billion in 1979, $1.786 billion in 1980 and $2.164 billion in 1981; see *New York Times,* 8/8/82.

[15]Sheehan, *The Arabs, Israelis, and Kissinger,* p. 192. Peres refused to be identified in the article but the author was head of the *Time* bureau at the time and one of his reporters interviewed Peres for the quote.

Chapter 43

1963: Johnson Aligns U.S. Policy With Israel

O N NOV. 22, 1963, President John F. Kennedy was assassinated in Dallas. While a traumatized nation grieved for
its youngest president, he was succeeded by Vice President Lyndon B. Johnson, who was to become the most pro-Israel
president up to that time. A sea change was about to take place in
America's relations with Israel.

Johnson was quick to declare his support for the Jewish state.
Shortly after being sworn in as president, Johnson reportedly remarked to an Israeli diplomat:

"You have lost a very great friend, but you have found a better
one." Commented Isaiah L. Kenen, one of the most effective lobbyists for Israel in Washington: "...I would say that everything he
did as president supported that statement."[1]

Up to Johnson's presidency, no administration had been as
completely pro-Israel and anti-Arab as his. Harry S Truman, while
remembered as a warm friend of Israel, was more interested in his
own election than Israel's fate. After winning office on his own in
1948 with the support of the Jewish vote, he seemed to lose interest in the Jewish state.[2]

Dwight D. Eisenhower was distinctly cool toward Israel, seeing
it as a major irritant in America's relations with the Arab world and
U.S. access to oil. There were no powerful partisans of Israel in his
administration and his secretary of state, John Foster Dulles, was a
frequent critic of Israel. Kennedy was considerably warmer toward
the Jewish state and became the first president to begin providing

major weapons to it, breaking an embargo in place since 1947.[3] Yet he valued the U.S. position in the Arab world, particularly with Egypt's Gamal Abdel Nasser, and as a result maintained a fairly even-handed policy despite having a number of pro-Israel officials in his administration.

All this changed dramatically under Johnson. Not only was he personally a strong supporter of the Jewish state but he had a number of high officials, advisers and friends who shared his view. These included officials within the administration such as McGeorge Bundy, Clark Clifford, Arthur Goldberg, Harry McPherson, John Roche, the Rostow brothers, Walt and Eugene, and Ben Wattenberg.

These officials occupied such high offices as the ambassador to the United Nations, the head of the National Security Council and the number two post at the State Department. They were assiduous in putting forward Israel's interests in such memoranda as "What We Have Done for Israel"[4] and "New Things We Might Do in Israel"[5] and "How We Have Helped Israel."[6]

The president was repeatedly urged by Israel's supporters to embrace Israeli policy, give the Jewish state increased aid, and distance America from the Arab world. So pervasive was the influence of Israel's supporters during Johnson's tenure that CIA Director Richard Helms believed there was no important U.S. secret affecting Israel that the Israeli government did not know about in this period.[7]

So closely allied were U.S. and Israeli interests in the mind of "Mac" Bundy, the special coordinator of Middle East policy during the 1967 war, that he once sought to buttress a recommendation to Johnson by remarking: "This is good LBJ doctrine and good Israeli doctrine, and therefore a good doctrine to get out in public."[8] When initial war reports showed Israel making dramatic gains and several officials in the State Department Operations Room outwardly showed satisfaction, Undersecretary of State Gene Rostow turned to them with a broad smile on his face and said ironically: "Gentlemen, gentlemen, do not forget we are neutral in word, thought and deed."[9] In the State Department's summary of the start of the war, Rostow's brother, Walt, the national security adviser, wrote on a covering letter to Johnson: "Herewith the account, with a map, of the first day's turkey shoot."[10]

Beyond the administration's supporters of Israel, one of Johnson's closest informal advisers was Supreme Court Justice Abe Fortas, another warm friend of Israel's. Two of Johnson's closest outside advisers were Abraham Feinberg and Arthur B. Krim, both strong supporters of Israel. Feinberg was president of the American Bank & Trust Company of New York and the man whose "activities started a process of systematic fund-raising for politics [in the late 1940s] that has made Jews the most conspicuous fund-raisers and contributors to the Democratic Party," according to a study by Stephen D. Isaacs, *Jews and American Politics.* Johnson routinely consulted Feinberg on Middle East policy.

Feinberg was a vocal supporter of increased aid to Israel. Although an American, Feinberg at various times owned the Coca-Cola franchise in Israel and was a part-owner of the Jerusalem Hilton Hotel. When his bank fell into trouble in the 1970s and two of its officers were convicted of misappropriating funds, the Israeli Company, in a generous act of reverse aid, purchased Feinberg's American Bank & Trust Company.[11]

Arthur Krim was president of United Artists Corporation of Hollywood, a New York attorney and another major Democratic fund-raiser. He served as chairman of the Democratic Party National Finance Committee and chairman of the President's Club of New York, the most potent source of Johnson's campaign funds. Krim was married to a physician, Mathilde, who in her youth had briefly served as an agent for the Irgun, the Jewish terrorist group led by Menachem Begin.

The Krims were so close to Johnson that they built a vacation house near his Texas ranch to be close to him on long weekends and were regular guests at the White House. Mathilde Krim stayed at the White House during much of the 1967 war and was a regular caller at the Israeli Embassy, passing reports and gossip back and forth. The Krims, like other Johnson friends, did not hesitate to advise the president on Middle East policy.[12]

How influential the Krims were in forming Johnson's Middle East policy was hinted at by notes in the president's daily diary for June 17, 1967. The notes reported that at a dinner with the Krims and others at Camp David, Johnson openly discussed a speech he was working on that was to establish the nation's Middle East policy for the years ahead.

According to the notes, Johnson read from various drafts of the speech around the dinner table, "inserting additions and making changes, also accepting comments and suggestions from all at the table." Thus two passionate partisans of Israel, the Krims, helped Johnson refine what was later called the "five great principles of peace," the pillars of U.S. policy in the Middle East for the next two decades.

After Johnson delivered the speech on June 19, he received a report of an enthusiastic phone call from Abe Feinberg saying that the Jewish community was delighted with the speech. "Mr. Feinberg said he had visited with Israelis and Jewish leaders all over the country and they are high in their appreciation."[13]

Under Johnson, aid to Israel increased and the old arms embargo was completely shattered, portending the massive transfer of treasure, technology and weapons that began in the next administration of Richard M. Nixon. That, of course, was only the beginning of the age of total support of Israel, which reached new heights under Bill Clinton. ❧

RECOMMENDED READING:

Donovan, Robert J., *Conflict and Crisis: The Presidency of Harry S Truman, 1945-1948*, New York, W.W. Norton, 1977.

*Green, Stephen, *Taking Sides: America's Secret Relations with a Militant Israel*, New York, William Morrow and Company, Inc., 1984.

*Hersh, Seymour M., *The Samson Option: Israel's Nuclear Arsenal and American Foreign Policy*, New York, Random House, 1991.

Isaacs, Stephen D., *Jews and American Politics*, Garden City, NY, Doubleday & Company, Inc., 1974.

Khalidi, Walid (ed.), *From Haven to Conquest: Readings in Zionism and the Palestine Problem until 1948*, Washington, DC, Institute for Palestine Studies, second printing, 1987.

Miller, Merle, *Lyndon: An Oral History*, New York, G. P. Putnam's Sons, 1980.

*Neff, Donald, *Warriors for Jerusalem: The Six Days that Changed the Middle East*, New York, Linden Press/Simon & Schuster, 1984.

*Neff, Donald, *Fallen Pillars: U.S. Policy towards Palestine and Israel since 1945*, Washington, DC, Institute for Palestine Studies, 1995.

Rubenberg, Cheryl A., *Israel and the American National Interest: A Critical*

Examination, Chicago, University of Illinois Press, 1986.

Wilson, Evan M., *Decision on Palestine: How the U.S. came to Recognize Israel*, Stanford, CA, Hoover Institution Press, 1979.

*Available through the AET Book Club.

NOTES:

[1]Miller, *Lyndon*, p. 477. This was generally the assessment in Israel as well; see Green, *Taking Sides*, pp. 184-86.

[2]See for instance: Wilson, *Decision on Palestine*, pp. 148-49; Rubenberg, *Israel and the American National Interest*, pp. 9-10, 31; Khalidi, *From Haven to Conquest*, pp. liii-lxvii; Donald Neff, "Palestine, Truman and America's Strategic Balance," *American-Arab Affairs*, No. 25, Summer 1988, pp. 30-41.

[3]Neff, *Fallen Pillars*, pp. 170-71.

[4]State Dept., NEA/IAI:2/8/67; confidential, declassified 4/16/81.

[5]W.W. Rostow, Memorandum for the President, 5/21/66; secret, declassified 3/13/79.

[6]Unsigned, White House papers, 5/19/66; secret, declassified 3/13/79.

[7]Neff, *Warriors for Jerusalem*, p. 110.

[8]*Ibid.*, p. 273.

[9]*Ibid.*, p. 213.

[10]Rostow to the President, 6/5/67, secret.

[11]Isaacs, *Jews and American Politics*, p. 83. Detailed information on Feinberg, including his aid to Israel's nuclear program, is in Hersh, *The Samson Option*, pp. 93-111.

[12]Neff, *Warriors for Jerusalem*, pp. 83, 156-58.

[13]"Marvin to the President," memorandum, 6:30 PM, 19 June, 1967, reprinted in Neff, *Warriors for Jerusalem*, pp. 307-08.

Chapter 44

1970: Jews Call Fulbright Anti-Semitic

O N AUG. 22, 1970, Democratic Senator J. William Fulbright of Arkansas proposed that the United Nations
impose peace on Israel and Arab states and that the
United States guarantee Israel's borders within its pre-1967
boundaries. His proposal also urged that the Palestinians living
under Israeli occupation be granted self-determination, that
Jerusalem become an international city, as mandated in the original U.N. partition of Palestine, and that Israeli ships be guaranteed
passage through the Strait of Tiran and the Suez Canal.[1]

Fulbright was the respected chairman of the Senate Foreign
Relations Committee and generally a foe of U.S. commitments
abroad. Nonetheless, in a 15,000-word speech titled "Old Myths and
New Realities—the Middle East," he said it may be necessary to
commit U.S. troops to the Middle East in order to gain peace. He
proposed that the United States enter into a bilateral treaty with
Israel to "guarantee the territory and independence of Israel within
the borders of 1967."

Fulbright added: "The supplementary, bilateral arrangements
with Israel would obligate the United States to use force if necessary,
in accordance with its constitutional processes, to assist Israel
against any violation of its 1967 borders which it could not repel
itself, but the agreement would also obligate Israel, firmly and unequivocally, never to violate those borders herself."

It was an extremely favorable proposal for Israel, giving it recognized sovereignty over the Palestinian land it had captured and
held by force before 1967, free naval passage through the Red Sea
to the Indian Ocean, and a formal defense treaty with the United

States, which it had long sought. But it did not give Israel sovereignty over Jerusalem and, significantly, it would mean the return of vast areas of Arab territory it had captured in 1967 and on which it already was constructing illegal settlements.

Instead of using Fulbright's plan to talk peace, Israel sharply rejected it as unfair, and Israel's U.S. supporters increased their personal attacks on the senator. Fulbright had long been characterized as an "anti-Semite" by American Jews because of his critical views of Israel's aggressive policies and its enormous influence in Washington. His critics, and there were many, particularly on the right after he spoke out against the Vietnam War in the mid-1960s, delighted in referring to him as "Senator Halfbright."

But it was Zionists who especially despised him. Fulbright had earned the ever-lasting enmity of Israel and its friends as early as 1963, when his Foreign Relations Committee held hearings on foreign lobbies, including Israel's lobby. The hearings concluded that Israel operated "one of the most effective networks of foreign influence" in the United States. It found that Israel used tax-free dollars donated to the United Jewish Appeal for charities in Israel in the United States to influence U.S. opinion.

These funds eventually were used to purchase the Jewish Telegraphic Agency, to establish and maintain the Conference of Presidents of Major American Jewish Organizations, and to pressure U.S. newspapers to support Israel and to attack critics of Israel, among other activities. Fulbright revealed that the Zionist pursuit of promoting Israel included "placement of articles on Israel in some of America's leading magazines," arranging for radio and TV programs sympathetic to Israel, and subsidizing trips to Israel by such "public opinion molders" as Christian clergymen, academics and mass media representatives.[2]

As the years went on, Fulbright became an increasingly outspoken critic of Israel. During the 1973 war in the Middle East, he said that the best way to have peace was for the United States and the Soviet Union to refuse to provide Arabs and Israelis weapons, adding: "but we are not going to do that....Somewhere around 80 percent of the Senate of the United States is completely in support of Israel and of anything Israel wants." In December, while the Senate debated the award to Israel of more aid, Fulbright observed that "instead of rearming Israel, we could have peace in the Middle East at once if we just told Tel Aviv to withdraw behind the 1967 borders and guarantee them."[3]

When Fulbright stood for re-election the next year, he was defeated, ending a 32-year congressional career. He believed his criticisms of Israel largely caused his loss, noting that "any member of Congress who does not follow the wishes of the Israel lobby is bitterly denounced and can be assured of finding his opponent richly funded in the next election."[4]

Indeed, major Jewish contributions flowed to his opponent, Dale Bumpers. A Bumpers' aide bragged: "I could have bought central Arkansas with the offers of money from the Jewish community—they came particularly from people in New York and California who have raised a lot of money in the Jewish community for political purposes."[5]

Although out of office, Fulbright maintained his interest in the Middle East and Israel's influence in America. He joined a Washington law firm, where he was well situated to keep an eye on the Israel lobby's activities. In a 1989 book, *The Price of Empire*, he wrote: "The [Israel] lobby can just about tell the president what to do when it comes to Israel. Its influence in Congress is pervasive and, I think, profoundly harmful—to us and ultimately to Israel itself...So completely have many of our principal officeholders fallen under Israeli influence that they not only deny today the legitimacy of Palestinian national aspirations, but debate who more passionately opposes a Palestinian state."

He added: "AIPAC [the American Israel Public Affairs Committee] and its allied organizations have effective working control of the electoral process. They can elect or defeat nearly any congressman or senator that they wish, with their money and coordinated organizations. They are the really important power to negotiate with in the Middle East if you want an agreement.

"The Israelis and their supporters here—especially the latter— have long taken the position that if you do not do exactly as they wish, you are anti-Israel and anti-Semitic. Accordingly, since no one welcomes these charges and the political sanctions that go with them, it has been impossible to follow what I would call an evenhanded policy in the Middle East. It has not been possible in the past; and it still isn't."[6]

Anyone doubting his claims about the influence of Israel's lobby had only to read the obituaries written about Fulbright following his death at age 89 on Feb. 9, 1995. The lengthy obituaries recounted his distinguished career as the president of the University of Arkansas at age 34, then being elected to the House of Representatives in 1942 and to the Senate in 1944, where he introduced legislation that led to the Fulbright Scholarship program. He became chairman of the Senate Foreign Relations Committee in 1959 and retained that position for 15 years, the longest tenure in history.

For all that, no mention was made in either *The New York Times* or *The Washington Post* about his views toward the Middle East. It was as though his critical positions on Israel had been sucked into a black hole, totally forgotten. Yet here was an issue on which Fulbright had provided a major voice, and which directly contributed to the end of his political career. Clearly the Middle East constituted an important part of his life. Indeed, his career and his loss of office could not be understood without mention of it.[7]

That the omission of this vital subject was no oversight became clear in succeeding weeks. Both newspapers printed a number of letters from readers recalling various aspects of Fulbright's long career. But none of the letters sent to the two papers reminding them about Fulbright's record on Israel were deemed fit to print.[8]

❧

RECOMMENDED READING:

*Fulbright, J. William, *The Price of Empire*, New York: Pantheon Books, 1989.

*Lilienthal, Alfred M. *The Zionist Connection: What Price Peace?*, New York: Dodd, Mead & Company, 1978.

*Available through the AET Book Club.

NOTES:

[1]Excerpts are in *New York Times*, 8/23/70.

[2]Alfred M. Lilienthal, "J. William Fulbright: A Giant Passes," *Washington Report on Middle East Affairs*, April/May, 1995.

[3]*Ibid.*

[4]See Fulbright's last book, *The Price of Empire*.

[5]Alfred M. Lilienthal, "J. william Fulbright: A Giant Passes," *Washington Report on Middle East Affairs*, April/May, 1995.

[6]Richard H. Curtiss, "U.S. Obituaries on Senate Leader Omit His Mideast Views," *Washington Report on Middle East Affairs*, April/May, 1995.

[7]*Ibid.*

[8]Donald Neff, *Middle East International,* 4/9/95.

Chapter 45

1973: Origins of the Disastrous Oil Boycott

ON OCT. 20, 1973, Saudi Arabia announced it was imposing a total oil boycott against the United States in retaliation for its support of Israel during the October war. The action caused an economic earthquake around the world.[1] Suddenly Americans and others were forming long lines at gas stations, and the greatest transfer of wealth in world history began. The price of gasoline soared, briefly up tenfold. It was a devastating added cost for governments, corporations and families.

The embargo, Henry A. Kissinger later admitted, had "the most drastic consequences" for the United States, adding, "It increased our unemployment and contributed to the deepest recession we have had in the postwar [World War II] period."[2] What Kissinger failed to say was that he bore major responsibility for the boycott.

The boycott could not have come as a surprise, as so many U.S. officials of the period have pretended. Since the beginning of 1973, Saudi Arabia's King Faisal ibn Abdul Aziz had been warning the Nixon administration with increasing urgency that he would employ the oil weapon unless Washington forced Israel to return Arab land it had been occupying since 1967. As guardian of Islam's holy sites, Faisal was particularly perturbed that Israel continued to occupy the Haram Al-Sharif with the Al Aqsa and Dome of the Rock mosques in Arab East Jerusalem. Haram Al-Sharif is the third holiest site, after Mecca and Medina, to the world's one billion Muslims.

Faisal, a proud and pious man, knew Egypt and Syria were planning war if Israel did not end its occupation. He thought war might be averted and Arab rights restored if he could influence President Richard Nixon to moderate U.S. support of Israel. In April the king sent one of his top aides, Oil Minister Ahmad Zaki Yamani, to Washington to warn officials of his seriousness about imposing an oil boycott.[3]

Among other Nixon officials, Yamani met with Kissinger, who at the time was the national security adviser in the White House. Instead of heeding Yamani, however, Kissinger strongly advised the Saudi not to mention the threat of an oil boycott to anyone else because it would make the Saudis look domineering and extreme. Kissinger was outwardly disturbed when Yamani informed him he had already talked with some officials, including Treasury Secretary George P. Shultz.

Nonetheless, Kissinger said, Yamani should not repeat his threat. The Saudi suspected that Kissinger's Jewishness prevented him from being impartial on Middle East matters and believed Kissinger was trying to keep the facts from the American people. Yamani continued to voice the king's message, including granting an interview to *The Washington Post*. He pointed out to the newspaper that the West was pressing Saudi Arabia to increase its oil production up to 20 million barrels a day from its current 7.2 million. Yamani said: "We'll go out of our way to help you. We expect you to reciprocate."[4]

The *Post* was no more impressed by the Saudi message than Kissinger. On April 20, the *Post* editorially criticized the Saudis for threatening an oil boycott and added that "it is to yield to hysteria to take such threats as Saudi Arabia's seriously."[5]

Faisal was so disturbed by the U.S. rejection of his message that he granted for the first time in his life an interview to American TV. He warned: "America's complete support of Zionism against the Arabs makes it extremely difficult for us to continue to supply U.S. petroleum needs and even to maintain friendly relations with America."[6]

Israel was particularly active in encouraging Washington to ignore Faisal. Foreign Minister Abba Eban asserted that there was not "the slightest possibility" of an oil boycott. He added: "The Arab states have no alternative but to sell their oil because they have no other resources at all."[7]

In May, Faisal summoned to his Riyadh palace Frank Jungers, the board chairman of the Arabian American Oil Company. He warned the oilman about the possibility of an oil boycott. Jungers knew the king and believed that "he never acts on a whim. He never breaks his word. When he speaks, he never tells you anything unless he means it." Jungers passed on Faisal's message to both the White House and the State Department. It was ignored.[8]

That same month Faisal also called in four other leading oilmen and warned them that Arab resentment of U.S. support of Israel was rising, adding: "You may lose everything. Time is running out." They tried to relay that message. No one in the White House, the State Department or the Pentagon took it seriously. When they sought to meet with Kissinger, he refused to see them.[9]

Otto N. Miller, the board chairman of Standard Oil of California, tried to make the matter public by discussing it in a company letter to the firm's nearly 300,000 shareholders and employees. He wrote that Americans should foster "the aspirations of the Arab people [and] their efforts toward peace in the Middle East. There is now a feeling in the Arab world that the United States has turned its back on the Arab people."

Miller made no direct mention of Israel. Yet such was the explosion of protest by Israel's supporters—they threatened a boycott of Standard products—that he was forced to issue a statement saying that, of course, peace had to be based on "the legitimate interests of Israel and its people as well as the interests of all other states in the area."[10]

Another oilman, Maurice F. Granville, board chairman of Texaco, also sought to take the issue directly to the American people. He appealed to Americans "to review the actions of their government in regard to the Arab-Israeli dispute and to compare those actions with its stated position of support for peaceful settlement responsive to the concerns of all the countries involved." Such opaque language had no more influence than Granville.[11]

The warnings by oilmen, Arab leaders and Faisal to the Nixon administration continued throughout the summer. In another rare interview in September, Faisal told *Newsweek* that "logic requires that our oil production does not exceed the limits that can be absorbed by our economy." He meant that Saudi Arabia was already earning enough money to meet its needs and that to honor the U.S. request to produce more oil would be a favor to the West at the expense of depleting Saudi Arabia's only natural resource. He added that Washington should show its gratitude by disavowing "Zionist expansionist ambitions."[12]

Despite these repeated warnings, the Nixon administration continued to echo the Israeli claim that Saudi Arabia was not serious. George Shultz, who later as secretary of state proved completely incompetent in dealing with the Middle East, dismissed Faisal's warnings as Arab "swaggering."[13] Nixon himself repeated the Israeli mantra that "oil without a market...does not do a country much good." No one in the Nixon administration, certainly not Kissinger or Shultz, seemed to be willing to consider that America and most of the rest of the industrialized world were so dependent on oil that even its partial denial would be devastating.[14]

That blind attitude prevailed in Washington and Tel Aviv up to, and beyond, the successful attack by Egypt and Syria on Oct. 6 against territories occupied by Israel. It was a traumatic event. The Arabs caught Israel totally unprepared. Egyptian troops successfully crossed the Suez Canal, an amphibious operation thought impossible by Israel and U.S. military experts, and the Syrians captured back most of the Golan Heights in the first hours of the assault.[15]

Despite the initial Arab successes, Israel remained optimistic. So, too, did Washington. Even two hours after war had actually broken out, the combined intelligence agencies of the United States still did not believe hostilities were likely or that the Arabs were capable of such coordinated action.[16]

The first assumption of Henry Kissinger, who barely two weeks earlier had become secretary of state, was that Israel would quickly prevail. As he complacently said to Alexander Haig, President Nixon's chief of staff, America should let Israel "beat them up for a day or two and that will quiet them down."[17]

The reality was that by the second day of fighting the Syrians were threatening the very heartland of the Jewish state from the Golan Heights and the Egyptians were decimating Israel's forces in the Sinai Peninsula. Nonetheless, optimism continued in Tel Aviv and Washington.

During the second day of fighting Prime Minister Golda Meir sent a sedate message to the White House asking for a delay on a cease-fire vote in the U.N. Security Council for at least three or four days, time enough, it was thought, to repel the Arabs. The request was quickly granted. That same day Israel requested a modest amount of emergency supplies, which was also approved.[18]

By Oct. 9, it finally became clear to Israel that it was in desperate straits. So great was its fear that it reportedly armed its nuclear weapons.[19] Word of Israel's perilous position reached Israeli Ambassador Simcha Dinitz in Washington early in the morning. He met with Kissinger in the White House within hours and received assurances that Israel's needs would be promptly met.[20]

To be sure that Israel could quickly communicate with him, Kissinger ordered installed in Ambassador Dinitz's office at the Israeli Embassy a private, secure telephone line that directly linked the secretary of state with the ambassador, a unique privilege for a foreign country.[21]

Washington's blatant favoring of Israel caused acute fears among oilmen that Saudi Arabia might carry out its threatened boycott. On Oct. 12, the chairmen of Aramco's four parent companies—J.K. Jamieson of Essco, Rawleigh Warner of Mobil, M.F. Granville of Texaco and Otto N. Miller of Socal—sent a joint memorandum to President Nixon expressing their alarm at the possibility of an oil boycott and price rise if the United States continued its coddling of Israel.

Their memo said, in part: "We are convinced of the seriousness of the intentions of the Saudis and Kuwaitis and that any actions of the U.S. Government at this time in terms of increased military aid to Israel will have a critical and adverse effect on our relations with the moderate Arab oil-producing countries." The White House acknowledged receiving the memo but took no action on it.[22]

Instead, the next day, Oct. 13, the Nixon administration began a massive airlift of weapons and ammunition to Israel.[23] However, America's European allies, more cautious about provoking a boycott, refused to allow U.S. planes en route to Israel to overfly their airspace. The planes had to use America's leased base at the Portuguese island of Lajes, neither the best nor the cheapest route.[24]

By this time, Israeli forces, their morale bolstered by open U.S. support, were slowly gaining the upper hand. They had pushed the Syrians back beyond the 1967 cease-fire line on the Golan Heights and, on Oct. 16, they finally broke through the Egyptian line and a small contingent crossed the Suez Canal into Egypt proper. The Israeli military force was now not only successfully holding onto the Arab land it had captured in 1967 but it was threatening the ancient capitals of Cairo and Damascus.

On the day of the Israeli crossing of the Suez Canal, the Arab oil countries met in Kuwait and raised the price of crude 70 percent, from $3.01 to $5.11 a barrel.[25] Despite that dramatic gesture, Kissinger continued to insist that an oil boycott was not likely. He met on Oct. 17 with a delegation of Arab foreign ministers from Algeria, Kuwait, Morocco and Saudi Arabia. Afterwards he somehow concluded that there would not be an Arab oil boycott despite America's open resupplying of Israel.[26]

The next day King Faisal sent a stern warning to Washington. He said bluntly that an embargo would be placed on all oil shipments to the United States unless Israel returned to the 1967 lines and the U.S. stopped its arms supply to Israel.[27] Despite the Saudi warning, Kissinger decided that a way must be found for Washington "to gain a little more time for Israel's offensive...."[28] This implicitly meant that the U.S. supply operation would continue in defiance of Faisal's warning.

Instead of returning to the former lines as the Arabs were demanding, a massive Israeli force crossed the canal on Oct. 18, directly threatening Cairo. The invasion not only stunned the Arabs but the Soviets too. Soviet Chairman Leonid Brezhnev sent an urgent message to Nixon proposing a cease-fire in place and Israeli withdrawal to the 1967 lines. Kissinger stalled to give the Israelis more time to press their counterattack.[29]

Libya retaliated on the same day by announcing a total cutoff of oil shipments to the United States and a rise in the price of its premium oil to other countries from $4.90 to $8.25 a barrel.[30] The final straw for Faisal came the next day. On Oct. 19, President Nixon requested from Congress $2.2 billion in emergency aid to Israel, a huge sum far beyond any previous aid to Israel.[31]

In effect, the United States was now saying to the Arabs that it would finance Israel's fight to retain its illegal occupation of their land. At no time during the war did combat take place inside Israel itself. All the fighting was on Egyptian and Syrian soil.

An explanation for Nixon's reckless action can be found in the fact that in October Nixon was thinking less of foreign relations than of himself. By this time he was deep in the quagmire of the Watergate scandal and the devastating disgrace of his vice president. Spiro Agnew had resigned Oct. 10 after being accused of corruption. Nixon was desperate for political support, leaving Kissinger basically in charge of U.S. foreign policy throughout the October war.[32]

The next day Saudi Arabia carried out its longstanding threat. From April to as late as Oct. 18, Faisal had been insistently warning Washington to temper its bias toward Israel. Now he acted. Riyadh announced at 9 p.m. local time on Oct. 20 that it was imposing a total oil boycott against the United States, its closest Western friend. The Saudi action had a domino effect. Abu Dhabi, Algeria, Bahrain, Kuwait and Qatar quickly followed suit, violently disrupting international commerce.[33]

As a result of the boycott, the Arabs became enormously wealthy, largely at the expense of the United States and the West. Yet the boycott and the war had little effect on Israel's colonial policies. Even today it retains Syrian and Jordanian land—if not Egypt's, which America essentially bought back from Israel with the Sinai agreements.[34] Washington not only continued its close support of the Jewish state but grew closer to it, despite the heavy costs and the fact that Israel's occupation violated international law and America's own policies.

The boycott was lifted on March 18, 1974, leaving economies around the world shattered and many individuals living poorer lives, Kissinger admitted: "I made a mistake."[35] Skeptics might wonder whether it was a mistake, or wanton disregard of U.S. interests during a passionate effort to help Israel. ᵃ

RECOMMENDED READING:

*Cockburn, Andrew and Leslie, *Dangerous Liaison: The Inside Story of the U.S.-Israeli Covert Relationship*, New York, HarperCollins Publishers, 1991.

*Green, Stephen, *Living by the Sword: America and Israel in the Middle East, 1968-*

87, Brattleboro, VT, Amana Books, 1988.

*Hersh, Seymour M., *The Samson Option: Israel's Nuclear Arsenal and American Foreign Policy*, New York, Random House, 1991.

Kalb, Marvin and Bernard, *Kissinger*, Boston, Little, Brown and Company, 1974.

Kelly, J.B., *Arabia, the Gulf and the West*, New York, Basic Books, Inc., Publishers, 1980.

Kissinger, Henry A., *Years of Upheaval*, Boston, Little, Brown and Company, 1982.

Lacey, Robert, *The Kingdom*, London, Hutchinson & Co. (publishers) Ltd., 1981.

*Neff, Donald, *Warriors Against Israel: How Israel Won the Battle to Become America's Ally 1973*, Brattleboro, VT, Amana Books, 1988.

Nixon, Richard M., *The Memoirs of Richard Nixon*, New York, Grosset & Dunlap, 1978.

Rubenberg, Cheryl A., *Israel and the American National Interest: A Critical Examination*, Chicago, University of Illinois Press, 1986.

Sheehan, Edward R.E., *The Arabs, Israelis, and Kissinger: A Secret History of American Diplomacy in the Middle East*, New York, Reader's Digest Press, 1976.

*Available through the AET Book Club.

NOTES:

[1]Lacey, *The Kingdom*, p. 413; State Department Middle East Task Force, "Situation report #51," 10/21/73, secret; declassified 12/31/81. Also see Neff, *Warriors Against Israel*, p. 260. [2]Rubenberg, *Israel and the American National Interest*, p. 173.

[2]Rubenberg, *Israel and the American National Interest*, p. 173.

[3]Lacey, *The Kingdom*, p. 398; also see Neff, *Warriors Against Israel*, pp. 110-11.

[4]Lacey, *The Kingdom*, p. 399.

[5]*Washington Post*, 4/20/73.

[6]Lacey, *The Kingdom*, p. 400.

[7]*Ibid.*

[8]Sheehan, *The Arabs, Israelis, and Kissinger*, p. 69.

[9]Lacey, *The Kingdom*, pp. 400-02.

[10]*Facts on File 1973*, p. 654.

[11]*Ibid.*, p. 780.

[12]Sheehan, *The Arabs, Israelis, and Kissinger*, p. 67.

[13]*Ibid.*, p. 68.

[14]*Facts on File 1973*, p. 741.

[15]Neff, *Warriors Against Israel*, p. 153; Kissinger, *Years of Upheaval*, p. 458.

[16]"Pike Report on the Hearings of the House Select Committee on Intelligence," written in 1976 and published in the *Village Voice*, 2/16/76. Also see Kissinger, *Years of Upheaval*, p. 458.

[17]*Ibid.*, p. 472.

[18]*Ibid.*, p. 477.

[19]Hersh, *The Samson Option*, pp. 223-30. Also see Cockburns, *Dangerous Liaison*, p. 173; Green, *Living by the Sword*, pp. 90-92. *Time* reported the story as early as 1976. None of the principals involved has ever admitted the nuclear arming incident, although former Ambassador to Egypt Herman Eilts says Kissinger years later casually referred to it; see Hersh, *The Samson Option*, p. 230.

[20]Kissinger, *Years of Upheaval*, pp. 492-96.

[21]Kalb and Kalb, *Kissinger*, p. 467.

[22]Kelly, *Arabia, the Gulf & the West*, p. 396.

[23]Kissinger, *Years of Upheaval*, p. 514.

[24]Rubenberg, *Israel and the American National Interest*, p. 166.

[25]Kelly, *Arabia, the Gulf & the West*, p. 397; Lacey, *The Kingdom*, p. 406.

[26]Kissinger, *Years of Upheaval*, p. 536.

[27]Kelly, *Arabia, the Gulf & the West*, p. 397.

[28]Kissinger, *Years of Upheaval*, pp. 538, 541.

[29]*Ibid.*, pp. 539-40. Also see Neff, *Warriors Against Israel*, pp. 249-50, 253.

[30]Neff, *Warriors Against Israel*, p. 257.

[31]Lacey, *The Kingdom*, p. 413; Nixon, *The Memoirs of Richard Nixon*, p. 932. Up to 1973, the largest amount of combined economic and military aid to Israel in one year had been $634.3 million in 1971. Israel's regular aid for 1973 had been budgeted at $492.8 million.

[32]Neff, *Warriors Against Israel*, pp. 218, 261-62.

[33]Lacey, *The Kingdom*, p. 413; State Department Middle East Task Force, "Situation report #51," 10/21/73, secret; declassified 12/31/81.

[34]See Donald Neff, "Middle East History: It Happened in January, Unprecedented U.S. Aid to Israel Began under the Sinai Agreements," *Washington Report on Middle East Affairs*, January, 1997 (see following chapter).

[35]Sheehan, *The Arabs, Israelis, and Kissinger*, p. 69.

Chapter 46

1974: Sinai Accords Start Major Aid to Israel

ON JAN. 18, 1974, Egypt and Israel signed an armistice agreement officially ending their 1973 war. The agreement became known as Sinai I because it was signed in the Sinai peninsula and involved Israel's occupation of that strategic desert.[1] Sinai I had been achieved after a heavily publicized week of shuttling between the two countries by Secretary of State Henry Kissinger, who for his efforts was hailed in the U.S. media as the Superman of diplomacy. It was only later that American taxpayers would learn that Sinai I laid the groundwork for the start of unprecedented massive aid to Israel by the United States, which continues to this day.

The aid program to Israel has amounted to the largest voluntary transfer of wealth and technology in history, far more than all American aid given to rehabilitate Western Europe under the Marshall Plan after World War II.[2]

Sinai I was widely hailed in the West as a major diplomatic accomplishment. The Arab world more realistically considered it merely a modest first step in ending Israel's occupation of Arab lands, held since 1967 and some of which remain under Israeli occupation today. Under the pact, Israel agreed to withdraw its forces west of the Suez Canal, thus liberating the Egyptian Third Army, which had remained surrounded by Israeli troops since the October war, and withdraw all its forces back 15 miles from the eastern side of the canal to positions west of the Gidi and Mitla passes. Between the two armies would be stationed a U.N. peace force.[3]

While Kissinger's diplomatic prowess was loudly credited in the United States for Sinai I, it was actually a secret agreement that he signed with Israel that had achieved the breakthrough. This secret commitment foreshadowed what was to become America's huge aid program to Israel. The covert Memorandum of Understanding contained 10 detailed points, the most important being a far-reaching pledge that Washington would be responsive to Israel's defense needs on a "continuing and long-term basis."[4]

The potential massive dimensions of that pledge began to become clear less than two years later when Kissinger, after another highly publicized shuttle between Cairo and Jerusalem, achieved what became known as Sinai II, signed on Sept. 4, 1975.[5] The agreement was especially favorable to Israel, and considerably less so to Egypt. The major article involving Egypt committed that most powerful of Arab countries to abstain from the use of force to resolve the Arab-Israeli conflict, meaning in the words of scholar Abdel Safty: "Thus, the agreement marked Egypt's military abandonment of its commitment to the right to liberate occupied Arab territories."[6]

For the Arabs, there was the bitter realization that Israel's continued occupation of their territory was against official U.S. policy and the major instruments guiding international civilized behavior since World War II: the U.N. Charter and the 1949 Geneva Convention Relative to the Protection of Civilian Persons in Time of War. Yet it was Israel, not Egypt, that profited far more from Kissinger's diplomacy.

Kissinger made no effort to demand that the occupation end in exchange for the treasury he was about to give Israel. Instead he assured Israel a level of annual aid at around $2 billion for the next five years and opened to Israel a cornucopia of other U.S. assets never imagined by the average U.S. taxpayer.[7] The irony was that the amount of aid was of such magnitude that it allowed Israel to maintain the very occupation that the United States said it opposed.

It goes without enumeration that the staggering amount of money given to Israel would have been of significant impact in helping America address its own domestic problems, especially those in the ghettos of the crumbling cities.

Kissinger's series of secret understandings included a memorandum of understanding (MOU) with Israel in which he committed the United States to "make every effort to be fully responsive...on an on-going and long-term basis to Israel's military equipment and other defense requirements, to its energy requirements and to its economic needs." This was made at a time when the U.S. economy itself was reeling under the staggering costs of the oil boycott, which in turn had been imposed as a direct result of Washington's ostentatious support of Israel during the 1973 war.

The memorandum also officially committed American support against threats by a "world power," meaning the nuclear-equipped Soviet Union, and among other things promised:

- America would guarantee for five years that Israel would be able to obtain all its domestic oil needs, from the United States if necessary.

- America would pay for construction in Israel of storage facilities capable of storing a one-year's supply of reserve oil needs.

- America would conclude contingency planning to transport military supplies to Israel during an emergency.

- America shared Israel's position that any negotiations with Jordan would be for an overall peace settlement, that is, there would be no attempt at step-by-step diplomacy on the West Bank.

- In a secret addendum to the secret MOU, America promised that the administration would submit every year to Congress a request for both economic and military aid for Israel. It also asserted that the "United States is resolved to continue to maintain Israel's defensive strength through the supply of advanced types of equipment, such as the F-16 aircraft." In addition, America agreed to study the transfer of "high technology and sophisticated items, including the Pershing ground-to-ground missile," which is usually used to deliver atomic warheads.

- In another secret memorandum, Kissinger committed America not to "recognize or negotiate with the Palestine Liberation Organization as long as the Palestine Liberation Organization does not recognize Israel's right to exist and does not accept Security Council Resolutions 242 and 338."[8] This language was passed into law by Congress in 1985.

- The United States would coordinate fully on strategy for any future meetings of the Geneva Conference. Thus, with Israel and the United States refusing to recognize the PLO and with powerful groups within the PLO refusing to accept Resolutions 242 and 338, the stalemate on the West Bank was set in concrete, much to Israel's satisfaction.

- In a separate secret letter signed by President Ford, the United States promised Israel that it would not put forward any peace proposals without first discussing them with the Israelis. This was a significant concession since it gave Israel, in effect, a direct input to formulation of U.S. policy in the Middle East.[9]

- In addition, President Ford signed a secret letter promising that the United States "will lend great importance to Israel's position that any peace treaty with Syria must be based on Israel's remaining on the Golan Heights."[10]

For this colossal commitment of U.S. wealth, technology and diplomatic support, Israel agreed to withdraw its forces between 20 to 40 miles east of the Suez Canal. This left well over half of Sinai under continuing Israeli occupation. Israel's major concession was to give up Egypt's oil fields, which lay on the western edge of the Sinai. The withdrawal resulted in Israeli forces being deployed east of the Gidi and Mitla passes, which were turned into observation posts. The United States pledged to set up and pay for stations manned by 200 Americans to protect both sides from violations. The arrangement replaced U.N. peacekeepers, who Israel opposed as being prejudiced against it even though U.N. reports from the field had proved to be rigorously objective over the decades.[11]

Defense Minister Shimon Peres summed up the benefits to Israel of Sinai II: "The...agreement [assures] us arms, money, a coordinated policy with Washington and quiet in Sinai...We gave up a little to get a lot."[12]

Indeed, there is no example in history when one nation granted to another such enormous amounts of wealth and array of commitments as Henry Kissinger's Sinai II agreement. This perhaps helps explain the tantalizing reference to Kissinger in the memoirs of Yitzhak Rabin, prime minister at the time of Sinai II, in which he wrote: "The story of Kissinger's contribution to Israel's security has yet to be told, and for the present suffice it to say that it was of prime importance."[13]

RECOMMENDED READING:

Kissinger, Henry A., *Years of Upheaval*, Boston, Little, Brown and Company, 1982.

Medzini, Meron, *Israel's Foreign Relations: Selected Documents, 1974-1977* (vol. 3), Jerusalem, Ministry of Foreign Affairs, 1982.

*Neff, Donald, *Warriors Against Israel: How Israel Won the Battle to Become America's Ally 1973*, Brattleboro, VT, Amana Books, 1988.

Riad, Mahmoud, *The Struggle for Peace in the Middle East*, New York, Quartet Books, 1981.

Quandt, William B., *Decade of Decisions: American Policy Toward the Arab-Israeli Conflict, 1967-1976*, Berkeley, University of California Press, 1977.

Rabin, Yitzhak, *The Rabin Memoirs*, Boston, Little, Brown and Company, 1979.

Safty, Abdel, *From Camp David to the Gulf: Negotiations, Language & Propaganda, and War*, New York, Black Rose Books, 1992.

Sheehan, Edward R.E., *The Arabs, Israelis, and Kissinger: A Secret History of American Diplomacy in the Middle East*, New York, Reader's Digest Press, 1976.

Yodfat, Aryeh Y. and Yuval Arnon-Ohanna, *PLO: Strategy and Tactics*, London, Croom Helm, 1981.

*Available through the AET Book Club.

NOTES:

[1] Kissinger, *Years of Upheaval*, pp. 809-21; the text is in Sheehan, *The Arabs, Israelis, and Kissinger*, Appendix Six.

[2] Robert W. Gibson, *Los Angeles Times*, 7/20/87. Gibson reports that by fiscal year 1988, total U.S. aid to Israel since 1948 had equalled in inflation-adjusted dollars $58.8 billion. Under the Marshall Plan, Congress in 1947 voted some $12 billion to be given to friendly European countries to rebuild their war-ravaged economies. The major difference with U.S. aid to Israel is that Marshall Plan aid was limited to a three-and-a-half-year period, while aid to Israel has been open-ended both in terms of time and amounts. Moreover, all aid to Israel since 1985 has been in the form of nonrepayable grants, averaging $3 billion a year in economic and military funds.

[3] Riad, *The Struggle for Peace in the Middle East*, pp. 274-75. Also see Safty, *From Camp David to the Gulf*, pp. 55-56.

[4] Sheehan, *The Arabs, Israelis, and Kissinger*, p. 112. Also see Quandt, *Decade of Decisions*, p. 228.

[5] Text of the agreement and of the MOU and its secret addenda are in Medzini, *Israel's Foreign Relations, Selected Documents, 1974-77*, vol. 3, pp. 281-90. Also see Sheehan, *The Arabs, Israelis, and Kissinger*, Appendix Eight.

[6] Safty, *From Camp David to the Gulf*, pp. 56-57.

[7] Over the next five years the State Department reported total aid to Israel equalled $1.742 billion in 1977, $1.792 billion in 1978, $4.790 billion in

1979 (reflecting the costs to move Israel out of the Sinai, where it had no right to be in the first place), $1.786 billion in 1980, and $2.164 billion in 1981; see *New York Times*, 8/8/82. By contrast, total U.S. aid to Israel in fiscal 1970 had totaled less than $100 million.

[8]Text is in Yodfat and Arnon-Ohanna, *PLO*, p. 191, and Sheehan, *The Arabs, Israelis, and Kissinger*, pp. 256-57.

[9]Quandt, *Decade of Decisions*, p. 201.

[10]The text is in *Journal of Palestine Studies*, Autumn 1991, pp. 183-84.

[11]Neff, *Warriors Against Israel*, pp. 302-03; Sheehan, *The Arabs, Israelis, and Kissinger*, p. 190.

[12]Sheehan, *The Arabs, Israelis, and Kissinger*, p. 192. Peres refused to be identified as the source of the quote, which originally appeared in *Time* magazine. However, the author was head of the *Time* bureau in Jerusalem during this period and Peres made the statement to one of his reporters.

[13]Rabin, *The Rabin Memoirs*, p. 261.

Chapter 47

1981: Israel Becomes Strategic Partner of U.S.

ON SEPT. 10, 1981, the Reagan administration conferred an extraordinary privilege on Israel. It formally announced that the tiny nation of well under four million Jews and the mighty United States had a "strategic relationship."[1] On Nov. 30, the United States made the compact official by signing a Memorandum of Understanding on Strategic Cooperation with Israel.[2]

The rationale for the unique relationship was that Israel would cooperate to counter threats in the Middle East "caused by the Soviet Union or Soviet-controlled forces from outside the region." Since Israel had shown a decade earlier that it could not stand up to Soviet air power in Egypt during the war of attrition, this was not exactly a major gain for the United States.[3] But it had great benefits for Israel.

The agreement brought the Jewish state a large array of new claims to U.S. assets and technology and diplomatic prestige. The memorandum created a coordinating council and working groups on weaponry research, military cooperation, maintenance facilities and other areas of so-called "mutual interest," in effect giving Israel American expertise at the working level. In addition, the United States agreed to buy up to $200 million a year of Israeli military products, thus opening the lucrative U.S. arms market to Israel. The irony was that Israel had founded its industry on U.S. technology transferred to Israel as aid or purloined by Israeli spies.[4]

Not surprisingly, the pact angered Arabs, who charged the

United States was directly helping Israeli "aggression and expansionism."[5] The Arabs were particularly disturbed by the timing of the announcement. It came barely a month after Crown Prince Fahd bin Abdul Aziz put forward the first comprehensive peace plan ever offered by Saudi Arabia.[6]

The U.N. General Assembly also criticized the agreement, saying it would "encourage Israel to pursue its aggressive and expansionist policies and practices in the occupied territories" and would have "adverse effects on efforts for the establishment of a comprehensive, just and lasting peace in the Middle East and would threaten the security of the region."[7]

Despite the enormous prestige and profit the United States had conferred on Israel by adopting it as a strategic partner, Israel then turned around and caused tremendous embarrassment to Washington two weeks later by annexing Syria's Golan Heights.[8] Israel's action on Dec. 14 directly defied U.S. policy and came at considerable cost to itself. In a rare show of anger at Israel, the Reagan administration joined in a unanimous U.N. Security Council resolution condemning the annexation and calling it "null and void."[9] More dramatically, on Dec. 18 Washington unilaterally suspended the Memorandum of Understanding on Strategic Cooperation.

With that action, there also were suspended a series of special privileges enjoyed by Israel. These included halting technical advice to Israeli concerns seeking to sell military equipment to the United States, barring Israel's use of U.S. aid to buy supplies from Israeli rather than American firms, and rescinding permission for third countries to use U.S. aid to buy military equipment from Israeli firms.[10]

Washington also had strong words for Israel. A State Department spokesman said: "We do not recognize Israel's action, which we consider to be without international legal effect. Their action is inconsistent with both the letter and the spirit of U.N. Security Council Resolutions 242 and 338."[11]

Prime Minister Menachem Begin reacted to the U.S. actions with outrage and arrogance. He summoned U.S. Ambassador to Israel Samuel W. Lewis to his Jerusalem home and declared:

"You have no moral right to preach to us about civilian casualties. We have read the history of World War II and we know what happened to civilians when you took action against an enemy. We have also read the history of the Vietnam War and your phrase 'bodycount'....Are we a vassal state? A banana republic? Are we 14-year-old boys, that if they don't behave they have their knuckles smacked?...The people of Israel has lived for 3,700 years without a memorandum of understanding with America—and it will continue to live without it for another 3,700 years."[12]

The ironies of the scene were many, not the least of which was that Begin himself was a notorious schemer more than willing to break agreements and that Lewis was one of America's most pro-Israel ambassadors.[13]

As a result of such harsh words and emotions, the strategic relationship remained suspended as long as Begin was in power. He finally resigned on Sept. 15, 1983, and on Oct. 10 he was succeeded by Yitzhak Shamir. Nineteen days later Washington resurrected the memorandum of understanding with the signing by President Reagan of top-secret National Security Decision Directive 111. It called for strategic cooperation with Israel against Soviet moves in the region. The policy was opposed by Defense Secretary Caspar Weinberger and the CIA, but it had the strong backing of Secretary of State George Shultz, one of America's most pro-Israel secretaries ever.[14]

In return for its cooperation, Israel was given more aid and intimate access to American national security officials and technology. The United States and Israel established a Joint Military Political Group (JMPG) for strategic cooperation. Funding was provided for Israel's Lavi fighter, joint military exercises were scheduled, stockpiling of U.S. military equipment in Israel was authorized, more extensive sharing of intelligence was agreed to, use of Israeli ports to service ships of the U.S. Sixth Fleet was approved, and a unique free-trade zone which would give Israel duty-free access to U.S. markets was established.

It was a long and tortuous path from the original strategic partnership and its final confirmation. Among the twists and turns: In 1982, Israel, armed with U.S. weapons, committed another outrage by invading Lebanon, causing untold death and destruction. Other horrors followed—the massacre at Sabra and Shatila and the bombing of the U.S. Embassy in Beirut with the loss of 63 lives, including one of the CIA's top officials. Israel's refusal to withdraw caused the dispatch of U.S. Marines to Lebanon, where less than a week before the strategic partnership was finalized 241 servicemen were killed by an explosives-laden truck that penetrated the Marine barracks at Beirut airport, one of the worst losses in the corps' history.[17]

Although Reagan vowed that the Marines would remain, they were withdrawn early the next year. But that did not stop attacks against Americans. On Sept. 20, 1984, further evidence of American vulnerability was provided by the bombing of the American Embassy's new location in East Beirut, with the loss of 24 employees, most of them not Americans. That same year saw the start of long-term kidnappings of Americans by Iranian-funded Lebanese Muslim groups. Anti-Americanism became so bad that in 1985 Washington imposed a travel ban on Americans going to Lebanon, declaring it was too dangerous. By the end of 1988, the American presence in Lebanon was essentially finished except for a handful of embassy personnel, who kept a very low profile.[18]

While the strategic partnership could not be directly blamed for causing one of America's biggest setbacks in the Middle East—U.S. expulsion from Lebanon after having had a major presence there since 1866—it certainly did nothing to prevent it. If anything, the open association with Israel as a "partner" further encouraged Israel's enemies to become America's enemies. The only benefactor of the strategic relationship was Israel. It gained the stature of being a partner of America as well as the profits of additional aid and cooperation that allowed it to continue its occupation of Arab lands in defiance of the rest of the world. ✦

RECOMMENDED READING:

Aronson, Geoffrey, *Creating Facts: Israel, Palestinians and the West Bank*, Washington, DC, Institute for Palestine Studies, 1987.

Bar-Siman-Tov, Yaacov, *The Israeli-Egyptian War of Attrition, 1969-1970: A Case Study of Limited Local War*, New York, Columbia University Press, 1980.

*Cockburn, Andrew and Leslie, *Dangerous Liaison: The Inside Story of the U.S.-Israeli Covert Relationship*, New York, HarperCollins Publishers, 1991.

Cooley, John K., *Payback: America's Long War in the Middle East*, New York, Brassey's (U.S.), Inc., 1991.

Fisk, Robert, *Pity the Nation: The Abduction of Lebanon*, New York, Atheneum, 1990.

Frank, Benis M., *U.S. Marines in Lebanon: 1982-1984*, Washington, DC, History and Museums Division, Headquarters, U.S. Marine Division, 1987.

*Friedman, Thomas L., *From Beirut to Jerusalem*, New York, Farrar, Strauss, Giroux, 1989.

*Khouri, Fred J., *The Arab-Israeli Dilemma* (3rd ed.), Syracuse, NY, Syracuse University Press, 1985.

Kimche, David, *The Last Option: After Nasser, Arafat, and Saddam Hussein*, New York, Charles Scribner's Sons, 1991.

*Mallison, Thomas and Sally V,. *The Palestine Problem in International Law and World Order*, London, Longman Group Ltd., 1986.

Moore, John Norton (ed.). *The Arab-Israeli Conflict* (vols I-IV), Princeton, NJ, Princeton University Press, 1974, 1991.

*Ostrovsky, Victor and Claire Hoy, *By Way of Deception*, New York, St. Martin's Press, 1990.

Raviv, Dan and Yossi Melman, *Every Spy a Prince: The Complete History of Israel's Intelligence Community*, Boston, Houghton Mifflin Company, 1990.

Rubenberg, Cheryl A., *Israel and the American National Interest: A Critical Examination*, Chicago, University of Illinois Press, 1986.

Sherif, Regina S., *United Nations Resolutions on Palestine and the Arab-Israeli Conflict: 1975-1981*, vol. 2, Washington, DC, Institute for Palestine Studies, 1988.

Silver, Eric, *Begin: The Haunted Prophet*, New York, Random House, 1984.

Woodward, Bob, *Veil: The Secret Wars of the CIA 1981-1987*, New York, Simon and Schuster, 1987.

*Available through the AET Book Club.

NOTES:

[1] The text is in *New York Times*, 12/1/81; "International Documents on Palestine 1981," *Journal of Palestine Studies*, pp. 405-06; Moore, *The Arab-Israeli Conflict*, IV (part 1): pp. 1065-66.

[2] *New York Times*, 12/1/81.

[3] Bar-Siman-Tov, *The Israeli-Egyptian War of Attrition*, p. 154.

[4] Cockburns, *Dangerous Liaison*, p. 7; Duncan L. Clarke, "The Arrow Missile: The United States, Israel and Strategic Cooperation, *Middle East Journal*, Summer 1994, pp. 483-84.

[5]Khouri, *The Arab-Israeli Dilemma* (3rd ed.), pp. 426-27. Also see Bishara A. Bahbah, "The U.S. Role in Israel's Arms Industry," *The Link*, December, 1987. Official Arab reaction is in *Journal of Palestine Studies*, Winter 1982, p. 194. Also see Rubenberg, *Israel and the American National Interest*, 268-69, who claims Washington saw the relationship as having Israel act as its proxy around the world. Certainly it quickly got the United States into trouble when Washington agreed to an Israeli plot to secretly trade weapons for hostages in what turned out to be the Iran-contra scandal of the mid-1980s, the greatest embarrassment of President Reagan's two terms and a classic example of the perils of letting one's policy become entangled with another country's interests.

[6]The text is in "Documents and Source Material," *Journal of Palestine Studies*, Autumn 1981, pp. 241-43. See Kimche, *The Last Option*, pp. 270-71; Khouri, *The Arab-Israel Dilemma* (3rd ed.), p. 425.

[7]Resolution 36/266 A. The text is in Sherif, *United Nations Resolutions on Palestine and the Arab-Israeli Conflict 1975-1981*, pp. 175-77.

[8]Aronson, *Creating Facts*, pp. 276-78; a partial text of Israel's announcement is in "International Documents on Palestine 1981," *Journal of Palestine Studies*, p. 414.

[9]Resolution 497; the text is in Sherif, *United Nations Resolutions on Palestine and the Arab-Israeli Conflict 1975-1981*, p. 200; Mallisons, *The Palestine Problem*, pp.476-77.

[10]David K. Shipler, *New York Times*, 12/24/81. The text of the State Department statement and Prime Minister Begin's response are in "International Documents on Palestine 1981," *Journal of Palestine Studies*, pp. 428-29.

[11]"International Documents on Palestine 1981," *Journal of Palestine Studies*, pp. 428-29.

[12]*New York Times*, 12/21/81; "International Documents on Palestine 1981," *Journal of Palestine Studies*, pp. 429-31. Also see Silver, *Begin*, pp. 245-46.

[13]When he retired from the State Department in 1985, after having served in Tel Aviv since 1977, Lewis took up residence part time in Israel and was made a board director of the New York branch of Bank Leumi, Israel's largest bank, as well as an international fellow at the Dayan Center at Tel Aviv University and chairman of the board of overseers at the Truman Institute for International Peace at Hebrew University in Jerusalem. He later became an adviser to the Washington Institute for Near East Policy, an Israeli lobby spinoff that had been co-founded by Martin Indyk, a future U.S. ambassador to Israel. Thus the Zionist promoters go round and round.

[14]William Safire, *New York Times*, 6/16/83. Also see Donald Neff, "The Remarkable Feat of George Shultz," *Middle East International*, 3/5/88. For

a description of Shultz's style on dealing with Israel, see Friedman, *From Beirut to Jerusalem*, pp. 500-01.

[15]Bernard Gwertzman, "Reagan Turns to Israel," *New York Times Sunday Magazine*, 11/27/83. Also see John M. Goshko, *Washington Post*, 11/22/83; Charles R. Babcock, *Washington Post*, 8/5/86; "Free Trade Area for Israel Proposed," *Mideast Observer*, 3/15/84; Khouri, *The Arab-Israeli Dilemma* (3rd ed.), pp. 449-500.

[16]*New York Times*, 4/22/83 and 4/26/83. For more details on CIA victims, see Charles R. Babcock, *Washington Post*, 8/5/86; Woodward, *Veil*, pp. 244-45. Also see Cooley, *Payback*, pp. 76-81; Fisk, *Pity the Nation*, pp. 478-90; Friedman, *From Beirut to Jerusalem*, p. 198.

[17]Philip Taubman and Joel Brinkley, *New York Times*, 12/11/83. Also see *New York Times*, 10/23/83; Cooley, *Payback*, pp. 80-91; Fisk, *Pity the Nation*, pp. 511-22; Frank, *U.S. Marines in Lebanon: 1982-1984*; Friedman, *From Beirut to Jerusalem*, pp. 201-04; Woodward, *Veil*, pp. 285-87; Ostrovsky, *By Way of Deception*, p. 321, who claimed Israel had early information about the attack but declined to pass the information on to the United States.

[18]Associated Press, *Washington Post*, 12/2/88.

Chapter 48

1983: How George Shultz Became the Most Pro-Israel Secretary of State

ON APRIL 14, 1983, a chorus of criticism of Secretary of State George Pratt Shultz reached a crescendo in *The Washington Post*. The newspaper wrote that "there is a growing body of thought that Shultz may be too quiet, that he may not be forceful enough."[1] Similar comments had appeared in *The New York Times, Time, Newsweek* and by columnists Rowland Evans and Robert Novak, to name only some of the major critics.

The criticism had gathered speed after an interview in *The New York Times* on Feb. 19 by Moshe Arens, Israel's new defense minister. He complained there was "such a degree of frustration and impatience and anger" that relations between the United States and Israel were perhaps the worst in history.[2]

All this preceded an astonishing change in Shultz. Within months he became a passionate supporter of Israel and spent much of the rest of his time in office promoting Israel's interests and forging a relationship that turned the United States into the tiny Jewish state's closest friend at all levels of government.

The change was so noticable by June that *New York Times* columnist William Safire was writing, "the Reagan administration has suddenly fallen passionately in love with Israel."[3]

After that most of the media criticism of Shultz not only ceased but his praise as a supporter of Israel grew proportionately.[4] Sources in Washington explained that two of Shultz's closest colleagues, his executive secretary, Charles M. Hill, and Under Secretary of State for Political Affairs Lawrence S. Eagleburger, later secretary of state in the last days of the Bush administration, suggested to Shultz in the spring of 1983 that he try treating Israel more circumspectly to see if the media criticism would wane.[5]

Whatever the facts, the record clearly shows that from this time forward there was a sea change in Shultz's attitude toward Israel. He never again seriously opposed Israel, or treated the Palestinians with anything more than contempt. By 1985 Shultz was openly proclaiming his Zionist credentials. At the annual conference of AIPAC, the American Israel Public Affairs Committee, he declared: "Our original moral commitment to Israel has never wavered, but over the years Americans have also come to recognize the enormous importance of Israel—as a partner in the pursuit of freedom and democracy, as a people who share our highest ideals, and as a vital strategic ally in an important part of the world....Every year we provide more security assistance to Israel than to any other nation. We consider that aid to be one of the best investments we can make—not only for Israel's security but for ours as well."[6]

The next month in Israel, Shultz declared that "Israel is the true witness to the Holocaust and the truest symbol of the victory of good over evil. Never again. Never again would we fail to confront evil. Never again would we appease the aggressor. Never again would we let the Jewish people stand alone against persecution and oppression. Today, we honor that pledge by standing beside the state of Israel."[7]

Shultz had been appointed by President Reagan on June 25, 1982.[8] Born Dec. 13, 1920, Shultz had been an economics professor at MIT and the University of Chicago before President Nixon appointed him to his cabinet as secretary of labor, then director of the Office of Management and Budget, and finally as secretary of the treasury, in which job he had completely failed to see the disastrous 1973 Arab oil boycott coming.

He left the government in 1974 to join the huge international construction company Bechtel Group Inc. and soon became president of Bechtel. His work at Bechtel brought him into close contact with many Arab leaders, and when he returned to government it was believed that he would be more even-handed in the Middle East than some of his predecessors.[9]

In fact, he became the most pro-Israel secretary ever except for Henry Kissinger. Shultz got off on the wrong foot with Israel when, after less than a month in office, he signed off on a presidential warning to Israel on July 15 accusing it of violating the Arms Export Control Act because of its use of U.S. weapons in its invasion of Lebanon. He further provoked Israel in September when he put forward the comprehensive peace plan that subsequently became known as the "Reagan plan." Israel disdainfully rejected it out of hand the next day.

All that had changed by the middle of 1983. How profound the change was became clear within five months, when Shultz backed the signing of a strategic alliance agreement with Israel, in effect elevating Israel to the status of a strategic ally of America.[10] By mid-1984, Moshe Arens was describing relations between the two countries as "probably better" than ever before.[11] That description continued to be made throughout Shultz's time in office.

Perhaps more telling were the heaps of praise bestowed on Shultz and Reagan by AIPAC. In 1986, AIPAC executive director Thomas Dine reported at the group's 27th annual policy conference that relations had never been better between the United States and Israel.[12] Dine said that in the process of this development "a whole new constituency of support for Israel is being built in precisely the area where we are weakest—among government officials in the state, defense and treasury departments, in the CIA, in science, trade, agriculture and other agencies." Israel, Dine added, was now treated by the United States as an "ally, not just a friend, an asset rather than a liability, a mature and capable partner, not some vassal state."

He added that President Reagan and Shultz were going to "leave a legacy that will be important to Israel's security for decades to come." Shultz, he said, had vowed to him to "build institutional arrangements so that eight years from now, if there is a secretary of state who is not positive about Israel, he will not be able to overcome the bureaucratic relationship between Israel and the U.S. that we have established."

Later in 1986, former AIPAC staffer Richard B. Straus wrote in *The Washington Post* that "American Middle East policy has shifted so dramatically in favor of Israel" that now it could only be described as "a revolution." He quoted Dine as saying that Shultz was the "architect of the special relationship," which, Dine said, "is a deep, broad-based partnership progressing day-by-day toward a full-fledged diplomatic and military alliance." Straus added: "State Department Arabists acknowledge that Arab interests hardly get a hearing today in Washington. 'We used to have a two-track policy,' says one former State Department official. 'Now only Israel's interests are considered.'" While Straus credited Reagan's "gut" support for Israel as a major reason for the change, it was, Straus observed, only after George Shultz finally decided to throw his full weight behind Israel that the "revolution was complete."[13]

By the next year, 1987, Dine declared Reagan and Shultz among Israel's greatest friends who had immeasurably helped Israel.[14]

In his address, Dine declared that "there is wide agreement that Ronald Reagan is among the best friends of Israel ever to sit in the Oval Office, and that George Shultz has been a friend beyond words as secretary of state....These stalwarts have truly transformed U.S. policy over the past five years, raising the relationship to a new level."[15]

Dine said that despite a year in which there was the Pollard spy scandal, Israel's entanglement in the Iran-Contra scandal, Israel's selling of weapons to South Africa, speculation about Israel's nuclear policy and leadership confusion in Israel, "We have had one of the best years on record in terms of concrete legislation, in the strategic relationship between our country and Israel, and in the gains scored by our cause in the results of the 1986 elections."[16]

The New York Times reported in July that "AIPAC has become a major force in shaping United States policy in the Middle East....the organization has gained power to influence a presidential candidate's choice of staff, to block practically any arms sale to an Arab country and to serve as a catalyst for intimate military relations between the Pentagon and the Israeli army. Its leading officials are consulted by State Department and White House policymarkers, by senators and generals." It concluded that AIPAC "has become the envy of competing lobbyists and the bane of Middle East specialists who would like to strengthen ties with pro-Western Arabs."[17]

AIPAC's rise was accomplished in part by Shultz's willingness to support it by speaking at its annual meeting and, more significantly, consulting it on policy matters. Former CIA analyst Kathleen Christison observed: "...the Reagan years have witnessed a marked change in the lobby's influence on policymaking. If in past administrations it was thought to have a major limiting impact on policy formulation, the magnitude of its influence today is so great that it can no longer be considered merely a constraint on policy. Under Reagan, AIPAC has become a partner in policymaking." She quoted former Carter administration National Security Council Middle East analyst William

Quandt as saying: "We would sometimes go to the Israelis in advance of some action and ask them not to make trouble, but we never went to AIPAC. The Reagan administration has elevated AIPAC to the level of a player in this game."[18]

Just how total Shultz had become in his passionate embrace of Israel was demonstrated a few months later. While in Israel in mid-October, 1987, Shultz inaugurated the George Shultz Doctoral Fellowships at Tel Aviv University. He personally contributed $10,000 to the program, an extraordinary gesture by a secretary of state claiming to be a mediator in the Arab-Israel conflict.[19]

Little wonder that Shultz's reception in Arab countries was no more than diplomatically polite. During nearly seven years in office, his principal influence on the Arab-Israel conflict was to prolong it by his blatant partisanship toward Israel and thereby to contribute to the explosion of Palestinian frustration that erupted as the intifada later in 1987 with untold cost in suffering and blood. ✺

RECOMMENDED READING:

*Friedman, Thomas L. *From Beirut to Jerusalem*, New York: Farrar, Strauss, Giroux, 1989.

*Neff, Donald, *Fallen Pillars: U.S. Policy towards Palestine and Israel since 1945*, Washington, DC: Institute for Palestine Studies, 1995.

*Schiff, Zeev, and Ehud Ya'ari. *Israel's Lebanon War*, New York: Simon and Schuster, 1984.

*Available through the AET Book Club.

NOTES:

[1]Michael Getler, *Washington Post*, 4/24/83.

[2]Bernard Gwertzman, *New York Times*, 2/20/83.

[3]William Safire, *New York Times*, 6/16/83.

[4]Donald Neff, "The remarkable feat of George Shultz," *Middle East International*, 3/5/88. For a description of Shultz's meek style henceforth in dealing with the Israelis, see Friedman, *From Beirut to Jerusalem*, pp. 500-01.

[5]Neff, *Fallen Pillars*, pp. 121-24.

[6]The text is in *Journal of Palestine Studies*, "Special Document," Summer 1985, pp. 122-28.

[7]Bernard Gwertzman, *New York Times*, 5/11/185; excerpts of his remarks in same edition.

[8]Excerpts of Shultz's testimony in his confirmation hearings on 7/13/82 in *Journal of Palestine Studies*, "Documents and Source Material," Summer/Fall 1982, pp. 333-35.

[9]*Time*, 7/5/82, pp. 15-16.

[10]Donald Neff, "The remarkable feat of George Shultz," *Middle East International*, 3/5/88; Friedman, *From Beirut to Jerusalem*, pp. 500-01.

[11]*New York Times*, 5/31/84.

[12]The text of Dine's speech, "The Revolution in U.S.-Israel Relations," is in *Journal of Palestine Studies*, "Special Document," Summer 1986, p. 134-143.

[13]Richard B. Straus, *Washington Post*, 4/27/86.

[14]Middle East Policy and Research Center, May/June, 1987, 5/6-IV-3-pages 16/17; also see a special report on the meeting in the *Journal of Palestine Studies*, Autumn 1987, pp. 107-13.

[15]The text of Dine's speech is in the *Journal of Palestine Studies*, Vol. XVI, No. 4, Summer 1987, pp. 95-106; the same issue also carries the text of AIPAC's 1987 policy statement, pp. 107-114.

[16]Middle East Policy and Research Center, May/June, 1987, 5/6-IV-3-page 12.

[17]David K. Shipler, *New York Times*, 7/6/87.

[18]Kathleen Christison, "Blind Spots: Official U.S. Myths About the Middle East," *Journal of Palestine Studies*, Vol. XVII, No. 2, Winter 1988, p. 50.

[19]Glenn Frankel, *Washington Post*, 10/19/87.

Chapter 49

1987: U.S. Pays Israel to Drop Lavi Warplane

O N AUG. 30, 1987, Israel bowed to pressure from Washington to drop its effort to build its own advanced warplane, the Lavi. Despite Israeli claims to the contrary, the Lavi program was an embarrassing failure.[1] American and Israeli studies showed it was poorly designed, under-researched, behind schedule and vastly over budget. Moreover, a study had recently revealed that the United States had paid $1.75 billion, more than 90 percent of the Lavi's costs, and had contributed more than 50 percent of its technology. By contrast, Israel had invested only $133 million of its own funds.[2]

The decision to terminate the Lavi was long in coming and welcome—if belated—news to some U.S. plane makers such as the Northrop Corporation. Northrop's chairman, Tom Jones, had been a consistent critic of the Israeli project ever since it was first embraced by the White House in early 1983. At the time, he had noted that it was unprecedented for the United States to finance a weapons program by a non-NATO foreign country and one that would be in direct competition on the world market with U.S. warplanes. But, more specifically, he was unhappy because since 1980 a presidential directive had established that although there was a need for a new U.S. fighter plane, the White House had decided that "the U.S. Government will not provide funding for development of the aircraft, and aircraft companies will assume all financial and market risks."

Jones noted that Northrop had accepted the directive and invested its own funds to develop the F-20 Tigershark—around $600 million, far more than Israel contributed to the Lavi. But, he added, "the development of a Lavi fighter program, supported by U.S. technology and U.S. funds, clearly changes the market risks we were asked to take." He added:

"The policy and political issues raised by such a precedent are indeed profound. They involve the exporting of U.S. jobs at a time of high unemployment and difficult economic conditions. Additionally, this precedent could well discourage not only those on the F-20 industrial team but also those involved in other programs from investing their own funds for achieving U.S. security objectives."[3]

Despite such complaints, the Reagan White House announced on April 17, 1983, that it would allow Israel access to U.S.-made components to build the Lavi, in effect meaning Israel would depend on American technology, including engines, wings, tails and flight controls, to build a plane that, if it ever went into production, would compete directly with the U.S. aerospace industry.[4]

Jones again wrote protest letters after the technology transfer, but with no more success.[5] Instead, Israel and its Washington lobby, AIPAC, the American Israel Public Affairs Committee, swung into full action to win the administration's support for not only advanced technology but for financing too. AIPAC sent memoranda on the Lavi's virtues to every member of Congress and its agents visited top legislators to argue the deal personally.[6] The aim was to convince Congress that the legislation would provide extra jobs in America and Israel and that American industry would profit from sharing by Israel of technical innovations developed during the plane's research and production.

How successful the lobby was became clear in the late spring of 1983, when Congress approved an amendment to the pending foreign aid bill allowing Israel to spend $550 million of its $2.61 billion in total aid for fiscal 1984 for the Lavi. The terms allowed Israel to spend $300 million of the Lavi money in the United States—but it also would be allowed to use an additional $250 million in Israel itself.[7]

Although this amounted to the breaching of the Buy American Act by the use of U.S. aid funds outside America, there was not one committee hearing devoted to the amendment nor was there any substantial discussion of it in Congress. Observed Democrat Representative Charles Wilson of Texas, who introduced the amendment:

"When the Israeli lobby got working on it, when it became quite clear that it was a big priority for them, resistance suddenly melted."[8]

In fact, with official U.S. funding, the sky seemed the limit for the Lavi. Israeli Defense Minister Moshe Arens was so optimistic that he even foresaw the possibility that not only would America give the technology and the funds to develop and produce the Lavi but that eventually Israel might even find a lucrative market for the Lavi in America. "It could conceivably happen if the airplane turns out to be as good as we hope it's going to be," he said.[9]

From the beginning, Israel's cost projections were wildly off. Originally it had estimated the cost of research and development at $750 million and the cost for each of 300 airplanes at $7 million.[10] Soon Israeli technicians realized that R&D alone would probably cost $1.5 billion and that the actual cost per unit would be $15.5 million. This was far more than the $12 million unit cost for the superior U.S.-made F-16.[11]

Nonetheless, Congress again awarded Israel $2.61 billion in economic and military aid for fiscal 1985, but with a significant difference: all of it was in the form of non-repayable grants. Hereafter, all aid to Israel was in the form of grants instead of loans. In addition, Congress also earmarked $400 million of the military aid for the Lavi. Of that amount, Israel was given the right to spend $250 million in Israel and only $150 million in the United States, denying jobs to about 6,000 more American workers.[12]

Thus, within a year, Congress had donated $950 million to the Lavi—while Northrop was still spending its own funds on the jinxed F-20. An unnamed lobbyist told The Wall Street Journal: "This is amazing. Almost $1 billion for a new weapons system and not even one hearing on it. If the Pentagon tried to do that, they'd be laughed off Capitol Hill."[13]

Despite the continuing objections of the Lavi's many critics in industry and the State and Defense Departments, Congress continued granting large amounts of funds for the project. Israel was awarded total aid packages of $3.6 billion for fiscal 1986 and $3 billion for fiscal 1987, including for each year $400 million for the Lavi; $250 million was allowed to be spent annually in Israel itself.[14] Through fiscal 1987, over a four-year period, Congress had voted $1.75 billion for the Lavi.

But despite such lavish funding, all was not well with the Lavi. It was disastrously behind schedule and over budget. A special study by the General Accounting Office concluded in early 1987 that the likely cost for each Lavi—if 300 were produced—would be $17.4 million, rather than $14.5 million as Israel was then contending. In addition, the GAO estimated that cash flow requirements for the project would be over $1 billion a year by 1990 and would climb to $1.4 billion by 2000.[15] That would mean the total cost of the project would be around $15 billion—compared to Israel's updated estimate of $8 billion.[16]

In addition, the GAO determined that although Israel had promised that more than 50 percent of the Lavi costs would be spent in the United States, as of the end of November, 1986, only 28 percent had actually been spent in America.[17]

When U.S. officials pointed out to Israel that the costs of the Lavi would soon eat up most of Israel's military aid from America, the GAO study reported: "Israeli officials expressed the hope that by the early 1990s, U.S. budgetary constraints will have run their course and that additional funding will be available from the U.S. government to ensure successful completion of the Lavi program."[18] In other words, Israel was content to accept excessive cost overruns because it expected the United States to continue to pick up the tab.

Under such circumstances, it was not surprising that Israel continued to refuse to drop the Lavi. However, in July, 1987 the Israel State Comptroller issued a withering criticism of Israel's handling of the Lavi project. The 40-page report essentially confirmed U.S. suspicions and studies. Comptroller Yaacov Maltz reported:

"A great many of the significant and essential decisions were made with information that was without basis, inadequate, tendentious and lacking proper cost estimates."[19] He charged, in the paraphrase of the *Jerusalem Post*, that Israeli officials did not "consider the plane's purpose, size or cost....Nor did they have details regarding cost, export potential and other aspects of the program."[20] Maltz's report said Lavi cost projections were already so high it would have cost $2.5 billion more to produce it than to buy an equivalent number of F-16s.[21]

Amazingly, Israel continued to refuse to terminate the Lavi until it negotiated extremely favorable severance conditions with Secretary of State George Shultz, an effusive supporter of Israel. During the summer of 1987, he officially informed Israeli Finance Minister Moshe Nissim that America would agree Israel could use $450 million in its military aid to pay termination charges of contracts, approve continuation of Israel's "offset" practices in which U.S. companies had to buy up to $150 million of Israeli products in return for receiving Israeli contracts, which were paid by American aid, and allow as much as $400 million in U.S. aid to be spent annually in Israel.[22]

Rabbi Dov S. Zakheim, the U.S. deputy undersecretary of defense for planning and resources, had earlier paid a three-day visit to Israel to offer other imaginative inducements, including 300 F-16s and allowing Israel to provide the engine and make the final assembly in Israel. Also, he offered Israel the opportunity to provide the avionics for future U.S. F-16s, a lucrative contract. Both options would be as much as half as costly as the Lavi and would provide jobs for thousands of Israelis.[23]

How much Israel finally ended up getting remains hidden in government archives. But there can be no doubt that the country was given significant rewards for what amounted to a botched airplane project that had been enormously costly to the U.S. taxpayer.

Northrop was not so lucky. It failed to find any buyers for its F-20, including the U.S. Air Force, which in October, 1986, turned it down—for economic reasons. The next month Northrop announced that it was halting all investments in its plane and was concluding F-20 contracts with its subcontractors and suppliers. Total cost to Northrop and its stockholders: $1.2 billion.[24] ᴥ

RECOMMENDED READING:

*Ball, George W. and Douglas B. Ball, *The Passionate Attachment: America's Involvement with Israel, 1947 to the Present,* New York, W.W. Norton & Company, 1992.

*Cockburn, Andrew and Leslie, *Dangerous Liaison: The Inside Story of the U.S.-Israeli Covert Relationship,* New York, HarperCollins Publishers, 1991.

*Findley, Paul, *Deliberate Deceptions: Facing the Facts about the U.S.-Israeli Relationship,* Brooklyn, NY, Lawrence Hill Books, 1993.

Rubenberg, Cheryl A., *Israel and the American National Interest: A Critical Examination,* Chicago University of Illinois Press, 1986.

*Available through the AET Book Club.

NOTES:

[1]Ball, *The Passionate Attachment*, pp. 264-68; Cockburn, *Dangerous Liaison, p.* 191; Findley, *Deliberate Deceptions*, pp. 213-16; Rubenberg, *Israel and the American National Interest*, p. 368.

[2]U.S. General Accounting Office study, "Foreign Assistance: Analysis of Cost Estimates for Israel's Lavi Aircraft," January, 1987, pp. 3-4. Also see Clyde Mark, "Israel: U.S. Foreign Assistance Facts," Foreign Affairs and National Defense Division, Congressional Research Service, updated 7/5/91.

[3]Tom Jones letters to Secretary of State George R. Shultz and Defense Secretary Caspar W. Weinberger, 1/17/83.

[4]Bernard Gwertzman, *New York Times*, 4/18/83.

[5]Jones letter to Weinberger and Shultz, 4/18/83.

[6]William M. Kehrer, "U.S. Funding for the Israeli Lavi Project," *Middle East Insight*, Vol. 3, No. 6, 1984, p. 11.

[7]*Ibid.*, p. 11.

[8]John J. Fialka, *Wall Street Journal*, 6/22/84.

[9]*Ibid.*

[10]"U.S. Assistance to the state of Israel:" Report by the Comptroller General of the United States, GAO/ID-83-51, June 24, 1983, U.S. Accounting Office, pp. 56-57.

[11]U.S. General Accounting Office study, "Foreign Assistance: Analysis of Cost Estimates for Israel's Lavi Aircraft," January, 1987, p. 1.

[12]Middle East Policy and Research Center, "Israel's Embattled Lavi," March, 1986, 3-IV-2-page 4.

[13]John J. Fialka, *Wall Street Journal*, 6/22/84.

[14]Clyde Mark, "The Israeli Economy," Foreign Affairs and National Defense Division, Congressional Research Service, 10/31/86.

[15]U.S. General Accounting Office study, "Foreign Assistance: Analysis of Cost Estimates for Israel's Lavi Aircraft," January, 1987, pp. 1,6.

[16]Glenn Frankel, *Washington Post*, 1/8/87.

[17]U.S. Assistance to the state of Israel, Report by the Comptroller General of the United States, GAO/ID83-51, June 24,1983, U.S. Accounting Office, p. 4.

[18]U.S. General Accounting Office study, "Foreign Assistance: Analysis of Cost Estimates for Israel's Lavi Aircraft," January, 1987, p. 1.

[19]David Rosenberg, *Jerusalem Post* international edition, 7/11/87.

[20]Joshua Brilliant, *Jerusalem Post* international edition, 7/11/87.

[21]Andrew Meisels, *Washington Times,* 7/1/87.

[22]Charles R. Babcock, *Washington Post,* 9/11/87.

[23]Glenn Frankel, *Washington Post,* 1/8/87.

[24]Northrop announcement, 11/17/86.

Chapter 50

1989: Congress Has Been Irresponsible on Jerusalem

O N JAN. 18, 1989, U.S. Ambassador to Israel William Brown and Israeli Lands Authority Deputy Director Moshe Gatt signed an international executive agreement providing for the construction of two new U.S. diplomatic facilities in Israel, one in Tel Aviv and the other in Jerusalem. Signing of the "Land Lease and Purchase Agreement" occurred on the last full day in power of Ronald Reagan, the most pro-Israel U.S. president before Bill Clinton.

Although the agreement was kept extremely quiet and almost no publicity resulted from the signing, critics later claimed that its effect could result in the eventual moving of the U.S. Embassy from Tel Aviv to Jerusalem by mid-1999 despite fierce opposition from the Islamic world and America's own long-held opposition to such a move.[1]

The agreement was based on the "Helms Amendment," named after Republican Senator Jesse Helms of North Carolina. Never one to be upstaged in his public support of Israel ever since Israel's supporters poured huge amounts of money into his difficult 1984 campaign for re-election (he was able to outspend his opponent almost two to one), Helms added his amendment on Oct. 1, 1988, to the Department of State Appropriations Act. It called for the construction of two separate diplomatic facilities in Israel, one in Tel Aviv and one in Jerusalem "or the West Bank," a clear effort to satisfy Israel's desire to move the embassy to Jerusalem as an effort to legitimize its claim to the city.[2]

The amendment said that each facility should be able to serve as an embassy or consulate but "shall not be denominated as the United States Embassy or Consulate until after construction of both facilities has begun, and construction of one facility has been completed, or is near completion...." Critics claimed that the purpose of this language was to inject the issue into later presidential campaigns when candidates could be placed under pressure to approve the move.[3]

In his remarks on the Senate floor, Helms made clear the purpose of his amendment was to bring about the move of the embassy to Jerusalem. He said: "Many of us here in the Senate—I venture to say most of us here—believe that Israel has a right to choose its own capital, and that the United States should locate its Embassy accordingly."[4]

Professor of International Law James A. Boyle of the University of Illinois College of Law advised on July 21, 1989, in a letter to Rep. Lee Hamilton, chairman of the House Subcommittee on Europe and the Middle East, that the signing of the agreement could "only be interpreted as a last-minute attempt by the Reagan Administration to lock its successors into a policy of moving the United States Embassy from Tel Aviv to Jerusalem by a date-certain."

Boyle advised that the agreement "raises serious problems under international law, which in turn create a severe threat to the further development of the Middle East peace process that the Bush Administration is publicly committed to. For this reason, the United States government should not proceed with the implementation of this agreement, and the United States Congress must not provide any funding for the implementation of this agreement."

In his supporting arguments, Boyle listed among other objections the inapplicability of Israeli domestic law to Jerusalem, the applicability of international laws of belligerent occupation to Jerusalem, and the illegality of expropriating Waqf (Muslim communal) property in Jerusalem.

Despite such warnings, the Congress has consistently supported Israel's effort to claim all of Jerusalem as its capital. Yet since Israel's establishment, every administration, whether Democrat or Republican, has opposed moving the embassy to Jerusalem. The reasons were primarily legal as cited by Professor Boyle, mainly that Israel could not claim as its capital territory occupied by force.

But there was also an element of self-interest involved. Since Jerusalem is the third most holy city in Islam, U.S. acquiescence in Israel's occupation of it would jeopardize America's commercial relations with Muslim nations, and especially its access to oil.

But politicians have consistently shown less interest in America's welfare than their own futures. For example, on May 9, 1995, Congress's two top Republican leaders, House Speaker Newt Gingrich of Georgia and Senate Majority Leader Bob Dole of Kansas, introduced identical bills—The Jerusalem Embassy Relocation Implementation Act of 1995. It required that the U.S. Embassy be moved to Jerusalem by May 31, 1999, adding that half of the State Department's construction funds would be withheld if the deadline was not met.[5]

At the time, only Costa Rica and El Salvador had their embassies in Jerusalem. The rest of the international community agreed with the official U.S. position that Israel did not have a legal right to all of Jerusalem. Palestinians and Arab states were critical of the congressional action, with the Palestinian daily *An Nahar* of East Jerusalem writing that "there can be no homeland without land and no peace without Jerusalem."[6]

Dole, who previously had criticized Congress for playing politics with Jerusalem,[7] was now running for the Republican presidential nomination and needed the deep-pocket aid of Israel's supporters. He had announced his intention to introduce the bill during an address the day before at the annual meeting of Israel's lobby, AIPAC, the American Israel Public Affairs Committee. Over the years it had repeatedly echoed Israel's desire to have the embassy moved.[8]

Dole said: "Jerusalem is today as it has been for three millennia the heart and soul of the Jewish people. It is also, and should remain forever, the eternal and undivided capital of the state of Israel....The time has come...to move beyond letters, expressions of support, and sense of the Congress resolutions. The time has come to enact legislation that will get the job done."

Dole acknowledged at the AIPAC meeting that he had previously opposed moving the embassy, adding: "Today, however, much has changed....The peace process has made great strides, and our commitment to that process is unchallengeable. Delaying the process of moving the embassy now only sends a message of false hopes."[9]

Gingrich also appeared before the AIPAC convention, strongly endorsing the move. Gingrich's support of the bill was as transparent as Dole's: His wife, Marianne, was hired in September, 1994 as vice president of an Israeli company, the Israeli Export Development Corp. of Jerusalem.[10] Both men's speeches supporting the Jerusalem move were received with standing ovations by the AIPAC audience.

Secretary of State Warren Christopher responded by saying: "There is no issue related to the Arab-Israeli negotiations that is more sensitive than Jerusalem. It is precisely for this reason that we think an effort to bring the Jerusalem issue to the forefront at this time is ill-advised and damaging to the success of the peace negotiations."[11]

Although the peace process looked considerably bleaker in mid-1998 than it did in mid-1995, in part because of the hard line toward Jerusalem maintained by Israel's Likud government, that has not prevented Congress from interfering in this extremely emotional issue. A later example came on June 10, 1997, when an overwhelming total of 406 Democrats and Republicans voted in the House of Representatives to recognize Jerusalem as the undivided capital of Israel. Only 17 voted against.[12]

The representatives also allocated $100 million to move the U.S. Embassy from Tel Aviv to Jerusalem and called on—but did not demand—President Clinton to affirm publicly that Jerusalem must remain Israel's undivided capital.[13]

Despite his pro-Israel record, Clinton has not taken that opportunity. He expressed his view during the 1992 presidential campaign: "I believe in the principle of moving our embassy to Jerusalem." But he cautioned that he did not think "we should do anything to interfere with the peace process."[14] That has been a cautionary sentiment not shared by Congress in its rush to embrace Israel at the expense of U.S. interests. &

RECOMMENDED READING:

*Bookbinder, Hyman and James Abourezk, *Through Different Eyes: Two Leading Americans—a Jew and an Arab—Debate U.S. Policy in the Middle East*, Bethesda, MD, Adler & Adler, 1987.

*Curtiss, Richard, *Stealth PACs: Lobbying Congress for Control of U.S. Middle East Policy*, Washington, DC, American Educational Trust, 1996.

*Findley, Paul, *They Dare to Speak Out: People and Institutions Confront Israel's Lobby*, Westport, CT, Lawrence Hill & Co., 1985.

Kenen, I.L., *Israel's Defense Line: Her Friends and Foes in Washington*, Buffalo, NY, Prometheus Books, 1981.

*Lilienthal, Alfred M., *The Zionist Connection: What Price Peace?*, New York, Dodd, Mead & Company, 1978.

*Neff, Donald, *Fallen Pillars: U.S. Policy towards Palestine and Israel since 1945*, Washington, DC, Institute for Palestine Studies, 1995.

Rubenberg, Cheryl A., *Israel and the American National Interest: A Critical Examination*, Chicago, University of Illinois Press, 1986.

Smith, Hedrick, *The Power Game*, New York, Ballantine Books, 1989.

Tivnan, Edward, *The Lobby: Jewish Political Power and American Foreign Policy*, New York, Simon and Schuster, 1987.

*Available through the AET Book Club.

NOTES:

[1]Francis A. Boyle memorandum to Rep. Lee Hamilton, July 21, 1989, *American-Arab Affairs*, No. 30, Fall 1989, pp. 125-38. For a review of U.S. policy on Jerusalem, see Donald Neff, "Jerusalem in U.S. Policy," *Journal of Palestine Studies*, Vol. XXIII, No. 1, pp. 20-45; Neff, *Fallen Pillars*, pp. 129-50.

[2]Francis A. Boyle memorandum to Representative Lee Hamilton, July 21, 1989, *American-Arab Affairs*, No. 30, Fall 1989, p. 126.

[3]*Ibid.*, p. 126.

[4]Complete text of Helms' remarks is in *Congressional Record—Senate*, SS9919, 7/26/88.

[5]Katharine Q. Seelye, *New York Times*, 5/10/95. Text of the Senate bill is in *Journal of Palestine Studies*, summer 1995, pp. 158-60.

[6]Barton Gellman, *Washington Post*, 5/12/95.

[7]Katharine Q. Seelye, *New York Times*, 5/18/95.

[8]Mark H. Milstein, "AIPAC Considered One of Top U.S. Lobbies," *The Washington Report on Middle East Affairs*, May/June, 1991. Also see Bookbinder and Abourezk, *Through Different Eyes*; Findley, *They Dare to Speak Out*; Kenen, *Israel's Defense Line*; Lilienthal, *The Zionist Connection*; Rubenberg, *Israel and the American National Interest*; Smith, *The Power Game*, Tivnan, *The Lobby*.

[9]The text of Bob Dole's AIPAC speech was distributed by his office, 5/8/95.

[10]*Middle East Labor Bulletin*, Spring 1995, p. 25; *Kansas City Star*, 2/10/95.

[11]Thomas W. Lippman, *Washington Post*, 5/10/95.

[12]H. Res. 60.

[13]Associated Press, 6/11/97.

[14]Martin Gellman, *Washington Post*, 10/28/94.

Chapter 51

1991: $10 Billion U.S. Loan Guarantees to Israel

ON MAY 5, 1991, Israeli Ambassador to the United States Zalman Shoval said Israel would soon ask America for $10 billion in loan guarantees to help provide housing for as many as a million Soviet immigrants expected to arrive in Israel over the next five years.[1] His statement marked the beginning of the sharpest clash ever between Washington and Tel Aviv over the question of Jewish settlements in the Palestinian territories occupied by Israeli troops. The battle raged over the next 16 months, with President George Bush seeking to do what no president had ever had the courage to attempt—link U.S. aid to Israel's settlement policy.

Despite a heroic effort, in the end the president's effort to link U.S. aid to restrictions on Jewish settlements was lost. Israel got its $10 billion in guarantees and at the same time went ahead with a vigorous program to establish settlements on Palestinian land.[2]

Ambassador Shoval's warning about Israel's pending request for loan guarantees came at a delicate time in the Middle East. America had just led a coalition of forces to turn back Iraq's invasion of Kuwait and Bush's popularity was at an all-time peak. He and Secretary of State James A. Baker III were deep in an active campaign to take advantage of the high standing of the United States in the region by trying to jump-start the peace process.

But a new disturbing factor had appeared. It was at this time that unprecedented numbers of Jews from Russia were pouring into Israel. More than 200,000 had arrived between mid-1989 and mid-1991. The massive immigration alarmed Arabs, who feared the new immigrants would settle in the occupied territories and thereby further deprive Palestinians of their land.

Bush and Baker were caught in a dilemma. For humanitarian and domestic political reasons, they wanted to aid Israel in its efforts to house the new immigrants. But at the same time they did not want to sidetrack the peace process by having the Russians housed in occupied territory, thereby alienating the Arabs and undermining the peace process.

Arab criticism was already high from an earlier loan guarantee granted Israel. In October, 1990, Washington had agreed to provide Israel with $400 million in loan guarantees for the Russian immigrants to be housed within the frontiers of Israel. But it quickly became obvious that Israel was cheating on its written promise not to use the money to build housing in the occupied territories. Although Israel denied any wrongdoing, a report by its own Housing Ministry on March 3, 1991, revealed that plans called for more than 10,000 immigrants to be located in housing in the occupied territories.[3]

Later, a study by the General Accounting Office reported that Israel's pledges had been meaningless.[4] Democratic Senator Robert C. Byrd of West Virginia, chairman of the Senate Appropriations Committee, summed it up succinctly by observing that trying to keep Israel from using the $400 million in loan guarantees in the occupied territories was like "an exercise in building a paper dam. The money that Israel borrowed under the guarantee program went straight into the Israeli treasury and immediately lost its identity."[5]

The loan guarantees emerged as a test of strength between Israeli Prime Minister Yitzhak Shamir and Bush.

It was within this context of conflicting currents that Baker made the Bush administration's major effort to bring Arabs and Israelis to the negotiating table at Madrid later in the year. In order to defuse the loan guarantee issue, he got Israel to delay its official request for the $10 billion package until late summer. The Arabs were further reassured when Bush and Baker let it be known privately and publicly that if any new loan guarantees were to be granted they would be linked to a commitment by Israel not to use the money in the occupied territories.

But Israel's hard-line Prime Minister Shamir was equally determined to resist linkage. He had become Israel's leader in 1983, vowing in his inaugural speech to continue the "holy work" of establishing settlements in the occupied territories.[6] During the summer of 1991, as Secretary of State Baker repeatedly traveled to the Middle East and bargained with Arab and Israeli in the quest for peace, Shamir left no doubt that he was determined to continue his holy work. By that time Israel was engaged in its most ambitious building campaign ever in the territories, with thousands of units going up.[7]

Shamir was confident to the point of arrogance that the influence of the Israeli lobby in the United States was so great that ultimately Bush would succumb to Israel's wishes. Shamir said on June 12: "Settlement in every part of the country continues and will continue. They try to link the two things but no one said that aid will end. I don't think it will happen."[8] A week later Shamir warned: "Creating such a linkage is dangerous, and I hope that the American people won't accept the linkage that the administration is trying to create between the two...Settlement momentum in [the West Bank] and Gaza is unstoppable."[9]

Implicit in these remarks was a direct challenge to President Bush not to link the loan guarantees to Israel's settlement program. By this time the stakes involved were not only the peace process but presidential pride as well. On July 1, 1991 Bush declared:

> "We're not giving one inch on the settlements question... We're not going to change our position on settlements. So please, those in Israel, do what you can to see that the policy of settlement after settlement is not continued. It is counterproductive."[10]

The next day, Israel coldly defied Bush by increasing its settlement activities. Housing Minister Ariel Sharon dedicated a new neighborhood in Mevo Dotan in the northern part of the West Bank, saying Israel would continue expanding settlements. He added: "Jewish settlements are not an obstacle to peace, they are an obstacle to war." A Mevo Dotan settler, Yael Ben Yakov, said: "We here are the answer to Bush. The building will continue."[11]

Nonetheless, Bush's tough remarks impressed the Arabs and the peace process began to move forward. On July 14, Syria announced it found Baker's ideas an "acceptable basis for achieving a comprehensive solution" to the Arab-Israeli conflict.[12] Five days later, five major Arab states—Egypt, Jordan, Lebanon, Saudi Arabia and Syria—officially signed on to a U.S. proposal for holding a peace conference.[13]

The only holdout was Israel. Despite heavy pressure from Washington, Shamir repeatedly found excuses why Israel could not meet with the Arabs. August turned to September and still Shamir could not be budged. Meanwhile, another crisis loomed. Shamir had agreed to delay Israel's official request for loan guarantees only until Sept. 6. As the day neared, the loan guarantees suddenly emerged as a symbolic test of strength between Shamir and Bush and, by extension, whether Israel was strong enough to continue to defy Washington's demand that it join the peace process.

It was clear that if the United States granted Israel the $10 billion in guarantees at this delicate juncture the Arabs would see it as favoritism to Israel and probably withdraw their support for a peace conference. Baker personally appealed to Shamir for a delay, but with no success. Bush then took the extraordinary action of calling the press to the Oval Office hours before Israel's scheduled presentation of its official request to plead for delay. He said debate over a loan guarantee at this time could "inflame passions," adding:

"We don't need an acrimonious debate just as we're about to get this peace conference convened. It is in the best interest of the peace process and of peace itself that consideration of this absorption aid question for Israel be deferred for simply 120 days...This is not the time for a debate which can be misunderstood, a debate that can divide."[14]

Despite the president's impassioned plea, Israeli Ambassador Zalman Shoval showed up at the State Department several hours later and officially delivered Israel's request to Secretary of State James Baker.

The battle was now joined. Major Jewish groups led by AIPAC, the American Israel Public Affairs Committee, vowed they would call a crusade of prominent Jewish Americans to travel to Washington to personally lobby congressmen. The Religious Action Center of Reform Judaism urged rabbis to use their pulpits during the Rosh ha-Shanah New Year's high holy days, which began Sept. 9, to mobilize grassroots support for the loan guarantee.[15]

The confrontation came on Sept. 12. More than 1,000 Jews from around the country descended on Capitol Hill personally to lobby lawmakers. President Bush retaliated by calling another news conference that same day to warn that he would veto loan guarantees if Congress insisted on approving the measure despite his plea for a 120-day delay. He also criticized the pro-Israeli lobbyists, saying:

"We're up against very strong and effective, sometimes, groups that go up to the Hill. I heard today there were something like a thousand lobbyists on the Hill working the other side of the question. We've got one little guy down here doing it...The Constitution charges the president with the conduct of the nation's foreign policy...There is an attempt by some in Congress to prevent the president from taking steps central to the nation's security. But too much is at stake for domestic politics to take precedence over peace."[16]

During the news conference, Bush bristled at questions implying he was not a supporter of Israel, saying:

"Just months ago, American men and women in uniform risked their lives to defend Israelis in the face of Iraqi Scud missiles, and indeed, [Operation] Desert Storm, while winning a war against aggression, also achieved the defeat of Israel's most dangerous adversary. And during the current fiscal year alone, and despite our own economic problems, the United States provided Israel with more than $4 billion in economic and military aid, nearly $1,000 for every Israeli man, woman and child, as well as with $400 million in loan guarantees to facilitate immigrant absorption."[17]

Bush's strong remarks brought attacks from Israeli officials. On Sept. 15, Israeli Minister without portfolio Rehavam Zeevi called Bush a "liar" and an "anti-Semite" during a cabinet meeting. The government insisted it would continue to press for the guarantees.[18]

It was not until Oct. 2 that the Senate finally acceded to Bush's call for a four-month delay in considering the loan guarantees. It was a rare defeat for the Israeli lobby. Although 70 senators co-sponsored a bill to grant the guarantees—three more than necessary to override Bush's threatened veto—they did so only with the understanding that the matter would be delayed. Said an unnamed administration official: "The assumption that the pro-Israel lobby could not be beat is now gone."[19]

Finally, on Oct. 20, Israel's cabinet voted 17 to 3 to approve Israel's participation in an international peace conference in Madrid on Oct. 30.[20]

But still the battle was not over. Shamir stood tough, declaring on Jan. 20, 1992, that Israel would "tell the Gentiles of the world" that nothing can stop establishment of settlements in the occupied territories. His aides said Shamir was ready to reject the loan guarantees if they meant a freeze of settlement activity.[21]

Although the Congress signaled its willingness to grant the guarantees, Bush continued to threaten a veto and the $10 billion were held up. The friction between the United States and Israel grew as elections approached in the Jewish state. Shamir's inability to gain the loan guarantees and his poor relations with Washington contributed heavily to his defeat on June 23.[22]

Bush appeared to have won. But in the end he failed. By the summer of 1992 Bush's own campaign for re-election was in deep trouble. On Aug. 12 he granted the $10 billion package to Yitzhak Rabin even though the new prime minister insisted some settlement activity had to continue. In this Bush agreed, thus destroying his effort to link U.S. aid to settlements.

Not only did the Rabin government go on expanding settlements but in the process it practically doomed the 1993 peace accord with the Palestinians. As *New York Times* columnist Thomas L. Friedman wrote in early 1995: "[Rabin's] government has increased settlements in the West Bank by ten percent in two years. That's crazy. It undermines Mr. Arafat's credibility and leaves Palestinians feeling they are being duped. It's time for Mr. Rabin to draw them a line where Israel stops and they start."[23]

The final irony was that it turned out Israel did not need the money anyway. By June, 1993, none of the money had yet been spent and in early June a symposium was held in Tel Aviv under the theme of "What Do You Do with $10 Billion?" Although Israel had sought the guarantees on the basis of helping resettle Soviet immigrants and building new housing for them, none of the money was being planned for that use. Reported *Washington Post* correspondent David Hoffman:

"Israelis say it was important to win the fight for the loan guarantees as a political reaffirmation of the country's alliance with the

United States. But from an economic standpoint, no one in the government is claiming any longer that the loans are 'vital' to Israel's survival. Now, the money is viewed as a nice cushion, rather than a lifejacket, and there are plans to use it to expand the country's highway system and as a pool for low-interest private business loans."[24]

One reason the money had become less vital was because when Israel originally made its request it anticipated the arrival of one million Soviets. In reality, less than half that number chose to go to Israel.[25]

It had all been a symbolic struggle to prove whether Tel Aviv or Washington would prevail. In the end, it was not Washington. Reports that the Israeli lobby could be beaten were premature. ✺

RECOMMENDED READING:

*Ball, George W. and Douglas B. Ball, *The Passionate Attachment: America's Involvement with Israel, 1947 to the Present*, New York, W.W. Norton & Company, 1992.

*Findley, Paul, *Deliberate Deceptions: Facing the Facts about the U.S.-Israeli Relationship*, Brooklyn, NY, Lawrence Hill Books, 1993.

Quigley, John, *Palestine and Israel: A Challenge to Justice*, Durham, Duke University Press, 1990.

*Available through the AET Book Club.

NOTES:

[1]Reuter, *Washington Post*, 5/6/91. For background, see Findley, *Deliberate Deceptions*, pp. 116-123.

[2]Rachelle Marshall, "To Israeli Leaders, Permanent Occupation Comes Before Peace," *Washington Report on Middle East Affairs*, March, 1995.

[3]Jackson Diehl, *Washington Post*, 3/11/91.

[4]General Accounting Office, "Israel: U.S. Loan Guaranties for Immigrant Absorption," GAO/NSIAD 2/12/92, pp. 92-119.

[5]John M. Goshko, *Washington Post*, 2/20/92.

[6]Quigley, *Palestine and Israel*, p. 176.

[7]Jackson Diehl, *Washington Post*, 9/8/91.

[8]Alan Elsner, Reuters, *Washington Times*, 6/13/91.

[9]Jackson Diehl, *Washington Post*, 6/23/91.

[10]Linda Gradstein, *Washington Post*, 7/3/91. Excerpts of Bush's remarks are in *Journal of Palestine Studies*, "Documents and Source Material," Autumn 1991, pp. 185-86.

[11]Linda Gradstein, *Washington Post*, 7/3/91.

[12]Thomas L. Friedman, *New York Times*, 7/15/91.

[13]Thomas L. Friedman, *New York Times*, 7/23/91.

[14]Thomas L. Friedman, *New York Times*, 9/7/91.

[15]John M. Goshko and John E. Yang, *Washington Post*, 9/7/91.

[16]Thomas L. Friedman, *New York Times*, 9/13/91.

[17]Text in *New York Times*, 9/13/91.

[18]Clyde Haberman, *New York Times*, 9/16/91.

[19]Helen Dewar, *Washington Post*, 10/3/91; Thomas L. Friedman, *New York Times*, 10/6/91.

[20]Jackson Diehl, *Washington Post*, 10/21/91. Also see Ball, *The Passionate Attachment*, p. 150.

[21]Jackson Diehl, *Washington Post*, 1/21/92.

[22]Don Oberdorfer, *Washington Post*, 6/25/92.

[23]Thomas L. Friedman, *New York Times*, 2/5/95.

[24]David Hoffman, *Washington Post*, 6/10/93.

[25]*Ibid.*

Chapter 52

1991 : All American Hostages Released in Lebanon

ON DEC. 4, 1991, the agony of America's hostages in Lebanon finally came to an end. The moment arrived with the release of newsman Terry Anderson, 44, after 2,454 days in captivity—the longest confinement suffered by any of the hostages.[1]

At least three Americans had been kidnapped in 1975 and 1976, early in Lebanon's civil war. All eventually had been released unharmed, and there was relatively little media attention given to these seemingly random events.

That was not the case with the total of 17 Americans kidnapped after early 1984, when five were taken. Four more were captured in 1985, three in 1986, four in 1987 and one in 1988. After 1988, the kidnappings ended in large part because Americans essentially had been chased out of Lebanon.

Three of the American hostages were killed or died in captivity: CIA Station Chief William Buckley, Marine Lt. Col. William R. Higgins and librarian Peter Kilburn. The remains of Buckley and Higgins were left on Beirut streets in the three weeks after Anderson's release and brought back to the United States for burial.[2] Kilburn's body had been similarly found in 1986.[3]

Three escaped: Charles Glass, Jeremy Levin and Frank Regier. Three were ransomed in the Reagan administration's Iran arms-for-hostages scandal: David Jacobsen, Lawrence Jenco and Benjamin Weir. Two were released in 1990: Robert Polhill and Frank

Reed. And six were released in the final four months of 1991: Joseph Cicippio, Thomas Sutherland, Alann Steen, Edward Tracy, Jesse Turner and Anderson.

The 1980s kidnappings were part of a highly successful campaign by Shi'i Muslims belonging to Hezbollah (Party of God) and supported by Iran to rid Lebanon of all Americans. It began in retaliation for Israel's 1982 invasion of Lebanon with the massive use of U.S.-made weapons and accelerated after Washington's decision to use U.S. warplanes and ships of the U.S. Sixth Fleet against Muslim and Druze targets in late 1983.

Early Hezbollah attacks included the bombing in 1983 of the U.S. Embassy in Beirut, with the loss of 63 lives including some of the CIA's top Mideast experts, and the bombing of the Marine barracks at Beirut Airport, with the initial loss of 241 lives.

On Jan. 18, 1984, President Malcolm Kerr of the American University of Beirut, a distinguished scholar of the Arab world, was gunned down outside his AUB office.[4]

At that point Hezbollah openly proclaimed its goal was to "drive all Americans from Lebanon."[5]

This seemed an unlikely prospect at the time, since Americans had a long and well-established position in Lebanon's educational, business and international refugee relief communities. The American University of Beirut had been founded in 1866 by U.S. missionaries and Americans had been intimately involved with it ever since. Yet by the end of 1988, Hezbollah had won and the U.S. presence in Lebanon essentially was gone.

In reality, Hezbollah was successful against the United States.

The first major retreat was by the 1,400 U.S. Marines then stationed in Lebanon as a result of Israel's invasion nearly two years earlier.[6] President Reagan on Feb. 5, 1984 made one of his stand-tall speeches, saying that "the situation in Lebanon is difficult, frustrating and dangerous. But this is no reason to turn our backs on friends and to cut and run."[7]

However, the next day Prof. Frank Regier, a U.S. citizen teaching at AUB, was kidnapped. The day after that, Reagan suddenly reversed course and said that all U.S. Marines would shortly be "redeployed," a euphemism for total withdrawal.[8] All the Marines except those guarding the U.S. Embassy were gone by Feb. 26, never to return.

The Marine retreat began a series of strategic withdrawals of the official American presence in Lebanon. On Sept. 20, 1984, 24 persons, including two Americans and seven other employees of the U.S. Embassy, were killed when a Hezbollah suicide bomber drove a car laden with explosives into the East Beirut annex of the U.S. Embassy.[9]

The next month, on Oct. 21, Washington announced it was reducing the official roster of American staff at the U.S. Embassy in Beirut from 45 to 30, with further cuts to come.[10]

The next major step came on July 1, 1985, when the United States imposed a ban on travel by Americans to Lebanon in retaliation for the skyjacking of a TWA flight on June 14. The State Department declared: "Beirut International Airport has become a source of danger to all air passengers. The United States has been singled out for air piracy and can no longer permit such actions to go unpunished. As of today, the U.S. will initiate efforts with all countries concerned to stop flights to and from the said airport; the U.S. will attempt to influence Lebanon's neighbors to stop providing air information on flights passing through Lebanon's airspace; the U.S. will attempt to cut off all aviation fuel from reaching Beirut."[11]

The only one of those threats that was fully realized was to keep Americans from traveling to Lebanon.

The final withdrawal came on Dec. 2, 1988, when Washington announced that all U.S. military representatives with the United Nations observer team in Lebanon had been withdrawn over the previous several days because of danger to their safety.[12]

The 16 Americans had been assigned to the U.N. Observer Group in Lebanon, the same group to which Lieutenant Colonel Higgins had belonged when he was kidnapped by Hezbollah the previous February and later hanged. The officers routinely patrolled southern Lebanon where troops of the U.N.'s Interim Force in Lebanon, UNIFIL, sought to keep the peace between Israeli, Lebanese and Palestinian fighters.

UNIFIL had been created in 1978 after Israel's earlier invasion of southern Lebanon that year and its establishment of a "security zone" on Lebanese territory.[13]

It was as a result of this expansion by Israel into Lebanese territory (the "North Bank," as critics of Israel's expansionist policies called it) and then its 1982 invasion that caused the establishment of Hezbollah that same year with the help of Iran to rid Lebanon of Israel's occupation.[14]

On Feb. 16, 1985, Hezbollah issued a statement of its ideology called an "Open Letter to the Downtrodden in Lebanon and the World." It said the "first root of vice is America...Israel is the American spearhead in the Islamic world and must be wiped out. All plans, including even tacit recognition of the Zionist entity, are rejected." It identified as other enemies the anti-Muslim Maronite Christian Phalange, and France.[15]

In reality, Hezbollah failed in its immediate purpose of ending the Israeli occupation of southern Lebanon. However, it was successful against the United States. The withdrawal of the U.S. military officers in 1988 removed almost all vestiges of the American presence. About the only American officials then left in Lebanon were the few members of a skeletal and secluded embassy staff, while the U.S. ambassador was forced to spend most of his time in Cyprus because of fears for his safety. The prohibition by the State Department on travel to Lebanon by Americans remained in effect until 1997. The Israeli occupation, however, continued into 1998, when Israel offered to withdraw under conditions which were unacceptable to Hezbollah and the governments of Lebanon and Syria.

This humiliating U.S. defeat in Lebanon was one of the hidden costs of Israel's 1982 invasion. Although the media have never bothered counting up these damages, they have been high for America: the assassination of AUB president Malcolm Kerr, the kidnappings of 17 Americans and deaths of three of them, the bombings of the U.S. Embassy and its annex and of the Marine barracks, with a total loss of more than 300 lives, and the final chasing out of Lebanon of Americans after a presence of more than a century.

As a final irony, Americans then essentially paid for Israel's invasion expenses. This came about thanks to special legislation by Congress that turned Israel's aid into non-repayable grants and hefty increases in total aid to Israel, including the notorious 1984

Cranston Amendment that stipulated economic aid to Israel each year must at least equal Israel's annual repayments (principal and interest) of its debt to the United States. In other words, after the invasion Israel was assured that it would always receive more than enough U.S. aid to cover its debt payments to America. Or put another way, henceforth Congress agreed to use U.S. taxpayer money to pay Israel's debt. 🙢

RECOMMENDED READING:

Chomsky, Noam, *The Fateful Triangle*, Boston, South End Press, 1983.

Cooley John K., *Payback: America's Long War in the Middle East*, New York, Brassey's (U.S.), Inc, 1991.

Fisk, Robert, *Pity the Nation: The Abduction of Lebanon*, New York, Atheneum, 1990.

*Friedman, Thomas L., *From Beirut to Jerusalem*, New York, Farrar, Strauss, Giroux, 1989.

*Randal, Jonathan, *Going All the Way*, New York, The Viking Press, 1983.

Sherif, Regina S., *United Nations Resolutions on Palestine and the Arab-Israeli Conflict: 1975-1981*, Washington, DC, Institute for Palestine Studies, 1988.

Woodward, Bob, *Veil: The Secret Wars of the CIA 1981-1987*, New York, Simon and Schuster, 1987.

*Available through the AET Book Club.

NOTES:

[1]William Claiborne, *Washington Post*, 12/5/91.

[2]Dana Priest and Nora Boustany, *Washington Post*, 12/28/91.

[3]White House announcement, 4/18/86.

[4]*New York Times*, 1/19/84.

[5]*New York Times*, 4/16/84; Cooley, *Payback*, p. 75. For a chronology of attacks against Americans in this period, see the *Atlanta Journal*, 1/31/85.

[6]See Donald Neff, "Middle East History: It Happened in March," *Washington Report on Middle East Affairs*, March, 1995 (chapter 23 of this book).

[7]*New York Times*, 4/16/84. Also see Cooley, *Payback*, p. 111; Fisk, *Pity the Nation*, p. 565.

[8]Fisk, *Pity the Nation*, p. 533.

[9] Cooley, *Payback*, p. 102; Fisk, *Pity the Nation*, p. 533; Friedman, *From Beirut to Jerusalem*, p. 220. The text of Reagan's report to Congress on the Marine mission is in *The New York Times*, 2/16/84.

[10] *Washington Post*, 9/21/84. For good background, see Cooley, *Payback*, pp. 104-8.

[11] *New York Times*, 10/22/84.

[12] Fida Nasrallah, "The US Travel Ban on Lebanon: in No One's Interest," *Middle East International*, 4/28/95.

[13] Associated Press, *Washington Post*, 12/2/88.

[14] UNIFIL was created by Security Council Resolution 425 of March 19, 1978. The text is in Sherif, *United Nations Resolutions on Palestine and the Arab-Israeli Conflict*, p. 184.

[15] Cooley, *Payback*, pp. 81-83, p. 228.

[16] Godfrey Jansen, "Hezbollah, Rabin's Main Target," *Middle East International*, 8/6/93.

[17] David R. Francis, *Christian Science Monitor*, 10/23/84. Also see Chomsky, *The Fateful Triangle*, p. 10; "U.S. Assistance to the State of Israel, Report by the Comptroller General of the United States," GAO/ID-83-51, June 24, 1983, U.S. Accounting Office.

Chapter 53

1992: Senator Byrd on Aid to Israel

ON APRIL 1, 1992, Democratic Senator Robert C. Byrd of West Virginia detailed for the first time on the Senate floor the vast array of aid and special benefits that Israel receives from the United States.[1] Although Israel had emerged in the early 1970s as the largest recipient of U.S. aid and other special favors, Byrd's carefully prepared speech was the first—and only— major delineation of the increasingly complex and costly relations America has with Israel. No other senator or congressman or executive branch official has ever reported to the American people the full details of aid and assistance that the United States provides to Israel. Despite the often astonishing revelations provided by Byrd, his remarks were generally ignored by the media.

Yet his remarks were as dramatic as the figures he cited and would have made headlines about any other country. To take just three: "Beyond the massive economic and military aid, however, in our so-called strategic relations with Israel, we have served as a protector almost in the same sense as the government of the United States would protect one of our 50 states."

At another point, he said: "We should wake up to the reality which has been slow to dawn on many, including our own Pentagon, that the Cold War is over and the real threat to stability in the Middle East lies in the tension between Israel and its Arab neighbors. And that tension only increases as a result of the continued expansion by Israel of settlements in the occupied territories." He also said: "We have poured foreign aid into Israel for decades at rates and terms given to no other nation on earth. And we are the only nation to have done so."

To support the latter statement, Byrd revealed that between 1949 and 1991, total U.S. aid to Israel amounted to $53 billion, equal to 13 percent of all U.S. economic and military foreign aid given during that period. Since the 1979 Egyptian-Israeli peace treaty, the amount totaled $40.1 billion, equal to 21.5 percent of all U.S. aid, including all multilateral as well as bilateral aid. By contrast, the Marshall Plan to rebuild Western Europe after World War II cost only some $12 billion.[2] Starting in 1985, all aid was converted from loans to cash grants, meaning that since then Israel has not had to pay back any money except interest on pre-1985 loans. In 1987, formal economic and military aid to Israel settled into a yearly grant of $3 billion. But it has routinely exceeded that. Byrd noted that in 1979 the aid total was $4.9 billion. In 1985 it reached $4.1 billion and in 1991 nearly $4 billion. But, added Byrd, "Despite this unmatched foreign aid program, this is only part of the story. Israel derives many other benefits, both direct and indirect, from its special relationship with the United States."

Byrd reported that in addition to Israel's regular economic and military aid, it also received funds in 1991 and 1992 under such programs as the American Schools and Hospitals Grant Program, representing $2.7 million for 1991; $7 million for Arab-Israeli cooperative programs, of which approximately half is spent in Israel; $42 million for joint research and development on the Arrow anti-tactical ballistic missile follow-on program. This amount was increased to $60 million in the fiscal year 1992 Defense Appropriations Act; also, authority was given Israel to use up to $475 million of its military aid in Israel instead of spending it in the United States.

Byrd observed that "although the president has the authority to allow countries to engage in non-United States procurement in certain limited cases, Israel is the only country that receives specific legislative authority and a designated dollar amount for such procurement; moreover, priority over every other country, except Turkey, to receive excess defense articles; additionally a major new petroleum reserve of 4.5 million barrels, worth $180 million, which is available for Israel's use in the case of an emergency; furthermore, $15 million to improve military facilities at the Israeli port of Haifa in 1991 and another $2 million in 1992 to study the costs of further improving the facilities to allow for full-scale maintenance and support of an aircraft carrier battle group; in addition thereto, specific inclusion in the Overseas Workload Program, allowing Israel to bid on contracts for the repair, maintenance, or overhaul of United States equipment overseas; and additionally $1 million in investment insurance in Israel, provided by the Overseas Private Investment Corporation."

Byrd added that there were additional large sums of aid provided Israel in times of crisis: "In 1990, the United States responded to the increased immigration of Soviet and Ethiopian Jews by providing $400 million in housing loan guarantees. The United States also rushed to provide additional assistance during the Persian Gulf war. Early in the war, President Bush used his emergency authority…to transfer to Israel two Patriot missile batteries valued at $117 million. The Congress appropriated an additional $650 million economic assistance grant, allowed the use of $200 million of Economic Support Fund money for the purchase of military equipment, and earmarked $300 million for the prepositioning in Israel of United States defense equipment that can be used by Israel in an emergency. Congress also authorized the president to transfer another $700 million in United States military equipment to Israel."

Byrd observed that in addition to such aid there were other legislative initiatives that provide continuing benefits to Israel. These included:

"Immediate transfer each year of the $1.2 billion Economic Support Fund grant and the $1.8 billion military assistance grant. Thus, our grants to Israel are turned into interest-bearing assets for Israel while our own budget deficit is increased, resulting in higher interest charges to us. This immediate transfer created approximately $86 million in interest income for Israel in fiscal year 1991. Such an arrangement has been in place for the Economic Support Fund since 1982 and was extended to military aid in fiscal year 1991 and applies to no other country; moreover, debt restructuring that took place in the late 1980s allowed Israel to lower interest payments by an estimated $150 million annually; additionally, the fair pricing initiative within the Foreign Military Sales Program that allows Israel to avoid certain administrative fees normally charged on foreign military sales. This benefit saved Israel an estimated $60 million in 1991…

"Since 1984, Israel has been allowed to use a portion of its foreign military financing credits for procurement of Israeli-made military items. Unlike other countries that receive United States military assistance, Israel does not have to spend all of those funds to purchase United States equipment. In 1991, of a $1.8 billion military assistance grant, we allowed Israel to use $475 million to buy the output of its own defense industry instead of American-made products. Moreover, Israel was allowed to spend an additional $150 million of the 1991 grant for its own research and development in the United States."

Despite this massive amount of aid, Byrd charged that Israel showed no willingness to change its policies to make them comply with U.S. policy. This was particularly true in the case of Jewish settlements established in the Arab territories occupied by Israel in 1967. Byrd noted that every United States President since Lyndon B. Johnson has called for Israel to withdraw from the occupied territories. Said Byrd:

"The Congress has always supported this policy, and, in 1990, when the United States provided $400 million in housing loan guarantees, it was explicitly linked to the settlements so that none of the money could be spent in the occupied territories. Unfortunately, this linkage was not enough to influence Israeli policy in any way...There is no restraint, as one might reasonably expect with the development of the peace process and the rising concerns from the United States over the settlement policy—no restraint whatsoever."

Byrd's conclusion was a wake-up call for both Israel and the Congress to reform the increasingly complex relations between the two countries:

"We have provided Israel with multibillion-dollar aid packages since 1974, and both the United States and Israel have very little progress to show for it. Israel has become dependent on both our economic and military assistance. Our aid has enabled Israel to maintain its enormous military capability, put off much needed economic reforms, and avoid making serious progress in solving its problems with its neighbors. Israel must, for its own good, start to stand on its own and cut itself free of a dependence that is really a road block to progress, both economically and from the standpoint of achieving security, and it is a dependence that will have no end otherwise...The United States must take steps to wean Israel from the pipeline of United States foreign aid....Israel's dependency on the United States is too deep, and such an overly dependent situation inevitably breeds resentment on the part of the dependent entity."

Byrd's thoughtful comments had no influence on Congress. Five months later, on Oct. 1, Congress approved $10 billion in loan guarantees over five years to Israel and lavished on Israel even more special favors. Israel was allowed to use its U.S. economic aid to pay the administrative and other costs of the guarantees running into the millions of dollars.

Congress also agreed to guarantee 100 percent of the $10 billion loan, an unheard-of concession. The usual practice is to guarantee only a certain percentage of both the principal and interest. Congress also reserved to itself the right to override any presidential suspension of the guarantees should Israel use them outside of its pre-June 5, 1967, frontiers, in effect eliminating any effort to link the guarantees to Israel's settlement program.

It further promised that America would "substantially increase" the amount of goods and services Israel could purchase inside Israel with U.S. aid. The same bill also gave to Israel $3 billion in economic and military aid, the same amount it has been receiving annually since 1987.[3] ✈

RECOMMENDED READING:

*Ball, George W. and Douglas B. Ball, *The Passionate Attachment: America's Involvement with Israel, 1947 to the Present,* New York, W.W. Norton & Company, 1992.

*Curtiss, Richard H., *Stealth PACs: Lobbying Congress for Control of U. S. Middle East Policy,* Washington, DC, American Educational Trust, 1992.

El-Khawas, Mohammed and Samir Abed-Rabbo, *American Aid to Israel: Nature and Impact,* Brattleboro, VT, Amana Books, 1984.

*Findley, Paul, *Deliberate Deceptions: Facing the Facts About the U.S.-Israeli Relationship,* Brooklyn, NY, Lawrence Hill Books, 1993.

Tivnan, Edward, *The Lobby: Jewish Political Power and American Foreign Policy,* New York, Simon and Schuster, 1987.

*Available through the AET Book Club.

NOTES:

[1]Robert Byrd, Congressional Record—Senate, April 1, 1992. The text was reprinted in "Special Document," *Journal of Palestine Studies*, Summer 1992; excerpts are in Findley, *Deliberate Deceptions*, Chapter 14 and the *Washington Report on Middle East Affairs*, June, 1992.

[2]Robert Gibson, *Los Angeles Times*, July 20, 1987.

[3]Helen Dewar, *The Washington Post*, Oct. 2, 1992; Gene Bird, "How Israel Got the Loan Guarantees Opposed by 89 Percent of Americans," *Washington Report on Middle East Affairs*, November, 1992. Text of the legislation is in *Journal of Palestine Studies*, "Documents and Source Material," *Winter 1993, 158-60.*

Chapter 54

1993: New Book Attacks Arabists

I N OCTOBER, 1993, Robert D. Kaplan's book *The Arabists* was published, yet another of a series of assaults launched by Zionists over the past century against the professionals on the Middle East in the State Department.[1] The big difference this time was that there were barely any "Arabists" left in government service. As Prof. Augustus Richard Norton, an expert on the State Department and the region, noted with gentle irony in his review of Kaplan's book, these days "to be labeled an Arabist is hardly career-enhancing."[2]

According to Kaplan, one definition of an Arabist is "someone who loves Arabs, often because he hated Jews."[3] Although Kaplan then distances himself from this racist slur because the "truth about them is far more subtle" and finds much to admire in the Arabists, he nonetheless leaves no doubt that Arabists in general suffered a common flaw in his view: They did not support Israel with the kind of unquestioning zeal he does.

A definition similar to Kaplan's was offered two decades earlier in another highly publicized assault on Arabists, this one by the late columnist Joseph Kraft in *The New York Times Magazine* titled: "Those Arabists in the State Department."[4] Kraft's central contention was that the Arabists harbored a "basic bias" against Israel.

The unspoken but clear message from both authors was that Arabists are an elitist class who are basically anti-Semites. The willingness of some Zionists to besmirch reputations with this malicious charge has taken its predictable toll, especially in the State Department. Ambassador Richard B. Parker, an Arabist who worked in the Bureau of Near Eastern Affairs during Nixon's presidency, later admitted: "If ever there was a body that was frozen out of the serious policy decisions it was the Arabists, who were regarded with suspicion by their American colleagues as well as by American Jews and other supporters of Israel, whose predominant influence in Congress and the White House on the Palestine issue has been well documented. Not only were the Arabists a fringe group within a Department of State that was itself largely powerless on this issue, but they were afraid to speak out for fear of being accused of anti-Semitism."[5]

Today, in their stead, has come what could fairly be called the New Israelites, or perhaps more fashionably, the neo-Israelites, after their political front, neo-Conservatism. They have had no compunction in speaking out in support of Israel. By definition, inclination and commitment they are intellectually and emotionally dedicated to Israel. They flourish today as never before in the environs of Bill Clinton's White House and Foggy Bottom, completely dominating the administration's Middle East policy.

Such Zionist dominance is an astonishing turn-about. Even in the Truman administration, which nurtured Israel to existence, supporters of the Jewish state were so few that they kept a low profile lest they be labeled Zionists, by general understanding to mean they were partisans committed to one side of the conflict.

In the 1940s, Arabists dominated—at least officially. They were highly professional diplomats who, for the most part, had worked in Arab lands, spoke the language and, when they returned to Washington, brought with them experience and insight into an exotic civilization unknown to most Americans but inhabited in the wider Islamic world by more than 900 million Muslims, by today's count. Thus the term Arabist was once a proud title denoting diplomatic and intellectual achievement. Today few young foreign service officers with ambition aspire to become Arabists. In 1990, the Foreign Service field school in Tunis graduated only a half-dozen Arabic speakers.[6]

It is not, of course, that the predominance of the neo-Israelites is new in guiding U.S. policy. Their policies largely have prevailed over the past half-century against the advice of the Arabists. The difference is that they accomplished this, as in the Truman administration, by exerting extraordinary political influence directly through the White House and Congress, thereby circumventing recommendations from the professional Arabists.

It is sobering to recall that every major U.S. foreign affairs or defense institution—the State Department, the Defense Department, and the Central Intelligence Agency—and all of the top foreign affairs advisers, including such a towering figure as Secretary of State George C. Marshall, opposed Truman's pro-Israel policies. Their opposition was not against the idea of Israel per se but rather what they recognized as the realities in the region. As they predicted, and history since has proven, these realities led to massive bloodshed, decades of turmoil and a skewing of U.S. interests after Truman's pro-Israel policies prevailed.

Whatever the complaints about the Arabists, lack of professionalism or failure to see clearly where U.S. national interests lie are not charges that can be made credibly. The Arabists were a highly trained and sophisticated elite, dedicated and loyal, who prided themselves on their language skills and meticulous professionalism. Any balanced review of their various reports and studies over the past half-century shows how stunningly prescient they often were. One has only to read Assistant Secretary of State Loy W. Henderson's perspicacious warnings in the turbulent 1947-48 period about the expectable troubles that would attend Israel's birth to realize how enormously talented and foresighted the Arabists were.[7]

These days, however, the neo-Israelites not only occupy the political high ground but the tentacles of the bureaucracy stretching deep into these same institutions as well. Throw a stone down any hallway of the White House or State Department and it would not hit an Arabist or, for that matter, anyone admitting the least bit of skepticism concerning the wisdom of the current close embrace of Israel.[8] The highest level any of the few remaining Arabists has reached in the Clinton administration is assistant secretary.

The neo-Israelites who have replaced the Arabists include the very top levels of the administration, meaning President Clinton himself and his vice president, Al Gore. Although neither Clinton nor Gore ever has been accused of having a serious understanding of any aspect of the contemporary Middle East, both are nonetheless blindly committed to Israeli viewpoints over those of the Arabs. Clinton repeatedly has shown himself sensitive to a fault to only the Israeli version of the conflict. He seldom seems to miss a chance to retell an anecdote about an old preacher who, on his death bed, warned the future president, as Clinton describes it, that "if I ever let Israel down, God would never forgive me." He concludes this tale with the vow that "I'll never let Israel down."[9]

Gore has described Israel as America's "strongest ally and best friend, not only in the Middle East, but anywhere else in the world."[10] He takes pride in the fact that on matters of the Middle East he is the protégé of Martin Peretz, the man who, after his wife bought the once respectable *New Republic*, became its editor and turned the magazine into an embarrassing apologist for Israel.[11]

The man the administration has chosen to be its chief Middle East negotiator is Dennis B. Ross. He has mainly kept a low profile as a behind-the-scenes player and so has less a public image as a neo-Israelite than two other early members of Clinton's Middle East team, former Ambassador to Israel Samuel W. Lewis, who headed the State Department's Policy Planning division during 1993, and Martin Indyk, a former paid lobbyist for Israel who was the National Security Council's Middle East expert for two years before becoming the first Jewish U.S. ambassador to Israel. Ross' sympathies are no secret, however, and his credentials include what the *Washington Post* has called his "strong pro-Israel convictions."[12] Or as author Robert Kaplan reported, Ross "traveled in pro-Israel, neo-Conservative circles."[13] In fact, Ross has been active for years in promoting pro-Israel positions in various studies and forums, in which he has had no kind words for what he called back in 1985 "traditional Arabists and their media supporters," a pathetically quaint sounding phrase these days.[14]

Secretary of State Warren Christopher, whatever his private thoughts, bought totally into the Zionist agenda. He was, of course, an ambitious man boxed in between a chief executive and politically appointed bureaucrats who shared the same biases favoring Israel. He could not retain his post without following their lead— nor did he display any public reluctance to do so.

Given the influence of the neo-Israelites, it is no surprise that the Clinton administration became the most pro-Israel ever. It demonstrated this by taking a number of actions that have abandoned U.S. ideals and reversed diplomatic positions that had formed America's basic policies since the 1967 war.

Under President Clinton, for the first time, the United States (1) publicly allowed U.S. funds to be used to finance growth of

Jewish settlements in Arab East Jerusalem and the other occupied territories; (2) called settlements neither illegal nor obstacles to peace but merely a "complicating factor"; (3) endorsed Israel's right to deport Palestinians; and (4) no longer referred to the Arab territories captured by Israel in 1967 as "occupied" but rather as in "dispute." On May 17, 1995, it went so far as to cast the first U.S. veto in five years in the U.N. Security Council against a resolution endorsed by all 14 other members urging Israel to halt its confiscation of Palestinian land in Jerusalem, an action the U.S. had declared many times before to be a violation of the Geneva Accords.

These are fundamental changes reaching to the very core of U.S. policy, turning it into an ever more dangerously narrow pro-Israel stance. Zionists finally have achieved this objective in large measure because of the essential disappearance of the once-proud breed of American diplomats known as Arabists. ✇

RECOMMENDED READING:

*Ball, George W. and Douglas B. Ball, *The Passionate Attachment: America's Involvement with Israel, 1947 to the Present*, New York, W.W. Norton & Company, 1992.

Kaplan, Robert D., *The Arabists: The Romance of an American Elite*, New York, Free Press, 1993.

Parker, Richard B., "The Arabists," *Journal of Palestine Studies*, Washington, DC, Institute for Palestine Studies, Autumn 1994.

Rubenberg, Cheryl A., *Israel and the American National Interest: A Critical Examination*, Chicago, University of Illinois Press, 1986.

U.S. Department of State, *Foreign Relations of the United States 1947* (vol. V), The Near East and Africa, Washington, DC, U.S. Printing Office, 1971.

U.S. Department of State, *Foreign Relations of the United States 1948* (vol. VI), The Near East, South Asia, and Africa, Washington, DC, U.S. Printing Office, 1975.

*Available through the AET Book Club.

NOTES:

[1]Kaplan, *The Arabists.*

[2]*Washington Post*, 10/24/93.

³Kaplan, *The Arabists*, p. 98.

⁴Joseph Kraft, "Those Arabists in the State Department," *New York Times Magazine*, 11/7/71.

⁵Parker, "The Arabists," *Journal of Palestine Studies*, Autumn 1994, p. 72.

⁶Kaplan, *The Arabists*, p. 308.

⁷See his numerous memoranda reprinted in the official *Foreign Relations of the United States* series. Even author Kaplan is awed by Henderson's talents and gives him grudging high marks: "Henderson's judgments—the Middle East aside—were incredibly prescient. And even in regard to the Middle East, Henderson's opinions, though in some cases incorrect, are not impossible to defend"; see Kaplan, *The Arabists*, p. 89.

⁸For a detailed discussion of the entanglements of the U.S.-Israeli relationship, see Ball, *The Passionate Attachment.*

⁹From his speech to the Jewish Leadership Council in Washington, DC, 6/30/93.

¹⁰*Near East Report*, 7/20/92.

¹¹Lloyd Grove, *Washington Post*, 1/20/93.

¹²David Hoffman, *Washington Post*, 10/28/91.

¹³Kaplan, *The Arabists*, p. 287.

¹⁴See, for instance, his study "Acting with Caution: Middle East Policy Planning for the Second Reagan Administration," Washington Institute for Near East Policy, Washington, DC, 1985.

Index

A

Abdel Rahman, Hassan: 101
Abdel Safty: 289
Abrams, Floyd: 157
Abu Ageila: 262
Abu Dhabi: 285
Abu Musa: 173
Abu Nidal: 90
Abu Sharif, Bassam: 103
Addis Ababa: 229, 231
Agnew, Spiro: 285
Aharonson, Shlomo: 171
Al Aqsa mosque: 223-24, 279
Al Hamishmar: 170
Al Saud, Fahd bin Abdul Aziz: 295
Al Saud, King Faisal bin Abdul Aziz:
    279, 284
Alami, Raghed: 190
Albany, NY: 129
Albina, A.P.: 11
Algeria: 238, 247, 284-85; Algerian
    rebellion: 112
Algerians: 237
Alphand, Hervé: 118
Altalena: 29-30
Ambrose, Stephen E.: 264, 265
American Bank & Trust Company: 271
American Educational Trust: 66, 140,
    317, 337
American Friends of Hebrew
    University: 20
American Friends Service Committee:
    216

American Hebrew Congregations: 216
American Israel Public Affairs
    Committee (AIPAC): 7, 172, 174,
    276, 302-05, 308, 316, 322
American Jewish Committee: 171
American Jews: 2-3, 5, 12, 16, 30, 33,
    111, 232, 252, 261, 275, 322, 340;
    in Israel: 231; leaders: 252, 261;
    organizations: 217
American diplomats: 101, 264, 343;
    educational institutions: 259;
    ideals: 7, 61, 265, 302, 342; melting
    pot: 3, 4; navy: 130; people: 263,
    280-81, 321, 333; support for the
    U.N.: 100; taxpayers: 253, 288;
    technology: 130-31, 166, 308;
    troops: 22, 125; Zionism: 2, 5-6;
    Zionists: 5, 7
American-European Beth El
    Messianic Mission Children's
    Hostel and School: 202
American Red Cross: 71
American Schools and Hospitals
    Grant Program: 334
American University: 166
American University Hospital: 201
American University of Beirut: 147, 328
Americans for Middle East
    Understanding: 46
Americans, kidnappings of: 148, 297,
    327-28, 330
Ames, Robert C.: 145
Amir, Yigal: 33, 266-67
Amman: 59, 259
Amnesty International: 195-96, 218

Ilan, Uri: 117
In the Final Analysis: 34
India: 11, 237
Indian Ocean: 274
Indyk, Martin: 172, 342
Inman, Bobby: 123
Inouye, Daniel: 227
International Atomic Energy Agency: 154
International Convention Against Torture: 194
International Court of Justice: 99, 102
International law: 61
International Red Cross: 53
Intifada: 91, 102, 192, 196, 215-20, 305
Iran-Contra arms-for-hostages affair: 161, 304, 327
Iranian-backed Islamist militants: 145, 147, 171, 297, 328, 330
Iraq, Atomic Energy Commission of: 124; invasion of Kuwait: 91, 125, 319; Osirak nuclear facility, Israeli bombing of: 122-25, 252; Scud missiles: 323; Soviet presence in: 239; weapons inspection crisis: 125
Irgun Zvai Leumi: 28-30, 37-38, 54, 70, 112, 271
"Iron fist" policy: 217-18
Isaacs, Stephen D.: 271
Islam: 146, 215, 223, 238, 243, 279, 315; Alawite sect of : 243
Islamic Jihad: 145
Islamic Mufti of Jerusalem: 223
Islamic world: 12, 314, 330, 340
Ismailiya: 248
Israel Defense Forces: 59, 137, 142, 252
Israel, aid to: 101, 148, 217, 265, 271-72, 283-84, 288-89, 291, 309, 319, 330-31, 334; American supporters of: 30, 102, 111, 123, 135, 170, 196, 216, 250, 263, 270, 275, 281, 314, 316; Arab population of: 43; as weapons exporter: 164, 304; border police: 212; borders of: 42-43, 76, 79, 82, 122, 185, 274, 276; criticism of: 55, 60, 63, 88-91, 101-02, 118, 122-23, 130, 161, 181-82, 185, 190, 194-95, 197, 212, 216-19, 225-26, 269, 275-77, 295, 310, 330; declaration of independence: 42-43; Defense Ministry: 166; embassy in Argentina: 172; embassy in

Washington: 144, 263, 271, 283; espionage: 128; expansionism: 43, 85, 184, 295; Government of National Unity: 65; Housing Ministry: 320; human rights violations: 196; Jewish settlements: 84-85, 89, 91, 184-87, 206, 249, 252-53, 319, 321, 336, 343; Labor Alignment: 33, 207; Labor governments: 185, 219, 245; lobby: 173, 275-77, 323; military courts: 196; "neutrality" of: 110-14; 1982 invasion of Lebanon: 63-65, 90, 134-35, 252, 260, 266, 303, 328; nuclear weapons program: 152-55; occupation of Arab lands: 60, 63, 89, 99-100, 192, 211, 218, 244, 274, 288, 330; parliament: 199, 247; prisons: 89; recognition of: 104, 112; right to exist: 96, 101, 290; Soviet immigrants to: 319, 324; State Comptroller: 310; Supreme Court: 202; terrorist attacks on: 89, 105, 244-45; theft of U.S. technology: 128-30; torture: 194-97; war of independence: 65; wars of "choice": 63-66
Israel-Egypt armistice agreement: 79
"Israel: Foreign Intelligence and Security Services": 127
Israeli Academy of Sciences: 160; Air Force: 129, 135; Export Development Corp: 316; Lands Authority: 314; League for Human and Civil Rights: 191; National Defense College: 63; Palestinians: 43
Israeli Mazlat Ltd: 129
Israelis: 96; anti-Arab feelings of: 33, 180
Italy: 31, 124, 136, 143
Ivri, David: 166

J

Jabalya refugee camp: 192, 215
Jabarin, Shawan: 196
Jabotinsky, Vladimir Zeev: 29, 31-32
Jacobsen, David: 327
Jaffa: 28, 37-39, 48, 200-02
Jamieson, J.K.: 283
Jenco, Lawrence: 327
Jericho: 185

Samaria: 207-08, 211, 217, 249, 252
Satellite intelligence, Israeli: 123
Satellite photography, U.S.: 123
Saudi Arabia: 162, 172, 279-85, 295, 322; oil production: 280-81;
Saudis: 280, 283
Saunders, Harold H.: 95, 97; Saunders Document: 95-96
Schindler, Rabbi Alexander : 216
Scorpion Pass: 180
Scranton, William W.: 89, 185
Scud missiles: 323
Sea of Galilee: 119
Seale, Patrick: 242-43
Seersucker ground-to-ground missiles: 173
Segev, Tom: 43
Senate: 6, 102, 154, 165, 227, 250, 274-77, 315-16, 320, 323, 333; Appropriations Committee: 320; Armed Services Committee: 158; Foreign Relations Committee: 154, 274, 277; senators: 103, 250, 276, 304, 323, 333
Settlements, freeze of: 208
Settlers, Jewish: 33, 208, 211-13, 220
Shahak, Israel: 170
Shamir, Yitzhak: 29, 32-34, 53-54, 70-71, 128, 134, 153, 187, 206-08, 217-18, 220, 225-26, 229, 252, 296, 320-22, 324
Shapira, Yaakov S.: 43
Sharett, Moshe: 110, 117
Sharm el Sheikh: 65
Sharon, Ariel: 32, 118, 134, 136, 142-45, 181, 191-92, 226, 321
Shati refugee camp: 190, 192
Shatila refugee camp: 137
Sheikh Bader: 42
Sheikh Jarrah: 42
Sheikh Saad El Dine Alami: 223
Shifa Hospital: 216
Shin Bet: 195, 196, 197
Shoval, Zalman: 319, 322
Shultz, George P.: 90, 96-97, 99-105, 187, 280, 282, 296, 301-05, 311; George Shultz Doctoral Fellowships: 305
Shuqayri, Ahmad: 77
Shuttle diplomacy: 289
Silver, Eric: 31
Sinai I: 288-89

Sinai II: 101, 265-67, 285, 289-91
Sinai Peninsula: 65, 181, 190, 238, 249, 253, 266, 282, 288, 291; Israeli occupation of: 99, 249, 262, 265, 291
Sino-Israeli relationship: 160, 162
Six-Day War (see 1967 war): 184, 243
"60 Minutes": 224
Skyjackings, Israeli: 90, 117; Palestinian: 60, 329
Smilansky, Yizhar: 51
Smyth, Richard K.: 128
SNIA-Techint: 124
Society of Activists of the Torah Camp: 202
Solarz, Stephan J.: 155
Soldiers Against Silence: 64
Somi, Father Pierre: 200
Sonneborn, Rudolf G.: 16; Sonneborn Institute: 16
South Africa: 130, 163, 166, 219, 304
South Yemen: 248
Soviet Union: 60, 88, 128, 190, 239, 248, 266, 275, 290, 294; Israeli relations with: 110-14; Soviets: 284
Spaniards: 11
Sperry Corp.: 129
Sprinzak, Dr. Ehud : 33
St. Anthony Catholic Church in Jaffa: 201
St. Joseph convent: 202
Standard Oil of California (Socal): 281; boycott threat: 281
Star Wars: 129
State Department annual report on terrorism: 172; Arabists: 303, 339-43; Bureau of Near Eastern Affairs: 339; Israel and Arab-Israeli affairs: 186; Office of Near East and South Asian Affairs: 95; Office of Near Eastern and African Affairs: 21; Operations Room: 270; opposition to Zionism: 6, 12, 22-24; Policy Planning division: 342; position on Palestinian refugees: 70-73, 76-79, 208; supporters of Israel: 270, 303-04
Steen, Alann: 328
Steindler, Harold: 129
Stern, Avraham: 28; Stern Gang (see Levi): 28-29, 34, 53-54, 71, 112
Stockholm International Peace Research Institute: 152

Weizman, Ezer: 248, 249
Weizmann, Chaim: 12-13, 44
West Bank: 32, 44, 80, 84-85, 99, 105,
    184, 186, 201, 206-08, 212, 218, 220,
    249-52, 266, 290, 314, 321, 324
West Virginia: 227, 320, 333
Western Europe: 288, 334
Western powers: 11
"What Do You Do with $10 Billion?":
    324
"What We Have Done for Israel": 270
Wheeler, Keith: 48
White Paper of 1939: 17
Williams, Angela: 218
Wilson, Charles: 308
Wilson, Woodrow: 5-6, 12-14
Wisconsin Project on Nuclear Arms
    Control: 128
Wolpe, Howard: 231
Woolsey, James R.: 130, 165
World Court: 102
World Jewish Congress: 174
World opinion: 56, 60, 78, 106, 260,
    264
World War I: 2, 6, 110
World War II: 16-18, 41, 53, 64, 111,
    236, 279, 288-89, 295, 334
World Zionist Organization: 12
Wu Jianmin: 162

Y

Yad Le'Achim: 203
Yalchin, Huseyin Cahit: 77
Yamani, Ahmad Zaki: 280
Yang Fuchang: 161
Yaron, Amos: 134, 138
Yemenites: 11
Yesh Givul (There is a Limit): 64
YMCA: 201
Yom Kippur War (see 1973 war): 65
Yosef, Dov: 43
Yosef, Rabbi Ovadiah: 199
Yoseftal, Giora: 39

Z

Zakheim, Rabbi Dov S.: 311
Zamir, Itzhak: 195
Zeevi, Rehavam: 323
Zion: 5, 32; binational state in: 32
Zionism: 2-7, 30, 32, 258-59, 280;
    Revisionist: 28-30, 32; secular: 32
Zionist ambitions in Palestine: 12;
    Central Office: 2; Federation of
    Britain: 38; membership: 6
"Zionist entity": 248, 330
Zionists: 3- 7, 10-11, 17-19, 33, 85, 113,
    264, 275, 339-40, 343; anti-Zionists:
    10; mainline: 29-30; radical: 223;
    Revisionists: 29-30, 33-34

About the Author

Donald Neff was born in 1930 in York, Pennsylvania, and has traveled as a journalist over much of the United States and the world. During and after service in the U.S. Army from 1948 to 1950 he was a university student at Trinity College in San Antonio, Texas, York College in Pennsylvania, and New York University. His journalistic career included stints at the *York Dispatch* from 1954 to 1956, the *Los Angeles Mirror News* in 1956 and 1957, the Los Angeles bureau of United Press International from 1957 to 1961, and with the *Los Angeles Times* from 1961 to 1964, ending as the newspaper's Tokyo bureau chief.

Then he began 16 years of service with *Time* magazine, including Vietnam correspondent from 1965 to 1966, writer in New York City from 1966 to 1968, bureau chief in Houston from 1968 to 1970, in Los Angeles 1970 to 1973, in Jerusalem 1975 to 1978, and in New York City in 1978 and 1979. Between 1973 and 1975 he was a senior editor.

He was news services editor with the *Washington Star* from 1979 to 1980. During the 1980s and 1990s he also has been a regular contributor to *Middle East International*, published in London, and the *Washington Report on Middle East Affairs*, published in the U.S. national capital, and has contributed articles to other U.S. journals concerned with U.S. Middle East Policy. He has written four previous books on the Middle East.